BASIC *Professional Courses* IN EDUCATION

EDITED BY CHARLES H. JUDD

EDUCATIONAL PSYCHOLOGY
Charles H. Judd

THE AMERICAN EDUCATIONAL SYSTEM
John Dale Russell
AND
Charles H. Judd

THE TEACHER AND EDUCATIONAL ADMINISTRATION
William C. Reavis
AND
Charles H. Judd

IN PREPARATION
SCHOOLS AND THE SOCIAL ORDER
Newton Edwards

The AMERICAN EDUCATIONAL SYSTEM

AN INTRODUCTION TO EDUCATION

John Dale Russell
PROFESSOR OF EDUCATION
UNIVERSITY OF CHICAGO

AND

Charles H. Judd
PROFESSOR EMERITUS OF EDUCATION
UNIVERSITY OF CHICAGO

BOSTON
NEW YORK
CHICAGO

DALLAS
ATLANTA
SAN FRANCISCO

HOUGHTON MIFFLIN COMPANY
The Riverside Press Cambridge

PREFACE

For a quarter of a century the Department of Education at the University of Chicago has experimented with the organization of subject matter into a course designed to introduce students to the study of education. The course during that time has progressed through a number of different arrangements. In 1931 a selection and organization of materials was developed which has continued to the present and which seems to be serving its purposes satisfactorily. This book is the outgrowth of that course, which has been under the direction of one or the other of the authors ever since it was first given in 1931.

The general purpose of this book is to give an overview of the characteristic features of the American educational system and some explanation of the forces that have affected its development. The book is designed for three kinds of readers: (1) those who are intending to enter teaching service and who need as a part of their basic preparation an orientation in the American educational system; (2) those who have already had considerable professional preparation in education and who need to broaden their general acquaintance with the American educational system and to integrate the knowledge they have obtained through their study of various specialized topics in education; (3) those who are not especially interested in professional preparation for educational service, but who are concerned with general social problems and desire some acquaintance with the educational system as one of the important social institutions.

The emphasis in this book is on a broad and rapid survey of the characteristics of the educational system in the United States.

The book treats briefly a large number of topics which specialists have expanded into whole volumes or even series of volumes, and does not attempt to go farther in the treatment of any topic than is necessary for a general understanding of it. Students who are interested in a more elaborate treatment of certain details will be expected to refer to the numerous specialized works, some of which are listed in the bibliographies at the ends of the chapters.

The treatment of the American educational system in this book is descriptive and explanatory. It is not intended to be a history of education in the United States; when historical material is introduced, its purpose is always to facilitate an understanding of the present situation and to provide a basis for the estimation of future trends. Although the emphasis is on the present characteristics of the American educational system, the attention of the reader is constantly drawn to emerging trends and to the desirability of changes and modifications.

The fact that an important purpose of this book is to provide orientation in the field of education, either for the beginner or for the advanced student of educational problems, necessarily limits its application to the development of the student's general background for educational service. To state the same point negatively, this book does not intend to provide the reader with a bag of tricks or devices out of which he can produce an appropriate procedure for immediate application in the situations that arise in the classroom or in the school administrative office. Instead the aim is to enable those engaged in educational service to approach their tasks with a knowledge of the larger whole, to see how the work done by each staff member in the system articulates with the general plan of organization, to enable each to fit into his particular niche and fulfill his own round of duties with the consciousness of the part that his co-operation plays in achieving the general objectives expected by society from the school system, and to perform his functions with that intelligent understanding and appreciation of their meaning and significance which can come only from a knowledge of the way in which the system has developed and the manner in which it operates as an organic whole. In the opinion of the writers a broad understanding of the kind here described is necessary for the highest personal satisfaction of one who is engaged in any type of professional service.

This book is the product of many minds. Although the authors assume full responsibility for the text in its present form, they owe a great debt to their colleagues on the faculty of the Department of Education at the University of Chicago for assistance in shaping and criticizing the ideas that are herein set forth. Many of the members of the Department of Education at the University of Chicago participated in the original formulation of the course out of which this book has grown, and a number of them also in the early stages of the course delivered some of the lectures which have been developed into chapters in this book. The students who have taken the course have also assisted in its development in an important way by indicating the topics on which they wished information. To a considerable extent the list of topics included in this book represents an analysis of the needs of students as these needs have appeared in the questions brought up for discussion by students in class meetings.

The authors present this book with the hope that it will prove useful to the oncoming generation of school men and women. The educational problems that must be solved in the future are both numerous and difficult. These problems can be solved intelligently only by a generation of school people and citizens who have a thorough knowledge of the entire American educational system. It is the belief and hope of the authors that this volume may contribute to the future progress of education in the United States through the development of a clearer understanding of the system as it now operates and of the forces that have brought about the present organization.

JOHN DALE RUSSELL
CHARLES H. JUDD

Contents

as a School Subject; Vocational Education; Safety Education and Health Education; Thrift Education; Teaching the Constitution; Other Subjects Introduced by Legislation. Influence of Pupils on the Curriculum. Enrichment of the Subjects of the Curriculum. Defensible Attitude toward Curriculum Changes.

LIST OF FIGURES

LIST OF TABLES

THE AMERICAN
EDUCATIONAL SYSTEM

CHAPTER I

THE APPROACH TO THE STUDY OF THE AMERICAN EDUCATIONAL SYSTEM

EDUCATION in the United States is a large-scale enterprise. Some thirty million children and youth are enrolled in the schools, and more than a million teachers and administrators are engaged in the work of conducting schools. The total annual expenditures for educational purposes have in recent years ranged well above two billion dollars. In the years before 1930 expenditures reached the high figure of more than three billion dollars annually. Not only is the educational enterprise of great magnitude, but the service it renders is of vital importance to the future of the country and to all aspects of American life. The way in which a public service of such magnitude and importance is carried on is a worthy object of study for every citizen, especially for those who are engaged or expect to be engaged in some active way in this service. The purpose of this volume is to analyze the American educational system, to trace the social conditions under which it has developed, to describe its principal features, and to point out the trends of change that seem indicative of the course it will follow in the future.

THE SCHOOL AS A SOCIAL INSTITUTION

Most people are somewhat familiar with the school system because they have been enrolled in it as pupils, but they seldom see beyond the particular classrooms and courses of instruction with which they have had direct personal contact. They do not realize that education is only one phase of community life and that schools are organized and controlled by influences which originate outside the schools themselves. It usually requires comparison with educational practices belonging to other times and other peoples to focus the attention of one who has been a pupil in an American school on the unique characteristics of the educational system through which he has passed, and to give an understanding of the fact that all educational institutions and practices are determined by the general social setting in which they have developed.

In a primitive society education is markedly different from that which exists in a modern American or European community. In a primitive civilization the education is of a type dictated by the needs of that society. The following quotation illustrates this fact.

Utilitarian training naturally differs with special tribal requirements which may relate to hunting, fishing, or agriculture. A Kayan boy is taken, not only to the forest on hunting expeditions, but, in addition to this, he receives a useful training on the padi farms, where he is taught the routine of sowing, reaping, and garnering. Employment of the boy for scaring birds marks his first contact with agricultural work.

A consideration of evidence adduced with regard to the training of boys for tribal life reveals an idealism and a power of psychological analysis, combined with practical pedagogics which do credit to the intelligence of primitive man and the ancient civilizations from which he borrowed his culture.

First and foremost, tribal elders have considered stability of the social group when arranging courses of instruction and training. Sanctity of custom has decided that prescribed rules of conduct with regard to marriage, reverence for what is sacred, and dealings with fellow tribesmen shall be followed with precision. Hence the primary object of the training is a standardising of boys, who are expected suddenly to break away from the standards of childhood for the purpose of adopting criteria of manhood. Of these criteria obedience to tribal law is paramount, therefore special stress is placed upon the inculcation of precepts which are held to have been derived from ancestors of a remote period.

The inflexibility of communal traditions is probably thought to lead to a direct preservation of the unit, for breach of law by one who is initiated is regarded as a most serious offence, because of the possible suffering which it may cause to the social group. A feeling that breach of tradition will end in disaster for the tribe is always present, though not always verbally expressed.

Novices are taught the necessity for avoiding both sins and crimes. The former include all abrogations of tribal tradition respecting marriage, the approach of sacred places or objects, the use of prayers and formulae for seeking the aid of non-human powers, while the latter have a direct reference to duty toward a neighbour, usually a neighbour within the novice's own unit.[1]

At levels of society above the primitive the organization of education becomes more definitely institutionalized and its purposes come to clear expression through explicit statements issuing from some general authority. The early history of the Massachusetts Colony may be drawn upon to illustrate an official authorization for the establishment of educational facilities. The following statute was enacted as soon as the colony became sufficiently settled in its government to give attention to the needs of the younger generation.

It being one chief project of that old deluder, Satan, to keep men from the knowledge of the Scriptures, as in former times by keeping them in an unknown tongue, so in these later times by perswading from the use of Tongues, that so at least the true sense and meaning of the Originall might be clowded with false glosses of Saint-seeming-deceivers; and that Learning may not be buried in the graves of our fore-fathers in Church and Commonwealth, the Lord assisting our indeavours: it is therfore ordered by this Court and Authoritie therof:

That everie Township in this Jurisdiction, after the Lord hath increased them to the number of fifty Housholders shall then forthwith appoint one within their Town to teach all such children as shall resort to him to write and read, whose wages shall be paid either by the Parents or Masters of such children, or by the Inhabitants in general by way of supply, as the major part of those that order the *prudentials* of the Town shall appoint. Provided that those which send their

---

[1] W. D. Hambly, *Origins of Education Among Primitive Peoples*, pp. 195–96. New York, 1926. Reprinted by permission of The Macmillan Company, publishers.

children be not oppressed by paying much more than they can have them taught for in other Towns.

2. And it is farther ordered, that where any Town shall increase to the number of one hundred Families or Housholders they shal set upon a Grammar-School, the Masters therof being able to instruct youth so far as they may be fitted for the Universitie. And if any Town neglect the performance heerof above one year then everie such town shall pay five pounds *per annum* to the next such School, till they shall perform this Order. [1647] [1]

Not only is the general character of the educational system dictated by the social order of which it is a part, but in matters of detail, such as the content of the subjects taught and the methods of classroom teaching, forces entirely outside the school are determinative. If one visits a Mohammedan school, for example, one sees the pupils sitting on the floor swaying back and forth and repeating aloud some extract from the Koran which they are required to learn by heart. As compared with the discipline, mode of study, and content of instruction to be seen in an American school, the situation is so strikingly different that the observer recognizes at once that a school is a product and embodiment of a particular type of civilization.

Other illustrations to reinforce what has been said about the dependence of education on general social forces can be drawn from pronouncements regarding the control of education. The following official statement of a Catholic Pope expresses a view which is different from the doctrine held in countries that maintain secular educational systems.

I. To Whom Does Education Belong?
Education is essentially a social and not a mere individual activity. Now there are three necessary societies, distinct from one another and yet harmoniously combined by God, into which man is born: two, namely the family and civil society, belong to the natural order; the third, the Church, to the supernatural order.

---

[1] *The Laws and Liberties of Massachusetts Reprinted from the Copy of the 1648 Edition in the Henry E. Huntington Library*, p. 47. Cambridge, Massachusetts: Harvard University Press, 1929.

In the first place comes the family, instituted directly by God for its peculiar purpose, the generation and formation of offspring; for this reason it has priority of nature and therefore of rights over civil society. Nevertheless, the family is an imperfect society, since it has not in itself all the means for its own complete development; whereas civil society is a perfect society, having in itself all the means for its peculiar end, which is the temporal well-being of the community; and so, in this respect, that is, in view of the common good, it has pre-eminence over the family, which finds its own suitable temporal perfection precisely in civil society.

The third society, into which man is born when through Baptism he receives the Divine life of grace, is the Church; a society of the supernatural order and of universal extent; a perfect society, because it has in itself all the means required for its own end, which is the eternal salvation of mankind; hence it is supreme in its own domain.

Consequently, education, which is concerned with man as a whole, individually and socially, in the order of nature and in the order of grace, necessarily belongs to all these three societies, in due proportion, corresponding, according to the disposition of Divine Providence, to the co-ordination of their respective ends.

And first of all education belongs pre-eminently to the Church, by reason of a double title in the supernatural order, conferred exclusively upon her by God Himself; absolutely superior therefore to any other title in the natural order.[1]

In contrast to the view set forth in the foregoing quotation is the view expressed by Calvin E. Stowe in a report which he made in 1836 to the legislature of Ohio. Stowe had visited the schools of Prussia on a commission given him by the Ohio legislature to report on the organization of schools in that state. In his report he writes:

The participation of different sects in the management of schools, must be regulated on different principles here [in Ohio] from what it is there [in Prussia]. There are there, in fact, but two religious denominations of any extent — the protestant and the catholic; and one or the other of these predominates in every community. Besides, the religious differences there are not violent, and there is, comparatively, little of sectarian jealousy. Owing to these circumstances, it is easy

---

[1] Pope Pius XI, "Christian Education of Youth," *Catholic Mind*, XXVIII: 63–64, February 22, 1930.

to avoid encroachments on the rights and feelings of the different denominations, when legislating expressly with reference to them. But here religious denominations are numerous, of equal responsibility, and possessing equal rights. The district schools, instead of being made up of two, or, at most, of three religious sects, often comprehend six or eight; and it would be impossible to select teachers and school committees, with reference to the numerical proportions of these different sects, for the purpose of satisfying them. ...

... the same considerations of public good and of public safety, which make it every man's duty to bear his proportion in the making and repairing of roads, and sustaining the necessary expenses of the government, and oblige him to give his personal services for the defence of the country when invaded, also impose upon him the obligation to educate his children.

The Constitution of Ohio clearly recognizes this principle, by placing the superintendence of education among the legitimate objects of legislative action.[1]

Even where education is recognized as under the authority of governmental agencies, there are marked differences among nations with respect to the distribution of powers of control. Various levels of government, ranging from the local community to the nation as a whole, may participate in the control and operation of the schools. Among the countries of the world there are marked differences in the extent to which the central or federal government has control over education. In the United States the Federal Government participates relatively little in the control of the educational system. On the other hand, highly centralized control is exercised by the national governments in many other countries such as Germany and France.

Although the control of European school systems is different in many respects from the control of schools in this country, there are certain characteristics in which European and American schools are alike. The common characteristics are to be accounted for by the fact that the American continent was settled by emigrants

---

[1] Calvin E. Stowe, *The Prussian System of Public Instruction, and Its Applicability to the United States*, pp. 57–58, 60–61. Cincinnati, Ohio: Truman and Smith, 1836.

from Europe who brought with them the traditions of older civilizations.   Occasion will frequently arise in later chapters to point out respects in which American education has been influenced by European practices.

Enough has perhaps been said with regard to the relations of schools to the society in which they exist to justify and explain the reasons for the type of treatment of American education which is adopted in this book.   Instead of concentrating at first on a description of classrooms and methods of teaching, chapters immediately following will give an account of the broad social influences which have made American schools what they are.   The classroom will be approached as one of the last centers of consid-

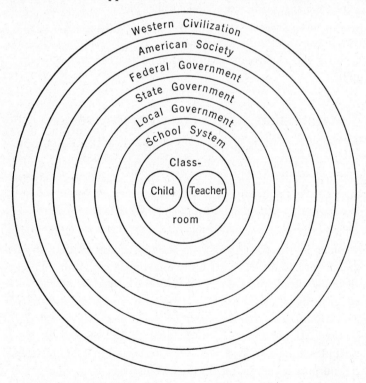

FIGURE I. THE HIERARCHY OF AGENCIES AFFECTING THE
EDUCATION OF THE CHILD

eration. The reader who has been a pupil in schools will be asked to step entirely outside of the institution which he knows and to study first the social order of which the school is a part. It is believed that this method of developing an understanding of the educational system will be far more illuminating than the method, frequently followed, of limiting discussion largely to the details of classroom management.

The plan of procedure which will be adopted can be made clear by a diagram such as that shown in the figure on page 9. The outermost circle represents the whole of Occidental civilization. Within this civilization is included that of the United States. Within American society is the governmental system with its several levels: federal, state, and local. The school system is set up as a part of the service of government and is especially close to the local community organization. Finally, within the school system is the classroom, composed of a teacher and a group of pupils.

THE SCHOOL AS A SOCIALIZING INSTITUTION

Not only is the school organized and controlled by society, but it is set up for the purpose of making its pupils adjusted members of society. This statement does not mean that the school is de-signed to make its pupils merely subservient individuals. It does mean that society recognizes that the only way by which harmonious life in the community can be assured is by transmitting to each newcomer in the social group an understanding of the essential requirements to which each individual must conform. Parents and young people are frequently more interested in personal advantages, that accrue or are thought to accrue because of educational attainments, than in any other ends to be achieved through schooling. In most cases the individual improvement of the pupil contributes to the welfare of the entire social group, and thus a social purpose is served, but in the last analysis, the school system is maintained not because the parents of pupils wish to have their children receive the personal benefits of an education, nor because pupils themselves wish to obtain personal advantages, but rather because the social group as a whole recognizes that the education of the oncoming generation is advantageous and necessary for the preservation and advancement of the society. If it ever comes to a choice, as sometimes happens in an educational organization, between benefits to the individual and benefits to society as a whole, the school fails in its mission unless it serves the larger purpose of benefiting the entire social order.

Failure to recognize the principle that the school is maintained for social purposes is perhaps found oftener among students at the level of professional education than among those at other levels. A teachers college or a university school of education does not exist primarily to provide opportunity for students to earn credits and degrees that will improve their salaries or that will enhance their professional prestige; rather, such facilities exist because society has need of people who are well prepared and competent to administer and carry on the increasingly complex processes of educating the younger generation. A school of medicine exists, not because some young men and women wish to prepare for the supposedly lucrative vocation of physician or surgeon, but because the social order has need of competent medical service. A law school which trains its graduates only to be shrewd in preying on the miseries of their fellow men is clearly not discharging its obligations as a social institution.

Throughout this book the view deliberately adopted and defended is that the school is a socializing as well as a social institution. The school was established originally to meet a social need, and its continued existence is justified only by its service to the social order in which it is maintained. Another and perhaps more instructive way of emphasizing the idea here expressed is to say that the major purpose of the school is to make available to the pupil all the experience which the race has accumulated, that is, to prepare him for civilized life. The individual pupil is in this way put in possession of skills and knowledge which he could never by his own unaided effort have acquired in a single lifetime.   He is socialized by being introduced to a system of culture.

THE AIM OF EDUCATION

If it is true that the aim of the educative process is to enable the oncoming generation to take full advantage of the culture into which it is born, the analysis of culture should show what the aims of the school are.   Thus an analysis of the culture of the Western civilization reveals the fact that such societies all lay great stress on communication through written language.   Hence in all schools maintained by societies in this civilization pupils are required to learn to read and write the vernacular.   In many primitive civilizations, by contrast, a written language does not exist or is not important as a part of the pattern of culture; therefore the education of the young in such societies does not include reading and writing.   Again, by way of illustration, the culture pattern of the United States is characterized by a general belief in the democratic form of government; a majority of the citizens therefore expect the schools to inculcate in the young an appreciation of democracy, an understanding of its institutions, and a desire to perpetuate it. In countries where other governmental forms dominate the culture pattern, the teaching in the schools is organized to develop in the young a firm belief in the desirability of the dominant form of government.

The view here expressed should not be interpreted to mean that education limits the development of the individual by compelling him to conform slavishly to the pattern of mature society.   It is true in some countries and in some times that individuals are coerced into the acceptance of modes of behavior which are dictated by a tyrannical government.   What is said here is that education passes on to the young people of a civilized nation what the culture of that nation offers.   Where that culture is liberal it leaves the learner free to adapt and even to improve through his own intellectual efforts the culture which he acquires.   A liberal culture is liberal in its treatment of individuals.   A dogmatic culture will reflect its dogmatism in its educational system.

In a society such as exists in the United States the members of the mature group are by no means in entire agreement with respect to many of the items of the culture pattern that is to be transmitted through the educational system.   While there is universal agreement in this country regarding the desirability of instructing children in the basic tools of communication, reading and writing, and while the great majority doubtless favor inculcation of the ideals of democracy, on other matters there is frequent and vigorous conflict of opinion.   For example, some would have the schools teach military training and would require every boy to be trained so as to be readily available for service in case of war; others would insist that this is not a pattern of culture that comports with the ideals of American democracy.   Some members of American society regard knowledge of the classical languages as indispensable; others do not.

There will always be discussions of the aims of education in a dynamic society where procedures, standards, and institutions undergo constant change.   There is no reason why disagreements with regard to the specific aims of education should confuse anyone.   Disagreements should be recognized as incentives to further study of the nature of civilization and its relations to individual life.   Teachers and those who are preparing to teach are sometimes perplexed by the fact that they are compelled to listen to various doctrines — sometimes opposing doctrines — about education.   They should learn to weigh the suggestions made by disagreeing authorities and to arrive, through a study of the social system in which the school exists, at independent judgments with respect to the validity of these suggestions.

EDUCATION THROUGH AGENCIES OUTSIDE THE SCHOOL

Society is by no means completely dependent on the school system for the entire task of educating the oncoming generation.

Such agencies as the home, the church, the movies, the radio, the newspaper or magazine, the street, the playground, and the shop, have very significant rôles to play in the total educational process affecting the child. The school system, however, is the institutionalized agency formally commissioned by society to perform the chief and most systematic educational service. Many other agencies operate casually and unsystematically; some of them operate in a directly antisocial manner. The school thus has the responsibility not only of instruction in the fundamentals but also of giving a balanced training and in some cases of providing education which definitely counteracts the effects of antisocial education.

Although non-school educational influences are widespread and although many of them have become increasingly important in recent decades, the general tendency for some time seems to have been toward centralizing more and more of the formal responsibility for the educational process in the school system. Many educational activities, such as training in social manners and in skills of hand, that were previously a function of other agencies, such as the home or industry, have been transferred in part or in whole to the schools. Formal schooling today occupies a larger percentage of the total lifetime of the individual than ever before in the world's history. In recent years there has appeared a distinct tendency to delay the entry of young people into productive employment and as a result to encourage them to spend additional years in the school system. Organized facilities for adult education are also increasing rapidly; this fact is another indication of the expanding emphasis of institutionalized education.

In former times when the school played a less important part in the total education of the individual than it does at present, the school system had a correspondingly insignificant place in the social order. Today the school system has attained vast proportions and importance. Questions of cost which were formerly of minor importance have become urgent in present-day society. The content of the curriculum, which was formerly restricted to a few rudimentary subjects, has expanded into many fields. Spoils sys-

tems of public politics have sometimes invaded the schools because the educational system has become so large and important that it invites interference.   In short, the school has become a significant subject of consideration from many points of view.   It is no longer possible for teachers and school administrators to think of them-selves as a special group isolated from the public and only remotely answerable to society for what they do.   The schools must be thought of as the centers of many converging influences and as responsible in many new ways to society in general.

BIBLIOGRAPHY

Burton, William H., *Introduction to Education*, pp. 1–116.   New York: D. Appleton-Century Company, 1934.

Chamberlain, Leo M., *The Teacher and School Organization*, pp. New York: Prentice-Hall, 1936.

Dewey, John, *The School and Society*.   Chicago: University of Chicago Press, 1900.   xvi + 164 pp.

Patterson, S. Howard, Ernest A. Choate, and Edmund de S. Brunner, *The School in American Society*, pp. 3–56.   Scranton, Pennsylvania: International Textbook Company, 1936.

Reeder, Ward, *A First Course in Education*, pp. 50–95.   New York: Macmillan Company, 1937.

Suzzallo, Henry, *Our Faith in Education*.   Philadelphia: J. B. Lippincott Company, 1924.   108 pp.

Tuttle, Harold S., *A Social Basis of Education*.   New York: Thomas Y. Crowell Company, 1934.   x + 590 pp.

CHAPTER II

THE AMERICAN EDUCATIONAL
SYSTEM AND ITS EUROPEAN
ANTECEDENTS

I~N ORDER~ to develop an understanding of the educational system of the United States it is necessary to consider briefly the history and present organization of the educational systems of Europe, from which many important features of American education have been borrowed. Ancient Greece and Rome had educational systems, and their cultures have exercised a profound influence on the subjects of instruction in modern schools, but the present-day organization of European and American educational institutions and school systems has no direct relation to the schools of antiquity.

The history which explains the organizational pattern of the leading educational systems of modern Western civilization begins with the appearance of the universities that grew up in Europe during and after the twelfth century A.D. After the fall of Rome a period known as the Dark Ages had ensued, during which cultural institutions other than those conducted by the Church were practically non-existent. Within the Church a limited number of so-called "cathedral schools" had existed and had administered meager curriculums designed to prepare for the services of the Church. In the twelfth century, however, the demand arose for special education for the ruling class in society; and the medieval universities developed in response to this demand.

By the twelfth century commerce and city organization had

progressed to the point where a settled culture of a higher type than that which had prevailed during the Dark Ages began to develop. Governments began to be strong enough to guarantee a measure of peace and order. The Church had grown powerful. An influx of new knowledge came into Western Europe, chiefly from Mohammedan scholars in Spain. At some time during the eleventh century a school of medicine at Salerno in southern Italy began to attract students, and at a later date a school of law, located at Bologna in northern Italy, became famous as a center where instruction was given in Roman law. Sometime before 1200 in Paris, where there had earlier been an important cathedral school, there began to develop a great university which became in the thirteenth century the chief center for instruction in theology. In other cities less conspicuous institutions were organized.

The students who attended the universities were for the most part sons of nobles and successful merchants or they were nephews of successful ecclesiasts. Now and then some bright boy from the lower levels of society, who had attracted the favorable attention of a churchman, was given the opportunity of a higher education, but such cases were exceptional and rare. The universities were exclusive institutions, offering professional education to the sons of upper class families.

Following the establishment of universities there developed in the provinces secondary schools that prepared young men for the work of the university. Instruction in the universities was given in Latin, and a student could not profit from attendance unless he understood the Latin language. For the medieval student Latin was as necessary as a knowledge of English is for an American student today. Much of the organization of these secondary schools and the subjects of their curriculum have tended to persist, and their influence is found today in the schools of Europe and the United States even though modern civilization has wrought great changes in educational demands. The secondary or preparatory schools that taught Latin ministered to the needs of the same select group of young men who attended the universities.

The peasant class had no share in such education as was provided in the medieval universities and secondary schools. The common people learned the practices of agriculture and of their simple trades by the direct method of imitating their elders. Not until the time of the Protestant Revolt did there come an effective realization of the need for education of the common people. It was a part of the fundamental belief of those who led the Reformation that a person must be able to learn for himself the truths of the Bible and thus acquire the religious knowledge necessary for his salvation. The Scriptures had been translated into the vernacular and Protestantism demanded that the common people be taught to read. Within the Catholic Church there grew up the so-called "Counter-Reformation," which also tended to improve conditions for the common people by providing them certain rudimentary educational facilities.

The demand for education of the common people so that they might read the Scriptures has ultimately resulted in a broad demand for participation of all people in the benefits of education. A document prepared by Martin Luther, addressed to the mayors and councilmen of German cities, may properly be described as the charter of the common schools. In the following extract from that document a vigorous revolt may be noted against the aristocracy and against the then established institutions of education which were not open to the common people.

Even if there were no soul, (as I have already said,) and men did not need schools and the languages for the sake of Christianity and the Scriptures, still, for the establishment of the best schools everywhere, both for boys and girls, this consideration is of itself sufficient, namely, that society, for the maintenance of civil order and the proper regulation of the household, needs accomplished and well-trained men and women. Now such men are to come from boys, and such women from girls; hence it is necessary that boys and girls be properly taught and brought up. As I have before said, the ordinary man is not qualified for this task, and can not, and will not do it. Princes and lords ought to do it; but they spend their time in pleasure-driving, drinking, and folly, and are burdened with the weighty duties of the cellar, kitchen and bedchamber. And though some would be glad to do it, they must stand in fear of the rest, lest they be taken for fools or heretics. Therefore, honored members of the city councils, this work must remain in your hands; you have more time and better opportunity for it than princes and lords.

But each one, you say, may educate and discipline his own sons and daughters. To which I reply: We see indeed how it goes with this teaching and training. And where it is carried to the highest point, and is attended with success, it results in nothing more than that the learners, in some measure, acquire a forced external propriety of manner; in other respects they remain dunces, knowing nothing, and incapable of giving aid or advice. But were they instructed in schools or elsewhere by thoroughly qualified male or female teachers, who taught the languages, other arts, and history, then the pupils would hear the history and maxims of the world, and see how things went with each city, kingdom, prince, man, and woman; and thus, in a short time, they would be able to comprehend, as in a mirror, the character, life, counsels, undertakings, successes, and failures, of the whole world from the beginning. From this knowledge they could regulate their views, and order their course of life in the fear of God, having become wise in judging what is to be sought and what avoided in this outward life, and capable of advising and directing others. But the training which is given at home is expected to make us wise through our own experience. Before that can take place, we shall die a hundred times, and all through life act injudiciously; for much time is needed to give experience.

Now since the young must leap and jump, or have something to do, because they have a natural desire for it which should not be restrained, (for it is not well to check them in everything,) why should we not provide for them such schools, and lay before them such studies? By the gracious arrangement of God, children take delight in acquiring knowledge, whether languages, mathematics, or history. And our schools are no longer a hell or purgatory, in which children are tortured over cases and tenses, and in which with much flogging, trembling, anguish and wretchedness they learn nothing. If we take so much time and pains to teach our children to play cards, sing, and dance, why should we not take as much time to teach them reading and other branches of knowledge, while they are young and at leisure, are quick at learning, and take delight in it? As for myself,[1] if I had children and were able, I would have them learn not only the lan-

---

[1] "Luther was not yet married."

guages and history, but also singing, instrumental music, and the whole course of mathematics. For what is all this but mere child's play, in which the Greeks in former ages trained their children, and by this means became wonderfully skillful people, capable for every undertaking? How I regret that I did not read more poetry and history, and that no one taught me in these branches. Instead of these I was obliged with great cost, labor, and injury, to read Satanic filth, the Aristotelian and Scholastic philosophy, so that I have enough to do to get rid of it.

But you say, who can do without his children and bring them up, in this manner, to be young gentlemen? I reply: it is not my idea that we should establish schools as they have been heretofore, where a boy has studied Donatus and Alexander [1] twenty or thirty years, and yet has learned nothing. The world has changed, and things go differently. My idea is that boys should spend an hour or two a day in school, and the rest of the time work at home, learn some trade and do whatever is desired, so that study and work may go on together, while the children are young and can attend to both. They now spend tenfold as much time in shooting with crossbows, playing ball, running, and tumbling about.

In like manner, a girl has time to go to school an hour a day, and yet attend to her work at home; for she sleeps, dances, and plays away more than that. The real difficulty is found alone in the absence of an earnest desire to educate the young, and to aid and benefit mankind with accomplished citizens. The devil much prefers blockheads and drones, that men may have more abundant trials and sorrows in the world.

But the brightest pupils, who give promise of becoming accomplished teachers, preachers, and workers, should be kept longer at school, or set apart wholly for study, as we read of the holy martyrs, who brought up St. Agnes, St. Agatha, St. Lucian, and others. . . .

There is consequently an urgent necessity, not only for the sake of the young, but also for the maintenance of Christianity and of civil government, that this matter be immediately and earnestly taken hold of, lest afterwards, although we would gladly attend to it, we shall find it impossible to do so, and be obliged to feel in vain the pangs of remorse forever.[2]

---

[1] "Donatus wrote a Latin grammar used as a textbook during the Middle Ages. Alexander was the author of a commentary on Aristotle."

[2] "Luther's Letter to the Mayors and Aldermen of All the Cities of Germany in Behalf of Christian Schools." Translated by F. V. N. Painter and published in *Luther on Education*, pp. 196–201. Philadelphia: Lutheran Publication Society, 1889. Used by permission of the United Lutheran Board of Publication.

THE DUAL SCHOOL SYSTEM OF EUROPE

The circumstances that have been described in the preceding section show how there grew up in Europe what is known as a dual school system.   One branch of the system was directed towards the education, in the secondary school and the university, of the members of the ruling classes who were later going into the professions or governmental service.   The other branch of the system was for the education of the common people and was intended chiefly to provide them with the knowledge necessary for religious purposes and also to make them useful as merchants, tradesmen, and tillers of the soil.   The clientele of the two types of schools was entirely separate, the subjects taught were different, and the purposes were different.   The schools for the common people and the schools for the upper classes therefore developed as separate institutions without relationship to one another.

The German System

The system of education in Prussia before the first World War was a school system of the strictly dual type, and may be taken as an example.   It must be noted that a dual type of school system existed there because society was organized into two classes, the upper and the lower classes.   Each of these classes had its distinct place in the social order and its separate school facilities.   In the German system prior to 1914 the *Volksschule*, or school for the common people, was attended by about 92 per cent of the population, while the other 8 per cent attended the secondary schools for the upper classes, known as the *Gymnasium*, the *Realgymnasium*, or the *Oberschule*.

The selection of pupils who were to attend the *Gymnasium* or other secondary schools was almost wholly on the basis of heredity. In later years economic status came to count somewhat, but pupils from the newly rich families were generally looked upon as intruders in the *Gymnasium*.   The separateness of the two schools is indicated by the fact that not more than one pupil in ten thousand attended the *Gymnasium* after completing the *Volksschule*.

The German *Volksschule* was an eight-year school, beginning with pupils at the age of six and ending at the age of fourteen. The last two years in this curriculum were devoted largely to training for confirmation in the church. In early times the pastor, or priest, was the authority who determined when a pupil was to leave the *Volksschule*. Thus the length of the curriculum in the school for the common people was determined in the first instance by the religious authorities and by the age at which children were accepted for confirmation in the church.

The *Gymnasium* [1] proper began with pupils at the age of nine and extended to the age of eighteen; it provided an education roughly comparable to that attained by students in this country through completion of the junior college. The first part of the education of a boy who was to attend the *Gymnasium* was given in a primary school three years in length, known as the *Vorschule*. From the *Gymnasium* the student passed directly into the university.

The purpose of the *Volksschule* was to prepare the children of the common people to be good peasants and tradesmen. The purpose of the *Gymnasium*, by contrast, was to prepare the children of the upper classes for the positions of leadership to which they could look forward by right of birth. The curriculums of the two schools were radically different and reflected these differences of objectives. The pupils who attended the *Volksschule* were not thought of as needing higher mathematics or foreign languages, and such subjects were not taught in the *Volksschule*. These subjects, by contrast, were useful for those who would take positions of leadership in the professions, in military and governmental service, and in the direction of commercial and industrial enterprises, so the *Gymnasium* included them in its curriculum.

Pupils who completed the *Volksschule* were given opportunity for vocational training in special schools organized for that purpose

---

[1] The *Gymnasium* is used here and in the rest of this chapter as the type of the German secondary school. The facts stated are true for the other kinds of secondary schools as well as for the *Gymnasium*.

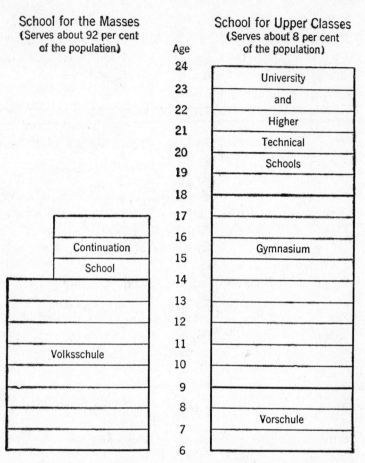

FIGURE 2. THE PRE-WAR GERMAN SCHOOL SYSTEM

in different parts of the country. These schools were adapted in their programs of instruction to the occupations common in the areas in which they were located.

Military requirements sharply distinguished the pupils in the two types of schools. The boy who completed the first six years of the *Gymnasium* had to spend only one year in military service, and he could elect where he would go for his period of training. He was eligible to become a commissioned officer upon the completion of the training period. The boy in the *Volksschule* had a longer period of military training, and he had no choice concerning the post to which he might go for training. Indeed, it was the policy of the government to send him far enough away from his home so that he would not be distracted by social connections. He was not eligible to become a commissioned officer; he might become a non-commissioned officer.

The preparation of teachers for the *Volksschule* and for the *Gymnasium* contrasted sharply. The teachers for the *Volksschule* were prepared in an institution known as the *Lehrerseminar*, which admitted pupils who had completed the *Volksschule* and a period of private study. In contrast, the teachers for the *Gymnasium* were prepared in the university; they were persons who had never attended a *Volksschule*. The teacher in the *Volksschule* was known as a *Lehrer*; the teacher in the *Gymnasium* was an *Oberlehrer*.

The pupils who attended the *Gymnasium* were under great pressure to do good academic work. To fail was to incur social disgrace and to wreck all possibility of a career befitting one's station in life. As a result, the schools of this type were able to require the most strenuous effort on the part of their pupils.

The French System

The school system in France before the first World War was similar to that in Germany; it was and still is set up as a dual system directly following the pattern of the class system of society. The common school in France was known as the *École Primaire*. The aristocratic or secondary school was known as the *Lycée* or in some instances as the *Collège*. Some opportunity was given those who completed the school for the masses to continue in vocational schools. The *Lycée* led directly to the university and to preparation for the professions.

The English System

In England the system was and is now somewhat more democratic than the systems in continental countries, although it also is fundamentally a dual school system. The masses of the population attend what are known as board schools. The sons of the upper classes attend the so-called secondary schools, which are institutions with rigorous standards of selection and with tuition fees. There is a system of competitive examinations which permits some transfer of bright pupils from the board schools to the secondary schools, but this possibility of transfer makes secondary education available for only a small percentage of the brighter children of the lower classes. Matthew Arnold, who was employed by the board of education as an inspector from 1851 to 1886, invented the phrase "the educational ladder" to describe the possibility of transfer by examination from the lower school to the secondary school.

In general the secondary schools in Europe are not coeducational. Separate institutions are provided for boys and girls, and the opportunities for girls have never equalled those open to boys. Girls were originally educated in the home and are now provided with only limited opportunities except at the lower levels.

Changes Following the First World War

The discussion has thus far centered on conditions which prevailed in the school systems of Europe prior to 1918. Since that date changes have occurred in social ideas and organization in many European countries, and the school systems have been correspondingly modified. The German Republic under the Weimar Constitution provided that all children should attend a single school, known as the *Grundschule*, for the first years of their education. Transfer from the *Volksschule* to the secondary schools was facilitated, and the whole system was democratized to a considerable extent. In countries such as Sweden the school system has been changed from the earlier dual pattern to one in which a pupil may pass from the lower to the higher schools much as in the United States. In other European countries the trend is in the direction of a unit school system, that is, a system where the higher schools are open — still with many restrictions — to boys and girls from all classes of society.

The history of schools and recent developments in Europe clearly support the thesis that the school system reflects the pattern of the society of which it is a part and which it is intended to serve. In European countries a dual educational system has been maintained because there has been a class society. In recent years, as the two-class system of society has weakened, the tendency has been away from the dual school system and toward a unified type of educational organization.

EARLY AMERICAN TRANSPLANTATIONS FROM ENGLAND

When educational facilities were first developed in America in colonial days, shortly after the original settlements were established, British civilization and culture were the dominant influences, and naturally the early schools in America were organized in imitation of British models. The system transplanted from England in colonial days was a dual system. Although the colonists desired education for the common people, especially in reading, it was not thought necessary to provide for the common people schools that taught the classical languages. The special schools that administered the traditional curriculum of the European higher schools were exclusive institutions for boys who were to become clergymen.

In the colonies of the southern part of this country, which were settled by owners of large plantations, the wealthy landowners usually sent their children back to England for education. The children of the poorer classes had practically no facilities for education except those provided by philanthropy. Later in the South there sprang up a system of private schools to take care of the educational needs of the wealthier classes, but the poorer classes were only meagerly supplied with education; there was no general public educational system until the middle of the nineteenth century.

MODIFICATIONS IN AMERICA

Although originally patterned after European models, the schools in America began to differ from those of Europe in certain important respects. Three of these significant differences will be made subjects of brief comment.

Control

Education in Europe was from the first controlled by the church or by the government. As nationalism developed in Europe the schools became highly centralized. France may be cited as an extreme example of federal control. The minister of education there even now prescribes in detail what is taught in the schools, when each subject is to be taught, and how it is to be taught. The German state also has always maintained a large measure of central control over both the *Volksschule* and the *Gymnasium*. A German teacher has never had to listen to the advice of parents or citizens in the local community about how the school should be operated; especially on what were known as "inner" school affairs, instruction, curriculum, methods, discipline, and the like, his orders come from above.

In sharp contrast with these European systems, the American schools began early and have continued throughout their history to exhibit a large measure of local autonomy. New England may be taken as an example, for that section of the country has been influential in determining the pattern of school organization in all other parts of the country.

The local communities in New England were small and isolated from one another. Although the colony, and later the state, passed laws requiring each local community to maintain schools, practically all details of organization were left to the community, and there was no machinery except that of the local government for the enforcement of the legislation. As settlement of the country proceeded, offshoots of local communities were established which were often widely separated from the parent community. Instead of the parent community retaining control over the school, a new school district was set up for each new center or settlement. There was thus established the district system of schools which is still characteristic of many sections of this country. The schools that developed under such conditions were controlled by local authorities. Although in later years the tendency toward centralization has become pronounced, even today there remains in the American educational system a large measure of local control, a feature entirely different from the strong central control found in European countries.

Unit Type of School System

In a second important respect the schools in America differ from those in Europe. The elementary and secondary schools in the United States are part of a single system rather than two separate systems as in Europe. Social organization is a prime cause of this difference.

Following the Revolutionary War there began the westward movement in the United States and the settlement of remote parts of the continent. During the early colonial period, as has already been noted, the schools imitated the dual pattern that was characteristic of the European schools. As the frontier became settled, all traces of aristocratic exclusiveness disappeared. There could really be no aristocracy under American frontier conditions. The result was that the so-called "common school" was developed as the single means of education for the children of all classes. The common school accepted children in some cases at the early age of four and allowed them to continue in attendance until they were married and assumed the responsibilities of adult life. Thus there grew up in this country a single or unit system of schools entirely different from the dual school system which had been originally transplanted from England.

Type of Instruction

In a third respect the American schools began to differ from those in Europe. The schools in this country emphasized from the first instruction in reading. In the common schools of Europe, even today, the method of instruction is largely that of oral teaching. For example, the European teacher using a wall map in the classroom describes to the pupils who have no geography textbook the various countries of the world. The pupils make notebooks of the items of information handed down by the teacher. The arithmetic lessons are of the type described in this country as "mental arithmetic," in which the teacher dictates the problem and the pupils solve it without writing it on slates or paper.

Emphasis on reading in American schools was due in part to the fundamental purpose of education, which was to prepare pupils to read the Scriptures. Another reason why reading continues to be emphasized is that many American teachers lack the training that prepares European teachers to give oral instruction. American education as a result of these circumstances has become largely dependent on textbooks.

Summary of Developments up to 1812

In summary it may be said that by the early years of the nineteenth century the American schools, which originally had been founded on European models, had come to differ sharply from the parent types of institution. The modifications that had been introduced in America were a direct result of the social conditions which were considerably different from those prevailing in Europe.

CHANGES FOLLOWING THE WAR OF 1812

By the second quarter of the nineteenth century the United States had reached the stage where its people were beginning to be conscious of the desirability of social improvements in many lines, especially in their educational institutions. This growing social consciousness seems to have been a direct result of the War of 1812, which through the application of embargoes encouraged the development of manufacturing enterprises and economic self-sufficiency in the United States.

State Boards Established

A number of the states in the second quarter of the nineteenth century established state boards of education to supervise the schools, and with this forward step in organization there began in America a long struggle toward the improvement of educational facilities. When the Massachusetts State Board of Education undertook its work after being established in 1837, it found need for an executive officer. It persuaded a young lawyer by the name of Horace Mann to undertake that office, with the title of Secretary of the Board of Education. The American school system was fortunate that so vigorous a personality as Horace Mann was brought face to face with the problems of education in that day.

Horace Mann visited the schools and found that they were at an extremely low level of efficiency; the equipment was poor, the teachers were untrained, the terms were short, and, in general, education was meagerly provided for the common people. He drew the conclusion that a large part of the difficulty could be charged to the district school system. He demanded standardization of the schools. At about the same time similar suggestions began to be heard in other states, and leaders such as Henry Barnard of Connecticut, Calvin Stowe of Ohio, Caleb Mills of Indiana, Calvin Wiley of North Carolina, and John Pierce of Michigan began to advocate reforms in education in their respective sections.

The Elementary School Reorganized

The reformers mentioned in the preceding paragraph, in looking around for methods of improving the schools, found in Europe, especially in Prussia, examples of well-organized schools for children. They began to reconstruct the district school of America, vigorously recommending an eight-year graded elementary school of the type then existing in Prussia. During the decades from 1840 on, the older district or common school of America was replaced by an elementary school with a graded organization and an eight-year curriculum. Some American scholars have expressed doubt as to the influence of the Prussian system in producing the new elementary school and have insisted that the reorganization of the common school was a native development. An analysis of the speeches and writings of American educational reformers of the 1830's and 1840's seems to leave little question that the graded system was actually borrowed from Prussia.

The graded elementary school as it now exists in the United States should be sharply distinguished from the common school which existed before the elementary school was organized. The common school was ungraded, and attempted to serve the needs of pupils of all ages up to the completion of formal education. The modern elementary school, by contrast, is a graded school and definitely ceases to serve the needs of pupils after they reach the end of the eighth grade.

It must be remembered that the Prussian *Volksschule* which set the pattern for the American elementary school was not the school for the upper classes, but the school for the masses. The *Volksschule* was based on the assumption that eight years would provide all the education needed by any boy or girl of the common people. The difficulties of importing a foreign institution and adapting a school originally designed for a two-class system of society to the needs of a single-class democratic society are still causes of important weaknesses in the American educational system. Certain of the significant reforms now in progress in the American school system are directed toward the correction of these weaknesses.

Institutions Established for the Preparation of Teachers

The early educational reformers in America also pointed out that suitable arrangements were lacking for the preparation of teachers. Up to the second quarter of the nineteenth century there were practically no special provisions for the education of teachers, although even before the time of Horace Mann the desirability of such facilities had been considered. A Frenchman,

Victor Cousin, had reported on the Prussian system of preparing teachers; an English translation of his report was reprinted in New York in 1835 and came into the hands of Americans interested in better schools.   Cousin's report was influential in stimulating the establishment of the first public normal schools in this country in 1839.

Until recent times there has been in this country a sharp distinction between the education carried on in colleges and the education of teachers for the common schools.   A number of colleges had been established in America before 1840, but no one thought of them as agencies for the preparation of teachers for the lower schools.   Colleges had been established originally as training schools for the ministry; that is, they were theological schools.   In the course of time they took on the function of training lawyers, and other professional groups.   The colleges, however, were not adapted to the preparation of teachers for the elementary schools, for none of the content of the college curriculum had any particular bearing on the subject matter taught in the elementary school.   The lack of emphasis on advanced study for the teachers of these early schools is well illustrated by a statement by the state superintendent of public instruction in Michigan, who in 1842 described the desirable quali fications of an elementary-school teacher as follows:

> An elementary school, where the rudiments of an English education only are taught, such as reading, spelling, writing, and the outlines barely of geography, arithmetic, and grammar, requires a female of practical common sense, with amiable and winning manners, a patient spirit, and a tolerable knowledge of the springs of human action.[1]

The curriculum of the first normal schools consisted largely of a review of the common-school subjects.   Their enrollees had no qualification higher than the completion of the common school. Since the beginning of the twentieth century the normal schools

[1] State Superintendent of Public Instruction, State of Michigan.   *Report*, 1842, p. 254.

have improved their equipment, raised their requirements for entrance, and broadened their curriculums. A large part of them now prepare secondary-school teachers, and many of them have evolved into teachers colleges, granting degrees. Although a considerable number of the students in the normal schools and teachers colleges of the United States are still graduated on the basis of curriculums two years in length, the short curriculums are rapidly being replaced by full college curriculums.

The fact that the normal schools were originally established as institutions unrelated to the existing system of higher education has been a cause of confusion — confusion that has by no means disappeared as the years have passed. Furthermore, the confusion is increased by the fact that many liberal arts colleges have changed their curriculums so as to include courses designed to prepare teachers and have as a result come into direct competition with teachers colleges.

Changes in Colleges and Secondary Schools

While the changes described were taking place in the lower schools and in the institutions for the preparation of teachers, equally important changes were occurring in the secondary schools and colleges which originally imitated the pattern of the exclusive higher institutions of Europe. Some of the changes in American upper schools are the direct consequences of the democratic tendencies which grew out of the awakening that came as a result of the War of 1812. Many of them are of later date and will be described in subsequent chapters. For the purposes of the present discussion it is enough to say that the secondary schools of America are no longer exclusive class schools designed for the few. They are schools for the common people to a degree unparalleled in the history of any other nation.

State Supervision of Education

The reforms which took place in education during the first half of the nineteenth century were accompanied by an ever-increasing participation in the control of schools by the state as distinguished from the local government.   The state has always been the ultimate source of all authority in educational matters but because of the scattered population of the states in their early history and because the personnel of state government was in former times limited, the local community was allowed to go its independent way in conducting its schools.   It became evident in the course of time that if standards were to be maintained there must be central supervision of a more vigorous type than that which was supplied through local government.   The state has as a result withdrawn in some measure the right of independent action by local governments and has assumed control in areas in which earlier it did not exercise its authority.

Financing Schools

Up to the middle of the nineteenth century the financial support of schools was meager.   Parents contributed in one way or another to the payment of the salary of the teacher.   Anything approaching complete public support through taxation was uncommon.   In many instances philanthropy provided schools. Sometimes the local governmental authority bore the costs of schooling only for the children who belonged to pauper families. The view was widely accepted that the state had no right to impose taxes for education on persons who were not parents of the children attending school.

One of the great struggles of the last century was the struggle to secure public tax support for schools.   Sentiment in favor of public support of education was not firmly established even in some of the northern states until after the Civil War.

BIBLIOGRAPHY

Butterweck, Joseph S., and J. Conrad Seegers, *An Orientation Course in Education*, pp. 25–79, 94–125, 336–39.   Boston: Houghton Mifflin Company, 1933.

Clapp, Frank L., Wayland J. Chase, and Curtis Merriman, *Introduction to Education*, pp. 1–154.   Boston: Ginn and Company, 1935.

Cubberley, Ellwood P., *The History of Education*, pp. 3–786.   Boston: Houghton Mifflin Company, 1920.

Cubberley, Ellwood P., *Public Education in the United States*, pp. 1–407. Boston: Houghton Mifflin Company, 1934.

Douglass, Aubrey A., *The American School System*, pp. 3–31, 60–92.   New York: Farrar and Rinehart, 1934.

Eby, Frederick, and Charles Flinn Arrowood, *The Development of Modern Education*.   New York: Prentice-Hall, 1934.   xxiv + 922 pp.

Educational Policies Commission of the National Education Association, *The Unique Function of Education in American Democracy*.   Washington: National Education Association, 1937.   vi + 130 pp.

Frasier, George Willard, and Winfield D. Armentrout, *An Introduction to the Literature of Education*, pp. 269–95.   Chicago: Scott, Foresman and Company, 1931.

Graves, Frank Pierrepont, *A Student's History of Education*.   New York: The Macmillan Company, 1936.   xix + 568 pp.

Judd, Charles H., *The Evolution of a Democratic School System*, pp. 1–70. Boston: Houghton Mifflin Company, 1918.

Knight, Edgar W., *Education in the United States*, pp. 1–460.   Boston: Ginn and Company, 1934.

Patterson, S. Howard, Ernest A. Choate, and Edmund de S. Brunner, *The School in American Society*, pp. 59–157.

Reeder, Ward, *A First Course in Education*, pp. 1–49.

Reisner, Edward H., *Historical Foundations of Modern Education*.   New York: The Macmillan Company, 1927.   xv + 514 pp.

Schachner, Nathan, *The Mediaeval Universities*.   New York: Frederick A. Stokes Company, 1938.   viii + 388 pp.

Wilson, Lester M., and I. L. Kandel, *Introduction to the Study of American Education*, pp. 3–36.   New York: Thomas Nelson and Sons, 1934.

CHAPTER III

SOCIAL, INDUSTRIAL, AND EDUCATIONAL CHANGES IN THE UNITED STATES SINCE 1870

THE WAR OF 1861–65 was a turning point in the development of the educational system of the United States. Like all major wars, the War Between the States resulted in a social upheaval. Men during their service in the army acquired new ideas of geographical relationships and social organization. Women had new opportunities opened to them in the economic world because of the large number of men called out of civilian occupations into military service. At the time of the demobilization of the armies at the end of the war the soldiers in many instances found occupations that were different from those in which they had been engaged in earlier peacetime. Often they took up residence in new parts of the country. In many ways the Civil War contributed to the radical modification of the social pattern of the country. The schools could not fail to be affected by these modifications in the general social structure.

Three very important educational changes in the United States since the Civil War may be briefly mentioned. The first of these was a general expansion in school facilities, including a lengthening of the school period, both in years of schooling per individual and in days of schooling per year. This expansion included the organization of the public secondary school. The second was in the introduction of improved methods of administration and the coming of organization and systematization in the management of schools. The third was the development of new methods of instruction and a new spirit of critical examination of the results of education.

In order to illustrate the effect of social change on the educational system, only the first of these important educational developments following the Civil War, the expansion in school facilities, will be discussed in this chapter. In later chapters attention will be paid to the development in school administration and to the movement for the critical study of education and its results.

EXPANSION OF SCHOOL FACILITIES

The expansion in school facilities in the United States in the years following 1870 is important chiefly because it resulted in the development of a new type of secondary school. Three types of secondary schools, the Latin grammar school, the academy, and the high school, have appeared in the history of this country.

The first secondary school in America was the Latin grammar school, patterned after the English model. The Latin grammar school was the only type of secondary school known in this country for more than a hundred years after colonization began, and it continued as a major factor in the educational system for a long period even after other types of secondary schools had been introduced.

About the middle of the eighteenth century, a new type of secondary school, the academy, came into existence. It was different in some respects from the Latin grammar school. It admitted young people who had attended the district schools and it conducted a more popular type of curriculum. It offered in many cases the subjects of the conventional classical secondary-school curriculum, but in addition gave courses in a number of practical and popular subjects, such as bookkeeping, surveying, navigation, and the fine arts. The academy was a privately controlled institution, and frequently was operated on a proprietary or profit-making basis.   The available statistics regarding the development of the academy are not entirely trustworthy, but it seems clear that by the middle of the nineteenth century this institution had become a very important part of the American educational system.   The academy continued to exert a strong influence until well after the Civil War; after 1880 it began to disappear rapidly, the established institutions either being closed or taken over by communities and converted into public high schools.   A few endowed academies remain today but for the most part they differ from the high school only in name and control; a privately controlled secondary school is today frequently called an academy.

Near the end of the first quarter of the nineteenth century the public high school, at that time a new type of secondary school, began to appear in the larger cities of the northern states.   This new institution developed slowly at first, but shortly after the Civil War it began to grow rapidly.   The rise of the public high school was the cause of the disappearance of the academy.

The development of the public high school was a direct consequence of the fact that the establishment of a graded system in the elementary schools, based upon the model of the Prussian *Volksschule*, fixed the terminal point of elementary education at the end of eight years of schooling.   Prior to the organization of the elementary school the common school, which was the school attended by the ordinary boys and girls of this country, accepted pupils up to the age of twenty-one, teaching them for the most part by the method of individual instruction.   Young people were permitted to attend the common school as long as they found attendance profitable and interesting, until they reached their majority, or until they were married.   But with the introduction of the graded system, the pupil who had completed the eighth grade could not go further, even if he desired to do so, unless he could afford to attend an academy, usually in a town in which he did not live, and unless he could afford to pay the tuition fees that were charged for education in the higher institution.

The public high school was a solution of the problem that faced the older youth of the country. It can properly be thought of as having come into existence in response to a democratic desire on the part of the American people for more education for the common people than was supplied by the graded elementary school.

An important milestone in the development of the high school was the Kalamazoo Decision, handed down by the Supreme Court of Michigan in 1874. The school authorities in the city of Kalamazoo had levied a tax in 1872 for the purpose of maintaining a high school. Certain citizens brought suit to prevent the expenditure of moneys collected by taxation for education above the elementary level. Specifically the suit was against the use of tax receipts for the teaching of foreign languages, these languages being the subjects characteristic of the secondary curriculum.

Judge Cooley in rendering the decision of the Court made the following sweeping decision.

> The bill in this case is filed to restrain the collection of such portion of the school taxes assessed against complainants for the year 1872, as have been voted for the support of the high school in that village, and for the payment of the salary of the superintendent. While, nominally, this is the end sought to be attained by the bill, the real purpose of the suit is wider and vastly more comprehensive than this brief statement would indicate, inasmuch as it seeks a judicial determination of the right of school authorities, in what are called union school districts of the state, to levy taxes upon the general public for the support of what in this state are known as high schools, and to make free by such taxation the instruction of children in other languages than the English. The bill is, consequently, of no small interest to all the people of the state; and to a large number of very flourishing schools, it is of the very highest interest, as their prosperity and usefulness, in a large degree, depend upon the method in which they are supported, so that a blow at this method seems a blow at the schools themselves. The suit, however, is not to be regarded as a blow purposely aimed at the schools. It can never be unimportant to know that taxation, even for the most useful or indispensable purposes, is warranted by the strict letter of the law; and whoever doubts its being so in any particular case, may well be justified by his doubts in asking a legal investigation, that, if errors or defects in the law are

found to exist, there may be a review of the subject in legislation, and the whole matter be settled on legal grounds, in such manner and on such principles as the public will may indicate, and as the legislature may prescribe.

The instrument submitted by the [Constitutional] convention to the people and adopted by them provided for the establishment of free schools in every school district for at least three months in each year, and for the university. By the aid of these we have every reason to believe the people expected a complete collegiate education might be obtained. The branches of the university had ceased to exist; the university had no preparatory department, and it must either have been understood that young men were to be prepared for the university in the common schools, or else that they should go abroad for the purpose, or be prepared in private schools. Private schools adapted to the purpose were almost unknown in the state, and comparatively a very few persons were at that time of sufficient pecuniary ability to educate their children abroad. The inference seems irresistible that the people expected the tendency towards the establishment of high schools in the primary school districts would continue until every locality capable of supporting one was supplied. And this inference is strengthened by the fact that a considerable number of our union schools date their establishment from the year 1850 and the two or three years following.

If these facts do not demonstrate clearly and conclusively a general state policy, beginning in 1817 and continuing until after the adoption of the present constitution, in the direction of free schools in which education, and at their option the elements of classical education, might be brought within the reach of all the children of the state, then, as it seems to us, nothing can demonstrate it. We might follow the subject further, and show that the subsequent legislation has all concurred with this policy, but it would be a waste of time and labor. We content ourselves with the statement that neither in our state policy, in our constitution, or in our laws, do we find the primary school districts restricted in the branches of knowledge which their officers may cause to be taught, or the grade of instruction that may be given, if their voters consent in regular form to bear the expense and raise the taxes for the purpose.[1]

The Kalamazoo Decision was by no means the only court decision which was rendered in support of the public high school

[1] *Stuart, et al.* v. *School District No. 1 of the Village of Kalamazoo*, 30 Mich. 69.

in the early days of its organization.   There was grave doubt in the minds of many people, including some of the leading educators of the country, with respect to the propriety of opening secondary schools to the common people.

For years following the early seventies the growth of the second-ary-school population was slow.   It was not until the present century that the ideal of public high schools was fully realized and the enrollments of the schools expanded to include the major-ity of the young people of appropriate ages.

Accurate statistics regarding the number of pupils enrolled in the public high schools are not available prior to 1890.   The reports before that year reflect the confusion that existed regard-ing the nature of this new institution.   The data in Table 1, reported by the United States Office of Education, indicate the

TABLE 1. SECONDARY-SCHOOL ENROLLMENTS IN THE UNITED STATES, 1890–1936 *

Year	Secondary-School Enrollment
1890	357,813
1900	695,903
1910	1,111,393
1920	2,494,676
1930	4,799,867
1936	6,424,968

* *Statistical Summary of Education, 1935–36,* p. 7 (being Chapter I of Volume II of the *Bien-nial Survey of Education in the United States: 1934–36*).   U.S. Office of Education Bulletin, 1937, no. 2, advance pages.   Washington, D.C.: Government Printing Office, 1939.

growth of high schools has doubled every decade.   Even the depression of the 1930's did not slow down this movement.   In 1938 it was estimated that 70 per cent of the total population between fourteen and seventeen years of age was actually en-rolled.   The corresponding figure in 1890 was only 7 per cent. No European country has ever reported 15 per cent of its youth of the appropriate ages actually enrolled in secondary schools.

The secondary-school period was not the only part of the educa-tional system which showed marked expansion in enrollment following the Civil War, although the increases were more striking at the secondary level than in any other part of the school system.

Colleges and universities also grew rapidly and by 1936 had between seven and eight times as many students enrolled as in 1890. The elementary schools also increased their enrollment, particularly in the upper grades. The increases in the elementary school were less striking than those in secondary schools only because there had already been a tendency toward universal education at the lower level. The ideal of a universal education at the elementary-school level may now be said to have been achieved in the United States, and universal secondary education has been approximated.

SOCIAL AND ECONOMIC FACTORS CONTRIBUTING TO THE EXPANSION OF EDUCATION

Educational changes of such unprecedented scope as those that have been outlined do not occur by accident. They are the product of definite causes within the economic and social system. A number of the social and economic changes since 1870 that have had an important bearing on educational development in the United States may be described briefly.

Mechanization of Industry

During the 1870's and 1880's the coal and iron of western Pennsylvania were extensively mined. They supplied the materials necessary for a rapid development of machine industry. Great strides were made during the last half of the nineteenth century in supplementing man power by mechanical power. The trend has continued at accelerated rate during the twentieth century. Data presented in *Recent Social Trends* [1] indicate that the amount of power available in 1929 was twenty-six times the amount available only thirty years before. Since this estimate includes passenger automobiles, not all the increase in power has

---

[1] *Recent Social Trends in the United States*, p. 61. Report of the President's Research Committee on Social Trends. New York: Whittlesey House (McGraw-Hill Book Co.), 1934.

been available for production. With passenger automobiles excluded from the computation, however, the amount of power available in 1929 was more than six times that available in 1899.

Partly because of this increase in power and partly because of other industrial developments, the individual worker can today produce a much larger quantity of goods and services than he could a generation or two ago. Between 1899 and 1925 the per capita output of labor increased 53 per cent in agriculture, 99 per cent in mining, 42 per cent in manufactures, and 56 per cent in railway transportation. For example, a worker produced about 4,000 pounds of copper metal in a year in 1860; in 1929 the production of copper per man-year was in the neighborhood of 45,000 pounds. Similar illustrations of the increased production per worker could be given from practically every line of industrial activity. In agriculture during the five-year period beginning in 1922 total production increased 27 per cent while the total amount of labor engaged in agriculture actually declined.

These increases in production are important because they indicate that higher standards of living in this country can be maintained with smaller and smaller demands on human labor. Where the labor of children of school age was employed two or three generations ago in producing enough raw materials and manufactured goods to maintain a reasonably satisfactory standard of living, the increased mechanization of agriculture and industry now permits ample production without requiring the labor of children of school age.

The Closing of the Frontier

Through the history of the colonial period and the history of national life up to 1880, there was a great unoccupied frontier to which anyone seeking new land and new opportunities might move. The census of 1880 contains a brief statement to the effect that the frontier no longer existed. The fact referred to in that statement is of profound significance for education. The public domain which lay to the west of the populated areas of the North

American continent was opened by the Federal Government to homesteaders on highly attractive terms. These pioneering immigrants were given land in large areas and were free to organize communities without any of the hampering restrictions which limited life in older parts of the country.

The spirit of social invention which characterized frontiersmen is one of the most important causes for many of the institutions which characterize the nation. The attitudes of independence and self-reliance which flourished among those who settled the new lands in the west explain many of the movements which have determined educational policies.

The schools of the colonies, of the early states, and of the frontier did not teach practical arts because these arts were taught in the home. The common schools of the early days had a limited program of instruction. The school was of comparatively small importance in preparing young people for their occupations. The school limited its ministrations to instruction in the subjects which the home did not teach.

The frontier had an important function in that it absorbed the population which could not find employment in the industries that were carried on in the eastern towns and cities. Indeed, young people who found the farms of the east overcrowded migrated to the west and there founded independent homes. The understanding of American life is quite impossible without reference to the frontier and its settlement.

It is equally true that an understanding of the problems of present-day American life is impossible without considering the all-important fact that there are now no valuable homesteads to give away. Tax receipts are necessary to provide for young people opportunities of a type corresponding to those which the Federal Government formerly could provide by giving away the public domain without taxing anyone.

The people of this country have gained a biased view on economic issues of many different kinds but especially on taxation because so much assistance could formerly be given young

people by the government without imposing taxes.   When it
becomes necessary, as it is now, to give practical training to boys
and girls in trade schools because these young people cannot be
trained for life on frontier homesteads, society begins to feel the
burden imposed by the educational system as it never did in
earlier times when the educational system performed only a minor
part in the upbringing of children.

Cityward Movement of Population

Another important social change in the United States that has
affected education is the movement of the population into the
cities.   This trend was under way long before the Civil War, but
it has been greatly accelerated since 1880.   Table 2, based on
data from the U.S. Census, shows the percentage of the total
population of the United States living in cities of 2500 or more,
by decades from 1880 to 1930.

TABLE 2. PERCENTAGE OF TOTAL POPULATION IN CITIES
OF 2500 OR MORE, 1880–1930*

Year	Percentage of Total Population that was Urban
1880	28.6
1890	35.4
1900	40.0
1910	45.8
1920	51.4
1930	56.2

* *Fifteenth Census of the United States: 1930, Population*, vol. II, p. 8.
Washington, D.C.: Government Printing Office, 1933.

This tabulation shows that in a period of fifty years the percentage of the population in the United States living under urban
conditions doubled.   Since 1920 more than half of the total population has lived in cities.   Surrounding the cities are extensive
suburban areas which supply to a large population the advantages
of city life.   Furthermore, with the building of good roads, the
development of automobile transportation, and the extension into
the rural regions of electric service, a family on the farm now

differs much less in its mode of living from a family in the city than was the case a generation or two ago.

The causes which have led to the urbanization of this country are closely related to the development of machine industry. Factories where steam power is used gather about them large numbers of workers. Because much of the work of agriculture may be performed by machinery, fewer people are required to work on the farm than were formerly necessary to produce the Nation's food and other raw materials.

The mechanization of industry and the concentration of population in urban centers have an important bearing on the development of educational facilities. In former times, when agriculture was the chief occupation of the American people, the school program was arranged to permit the release of children during certain seasons of the year, in order that their labor might be used when the demands for crop sowing, tending, or harvesting were imperative. No such seasonal cycle is found in the city. The number of days in the year the schools may be kept open is much longer in the city than it was earlier or than it is now in many rural districts. The compact nature of the population of the city makes possible also an efficient grouping of the pupils for instructional purposes, and permits the maintenance of more effective classes and the use of more elaborate equipment. The rapidity with which the population of urban centers has increased, however, has raised serious problems of organization of instruction and housing for the school population. Furthermore, classes have in some cases been allowed to increase in size to the point where they cannot be properly taught.

Changes in the Ratio of Adults to Children

A third notable social change in the United States is one that has occurred in the age-structure of the population. Ever since the first Census in 1790 a tendency has been exhibited toward a diminishing proportion of children in the population. This tendency may be stated statistically in terms of the number of

adults for a given number of children.   Table 3 shows the number
of white persons twenty years of age and over per thousand children under sixteen years of age, for each decade from 1790 to
1930.

TABLE 3. NUMBER OF ADULTS PER THOUSAND CHILDREN IN
THE UNITED STATES, 1790–1930 *

Year	Number of Adults
1790	782
1800	850
1810	847
1820	883
1830	931
1840	989
1850	1,118
1860	1,175
1870	1,244
1880	1,355
1890	1,502
1900	1,583
1910	1,765
1920	1,801
1930	2,013

* Data for 1790 to 1900, inclusive, from Bureau of Census, United States Department of
Commerce, *A Century of Population Growth, 1790–1900*, p. 103.   Data for 1910, 1920, and 1930
calculated from *Fifteenth Census of the United States: 1930, Population*, vol. II, Table 20, pp.
593–94.

It is apparent from these data that in 1930 there were more than
twice as many adults per thousand children in the United States
as there had been in the population a hundred years previously.
Although the tendency toward fewer children per thousand adults
has been manifest ever since 1790, the change in the population
structure has taken place much more rapidly in the period following the Civil War than in the decades of the first part of the
nineteenth century.

The causes of this tendency toward a smaller proportion of
children in the population are numerous, and the problem is one
of special concern to the sociologist.   Many of these causes are to
be found in the conditions referred to in earlier paragraphs.

Large families, for example, are more difficult to maintain in cities than in rural areas.

The schools have to deal with the practical phases of the present situation. It is obvious that the society of today, with an average of two adults per child, can care much better for its children, can feed, clothe, house, and educate them in a much more satisfactory manner, than the society of a century ago with its average of only one adult per child. The actual degree to which this change in the population structure makes possible increased educational opportunities for children without greater burden on the population in the age group responsible for the economic productivity of the country is difficult to determine, but it is probable that, other things being equal, a state with two adults per child can provide at least four times the educational facilities with the same strain on its economic resources that can be provided by a state with one adult per child. It may thus be surmised that the changing age structure of the population has had a considerable influence on the expansion of the enrollment in the schools during the period following the Civil War.

On the other hand, competition for places in industry has become acute between middle-aged individuals. Since a higher percentage of the population belongs to the producing group, the absorption of the products of labor becomes increasingly difficult and consequently industry has more workers than it can use to supply goods for popular consumption. The problem of unemployment of adults has become acute and unemployment of young people has become common.

Children in Gainful Employment

The statistics of school attendance are the counterparts of the statistics of gainful employment of young people. When a child cannot secure gainful employment he is very likely to be found in school. What is said in earlier paragraphs regarding increased enrollments in the upper grades is directly related to the facts reported in Table 4, the data for which are derived from the

TABLE 4. PERCENTAGE OF BOYS AND GIRLS 10–15 YEARS OF AGE IN
GAINFUL OCCUPATIONS IN THE UNITED STATES, 1870–1930 *

Year	Percentage of 10-15-Year-Olds Employed
1870	13.2
1880	16.8
1890	18.1
1900	18.2
1910	18.4
1920	8.5
1930	4.7

* *Ninth Census of the United States: 1870*, vol. I, p. 698.   *Fifteenth Census of the United States: 1930, Population*, vol. V, p. 345.

United States Census.   Table 5 shows that school enrollments have increased for older children as well as for those fifteen years of age or younger.

TABLE 5. PERCENTAGE OF VARIOUS AGE GROUPS ATTENDING SCHOOL
IN THE UNITED STATES, 1910–30 *

Age Group	Percentages Attending School In:		
	1910	1920	1930
5	17.1	18.8	20.0
6	52.1	63.3	66.3
7–13	86.1	90.6	95.3
14–15	75.0	79.9	88.8
16–17	43.1	42.9	57.3
18–20	15.2	14.8	21.4

* *Thirteenth Census of the United States: 1910*, vol. I, p. 310.   *Fourteenth Census of the United States: 1920*, vol. II, pp. 1044–45.   *Fifteenth Census of the United States: 1930*, vol. III, p. 10.

The causes of changes reported in Tables 4 and 5 are readily ascertainable.   One of the important causes has been a change in the methods of industry and a corresponding change in the attitude of manufacturers and employers.   Largely because of the mechanization of industry, child labor is today unprofitable. Industry is very sensitive to any condition that affects its profits and is quick to respond to it.   The attitude of manufacturers on this question is well illustrated in the statement contained in an article by Richard H. Edmonds: "Introduction to Facts about Child Labor." The statement is as follows: "Employers generally realize that child labor is not profitable. They do not want it. Immature children are not capable of handling to advantage expensive and complicated machinery." [1]

Another cause for the change in the attitude of manufacturers toward child labor lies in the increasing requirements for compensation to workers who suffer from accidents. A number of the states require all employers to carry compensation insurance which will reimburse the employee if he is injured while at work. Even where these requirements are not in effect, farsighted employers carry such insurance of their own volition in order to protect themselves against damage suits arising from injuries to workers. The companies which provide insurance operate on the basis of actuarial tables developed statistically from careful records of experience. The actuarial tables show that the accident rate is relatively high among young workers, so in many lines of industry the insurance company offers the employer a choice between a high rate for his insurance if he employs children under eighteen or twenty years of age, and a much lower rate if he agrees not to employ workers under these ages. The advantage in rates for insurance is commonly so large as to lead the employer to choose the alternative of the lower rate and the higher employment age.

Besides this change in the attitude of manufacturers, another important factor bringing about a decrease in employment of children is the attitude of organized labor. The labor group has always strongly opposed child labor and has worked actively for legislation to limit the employment of children in industry. Labor has of course looked upon the employment of children as competitive. Labor has also been opposed to anything which it regards as exploitation of workers, and the employed child is particularly open to exploitation by an unscrupulous employer. The fact that the children who formerly entered employment

[1] Printed in the *Manufacturers' Record*, vol. XC, for July 15, 1926.

were for the most part sons and daughters of workers explains in some measure the reason for labor's attitude on the question. Organized labor, because of these motives, has worked vigorously and successfully to obtain legislation forbidding employment under certain age limits.

Besides the employer and the labor group, a small but enthusiastic group of humanitarians has for many years worked at the task of eliminating child labor. The proper development of a child, this group points out, requires that he have opportunities for rest, recreation, and education to a degree that is impossible to a laborer. Humanitarians have been successful in educating the general public to the dangers of child labor, and have done much to mobilize sentiment for the support of legislation opposing the employment of children.

Change in the Status of Women

The place of women in the economic and social world has undergone a radical revolution since the time of the Civil War. This movement, sometimes referred to as the emancipation of women, has opened up hundreds of vocations to women which were formerly closed to them. From the period when the chief occupation of women was that of wife and homemaker, society has passed into the present-day period when it not only tolerates but demands the service of women in many kinds of productive employment. It is difficult today to realize, for example, that at the time of the Civil War a woman would have been considered entirely outside of the pale of social respectability should she have been so bold and daring as to take a position as a secretary in an office. Today commerce and industry depend almost exclusively upon the services of women in the field of stenography, typing, filing, and secretarial service.

The employment of women in clerical occupations and in many forms of labor outside the home has resulted in radical changes in the home life of the American people. The family is today much less than it formerly was the agency for the education of children.

The school has been called on increasingly to perform many of the services which were in earlier times performed by the family.

Mobility of Population

There are other social changes which have taken place in recent decades that have vitally affected education. The population of the United States is much more mobile than it was in earlier times. Transportation facilities have increased greatly and migration from locality to locality takes place on an ever-expanding scale. The cities of this country are constantly receiving people who come from the rural areas, and from the cities a smaller number of people are constantly moving back to rural areas. From North, South, East, and West, people continually move into a different part of the country in search of better economic opportunities or conditions better suited to their needs. As a result, every part of the country must be concerned with education in every other part, for those who will as adults comprise the citizenry of any one community are today receiving their education in many widely scattered places all over the country.

SOCIAL CHANGE CAUSES MODIFICATION IN THE EDUCATIONAL SYSTEM

Enough has been reported in this chapter with respect to the changes which have taken place during the past seventy years in the social and educational systems of the United States to support the position taken in the preceding chapters. It is quite impossible to understand schools without considering the general trends in the life of the nation. The special purpose of this chapter is to pave the way for an understanding of the present unsettled character of the organization and instructional program of the educational system of this country. The upheaval which followed the first World War has produced in the United States, as it did in the rest of the world, new social and intellectual conditions which affect every phase of culture. If one observes that new institutional units are appearing in the school system, such as the nursery school, the junior high school, the junior college, and classes for adult education, one must look behind these particular additions to the school system to discover the causes for their rise.   If one finds that the traditional subjects in the curriculum of schools are giving place to new subjects and that experimentation is going on in many quarters with materials and methods of instruction, one must again seek the social causes for these changes.

Perhaps the most striking series of innovations that are taking place in American education at present are those which appear in the curriculum.   It will be illuminating to study briefly the development of the instructional program of the United States and to note the causes which have brought about this development.

BIBLIOGRAPHY

Burton, William H., *Introduction to Education*, pp. 294–302.

Counts, G. S., *et al.*, *The Social Foundations of Education*.   American Historical Association, Report of the Commission on the Social Studies, Part IX.   New York: Charles Scribner's Sons, 1934.   xiv + 580 pp.

Cubberley, Ellwood P., *The History of Education*, pp. 787–839.

Cubberley, Ellwood P., *Public Education in the United States*, pp. 408–512, 663–87.

Educational Policies Commission, *The Purposes of Education in American Democracy*.   Washington: National Education Association, 1938. ix + 154 pp.

Judd, Charles H., *Education and Social Progress*, pp. 1–50.   New York: Harcourt, Brace and Company, 1934.

Judd, Charles H., *Problems of Education in the United States*, pp. 1–35. New York: McGraw-Hill Book Company, 1933.

Knight, Edgar W., *Education in the United States*, pp. 461–613.

Patterson, S. Howard, Ernest A. Choate, and Edmund de S. Brunner, *The School in American Society*, pp. 193–96, 431–63.

Research Bulletin of the National Education Association, *Population Trends and Their Educational Implications*, XVI:1:3–58 (January, 1938).

Shorling, Raleigh, and Howard Y. McClusky, *Education and Social Trends*. Yonkers-on-Hudson, New York: World Book Company, 1936. vi + 154 pp.

Smith, Payson, Frank W. Wright, and Associates, *Education in the Forty-Eight States*, pp. 1–18. Staff Study no. 1, Advisory Committee on Education. Washington: Government Printing Office, 1939.

Social Change and Education. *Thirteenth Yearbook* of the Department of Superintendence (now the American Association of School Administrators). Washington: National Education Association, 1935. 384 pp.

CHAPTER IV

WHAT THE SCHOOLS TEACH

THE CURRICULUM or organized subject-matter of instruction in schools has a long and complicated history. The so-called "trivium" or group of literary subjects, which was early accepted as the core of the secondary-school curriculum of European institutions, included grammar, rhetoric, and logic. These subjects were emphasized because they were thought to be essential to the preparation of the orator. Since the boys who attended the early secondary schools all expected to enter the services of government or of the church, it was essential that they be able to maintain themselves in public address and in the debates which were characteristic of the scholastic period. Paralleling the literary subjects were certain scientific subjects known collectively as the "quadrivium": arithmetic, geometry, astronomy, and music. These subjects were studied to a less degree than the literary subjects, and were pursued not so much because of interest in their content as because of the training they were supposed to give in methods of reasoning.

The units of the trivium and the quadrivium were called "the liberal arts" because they were appropriate to the education of the freeman or citizen, in contrast with the practical arts which were learned and practiced by slaves and craftsmen. The trivium included as its chief constituent Latin grammar and Latin rhetoric, since Latin was the medium of communication of the learned of all nations and of the church.

When in the sixteenth and seventeenth centuries the natural sciences developed through the thinking and writing of such scholars as Copernicus, Bacon, and Newton, these sciences found it difficult to make their way into the curriculum of the secondary schools. It was not until the middle of the eighteenth century that the natural sciences gained recognition in the secondary-school curriculum of Germany through the establishment of a special institution of secondary education known as the *Real-gymnasium*. The American secondary school continued to emphasize the trivium and the mathematical sciences of the quadrivium until the organization of the public high school after the Civil War and to some extent even up to the present.

RESISTANCE TO CHANGE IN THE CURRICULUM

The tenacity with which established subjects retain their places in the school curriculum is easy to explain. Teachers are disposed to teach the subjects with which they are acquainted, and parents demand that their children shall have the same kind of education that they themselves received when they attended school. Traditional subjects have a prestige which makes it difficult to displace them or even to modify their content.

The attack on traditional subjects usually comes through the vigorous advocacy of new subjects by some interested reformer or by a social group which organizes for the purpose of securing a place in the school program for a hitherto unrecognized body of instructional material. Whenever new subjects are injected into the curriculum a readjustment of the time and attention of teachers and pupils becomes necessary. Usually the readjustment takes place slowly, with the result that the curriculum is always to some extent behind the times. Often new subjects have to be greatly modified before they are finally and fully established as accepted phases of the school program.

It is possible to cite numerous instances of the way in which changes are effected in the curriculum. In 1693 John Locke, the English philosopher, pointed out the folly of overemphasis on the classical subjects in the English secondary schools. In 1855 Herbert Spencer, in an essay entitled: "What Knowledge Is of

Most Worth," made a plea for the study of the sciences, which he contended do as much as the study of a classical language for the discipline of the mind. Furthermore, said Spencer, the sciences give the learner far more practical knowledge than the classics.

The conclusion which Spencer presented is still a subject of vigorous disagreement among educators. It has been the habit of specialists, who represent a particular subject of instruction and who find that attention to the subject which they teach is falling off, to claim that their subject is of superior value because of the general intellectual training which it gives. Much evidence has been accumulated by psychology to show that no subject of instruction in itself compels efficient intellectual activity in a learner. Any subject can be learned in a routine way, and when so learned it becomes utterly formal and barren as an intellectual exercise. The propositions of geometry, for example, can be committed to memory without understanding on the part of the learner. In such a case the learner remains entirely incompetent in logical methods of thinking. Latin words can be translated without producing any beneficial effects in either the vocabulary or literary style of the learner.

The defense of a school subject which specialists offer when they say that the subject is good for the learner's mind is frequently, if not always, a device for protecting the place of that subject in the curriculum after it has lost real social significance. There can be no doubt that desirable changes in the curriculum are frequently inhibited by the efforts of specialists who are moved by their own personal interests rather than by a broad-minded solicitude for keeping the curriculum abreast of the times.

The preceding paragraph mentions only one of the causes which operate to keep the curriculum from complete adaptation to the needs of society. It has been pointed out repeatedly in earlier pages of this book that schools and the social order are related. It is true, however, that the relation which obtains is not always immediately effective. It is inevitable in the long run that schools conform to the demands of society, but the rate at which conformity is achieved varies greatly.

One can find an endless number of examples of resistance to change in the materials of instruction. When the Arabic numerals appeared in Europe in the fifteenth century and began to displace the Roman numerals, the voice of orthodoxy was raised in protest against the introduction of heathen methods of calculation. The Arabic numerals and the methods of computation which they made possible were stigmatized as crass and irreligious. The Arabic numerals were difficult for the older generation to understand. The older generation is always loath to be outdistanced by the younger generation and has to be converted to new ideas by the force of social necessity.

EXAMPLES OF THE EFFECTUATION OF CURRICULUM CHANGES

One need not appeal to remote history to find illustrations of the processes by which the curriculum develops and the difficulties which are encountered in introducing new subjects. The history of American institutions affords striking examples in abundance.

The Morrill Act

In the midst of the Civil War, when agriculture and its allied industries were in need of improvement through the application of scientific principles, the Congress of the United States took action. There had been debates in Congress during the 1850's with regard to the needs of agriculture and with regard to methods of improving it. A bill passed in 1858 providing federal aid to agricultural education had been vetoed by President Buchanan. In 1862, under the leadership of Justin Smith Morrill, then a representative of Vermont in the lower house and later a senator from that state, the Federal Government made liberal grants of land to the states for the establishment of institutions which were to cultivate and teach the science of agriculture and to give instruction in the mechanic arts. The institutions of higher learning of that period were wholly without such practical lines of instruction as were contemplated in the Morrill Act. New colleges were established — those which are now known as the land-grant colleges. The following quotations indicate the way in which the new colleges developed.

When the organization of the colleges was announced the public looked for the arrival of education as something new under the sun, an open sesame to greater prosperity, a panacea of industrial ills, and when it was announced that the courses of study in the Maine State College contained subjects previously taught in the classical institutions it was asked in public print: "Why this new college, these things are already taught?" It was charged that agriculture had been betrayed in the house of its friends and that the faculty was not in sympathy with the purposes for which the new institution was established. In addition, the arguments favoring vocational education exalted the skilled hand as an essential element in its development, a doctrine sound enough in theory but badly misapplied in practice.[1]

An idea of the inadequacy of scientific data and lack of knowledge with which the teachers in the land-grant colleges contended in these early days when they were attempting to provide industrial and agricultural education to the masses is given in the following typical account by Professor Isaac P. Roberts, teacher of agriculture in the Iowa State Agricultural College in 1869:

I began to tell the students what I knew about farming. It did not take me long to run short of material and then I began to consult the library. I might as well [have] looked for cranberries on the Rocky Mountains as for material for teaching agriculture in that library. Thus, fortunately, I was driven to take the class to the field and farm, there to study plants, animals, and tillage at first hand. . . . I fell into the habit of taking the students to view good and poor farms; to see fine herds and scrub herds in the country round about, even though they

---

[1] Statement by William H. Jordan, director of the Maine Agricultural Experiment Station, as reported in the *Survey of Land-Grant Colleges and Universities*, I:19. United States Office of Education Bulletin, 1930, No. 9.

had to travel in freight cars. I suppose I was the first teacher of agriculture to make use, in a large way, of the fields and stables of the countryside as laboratories.... One day, being short on lecture material, I went into the fields and gathered a great armful of common weed pests. Handing them around to the class I asked for the common and botanical names, and the methods of eradication.... This experiment provided material for a week's classroom talk.... [1]

Drawing Introduced as a School Subject

A second example of the process by which the school curriculum expands in response to a demand from outside the schools is supplied by the history of drawing as a school subject. Even at present there are critics who regard drawing as unnecessary and undesirable as a unit in the public-school curriculum. These critics challenge drawing as a tax-consumer, as a luxury, as a subject lacking in value, and as a pet hobby of a few sentimentalists.

The official records of the State Board of Education of Massachusetts show that drawing was introduced by legislation adopted by the state legislature:

> ... in response to a petition signed by several well known and highly respected citizens, distinguished for their interest in popular education, and for their connection with those great branches of mechanical and manufacturing industry which absorb large amounts of the capital, and give employment to great numbers of the residents of the Commonwealth. The petition is as follows:

> *To the honorable General Court of the State of Massachusetts.*

> Your petitioners respectfully represent that every branch of manufactures in which the citizens of Massachusetts are engaged, requires, in the details of the processes connected with it, some knowledge of drawing and other arts of design on the part of the skilled workmen engaged.

> At the present time no wide provision is made for instruction in drawing in the public schools.

> Our manufacturers therefore compete under disadvantages with the manufacturers of Europe; for in all the manufacturing countries of Europe free provision is made for instructing workmen of all classes in

---

[1] *Survey of Land-Grant Colleges and Universities*, I, 21.

drawing. At this time, almost all the best draughtsmen in our shops are men thus trained abroad.

In England, within the last ten years, very large additions have been made to the provisions, which were before very generous, for free public instruction of workmen in drawing. Your petitioners are assured that boys and girls, by the time they are sixteen years of age, acquire great proficiency in mechanical drawing and in other arts of design.

We are also assured that men and women who have been long engaged in the processes of manufacture, learn readily and with pleasure, enough of the arts of design to assist them materially in their work.

For such reasons we ask that the Board of Education may be directed to report, in detail, to the next general court, some definite plan for introducing schools for drawing, or instruction in drawing, free to all men, women and children, in all towns of the Commonwealth of more than five thousand inhabitants.

And your petitioners will ever pray.

Jacob Bigelow.	John Amory Lowell.
J. Thos. Stevenson.	E. B. Bigelow.
William A. Burke.	Francis C. Lowell.
James Lawrence.	John H. Clifford.
Edw. E. Hale.	Wm. Gray.
Theodore Lyman.	F. H. Peabody.
Jordan, Marsh & Co.	A. A. Lawrence & Co.

Boston, June, 1869.[1]

Vocational Education

In 1906 a group of manufacturers and educators organized an association, the National Society for the Promotion of Industrial Education, the purpose of which was to secure for the trades recognition in the educational system similar to that earlier accorded to agriculture. In 1914 this association persuaded Congress to create a commission to study the country's need for vocational education. The arguments presented to this commission

[1] J. White, "Appendix A to the Report of the Secretary," *Thirty-Fourth Annual Report of the Board of Education of the Commonwealth of Massachusetts, Together with the Thirty-Fourth Annual Report of the Secretary of the Board* (1869–70), pp. 163–64.

and later by the commission to Congress were effective in 1917 in securing the passage of the Smith-Hughes Act, which provided federal appropriations for the introduction of trade courses into the secondary schools of the country.   These courses were injected into the instructional programs of secondary schools under the supervision of a special federal agency — the Federal Board for Vocational Education.

A brief extract from the report of the Congressional commission that recommended appropriations for vocational education sets forth the grounds on which appropriations were asked:

Our National Prosperity is at Stake.   We have become a great industrial as well as a great agricultural nation.   Each year shows a less percentage of our people on the farms and a greater in the cities.

Our factory population is growing apace.   Our future as a nation will depend more and more on the success of our industrial life, as well as upon the volume and quality of our agricultural products.   It has repeatedly been pointed out that the time is not far distant when our rapidly increasing population will press hard upon an improved agriculture for its food supply, and force our industries to reach out over the entire world for trade wherewith to meet the demands for labor of untold millions of bread winners....

The battles of the future between nations will be fought in the markets of the world.   That nation will triumph, with all that its success means to the happiness and welfare of its citizenship, which is able to put the greatest amount of skill and brains into what it produces.   Our foreign commerce, and to some extent our domestic commerce, are being threatened by the commercial prestige which Germany has won, largely as the result of a policy of training its workers begun by the far-seeing Bismarck almost half a century ago.

France and England, and even far-off Japan, profiting by the schools of the Fatherland, are now establishing national systems of vocational education.   In Germany, within the next few years, there will probably be no such thing as an untrained man.   In the United States probably not more than 25,000 of the eleven or twelve million workers in manufacturing and mechanical pursuits have had an opportunity to acquire an adequate training for their work in life.[1]

---

[1] *Report of the Commission on National Aid to Vocational Education Together with the Hearings Held on the Subject,* I:22–23.   House of Representatives Document 1004, Sixty-Third Congress, Second Session, 1914.

Safety Education and Health Education

New lines of instruction have been added to the curriculum of the elementary school as well as to the curriculums of the secondary schools. One of the new subjects of instruction in the elementary school is called "safety education." The streets of a modern city and even the roads of the rural areas are beset by hazards because of motor vehicles. Children must be taught how to avoid these hazards. The National Safety Council was organized in 1913 by certain businessmen who realized the dangers of modern mechanical civilization and were desirous of preventing accidents as far as possible. The casualty insurance companies have been the principal influence behind the establishment and maintenance of the National Safety Council. These business interests created an educational division of the Council, which publishes a monthly magazine devoted to accident prevention and supplies outlines of courses in safety education to school systems. Indeed, it has even provided teachers who help to install such courses. The promoters of the movement are much gratified to note by the statistics of accidents that the cities which have been most receptive to their ministrations have comparatively low accident rates. The *Eighteenth Yearbook* of the American Association of School Administrators, published in 1940, is devoted to the topic of safety education.

Paralleling the efforts of the casualty-insurance companies are the commendable efforts of one of the major life-insurance companies, which has been active in publishing booklets for distribution to the schools in the interests of health education. These booklets are attractively illustrated and contain reading lessons on such subjects as "All About Milk," "How to Live Long," "A War on Consumption," "Child Health Alphabet," "Eyesight and Health," and "Hookworm Disease and How to Prevent It." Children in the schools are encouraged, through attention to their personal health, to join in the worthy undertaking of extending the length of human life. The booklets thus serve the double purpose of helping humanity and reducing the risks of the insurance companies.

Care of the teeth has been vigorously promoted in recent years in all well-organized school systems. A series of articles prepared by a dentist and addressed to dentists contains some revealing passages. The following paragraphs are extracts from one of these articles.

> The local dentists had already done something to educate a part of the public. As president of the Bridgeport Dental Society in 1909, Dr. Fones organized a group of dentists, each of whom was to take ten boys to his office and put their mouths in good condition. At the same time these boys were to be taught the principles of oral hygiene. It was felt that they would be centers of interest and information in their schools and homes. They doubtless were. To stimulate public interest further, Dr. Fones wrote a series of articles for the local newspapers and gave public clinics. Other members of the dental profession with convictions like his own came to Bridgeport and gave public addresses. Among these were Drs. T. P. Hyatt, M. L. Rhein, and G. B. Palmer.

> But Fones's plan went much farther than this initial effort. He realized from the beginning that this was a work of education. It had to begin with the powers at the head of municipal affairs, to utilize activities possible only to the Board of Education, and to awaken the public to personal efforts in its own behalf, or it could never reach full fruition. The best way to begin with the authorities was to get them to put some money into the plan, do some of the work and take an interest in what was accomplished. . . .

> Fones sought therefore to induce the Board of Education to desire a demonstration in the schools, to ask the Board of Apportionment for the necessary funds and to be willing to use them when obtained [1]

Thrift Education

The American Bankers Association introduced courses in thrift into the schools, and for this purpose it created a committee of propaganda. An extract from a book prepared by this com-

---

[1] George Wood Clapp, *The Rise and Fall of Oral Hygiene in Bridgeport*, pp. 11–12. New York: Dental Digest, 1929. Reprinted from the *Dental Digest*, XXXIV:91–92, February, 1928.

mittee and published by the American Bankers Association is as follows:

The Savings Bank Division of the American Bankers Association presents in this volume the method for operating school savings banking systems, together with its interpretation of experience extending over many years, and studies by various committees and officials of the Division. The method described contains no experimental suggestion. It has drawn freely upon both the century-old experience of the savings banks and the methods of the most successful school savings banking systems now operating.

The conviction is growing among our people that if thrift is to become general, we must begin to train the child while he is in school. The thought is that by wise organization of school savings banking as an educational project the habit of thrift may be inculcated, even before the pupil is old enough to grasp its full significance. By periodical repetition of the art of saving according to ability, the pupil can thus be led to develop a desire to save, an intention to have something to save, and a determination to avoid thriftless expenditures and waste in general.[1]

Teaching the Constitution

In 1922 the American Bar Association organized a citizenship committee, which had as its chief purpose the enactment of legislation requiring that the Constitution of the United States be taught in all publicly supported educational institutions. The records disclose that the Association was prompted to take this action by genuine fear of a radical socialistic uprising. Something of the purpose of the Association may be gathered from the following statement quoted from the report made by the Committee on American Citizenship to the Association in 1923.

The report of the Committee on the Promotion of American Ideals [1922]... showed the anti-American propaganda that was disseminated; the attacks upon our Constitution; the bitter prejudice manifested against the courts in every community; the fact that socialistic doctrines were being taught in many of our schools and colleges; the

---

[1] *School Savings Banking*, p. v. Published for the American Bankers Association, Savings Bank Division. New York: The Ronald Press Company, 1923.

gross indifference of our people to the duties of citizenship; and in
general the challenge that was being made as to our form of government, not only by "soap box orators," secret societies, and radicals
who work both openly and insidiously, but also members of the United
States Senate and others high in authority who attack the Supreme
Court of the United States and demand a radical change from the
government we have developed under a written constitution.

During the past year the conditions above named have not abated,
but if anything have grown more pronounced and threatening.   It is
stated on competent authority that there are 1,500,000 radicals in
this country who are clamoring for a change in the nature of our
government from its present form to one of various degrees of a com-
munistic state.   It is said there are four hundred newspapers and
periodicals that represent similar views and that are read regularly by
5,000,000 people.   It is also said that $3,000,000 was spent during the
past year on behalf of "Red" propaganda.[1]

The report of the Committee on American Citizenship continues with a quotation from an address made by General John
J. Pershing:

"Dangerous elements are actually moving toward a revolution in
America, both openly and secretly, because national problems have
not been thoroughly discussed.   There is a disruptive tendency toward
radicalism of all sorts.   The slump in patriotism and the consequent
increase in the dangerous elements among us must be checked."[2]

To check the alleged growth of radicalism, the American Bar
Association proposed that all public schools, colleges, and universities be required to offer a separate course in the Constitution of
the United States.   An attempt was made, seemingly with much
success, to organize a citizenship committee in every state and
local bar association in the country.   Members of the bar associations and members of the legal profession in general were urged
to become "Minute Men of the Constitution" and to work vigorously for the enactment of laws requiring the teaching of the
Constitution in all public educational institutions.

[1] "Report of the Committee on American Citizenship," *Report of the Forty-
Sixth Annual Meeting of the American Bar Association* (1923), pp. 443–44.
[2] *Ibid.*, p. 444.

The fundamental purpose of the American Bar Association was undoubtedly commendable, but the educational concept on which the Association acted is open to serious criticism. It was evidently the accepted idea of the Association that a formal knowledge of the Constitution is enough to influence the thought and behavior of citizens. The Association made no demand or provision for the cultivation of a critical understanding of American political institutions. The theory seems to have been that the teaching of the Constitution must be carried on with something of religious fervor, and that the mind of the prospective citizen must be molded while it is still plastic. "The ultimate purpose of the movement is to inspire the emotional culture necessary to give permanency to our democratic institutions." [1] Thus it was said in the report of the Committee on American Citizenship of the American Bar Association in 1922:

> In teaching citizenship, the real essential is "atmosphere." An appeal must be made to the heart, to the spirit and to the emotions, as well as to the intellect.
> Gratitude must be developed, pride must be aroused, love must be inspired. We doubt whether pride can be stirred or whether love can find a place, in any heart in which gratitude is not alive.
> The college or university which confers a degree upon any student until such person understands and *feels* that under our Constitution this is a government by the people, with self-imposed limitations based upon a recognition of inalienable individual rights, is sowing the seed of destruction of the faith of the fathers. . . .
> The schools of America should no more consider graduating a student who lacks faith in our government than a school of theology should consider graduating a minister who lacks faith in God.[2]

Other Subjects Introduced by Legislation

The account thus far presented of additions to the school curriculum does not include any reference to the legislation which

[1] Samuel P. Weaver, "Teaching the Constitution," *American Bar Association Journal*, XV:542, September, 1929.
[2] "Report of the Committee on American Citizenship," *Report of the Forty-Fifth Annual Meeting of the American Bar Association* (1922), p. 421.

has been enacted in many states requiring the teaching of patriotism, humane treatment and protection of animals, manners, and
like subjects, that have been urged on the attention of legislators
by well-meaning citizens who think of the children of the nation,
readily accessible because they are regimented in classrooms, as
a fortunate avenue for propagandizing in favor of the reformers'
moral and social purposes.

INFLUENCE OF PUPILS ON THE CURRICULUM

The social control of the curriculum is not merely external and
legislative.   A potent influence operating to modify the curriculum is that exercised by the pupils in the schools.   Any teacher
who has attempted to administer an unpalatable intellectual dose
to a group of pupils knows there is a strong tendency to modify
instruction so as to avoid the struggle involved in such an undertaking.   If modern pupils balk at translating the intricate passages in which Caesar reports in the form of indirect discourse
what the ambassadors of a half-civilized tribe said, teachers of
Latin are very likely to decide that only selected sections of the
Gallic Wars are necessary for the cultivation of the literary tastes
of their pupils.   Indeed, there are factual indications that many
secondary schools are at the point of sacrificing the classical traditions of the curriculum because of the effective opposition of
pupils.   Anyone who has attended schools knows that pupils can
wear down the devotion of almost any teacher to any part of the
curriculum.

ENRICHMENT OF THE SUBJECTS OF THE CURRICULUM

The curriculum expands not only through the introduction of
new subjects but through enrichment of the contents of established subjects.   The meagerness of some of the school subjects
which were taught in American schools less than a century ago is
almost unbelievable.   In geography, for example, there has been
such an enlargement of human knowledge through the develop-

ment of means of transportation and communication that the following extract from a textbook in common use in the period immediately preceding the Civil War seems antiquated and even ridiculous.

LESSON XI. THE WORKS OF GOD AND MAN

And now, kind readers, great and small,
Remember what I tell you, all.
God made the ocean and the land;
He placed the mountains where they stand;
He made the valleys and the hills;
The lakes, the rivers, and the rills;
He made all plants, all living things;
The beast that walks, the bird that sings,
The insect dancing in the breeze,
The fishes gliding through the seas;
He made the day, he made the night;
Darkness is his, and his the light;
Sun, moon, and stars, all sink or rise
As he appoints — in yonder skies.
He makes the seasons come and go,
The summer's shower, the winter's snow,
The storm that speaks in thunder-tone, —
All nature's works are God's alone.
In making these man takes no part —
His works are only those of art.
Canals, roads, bridges, carts, and cars,
Towns, cities, streets, with all their jars,
Houses and churches, paper, pens,
Books, hats, shoes, clothing, — these are men's.[1]

Some of the early attempts to introduce the study of nature into the curriculum of the elementary school are of the type illustrated by the following quotations:

BLOODY RAIN

There are on record several instances of a fall of red liquid, resembling blood in appearance, and which has often been accompanied by

---

[1] [S. G. Goodrich], *Peter Parley's Geography for Beginners*, pp. 18–19. New York: Sheldon & Co., 1859.

a descent of aerolites. On the 15th of November, 1755, there was a heavy shower of this kind at Ulm, in Germany, and several parts of Russia and Sweden. There was another, March 5, 1803, in Apulia, in Italy, where it seemed to fall from a reddish black cloud. A descent of large quantities of dry dust preceded the latter; and has on several occasions occurred by itself.

Some of the liquid, which fell at Ulm, and appearing like congealed blood, was examined. It was found to have a sour taste, owing, as it was thought, to the presence of sulphuric acid. When dried, the dust that remained, forming the coloring matter, was found to resemble the substance of the meteoric stones. It was therefore inferred that the dust was caused by the fracture and friction of the aerolites, and that the rain was made red by the dust falling upon the clouds from which it was precipitated.

In the year 1841, a shower of bloody rain was noticed in the State of Tennessee. This was confined to a small district, and, from the peculiar appearance of the liquid, was supposed to proceed from an immense quantity of insects taken up into the air and mingled with the clouds by a whirlwind.[1]

The six-threaded bird of paradise, is one of the most gorgeous and curious species; it has no less than five colors, some of them exceedingly brilliant. It has a ruff of feathers on its neck, and proceeding from the back are long feathers, six of them terminating in thread-like filaments. Nothing can be conceived, more fantastic than this bird, flying through the air, attired as if for a fancy ball.

The paradise pie, is a very curious and beautiful species, with a tuft of feathers on the head and a long graduated tail.

Birds of paradise were once thought to have no feet, to live always in the air until exhausted, and to feed only upon odors, nectar, and dew; but these fancies have been exploded. They feed on insects, fruits, carrion, and the young of other birds.

Thus it often happens that those who have got reputation for great delicacy, are found in fact to have pretty much the same tastes as other people.[2]

[1] S. G. Goodrich, *A Pictorial Natural History: Embracing a View of the Mineral, Vegetable, and Animal Kingdoms*, pp. 64–65. Philadelphia: E. H. Butler & Co., 1870 (new edition).

[2] *Ibid.*, pp. 271–72.

DEFENSIBLE ATTITUDE TOWARD
CURRICULUM CHANGES

The growth of knowledge which makes instruction of the type illustrated in the foregoing quotations unacceptable in this day and age, and the changes illustrated earlier, which have been made in the curriculum as a result of external pressures, are facts of social life quite as much as they are facts of school organization. No one who reviews the expansion of the curriculum can think of education as a static process or as a process which takes place in an independent institution. Education is the means by which society prepares young people to enter upon the life which exists around them. The future will undoubtedly see changes in the curriculum no less radical than those which have taken place in the past. The teaching profession should learn from the history of schools that it is an important part of the duty of this profession to give hospitable consideration to a great many proposals, and to apply to these proposals such carefully directed scientific criticism as will insure the development of a systematic and timely body of instructional material.

The time has passed when the curriculums of educational institutions can be left to the control of chance influences. Knowledge has increased on a vast scale. Selection of the items which can properly be taught to young people and the arrangement of these items in such a way as to insure economical and effective learning are problems which call for solution today more than they have at any previous time in the history of civilized society.

BIBLIOGRAPHY

Burton, William H., *Introduction to Education*, pp. 391–450.

Butterweck, Joseph S., and J. Conrad Seegers, *An Orientation Course in Education*, pp. 179–200.

Caswell, Hollis L., and Doak S. Campbell, *Curriculum Development*. New York: American Book Company, 1935. xvii + 600 pp.

Chamberlain, Leo M., *The Teacher and School Organization*, pp. 389–412.

Cubberley, Ellwood P., *Public Education in the United States*, pp. 539–62.

Douglass, Aubrey A., *The American School System*, pp. 214–39.

Judd, Charles H., *Education and Social Progress*, pp. 51–82, 209–28.

Judd, Charles H., *Problems of Education in the United States*, pp. 68–100.

National Society for the Study of Education, *Curriculum-Making: Past and Present*. Twenty-Sixth Yearbook, Part I. Bloomington, Illinois: Public School Publishing Company, 1927. xiv + 476 pp.

Norton, John K., and Margaret Alltucker Norton, *Foundations of Curriculum Building*, pp. 3–91. Boston: Ginn and Company, 1936.

Patterson, S. Howard, Ernest A. Choate, and Edmund de S. Brunner, *The School in American Society*, pp. 465–566.

Reeder, Ward, *A First Course in Education*, pp. 119–77.

Rugg, Harold O., editor, *Democracy and the Curriculum*. New York: D. Appleton-Century Company, 1939. xiv + 536 pp.

Smith, Payson, Frank W. Wright, and Associates, *Education in the Forty-Eight States*, pp. 49–75. Staff Study no. 1, Advisory Committee on Education.

Wilson, Lester M., and I. L. Kandel, *Introduction to the Study of American Education*, pp. 197–215.

CHAPTER V

Federal Participation in Education

THE ADMINISTRATIVE CONTROL over education in the United States differs radically from that in other civilized nations. In most other countries the central or federal government exercises a powerful and direct control over the school system; in this country the schools are controlled not by the Federal Government, but by the governments of states and local communities. The absence of direct central control over the general system of education does not mean, however, that the Federal Government of the United States is or has been without influence in educational affairs. In many and various ways the Federal Government has affected educational developments in the states, and extensive educational undertakings have been supported and carried on under federal auspices.

CONSTITUTIONAL PROVISIONS

The basic outlines of the federal system of government in the United States are set forth in the Constitution. It is in that document therefore that one must first look for a declaration of federal policies concerning education. A careful search of the Constitution discloses no mention of the word "education" and no reference to any specific educational function of the Federal Government. The Tenth Amendment to the Constitution, moreover, declares that all powers not specifically assigned to the Federal Government are reserved to the states. From these facts educators and legalists have long been accustomed to regard education as a function of the state, rather than a function of the Federal Government.

In practice, the educational system of this country has grown up as a service under almost complete control of the several states. It may be truthfully said that in the United States there is not a single system of education, but rather forty-eight separate and distinct systems, each completely autonomous and under the control of a state government. To these forty-eight state systems there may even be added the systems of the two territories, Alaska and Hawaii, and those of the half-dozen more important outlying possessions, such as Puerto Rico, Guam, and American Samoa, for each of these areas also has its own distinctive school system, unrelated organically to any of the state or territorial systems.

The reason for omitting any reference to education in the Federal Constitution can only be surmised.[1]   It may be pointed out that at the time the Constitution was framed the young states differed markedly in their attitude toward education and in their provisions for it.   If an article in the Constitution assigning educational powers to the Federal Government had been seriously proposed, a bitter controversy would probably have raged over its provisions.   Controversial questions enough, relating to important and inescapable issues, had to be decided, without inviting disagreement by discussion of public education, especially as education at the time of the Constitutional Convention was looked upon as a very minor phase of governmental responsibility.

Education was, in fact, given some consideration by a few members of the Constitutional Convention.   Madison's journal throws light on the disposition which was finally made of education.   Apparently, at one stage in the drafting of the Constitution, control over an educational system was actually included

[1] For an excellent analysis of source material on this question see W. F. Russell, "Federal Financing of Education," *School and Society*, 38:225-33, August 19, 1933.

in a long list of enumerated powers to be assigned to the Federal Government. The list was later condensed and specific reference to education deleted. Some of the delegates considered that the intention had been to include education under a clause relating to the general welfare. Hamilton, in 1791, specifically stated that education was covered in the general welfare clause of the Constitution.

A constitutional amendment granting the Federal Government power over education was urged by two of the early presidents, Jefferson in 1806 and Madison in 1817, but neither of these recommendations was accepted by Congress. With the coming of Jacksonian Democracy and the triumph of the doctrine of states' rights and local autonomy, the conviction came to be generally accepted that the control over education belongs exclusively to the states.

Recent Supreme Court decisions have indicated that the question of the power of the Federal Government over education is by no means a settled issue. Particularly in point are the decisions in the Agricultural Adjustment Act case and the Social Security Act case [1] in which the court indicated that any activity of the Federal Government which can be shown to be related to the general welfare of the country is clearly constitutional. Although by custom American schools have grown up under state and local auspices rather than under federal control, it seems that present interpretations of the Constitution clearly permit a large measure of federal activity in education if such activity can be shown to be in the interest of the general welfare of the country.

HISTORICAL DEVELOPMENT OF FEDERAL PARTICIPATION IN EDUCATION

Despite the lack of any explicit constitutional provision relating to education, the Federal Government from the beginning of its history has given attention to education and has provided support

[1] *United States* v. *Butler*, 297 U.S., 1, 65, 66; *Helving* v. *Davis* (May 24, 1937).

to it in increasing amounts.   The beginnings of federal interest in education antedate even the Constitution itself, for the Ordinance of 1785, providing for the survey of the Northwest Territory, contains a provision reserving the sixteenth section of every township for the support of education.   Two years later the Ordinance of 1787, which provided for the government of the Northwest Territory, made explicit the federal attitude toward education in the famous clause: "Religion, morality, and knowledge being necessary to good government and the happiness of mankind, schools and the means of education shall be forever encouraged." A few years later, when grants of land were made for settlement in Ohio, certain tracts were reserved for the benefit of schools and particularly for universities.   The evident intent of the measures adopted by Congress in these early enactments was to help the settlers who migrated into western territories to maintain the standards of culture which were characteristic of the communities in the older settlements along the Atlantic seaboard.

Organization and Admission of New States

With few exceptions, the states admitted to the Union since 1789 have first been organized as territories.   In the territorial stage, the people and their government are under more or less direct supervision of the Federal Government.   An act of Congress is required to organize the territory as a governmental agency, and this organic act becomes the basic law of the territory, its constitution, so to speak, until it is admitted to statehood.

A study of these acts reveals that in every instance Congress has required the maintenance of an educational system in the territories it has organized.   Inasmuch as these organic acts more or less set the pattern for the later state government when the territory achieves statehood, Congress may quite properly be said to have fathered the system of education in most of the present states of the Union.

Furthermore, a territory can be granted statehood only by satisfying Congress that it is capable of assuming the responsibilities of state government, and Congress in some cases has gone far in specifying the conditions under which the application of a territory for admission to the union of states will be accepted. In the case of at least one state, Congress in granting permission to apply for admission to statehood explicitly specified the maintenance of a public-school system as a part of the proposed state governmental organization.

It is significant that Congress, in exercising power to approve the proposed constitution of a new state, has never approved a state constitution which did not carry provision for an educational system. Although no constitution has ever been disapproved for the reason of lack of such provision, it seems clear that the citizens of territories, in drafting their constitutions, have well understood that the inclusion of provisions for education was necessary in order to obtain Congressional approval.

Land Grants to New States

Not only did the Federal Government provide by general statute for setting aside the sixteenth section of land for schools, but in 1802, when Ohio was admitted to statehood, a grant of federal land was explicitly made for school support. The original agreement in this case seems to have been a compromise or bargain by which the state gave up the right to tax federal lands within its jurisdiction, in return for a grant of land for school purposes. This same policy has been followed in the admission of every subsequent state in which the Federal Government has had any jurisdiction over land. The grants of federal land have been increasingly generous. Originally set at one section in each township, they were later increased to two sections and in the more recently admitted states four sections in each township have been reserved for school purposes.

In addition to these outright grants of sections of land for school purposes, several of the states have received other grants of federal lands which they have been permitted to use for school purposes. Among these grants are certain saline and swamp lands. The so-called "five per cent funds," arising from an allocation of that percentage of the net proceeds of the sale of public lands, have been used in some states for education, although not specified for that purpose by the Federal Government. During the twentieth century two new grants of this type have been added, the forest reserve grant and the mineral royalty grant. In general these grants of land and money have provided only minor sources of support for public education, although in two or three of the states they provide a relatively large income.

The federal land grants described in this section were made for education in general. Congress for the most part did not define the kind of education to be given with the funds produced, nor did it attempt in any way to influence the procedures in the schools supported from such funds.

The Founding of the Land-Grant Colleges

An entirely new policy was introduced in 1862 with the passage of the Morrill Act, which provided a grant of federal lands to each state in the amount of thirty thousand acres for each senator and representative from the state in Congress. As pointed out in the preceding chapter, these grants were for the specific purpose of establishing a new type of educational institution, a college in which agriculture and mechanic arts would be offered as subjects of instruction. Although Congress did not provide for any continuing control over these institutions, it did specify that agriculture, mechanic arts, and also military science should be taught in the institutions so established.

The so-called "land-grant colleges," founded by the states through these federal grants, have proved highly successful, and have rendered a great social and economic service to the country. Each of the states now maintains at least one institution of the land-grant type. In the southern states separate colleges of this type are maintained for Negro students and for white students. A total of sixty-nine institutions, seventeen of which are for

Negro students, are recognized as belonging to the category of land-grant colleges and universities.

In all of the cases described up to this point Congress aided education by grants of land. There existed in the early history of the United States a vast public domain. In allotting land to states to be used for education and other public purposes, Congress made no draft on the tax resources of the nation. This fact is of great importance, as pointed out elsewhere in this volume, because it has left its impression on the thinking of the American people to such an extent that the whole subsequent history of the relation of the Federal Government to subventions of public enterprises has been biased. The American public is today confronted by the fact that the Federal Government no longer has valuable public lands which it can dispose of freely. It must resort to taxation if it is to promote any public enterprise. If it attempts to promote any worthy social undertaking, it can do so only by bringing it to the consciousness of every taxpayer through levies of taxes of a type which were formerly unnecessary. An expectation of help from the central government has been developed in this country which can no longer be satisfied by grants of land. A turning point in the history of federal grants was reached shortly after the Civil War, as will appear in a later paragraph of this chapter when the history of federal participation in education in the last few decades is discussed.

United States Office of Education Established

The first case in which Congress took action with regard to education involving the expenditure of money was in the creation of an agency for the gathering of information about education in all parts of the United States. An act of Congress, passed in 1867, organized a Department of Education without a representative in the President's Cabinet. Two years later, in 1869, the Department of Education was changed to an Office in the Department of the Interior. In 1870 the title was changed to Bureau of Education, but in 1929 the earlier title, Office of Education, was

restored.   Under the executive reorganization in 1939 the Office
of Education was transferred to the Federal Security Agency.

The Office of Education is in charge of an executive director
known as the Commissioner of Education.   The Office has a relatively large staff engaged in fact-finding and research related to
educational problems.   Its support, like that of all federal agencies, is provided out of federal funds.   To be sure, appropriations
for the Office have always been limited, but they make it clear
that there are aspects of education which are of such general
interest to the whole country that only the Federal Government
can deal with them.

Extension of Services in the Land-Grant Colleges

In 1887 Congress contributed to the expansion of the land-
grant institutions, which it had made possible by gifts of land in
1862, by passing the Hatch Act, which allotted money to each
land-grant college for the establishment and maintenance of an
agricultural experiment station.   The amount of these money
grants was originally $15,000 a year to each state; subsequently
the amount was increased to $20,000, then to $30,000, and under
the Purnell Act of 1925 the amount reached $90,000 a year for
each state.   The Bankhead-Jones Act of 1935 made still further
increases.   The authorized grants to the states for experiment
stations reached a maximum, under existing legislation, of
$7,500,000 in 1939–40.

It should be noted that Congress in these grants for agricultural
experiment stations prior to 1935 followed the policy of giving the
same allotment to each state, instead of differentiating according
to the size of the state as in the case of the Morrill Act of 1862,
which made grants, it will be recalled, on the basis of the number
of senators and representatives in Congress.   The Bankhead-
Jones Act of 1935 again changed the basis of distribution, providing that 60 per cent of the grant for experiment stations is to be
distributed to the states according to their rural population, and
40 per cent is to be for research "conducted by such agencies of

the Department of Agriculture as the Secretary may designate or establish."

While the Hatch Act was the first instance in which Congress appropriated money to the land-grant colleges, the Act specified that the money was to be derived from the sale of land. This provision was discontinued in later acts, thus throwing the burden of support directly on tax receipts.

In 1890 there was passed the so-called "Second Morrill Act," which granted funds on an annual basis for the general maintenance of land-grant colleges. The amount originally provided for this purpose was $15,000 yearly to each state; subsequent amendments have increased the grants, first to $25,000 and then to $50,000 annually to each state. The Bankhead-Jones Act of 1935 made still further increases; the amounts now authorized annually for this purpose total $5,000,000. The allotments for general maintenance, like those for the experiment stations, are annual cash grants in a flat sum, each state receiving the same amount, except that the Bankhead-Jones Act provides some funds for general maintenance of the institutions on the basis of population.

Support of a new type of educational activity through federal funds was undertaken with the passage of the Smith-Lever Act in 1914. This legislation provided funds for extension services in agriculture and homemaking, to be carried on through the land-grant colleges. The appropriation made by the Smith-Lever Act increased gradually until it reached a maximum of $4,580,000. Subsequent legislation, particularly the Capper-Ketcham Act of 1928 and the Bankhead-Jones Act of 1935, increased the amount available for agricultural extension purposes. The sum of all federal funds authorized for extension services for the fiscal year ending June 30, 1937, was $17,256,203.67. Under legislation now in effect the grants authorized for extension purposes will ultimately reach in 1942–43 a total of approximately $18,500,000.

The Smith-Lever Act required the matching of federal grants by state and local funds so that for each dollar contributed by the federal treasury there must be an additional dollar contributed from state and local funds. This was the first major piece of educational legislation to adopt deliberately this new federal policy that had been introduced in a somewhat casual way three years earlier, in 1911, in the comparatively minor Marine School Act.

A new plan of making the allotments to the states was also introduced in the Smith-Lever Act. The Act first made a grant of $5000 in a flat sum to each state and then authorized the distribution of the remainder of the fund to each state in accordance with the ratio of the rural population of that state to the total national rural population. Later appropriation acts followed the same plan except that the amount of the flat grant was increased to $10,000 and finally to $30,000, and in the Bankhead-Jones Act the distribution of the remainder for extension services was on the basis of farm population instead of rural population.

Vocational Education and Rehabilitation

The series of specific federal grants of land and money made for educational purposes, beginning with the Morrill Act of 1862, all pertained to services in institutions of higher education. The Federal Government during the second decade of the twentieth century began to make grants-in-aid for other types of educational services. In 1917 Congress was persuaded to pass the Smith-Hughes Act providing federal aid for vocational education in schools of less than college grade. The Act included extensive prescriptions regarding the nature of the program to be maintained, and a federal agency was created to supervise the service. Like the earlier Smith-Lever law, the Smith-Hughes Act required matching of federal funds by state and local funds.

The amount of the federal appropriation in the Smith-Hughes Act increased gradually over a period of years until it reached an annual total of $7,367,000. These amounts were subsequently increased by the George-Reed Act (1929), the George-Ellzey Act

(1934), and the George-Deen Act (1936). The total amount authorized to be appropriated for vocational education under acts in force in 1939–40 was $22,335,000 annually, of which $21,-785,000 was for distribution to the states, and $550,000 for administration in the federal agency. The distribution to the states is on the basis of population ratios, with guaranteed minimums to each state. The Smith-Hughes and the George-Deen Acts and their appropriations are still in effect.

Closely associated with the provision of vocational education has been the program of vocational rehabilitation of the physically disabled. Although not carried on to any considerable extent through the public-school system, the service of rehabilitating disabled persons is in a very real sense an educational program. Rehabilitation was first provided for persons disabled in military service (1918) and later (1920) for those disabled in industry or by any cause. The amounts of the grants for this purpose have been relatively small, the total annual federal appropriation authorized at present being $1,938,000. The allotments are made to the states on the basis of total population, with a minimum of $10,000 to each state.

Military Training

Another new policy in federal relations to education was introduced in the National Defense Act of 1920. Among the many provisions of this act was one which authorized the co-operation of the Federal Government in providing military training in secondary schools and colleges for the preparation of reserve officers.

The educational institutions accepting this co-operation are furnished federal aid, not in money, but in personnel, equipment, and other facilities for conducting instruction in military science and tactics. The members of the teaching staff for military science are selected and assigned to the institution by federal authorities and their salaries are paid from federal funds. The course of study is drawn up in Washington and the entire program of instruction is under federal supervision and control. Examinations of the accomplishment attained by each institutional unit are made by officers of the United States Army. The equipment and uniforms are furnished by the Federal Government to the men who are enrolled as students in these courses. The college students enrolled in advanced courses in military science are given a stipend from federal sources. This whole program, which is in operation in a large number of secondary schools and colleges, is unique in that the federal grants are not in the form of lands or money but in the form of personnel, equipment, and other services. Furthermore, institutions under private control may, and do, participate in the federal program of military training.

Educational Activities as Relief Measures

The policies of federal participation in education described in the foregoing paragraphs continued through the decade of the 1920's with no important new developments other than additions to the amounts of the existing grants.

With the beginning of the Roosevelt administration in 1933, the Federal Government began to assume large responsibilities for the social and economic welfare of the people. One of the early discoveries was that the provision of education is an advantageous method of providing relief for unemployment. Certain of the agencies and activities established primarily for relief purposes began to develop important educational programs.

One of the first developments of the relief policy was the organization of the work camps of the Civilian Conservation Corps. At first education was very little emphasized in the program of the camps, but gradually this function has loomed larger and larger, until, in the later legislation establishing the Civilian Conservation Corps on a continuing basis for a period of years from 1938 on, Congress saw fit to lay considerable emphasis on the educational features of the program.

Under the Federal Emergency Relief Administration and the Works Progress Administration there was developed an extensive group of educational services known as the Emergency Educational Program. The teachers for this program were drawn from relief rolls and were paid from relief funds. Classes of many different types were maintained for adults; emergency freshman colleges were established in some centers; nursery schools were instituted; workers' education received considerable stress; and a large amount of research bearing on educational problems was fostered under this program.

The third type of federal activity in education initiated during the depression period was the program of grants to needy students, provided first through the Federal Emergency Relief Administration and later through the National Youth Administration. By means of small grants of funds, earned by the students in socially desirable work under the supervision of the institutions attended, hundreds of thousands of young people who could not otherwise have afforded to continue in high school or college have been enabled to attend these institutions. While the college students so aided were in most cases not actually from the relief rolls, they were, through these grants of funds, removed from the labor market and thus the grants served effectively to reduce unemployment.

The fourth type of federal emergency activities in education consisted of direct grants to keep schools open. It was early discovered that in some regions public funds were so limited by the depression that schools would necessarily be closed after a term of only a few months. This early closing of schools would in many instances throw the unemployed teachers on the relief rolls, besides denying educational opportunities to the children. To meet this situation the Federal Government provided grants of relief funds to keep schools open for the full term in the districts which would otherwise have had to close their schools early.

Finally, the Federal Government provided large funds for public works as a means of relieving unemployment. A total of more than a half-billion dollars from such funds has gone into the construction and renovation of public-school buildings. During recent years practically all the public-school building construction of the country has been financed by these federal grants or by federal loans to local school systems.

It should be borne in mind that in the case of all these federal emergency programs the primary objective has been relief. Education has been secondary or incidental. Furthermore, it must also be remembered that practically all of these programs were instituted with unprecedented haste. One can scarcely stop long to argue about the niceties of jurisdiction when people are starving. A result has been that the Federal Government has been drawn into an extensive program of participation in education without any close organic or directive relationship, in most instances, to the long existing state and local school systems.

Some voices have been raised in protest against what has been termed an invasion of state rights in education in connection with the emergency programs. As economic conditions begin to clear up, there will undoubtedly be a disposition to inquire whether the Federal Government is embarking permanently on a new policy of providing educational services, or whether these emergency programs are to be gradually taken over and merged with the established programs maintained by state and local school systems.

PRESENT FEDERAL ACTIVITIES IN EDUCATION

The foregoing sections have presented an account, roughly in chronological order, of the development of federal policies regarding participation in educational programs. The present status of federal activities in various forms of educational service may be briefly reviewed.

Grants of Funds

As has been indicated in the preceding sections, the Federal Government now makes relatively large annual grants of money for the support of educational programs. The total federal appropriations for three of these programs, vocational education, vocational rehabilitation, and the land-grant colleges, amounted in 1938–39 to $53,594,000. Besides the continuing programs, large amounts have been made available from federal funds for educational services carried on as relief activities. The amounts of such federal expenditures cannot be ascertained accurately, but they undoubtedly amounted to several hundred million dollars annually during the depression years from 1933 to 1939. Although the total amount of funds for educational purposes from federal sources is relatively small when compared with the grand total of either the federal budget or the entire educational expenditures of the country, the amounts are large enough to indicate a significant participation on the part of the Federal Government in educational activities.

Education in Areas under Special Federal Jurisdiction

The Federal Government is solely responsible for the education of children living in areas under its special jurisdiction. These include the District of Columbia, the territories of Hawaii and Alaska, the island possessions, such as Puerto Rico, the Virgin Islands, American Samoa, and Guam, the Panama Canal Zone, and the special federal reservations including such areas as national parks, national forests, military reservations, etc. In addition the Federal Government assumes full responsibility for the education of the Indians and of the Aleuts in Alaska.

The policies followed in federal educational services in these various areas differ markedly. Even a superficial analysis indicates that, in making provisions for these areas over which it exercises special jurisdiction, the Federal Government has the intention of providing excellent educational service. This fact indicates the basic concern of the Federal Government for education in the United States. No well-considered and unified policy, however, has ever been adopted for educational services in these areas under special federal jurisdiction. Instead, the problem of education for each area has been met as the occasion arose. The resulting confusion leaves much to be desired by way of educational provisions.

Training of Governmental Personnel

No complete inventory has ever been made of the educational services actually carried on under the auspices of the Federal Government for the training of its own personnel.   Conspicuous examples of such training facilities are the Military Academy at West Point, the Naval Academy at Annapolis, and the Coast Guard Academy at New London.   In academic circles the graduate school of the Department of Agriculture is widely recognized, and its certificates of credit are acceptable at practically all the better graduate schools of America.   The educational program of the Tennessee Valley Authority has developed as an important feature of this new governmental agency.   From these large-scale enterprises, the educational provisions of the departments of the Federal Government range all the way down to occasional training classes for accountants and clerical staff members maintained by numerous federal bureaus and offices.   The extensive program, mentioned earlier, of military training maintained for the preparation of reserve officers, in co-operation with public and private schools and colleges all over the country, is also a method of educating governmental personnel.

The educational activities of federal departments are at present entirely unco-ordinated.   The programs have been set up primarily as service agencies for the departments concerned, rather than with any thought of their contributions to education as such. Some duplication of service undoubtedly exists, and possibly greater efficiency and a more effective program might result if some federal agency were given the responsibility of co-ordinating these numerous educational services for the training of governmental personnel.

Research and Information Service in Office of Education

The United States Office of Education, ever since its establishment in 1867, has rendered a valuable service in collecting and publishing statistics of education, in conducting research studies, and in providing leadership in the solution of educational problems. The quality of the leadership in the Office has varied considerably from time to time, and its limited budget and restricted salary levels have not always permitted the assembling of a staff that was commensurate with the possibilities of service.

Furthermore, the Office of Education has been totally lacking in authority for the collection of the very statistics that are its object of special concern. The Federal Government at present has no legal power to require the state and local school systems and the many private educational agencies to make reports. The Office of Education is thus forced to depend chiefly on the cooperation of the operating agencies for such facts and figures as it is able to gather. As a result, its published statistics do not present as complete and well-analyzed a picture of the educational program in the United States as is desirable.

Commendable efforts have been put forth by the Office of Education for the development of the statistical reporting service, and in spite of the handicap which it encounters its published reports have shown steady improvement, particularly in late years. During the depression the Office of Education has been especially handicapped by restrictions in its budget for printing, and as a result many of the important documents and reports have been slow in appearing or their publication has had to be turned over to non-governmental agencies.

Support of Research

The Federal Government supports and maintains an extensive program of fundamental research in many varied fields. Almost every department of the Government undertakes research of a type that may broadly be classified as an educational service. Noteworthy examples of this type of research are the programs maintained by the Department of Agriculture, the Public Health Service, the Bureau of Standards, the United States Geological Survey, and hundreds of other bureaus and agencies. A recent report by the Science Committee of the National Resources Committee, which discusses these research services, states that the Federal Government in the fiscal year ending June 30, 1937, spent approximately $124,000,000 on research.

Judicial Decisions

One branch of the Federal Government which has a measure of direct control over education as carried on by the states is the Supreme Court.   The Supreme Court of the United States may declare unconstitutional any law of a state that is contrary to the Federal Constitution.   A single illustration may be cited.

Acting under the initiative provision of the state constitution, the legislature of Oregon passed a law in 1922 which required children between the ages of eight and sixteen to attend a public school.   Obviously, the practical effect of this law would have been to prohibit private elementary schools.   Two private institutions tested the constitutionality of the act before the Supreme Court of the United States.   The act was declared void on the ground that it violated the due-process-of-law clause of the Fourteenth Amendment.   In the opinion of the court, the challenged legislation unreasonably interfered "with the liberty of parents and guardians to direct the upbringing and education of children under their control. . . . The fundamental theory of liberty upon which all governments of this Union repose excludes any general power of the state to standardize its children by forcing them to accept instruction from public teachers only.   The child is not the mere creature of the state; those who nurture him and direct his destiny have the right, coupled with the high duty, to recognize and prepare him for additional obligations."   The court held, moreover, that if the act under consideration were enforced, the two corporations concerned would be deprived of property without due process of law.   Their business and property were "threatened with destruction through the unwarranted compulsion" which the state was seeking to exercise over present and prospective patrons of their schools.   The maintenance of private schools, it was pointed out, is an undertaking not inherently harmful, and the court found nothing in the records of such institutions to demand extraordinary measures.

UNSOLVED PROBLEMS OF FEDERAL RELATIONS TO EDUCATION

In recent years there have been two important reports by national committees dealing with the problems of the relations of the Federal Government to education. The first of these reports [1] was issued by a committee appointed in 1929 by President Herbert Hoover, consisting of fifty-two persons, practically all of whom were educators. Dr. Charles R. Mann served as chairman of this committee, and Dr. Henry Suzzallo was its director of studies. The report of this committee, consisting of a small volume of summary and recommendations and a larger volume containing the basic materials, appeared in 1931.

In 1936 President Franklin D. Roosevelt appointed the Advisory Committee on Education, consisting of twenty-two persons representing a wide variety of social groups, such as labor, industry, agriculture, home economics, and education. This committee, under the chairmanship of Dr. Floyd W. Reeves, published its summary report [2] in February, 1938.

Each of these reports presents a large amount of factual material bearing on the problems of federal relations to education, and each makes certain recommendations for legislation and executive action. In each of these reports certain of the unsolved problems of federal relations to education are discussed. Attention is here called to a few of the most important of these unsolved problems.

Shall There Be a Federal Department of Education?

Practically every important country in the world having a cabinet form of government has a ministry of education in the central government. As previously pointed out, the United

---

[1] National Advisory Committee on Education, *Federal Relations to Education*, Parts I and II.

[2] United States. The Advisory Committee on Education, *Report of the Committee*. Washington: Government Printing Office, 1938. Pp. xi + 244.

States has no federal department of education. The only official representation of education in the Federal Government is the relatively inconspicuous Office of Education, a subordinate bureau attached for a long time to the Department of the Interior, but lately transferred to the Federal Security Agency.

The committee appointed by President Hoover recommended in 1931 "that a Department of Education with a Secretary of Education at its head be established in the Federal Government," and the report further elaborated the specifications under which such an office should be established. A minority report, presented by two members of the committee representing the Catholic Church, opposed this recommendation. After the publication of the report certain groups of citizens and educators vigorously endeavored to have this recommendation enacted into a law. Bills were introduced in Congress, the purpose of which was to create a department of education, but none of them was passed.

The President's Committee on Administrative Management, which reported [1] in 1936, dealt with the place of education in the Federal Government in a very broad way. This committee recommended the creation of a new department of social welfare, which would include education. This recommendation, made by a competent group of scholars and research workers in the field of government, seems to have satisfied the groups which were formerly advocating the establishment of a separate department of education; and there seems now to be little sentiment in favor of setting up a department of education as a separate executive branch of the Federal Government. President Roosevelt's Advisory Committee on Education, reporting in 1938, made no suggestion for the establishment of a department of education. As previously noted, the executive order of 1939 made the Office of Education a part of the Federal Security Agency.

[1] United States. The President's Committee on Administrative Management, *Report of the Committee.* Washington: Government Printing Office. 1937. Pp. xiii + 382.

Shall Funds Be Granted for Education of a General Type?

The preceding discussion in which the development of federal participation in education has been traced indicates that up to this time the Federal Government has granted money only for the support of education of a very specific type. Money has been granted for colleges teaching agriculture and mechanic arts, for vocational education, for military training, and for various purposes of relief. In recent years there has been strong advocacy of a federal appropriation for education free from specification as to the type of the educational service to be rendered, available for the support of any activities carried on in the public elementary and secondary schools or in public libraries and state departments of education. Differences of opinion have appeared with reference to the amount which the Federal Government should appropriate and with reference to the manner in which funds thus appropriated should be distributed, but there is apparently a very strong belief among educators that financial aid of a general type should be granted as a necessary means of maintaining adequate education throughout the nation.

Degree of Federal Control

Perhaps the chief issue at present debated among educators with regard to federal appropriations for education of a general type is the question of the degree of federal control that may or should accompany such appropriations. Educators, accustomed only to state and local control of education, have repeatedly voiced their fears of a centralized federal control that might accompany federal appropriations.

Throughout the national history of grants for educational purposes it is readily possible to trace a gradual increase in federal control. The original land grants were accompanied by practically no control, but later, as it began to be evident that some of the states had not administered their funds wisely, Congress began to make some stipulations concerning the price at which land was to be sold or the manner in which the funds derived from sales were to be handled.

The first Morrill Act carried very few limitations, but the later acts which expanded the services of the land-grant colleges have carried an increasing number of restrictions and controls. The Smith-Hughes Act of 1917 went very far in the direction of specifying the details of the program of vocational education to be followed, and the federal administration of vocational education has exercised a large measure of authority in directing the programs of vocational education in state and local systems.

In the emergency educational programs initiated during the depression, the Federal Government has assumed major control, often complete control. There is some co-operation with state and local sponsors of educational projects, but the regulations for the maintenance of these programs are laid down in Washington or by the federally appointed officers assigned to the control of the programs in the states.

A review of the history of federal grants for educational purposes warrants the generalization that, as the amount of federal funds has increased, the federal controls over the programs that are supported by these funds have also increased. The increase in federal control is not due solely, however, to increases in the size of the grants. In many instances increases in federal control can be traced definitely to abuses or maladministration of the educational program by states.

The history of federal grants in education indicates clearly that support and control are not likely to be separated far. Whenever the Federal Government supplies funds for education, it may confidently be expected to follow these funds with more or less control. That certain types of federal control may be entirely beneficial has been amply demonstrated during the years since the grants were first made.

Is There to Be a Federal System of Education?

The establishment of the educational activities carried on by the Federal Government as relief measures has raised the issue as to whether there is to be a federal system of educational services conducted independently of and parallel to the educational systems of state and local communities. To a considerable extent this has been the case in the educational activities under the relief program, although in many parts of the program sponsorship has been required from state and local educational authorities. For the most part the Federal Government in its relief activities has undertaken educational services not provided, or at least not adequately provided, by the regular school system. The Civilian Conservation Corps program, in so far as its educational aspects are concerned, is operated entirely outside the sponsorship or co-operation of the regular school system. In some parts of the relief program, however, particularly in the provision of funds for school buildings, in the direct grants to keep schools open, and in the aid to students under the National Youth Administration, the Federal Government has acted only through the regularly constituted educational system.

The Advisory Committee on Education, reporting in 1938, strongly recommended that there should be explicitly reserved to the state and local educational agencies "the administration of the schools, the determination of the content and processes of education, and decision as to the best uses of the allotment within the type of expenditures for which federal funds may be made available."

Proposals for a National University

One educational enterprise which has frequently been discussed but never approved by Congress is the establishment of a national university in Washington. George Washington proposed that a national university be organized, and reinforced his proposal by making a bequest to be used for that purpose. In one form or another this proposal has been repeated by several Presidents of the United States and by leaders in Congress. Bills have been introduced on a number of occasions providing the support for such an institution. Opposition has frequently been expressed by the heads of the great universities of the country and by others, especially on the ground that an institution located in close proximity to policy-making governmental authorities would be distracted and biased and would be unable to devote its energies as it should strictly to the pursuit and dissemination of knowledge.

As a substitute for a national university, the effort has been made to render the intellectual resources of the national capital more readily accessible to scholars. The Library of Congress has organized a staff of consultants who are specialists in various fields, and has made the services of these consultants available to anyone who is engaged in research. Many of the other federal agencies have also organized their departmental libraries and resources for investigation in such a way as to encourage and assist scholarly work by other than the members of their staffs.

There can be no doubt that the vast intellectual resources present in Washington constitute one of the important assets of American education, and any type of organization that will open these resources to scholars and encourage their use is worthy of encouragement and support. Although the proposal for a federal university has been strongly opposed by the representatives of the existing universities, and although the proponents of the measures have never been able to muster sufficient strength to secure passage of the bill, the issue is by no means closed. There will doubtless continue to be further agitation in the future in favor of the establishment of such a university.

Retrospect and Prospect

Although the Constitution of the United States makes no specific mention of education as a function of the Federal Government, actually the Government is engaged in education in a large way. According to present interpretations of the Constitution, there seems no doubt whatever that educational activities are entirely within the scope of the proper functions of the Federal Government.

The outstanding educational activity of the Federal Government has been the granting of land and money for the support of education. In a less striking manner the Federal Government has displayed its interest in education through provisions for military training, by the establishment and maintenance of the Federal Office of Education, by the organization acts for the territories, by provisions of educational service in areas under special federal jurisdiction, and by providing through the regular departmental budgets for the training of its own personnel.

New policies in the relations of the Federal Government to education under state and local jurisdiction are being introduced at an ever-accelerating rate, and the evolution of policies in this area is undoubtedly far from complete. Without question the next decade or at least the next generation will witness still further development of federal policies in relation to public education. The trends now in evidence indicate that the direction of these new policies will probably be toward a larger participation of the Federal Government in the educational services which have heretofore been considered the special province of states and local communities.

BIBLIOGRAPHY

Advisory Committee on Education, *Report of the Committee.* Washington: Government Printing Office, 1938. xi + 244 pp.

Blauch, Lloyd E., *Educational Service for Indians.* Staff Study no. 18, Advisory Committee on Education. Washington: Government Printing Office, 1939. xii + 138 pp.

Blauch, Lloyd E., *Federal Cooperation in Agricultural Extension Work, Vocational Education, and Vocational Rehabilitation.* Office of Education, Bulletin, 1933, no. 15. Washington: Government Printing Office, 1935. xii + 208 pp.

Campbell, Doak S., Frederick H. Bair, and Oswald L. Harvey, *Educational Activities of the Works Progress Administration.* Staff Study no. 14, Advisory Committee on Education. Washington: Government Printing Office, 1939. xiv + 186 pp.

Chamberlain, Leo M., *The Teacher and School Organization*, pp. 25–36.

Cubberley, Ellwood P., *Public Education in the United States*, pp. 739–49.

Educational Policies Commission of the National Education Association, *Federal Activities in Education.* Washington: National Education Association, 1939.

Edwards, Newton, *Equal Educational Opportunity for Youth.* Report to the American Youth Commission of the American Council on Education. Washington: American Council on Education, 1939.   ix + 190 pp.

Federal Relations to Education. Report of the National Advisory Committee on Education, I, II.   Washington: National Advisory Committee on Education (744 Jackson Place), 1931.   viii + 140 pp; xvi + 448 pp.

Frasier, George Willard, and Winfield D. Armentrout, *An Introduction to the Literature of Education,* pp. 374–81.

Johnson, Palmer O., and Oswald L. Harvey, *The National Youth Administration.* Staff Study no. 13, Advisory Committee on Education. Washington: Government Printing Office, 1938.   x + 122 pp.

Judd, Charles H., *Research in the United States Office of Education.* Staff Study no. 19, Advisory Committee on Education. Washington: Government Printing Office, 1939.   viii + 134 pp.

Norton, John K., and Margaret Alltucker Norton, *Wealth, Children and Education.* New York: Teachers College, Columbia University, 1938. xviii + 138 pp.

Reeder, Ward, *A First Course in Education,* pp. 425–32.

Wesley, Edgar B., *Proposed: The University of the United States.* Minneapolis: University of Minnesota Press, 1936.   x + 84 pp.

CHAPTER VI

STATE CONTROL OF EDUCATION

As POINTED OUT at the opening of the preceding chapter, the major control of education is a function of the individual states, not of the national government. This fact must be kept in mind when one uses the phrase the "American educational system." There are in reality as many school systems in the United States as there are states, territories, and island possessions. Each state government is sovereign in its own area with respect to education, except in so far as the acceptance of grants from the Federal Government and the rulings of the United States Supreme Court have made federal policies effective in particular lines. Education in the United States is carried on, not in a single system, but in a complex organization made up of many unique units.

The result of autonomous control by the states of their own educational systems appears in many aspects of the school services. The form of organization of the central state office for education in each state depends on the constitution of the state and the statutes passed by its legislature. Similarly, the age at which pupils may leave school, the qualifications of teachers, the powers granted to local boards of education, and other characteristics of state school systems differ among the states according to the will of the people as expressed through their respective legislatures. To be sure, a certain fundamental similarity is found throughout the nation with respect to educational institutions and practices, resulting from intercommunication, imitation, and the common historical antecedents of American communities. In other words, American ideas and ideals pervade the whole country and give to the life of the people and their institutions a unity which is deep-seated and evident in spite of obvious, often obtrusive, differences.

SOCIAL IMPLICATIONS OF EDUCATIONAL LEGISLATION

No one can read with full understanding the history of the policies which the Federal Government has adopted at different periods without realizing that behind each act of Congress there were social forces which originated in the desires and motives of the people of the times. When the nation was in a pioneering stage and social conditions on the frontier were unsettled, grants of land were given by the Federal Government without strict specification of the subjects to be taught in schools and without dictation as to methods of teaching. Later, when agricultural activities came to play an important part in the lives of the people, federal legislation was directed to the improvement of agriculture. Still later, when manufacturing became a major factor in the national economy, trade training was organized and supported.

The language used in federal legislation in the three stages of educational evolution is significant. The Ordinance of 1785 uses terms of a general type. The Morrill Act of 1862 reflects the beginning of a scientific mode of thinking. The Smith-Hughes Act of 1917 is full of evidences of the intense competition of modern industry. Legislation before Congress at the present writing uses the phrase "equality of opportunity"; this suggests that national solidarity has reached the point where it is intolerable that any young person should be so limited in opportunity that he will enter upon adult life incompetent to contribute to the common good because of lack of education.

Much other evidence could be presented to emphasize the social implications of legislation and the intense human interest of people in the policies which legislation controls, but it is perhaps unnecessary to go further than to suggest that behind each public enactment regarding education there are urgent personal motives — motives of parents and of individual youths who are trying to find places in the complex civilization into which they have been born. Congress and state legislatures do not act in a vacuum. They are impelled by the needs of people. The influence exercised by legislative bodies in directing the course of education is effective because communities recognize the need of schools of a certain kind and insist on having schools as means of preserving organized social life.

The future, like the past, will undoubtedly see much national legislation relating to education. If this nation continues to develop in the general directions in which it has been developing, the recognition of the importance of maintaining a comprehensive educational system will certainly grow stronger and stronger. As it is, and will be, with the nation, so is it and so will it be with the states. Their policies with respect to education come to expression in the laws which they pass regarding schools and in the taxes which they levy for the support of schools. When states differ in their arrangements for education, the causes are to be sought in the varying social conditions in different parts of the nation. When states pass laws which are like those of neighboring commonwealths, the causes are the common social traits that make the states coherent parts of the United States.

STATE CONSTITUTIONAL AND LEGAL PROVISIONS

Each of the forty-eight states has in its constitution acknowledged its responsibility for education and made provision for a system of public schools. The general tendency has been toward increasing the number of provisions made about education in the constitutions of the states. The states admitted to the Union prior to 1820 had on the average only one provision about education in their first constitutions. The eleven states admitted between 1821 and 1860 had an average of more than five provisions regarding education in their first constitutions; the four states admitted between 1861 and 1880 averaged over nine provisions; the seven admitted between 1881 and 1900 averaged fourteen provisions; and the three states admitted since 1900 have made on the average approximately eighteen provisions about education in their constitutions. Although the constitutional provisions in the various states differ in form, in length, and in number of explicit details which are set forth, the universality of the arrangement for a school system in each of the state constitutions is a most significant testimony regarding the general attitude of American citizens toward education as a function of their government.

The fundamental principles on which state control of education depends have been repeatedly expressed. An examination of some of the pronouncements which have been made by legislative bodies and courts will reveal what these principles are. One of the earliest laws passed in the Massachusetts Colony makes it clear that the authority of a commonwealth is such that it may, if necessary, take children away from their parents. A part of this law is as follows:

For asmuch as the good education of children is of singular behoof and benefit to any Common-wealth; and wher as many parents and masters are too indulgent and negligent of their duty in that kinde. It is therefore ordered that the Select men of everie town, in the severall precincts and quarters where they dwell, shall have a vigilant eye over their brethren and neighbours, to see, first that none of them shall suffer so much barbarism in any of their families as not to indeavour to teach by themselves or others, their children and apprentices so much learning as may inable them perfectly to read the englishtongue, and knowledge of the Capital lawes: upon penaltie of twentie shillings for each neglect therin. Also that all masters of families doe once a week (at the least) catechize their children and servants in the grounds and principles of Religion, and if any be unable to doe so much: that then at the least they procure such children or apprentices to learn some short orthodox catechism without book, that they may be able to answer unto the questions that shall be propounded to them out of such catechism by their parents or masters or any of the Select men when they shall call them to a tryall of what they have learned in this kinde. And further that all parents and masters do breed and bring up their children and apprentices in some honest lawful calling, labour or imployment, either in husbandry, or some other trade profitable for themselves, and the Common-wealth if they will not or cannot train them up in learning to fit them for higher imployments. And if any of the Select men after admonition by them given to such masters of families shal finde them still negligent of their dutie in the particulars aforementioned, wherby children and servants become rude, stubborn and unruly; the said Select men with the help of two Magistrates, or the next County court for that Shire, shall take such children or apprentices from them and place them with some masters for years (boyes till they come to twenty one, and girls eighteen years of age compleat) which will more strictly look unto, and force them to submit unto government according to the rules of this order, if by fair means and former instructions they will not be drawn unto it. [1642] [1]

Court decisions have frequently defined the relation of the state to education. The Supreme Court of New Hampshire made the following statement regarding the right of the state to compel children to attend school.

The primary purpose of the maintenance of the common school system is the promotion of the general intelligence of the people constituting the body politic and thereby to increase the usefulness and efficiency of the citizens, upon which the government of society depends. Free schooling furnished by the state is not so much a right granted to pupils as a duty imposed upon them for the public good. If they do not voluntarily attend the schools provided for them, they may be compelled to do so. While most people regard the public schools as the means of great personal advantage to the pupils, the fact is too often overlooked that they are governmental means of protecting the state from the consequences of an ignorant and incompetent citizenship.[2]

---

[1] *The Laws and Liberties of Massachusetts, Reprinted from the Copy of the 1648 Edition in the Henry E. Huntington Library*, pp. 11–12. Cambridge, Massachusetts: Harvard University Press, 1929.

[2] *Fogg* v. *Board of Education*, 76 N.H. 296, 82 Atl. 173, 37 L.R.A. (N.S.) 1110, Ann. Cas. 1912c 758.

The Court of Appeals of Kentucky made the following pronouncement.

> The place assigned it [education] in the deliberate judgment of the American people is scarcely second to any. If it is essentially a prerogative of sovereignty to raise troops in time of war, it is equally so to prepare each generation of youth to discharge the duties of citizenship in time of peace and war. Upon preparation of the younger generations for civic duties depends the perpetuity of this government. Power to levy taxes is an essential attribute of sovereignty. That is so because the necessity of conducting the government requires that money be raised for the purpose by some sort of taxation. So is the power to educate the youth of the state, to fit them so that the state may prosper; else the taxes raised could scarcely meet demands made upon a government in these times. Whilst the power named [the power to levy taxes] is older in point of adoption as a legal maxim, the other is modernly found to be of no less importance. It may be doubted if the state could strip itself of either quality of its sovereignty.[1]

Laws compelling parents to provide education for their children and laws compelling children to attend schools are among the most fundamental expressions of the will of society. The states have enacted laws at different dates and in different forms according to their peculiar interests. The southern states, which were slower than the northern states in establishing a public-school system, were the last to pass laws making attendance at school compulsory. Furthermore, some of the southern states enacted laws compelling school attendance for only a comparatively few days in the year, because the dominant agricultural pursuits of the people in those states were supposed to require the labor of children, and these agricultural demands were there-fore thought of as in competition with schools.

The state assumes obligations with respect to the conduct of schools as soon as it passes laws requiring children to be educated. In the colonial days and in the early days of national history, the states as such took very little part in the actual conduct of

[1] *City of Louisville* v. *Commonwealth*, 134 Ky. 488, 121 S.W. 411.

schools. Teachers were employed by the local community, and the curriculum consisted of whatever the teacher was able to teach and whatever the local people wanted. Step by step the states have found it necessary to assume more and more general control through central state agencies.

A description of some of the stages through which state control has evolved is given in a report of the State Superintendent of Indiana. It will be noted that state control in this instance began with control of material resources and developed from that into control of instruction. Extracts from the report referred to are as follows:

In 1816 Indiana was admitted into the Union, with boundaries as at present. The Federal Government at the same time presented the new State an additional township in Monroe County, as a seminary endowment. In the ninth article of the State Constitution were the following educational provisions:

"Knowledge and learning generally diffused through a community being essential to the preservation of a free government, and spreading the opportunities and advantages of education through the various parts of the country being highly conducive to this end, it shall be the duty of the General Assembly to provide by law for the improvement of such lands as are, or hereafter may be, granted by the United States to this State for the use of schools, and to apply any funds which may be raised from such lands or from any other quarter, to the accomplishment of the grand object for which they are, or may be, intended; but no lands granted for the use of schools or seminaries of learning shall be sold by authority of this State prior to the year 1820; and the moneys which may be raised out of the sale of any such lands or otherwise obtained for the purposes aforesaid, shall be and remain a fund for the exclusive purpose of promoting the interest of literature and the sciences and for the support of seminaries and public schools.

"It shall be the duty of the General Assembly, as soon as circumstances will permit, to provide by law for a general system of education, ascending in a regular gradation from township schools to a State University, wherein tuition shall be gratis and equally open to all. And for the promotion of such salutary end, the money which shall be paid as equivalent by persons exempt from military duty, except in times of war, shall be exclusively and in equal proportion applied to the support of county seminaries; also, all fines assessed for any breach of the penal laws shall be applied to said seminaries in the counties wherein they shall be assessed."

No efficient school law was ever passed under that Constitution, and no requirement of any kind for the maintenance of schools was made for many years. Yet the General Assembly at once arranged for the care and improvement of the school lands, hoping that they would yield a substantial revenue in future years. An act of December 24, 1816, required the County Commissioners to appoint a Superintendent of the school section in each congressional township. This Superintendent was to lease the unimproved lands for any period not exceeding seven years, no more than one lessee to be admitted to a single quarter-section. He was to lease the improved lands for any period not exceeding three years, the lessee being required to set out, annually, twenty-five apple trees and twenty-five peach trees, until one hundred of each kind should have been planted. The Superintendent was to hold his office for a term of two years, and was to be paid such a sum as the County Commissioners might deem a reasonable compensation.

At the same time, the General Assembly went through the form of enacting a school law. It was very simple in its provisions. On petition of twenty householders in any congressional township, an election was to be called and three Township Trustees for school purposes were to be elected. These officers were given unrestricted powers to make by-laws, rules and regulations relating to education, and to encourage schools. But they possessed little means for such encouragement. The statute also provided for the appointment, by the Governor, of Superintendents for the seminary township reservation, and for their compensation at the Governor's discretion.

Notwithstanding the utter lack of public means for the support of education, a number of elementary schools were soon established. Of course they were not free. The need of more advanced instruction than these could ever supply was at once foreseen. The State capital was now Corydon, and less interest was taken in the "university" at Vincennes. Ere the year closed — December 23, 1816 — the Corydon Seminary was incorporated.[1]

After numerous moves in which the sale of lands and the management of funds were the main topics dealt with by the legisla-

[1] *Thirteenth Biennial Report of the Superintendent of Public Instruction of the State of Indiana* (1886), Part II, pp. 7–8.

ture, the history of lawmaking in Indiana takes another turn as indicated in the following:

It is time to mention a singular and somewhat romantic series of quasi-State papers, which influenced the school legislation of succeeding years. In the *Indiana State Journal* of December 7, 1846, as the members of the General Assembly were gathering at the capital, appeared a message to the Legislature on the subject of education. Evidently it was written by a learned and practical man; but by whom? It bore the signature, "One of the People." It presented startling facts, verified by official statistics, and pointed out the grave danger of the growing illiteracy to the State. By the terms of the existing school law there was no uniformity in educational matters throughout the State, or even throughout a single county or township. The maintenance of schools depended wholly upon the popular will of the school district. A neighborhood feud, a feeling of apathy, or an opposition to education might cause the total abandonment of educational work in any community. The "pure democracy" of the New England township (town) was not adapted to the educational progress of the West. One of the People pleaded for a school law securing the maintenance of schools in all parts of the state under a general system.

The General Assembly of 1847 received a similar message from the same mysterious source, and was influenced to pass an act submitting the question of free schools to the people of the State at the fall election of 1848. The legislators shrewdly required that the vote on this question should be *viva voce*, and not written upon the ballots. The votes given in favor of free schools numbered 78,523; those opposed numbered 61,887. Thus there was a clear majority of 16,636 in favor of a general system of public instruction. A third message appeared in the winter of 1848, analyzing the recent vote and pointing out the manner in which the popular desire should be carried out. By an act of January 17, 1849 the benefits of the schools were expected to be considerably increased. This act abolished the office of County Commissioner, limited the number of District Trustees to one in each district, and levied a tax of ten cents on the hundred dollars and a poll tax of twenty-five cents, and also a tax on insurance companies, for school purposes. It provided, moreover, for a special school tax for buildings and supplies, and also for a special tuition tax, to be levied by districts, where desired by the inhabitants.[1]

[1] *Thirteenth Biennial Report of the Superintendent of Public Instruction of the State of Indiana* (1886), Part II, pp. 13–14.

When the stage of development was reached which is described in the last paragraph of the foregoing quotation, the state was ready to extend its central supervision of school districts so as to deal with problems of the training and certification of teachers and the organization of the curriculum. There has been a marked tendency to centralize in state departments of education more and more authority and to extend supervision so as to insure higher standards in local schools than they would reach if left entirely to themselves.

Authorities are not in complete agreement regarding the wisdom of the tendency to centralize power in state departments. The centralized plan serves to keep the weakest communities up to a satisfactory minimum provision, but it sometimes handicaps the development of the more progressive local units. In some states it seems that willingness to leave matters to the control of the local community is directly related to the ability of the local community to provide itself with capable leadership in educational affairs. In general, the city schools have attracted a type of leadership of superior quality as compared with that in the rural schools; the city school systems are typically under somewhat less control by the state than the systems of rural areas.

At the level of state control of education three major agencies are typically active: the legislature, the state board of education, and the chief state school officer, who with his staff of assistants forms a group usually known as the state educational office. The functions of each of these state agencies in the control of education will be treated in turn.

THE LEGISLATURE

The legislature typically determines what local units for management of schools may be created; it provides the plan for the local administration of schools; it provides or authorizes the plan for financial support of the school system. Besides these matters of general administrative control, the legislature often fixes many details of educational policy.

Many schoolmen object to the details enacted into statute laws from time to time by state legislatures. The objection becomes particularly acute when the legislature invades the field of the curriculum, and passes laws stating that such and such subjects shall be taught in the schools for a specified number of minutes each day or week. Schoolmen point out that curriculum-making is a highly technical undertaking, one that should be entrusted only to those who have had special preparation for this work, as well as a broad knowledge of the store of human knowledge and the needs of society. Only rarely would there be found an individual member of the legislature who could be considered at all competent to have intelligent judgment with regard to the program of instruction. Furthermore, the legislature, in enacting such laws, usually gives little or no attention to the curriculum as a whole; it considers only the particular phase of subject matter immediately under consideration. Thus the entire curriculum may be thrown out of balance by such legislation and time may be taken from other subjects more important than the one covered in the special legislation.

Although there are these valid reasons for objecting to legislation covering details in fields requiring technical competence, it must be remembered that the legislature is the chief agency through which society may express its will in the management of the schools. If even so technical a matter as curriculum-making were committed exclusively to experts, it is entirely possible that they might at some time fail to meet the needs and the wishes of society. As long as the schools are a part of the social order and are subject to control through the process of democratic government, it seems inevitable that state legislatures will from time to time take a direct hand in some matters that are regarded by specialists as technical in character.

THE STATE BOARD OF EDUCATION

All but eight of the states have provided an agency, usually known as the state board of education, for the general oversight of the school system. This agency has the function of determining rules and regulations as authorized by the legislature. To a considerable extent the duties of the state board of education fall into the category known as sublegislation, that is the making of rules for carrying out of the laws enacted by the legislature. This function is midway between the function of legislation or policy-making, and execution or the carrying out of policies.

The legislature, for example, may determine that there shall be a process of certifying teachers who are eligible for positions in the public schools. Regardless of the details written into such a statute, there are likely to be many matters connected with the carrying out of this legislation that require the making of administrative rules. In some states, for example, the legislature has delegated to the board of education the duty of establishing the total amount of preparation required for certification for various types of school positions. It is altogether usual for the legislature to grant power to the state board of education to determine the specific curriculum to be followed for those who would receive certificates for various specialized types of teaching positions, and to accredit the institutions in which the preparation may be taken.

The power of administrative rule-making might in good administrative practice be delegated to some competent executive officer. The American political attitude, however, opposes the centering of any kind of legislative authority, even that of enacting sublegislation, in the hands of an individual officer. The general practice in this country is to assign such a function to a board rather than to an individual. In setting up the control for schools in the states the same principle has been followed as in other governmental functions, and the rôle of administrative rule-making has in most of the states been delegated to a board known as the state board of education.

In most of the states the state board of education deals directly only with the schools of elementary and secondary grade; entirely separate boards of control are provided for the state-supported institutions of higher education. In some cases, however, the state board of education has direct control over the institutions for the education of teachers, and only the state universities are under the control of a separate board of trustees. In a few states all of the public educational program, elementary, secondary, and higher, is under the control of a central state board of education.

Although eight states have not established a general board with authority over the elementary and secondary schools, without exception each of the states has a board for vocational education. A board for this purpose was required by the federal Smith-Hughes Act, passed in 1917, and every state in the Union in accepting the provisions of this Act has been required to set up its board for vocational education. The control of vocational education in a few states is assigned to a separate board, but most of the states, perhaps contrary to the ideas of those who fostered the Smith-Hughes legislation, have merely assigned the function of control over vocational education to the existing state board.

Many of the states have a system of multiple boards, each of which has charge of a separate educational function. Separate boards for the control of higher institutions, and in a few cases for vocational education, have already been mentioned. Other types of separate boards are those for the control of teacher-pension and retirement systems, and for school textbook selection. One state has as many as eighteen separate boards, while another has only two; the average per state is seven boards dealing with separate phases of the educational program.

Methods for selection of members of the state board of education differ widely among the states. One of the earliest methods provided for ex-officio membership; under this method the holders of certain offices were designated as those to serve on the state board of education. This plan is not now generally considered wise, inasmuch as the persons who hold the designated offices may not always be individuals who are well fitted to serve or interested in serving on a board dealing with educational affairs. In eight states all or a majority of the board members are ex officio.

In some states board members are appointed by the governor of the state. The members of the state board under such circumstances are usually laymen in the field of education, but they are typically persons of broad social outlook and wide information, and thus are able to bring to bear upon the educational problems the point of view of leaders in the social order. The plan of appointment by the governor has the advantage of centering in that office responsibility for effective state government and for the selection of competent persons. In many of the states that follow this plan the appointments of the governor must be confirmed by the legislature or by one of its houses. The governor has the power to appoint all or a majority of the members of the board of education in twenty-six states.

The third method of selecting members of state boards of education is direct election by the people. This usually has the disadvantage of throwing the choice into the political arena, for only those with good political connections are able to make the race for the office. In only four states are a majority of the board members elected.

Some of the states follow combinations of methods in the selection of members for the state board, having some places ex officio and others either appointed or elected. In general, appointment by the governor on a nonpolitical basis seems to provide the best arrangement.

THE CHIEF STATE SCHOOL OFFICER

The third major agency concerned with education at the state level is the chief state school officer. Every state in the Union has provided for such an office. The exact title of this officer varies, but he is most frequently given the title, state superintendent of public instruction. This officer is in every case equipped with a staff for carrying on the various functions assigned to him by statute. In most of the states the chief school officer and his staff function as one of the major departments of state government, co-ordinate with such offices as the secretary of state, the treasurer, and the attorney general.

The office of state superintendent was first established in New York in 1812. The office in that state was subsequently discontinued, but was later re-established. Michigan in 1829 established the first state school office that has been maintained continuously to the present. By 1850 every state in the North and some of those in the South had provided for a chief state school officer.

Method of Selection

In the original establishment of the office in the early days it was customary to name some state official as the superintendent of education ex officio. In a number of instances, however, a full-time officer was appointed to the position. The office attracted a number of notable men in the early development of the American educational system. The success of such men as Horace Mann and Henry Barnard in promoting the cause of public education made it clear that the office was one that would challenge the highest capabilities of a full-time officer. The setting up of the office on a real administrative basis with a staff of qualified assistants dates from the last half of the nineteenth century.

Three methods are in use for the selection of the chief state school officer. Thirty-two states elect the state superintendent on a party ballot in the same manner as other state officials such as the governor and the members of the legislature. In eight states the governor is empowered to appoint the chief state school officer. In the other eight states the chief state school officer is appointed by the state board of education.

Although the majority of the states choose their chief state school officers through the medium of a party ballot, educational authorities without exception are of the opinion that this is the poorest of the three methods. Election on a party ballot means as a rule that the man must seek the office rather than the office seek the man. Party regularity is nearly always a prime essential in securing the nomination and election, and effective tests of professional competence are usually not possible in the case of elected officers of this type. The successful party ticket must have its nominees from widely scattered parts of the state, and the nomination of the ablest man available in the party for the state superintendency of education is often prevented by the fact that a candidate for some other state office lives in his district.

The other methods of selection, appointment by the governor and appointment by the state board of education, are based on different theories regarding the responsibility of this officer. If the state superintendent of education is looked upon as the head of one of the departments of a centralized state government, sound theory of organization would require that he be directly responsible to the head of that government, namely, the governor. If, on the other hand, the state board of education is considered as the head of the state school system, which is a more or less independent branch of state government, the state superintendent is properly looked upon as the executive officer of the school system and therefore logically he should be responsible to the state board of education. In general, the opinions of political scientists lean toward the plan of appointment by the governor; most educational authorities favor the plan of appointment by the state board of education.

Duties of the State Superintendent

The general functions of the chief state school officer and his staff are to execute the laws and regulations passed by the legislature and by the state board of education. These duties involve many details. The state school office is the logical source to which the local school officials turn for information regarding the law on educational matters. In practically every state the chief state school officer is responsible for explaining and interpreting the school laws, and in most states these laws are published in bulletin form from the office of the state superintendent.

The collection and publication of all kinds of statistics regarding the schools of the state is another important function of the state superintendent. The hearing of appeals from the decisions of local school authorities on specific questions is frequently assigned by law to the chief state school officer. In most states the department of education is charged with the certification of teachers, and the staff of the state superintendent performs this function. The inspection and rating of the schools maintained by local communities is another important function of most of the state departments of education. The distribution of state school funds to local communities on the basis established by the legislature is another executive function usually assigned to the state superintendent or some member of his staff. In many states the inspection and approval of plans for new school buildings is made a function of the state educational office. Detailed supervision over the federally financed program of vocational education is assigned as a function of the state department of education in most of the states, although in a few states this duty is lodged in a separate state agency which deals only with vocational education.

The state office is called upon to give advice and counsel on all kinds of educational problems to local communities and local school officers. Usually the chief state school officer is expected to provide the governor or the legislature with suggestions regarding needed educational legislation.

Exercise of Leadership

The functions of the state school office, which include these many details, may be summed up in the general statement that the office is expected to provide the educational leadership for the state. Potentially the office is the most important position within the state educational system. Unfortunately the potentialities of the office have not been fully realized today. The state super-intendent of public instruction in most states is outranked in prestige by the presidents of institutions of higher education and even by the superintendents of many of the local school systems, especially those in the larger cities.

Several reasons may be given for the failure of the office of state superintendent to live up to its potentialities. The fact that in two-thirds of the states this officer is elected on a party ballot explains to some extent the failure to attract to the state superintendency as capable individuals as are attracted to some other educational positions. The tenure of office is usually rela-tively short, particularly in the case of the elected superintend-ents, and therefore capable men cannot consider this office as offering opportunities for a career.[1] Finally, the salary of the state superintendent of public instruction is typically low com-pared with the responsibilities of the office. Relatively few of the state superintendents receive annual salaries of more than five thousand dollars. In a number of states the salary of the state superintendent cannot readily be increased, because the amount is fixed by the state constitution.

In some states the department of public instruction enjoys prestige chiefly because of the excellent staff with which it is manned. The personnel of the staff is usually of a much longer tenure than the state superintendency, although in some states there is the unfortunate tendency to look upon the staff positions as subject to the fluctuations of political fortune. In a number of states, however, there has been built up over a period of years a personnel in the state educational office that is entirely compe-tent for the duties assigned to that agency. The state superin-tendent is, in many of these cases, left with responsibility chiefly for contacts with the general public and with the leaders of the political party to which he belongs, while the actual professional

[1] A majority of the states have a legal term of four years or more, but in fourteen states the term is two years or less. Two-thirds of the chief state officers in September, 1937, had been in office less than six years.

duties of the office are carried on by the staff, the members of which are recognized as experts in their respective fields by the school people of the state.

OTHER AGENCIES WITH EDUCATIONAL FUNCTIONS

Although the three agencies that have already been discussed, the legislature, the state board of education, and the chief state school officer with his staff, are the principal means by which the state discharges its responsibilities in the field of education, a number of other agencies are found with some responsibility for minor educational functions.   The library service of the state is commonly assigned to a separate agency, usually a library board.   The licensing of practitioners in the various professions other than education is in essence an educational function, but this is commonly assigned to separate boards for each of the various professions, such as medicine, law, and dentistry.   The state board of health in some of the states is given the power of condemning old school buildings that are no longer fit for use, of passing on the plans and specifications for proposed new buildings, and of general medical inspection of pupils.   Central authority over the financial accounting for all public funds, including those used for education, is sometimes assigned to a state officer known as the examiner of accounts.   In many states the power to tax for school purposes or to issue bonds is subject to some control through an independent agency known as the state tax board.

CONCLUSION

The expansion of education in the states has brought a realization that there are many functions which must be performed by the state as a whole rather than by separate communities.   A single school district cannot prepare its own teachers; the organization of normal schools is recognized, therefore, as a function of the state.   In recent times the financial support of schools is more and more dependent on contributions to local schools from

the state treasury.   The state is obliged in many cases to enforce
policies of consolidation of schools where local districts are incompetent to conduct schools of satisfactory grade or size.

In short, education is a state function, and increasingly the
state is forced by modern conditions to participate with local
communities in the organization and conduct of schools.

BIBLIOGRAPHY

Almack, John C., editor, *Modern School Administration*, pp. 299–324.
    Boston: Houghton Mifflin Company, 1933.

Burton, William H., *Introduction to Education*, pp. 363–80.

Chamberlain, Leo M., *The Teacher and School Organization*, pp. 21–25, 36–
    53.

Chambers, M. M., *Some Features of State Educational Administrative
    Organization*.   Washington: American Council on Education, 1936.
    vii + 284 pp.

Clapp, Frank L., Wayland J. Chase, and Curtis Merriman, *Introduction
    to Education*, pp. 155–73.

Cocking, Walter D., and Charles H. Gilmore, *Organization and Administra-
    tion of Public Education*.   Staff Study no. 2, Advisory Committee on
    Education.   Washington: Government Printing Office, 1938.   x + 184
    pp.

Cubberley, Ellwood P., *Public Education in the United States*, pp. 717–33,
    750–65.

Cubberley, Ellwood P., *Public School Administration* (third edition), pp.
    3–43, 132–46, 680–98.   Boston: Houghton Mifflin Company, 1929.

Cubberley, Ellwood P., *State School Administration*, pp. 3–135, 270–335,
    685–733.   Boston: Houghton Mifflin Company, 1927.

Douglass, Aubrey A., *The American School System*, pp. 372–94, 455–59.

Educational Policies Commission, *The Structure and Administration of
    Education in American Democracy*.   Washington: National Education
    Association, 1938.   128 pp.

Engelhardt, Fred, *Public School Organization and Administration*, pp. 563–
    86.   New York: Ginn and Company, 1931.

Frasier, George Willard, and Winfield D. Armentrout, *An Introduction to
    the Literature of Education*, pp. 381–83.

Judd, Charles H., *Problems of Education in the United States*, pp. 101–19.

Reeder, Ward, *A First Course in Education*, pp. 411–25, 432–38.

Wilson, Lester M., and I. L. Kandel, *Introduction to the Study of American
    Education*, pp. 39–67, 295–317.

CHAPTER VII

LOCAL CONTROL OF EDUCATION

THE THEORY of political organization on which the government of the United States rests, as has been pointed out in the previous chapter, recognizes the state as the sovereign governmental entity. All local governmental organizations exist only by sanction of the state, and the local community has no inherent right to any control over education, except as the state delegates such control to it.

Although the state has the right to exercise any and all control over education, almost all the states have chosen to delegate a large degree of control to their local communities. As explained in a previous chapter, local autonomy in educational affairs was customary in the early days because of frontier or pioneer conditions. As these conditions changed, and as it became evident that certain educational functions can be exercised more efficiently by the state as a unit, there has developed a general tendency toward the centralization of more power over educational functions in the state. Even though there has been this tendency, the local communities in most of the states in this country are still granted a large degree of autonomy over their school affairs, and most communities are conscious and even jealous of their powers over their schools.

THE DEVELOPMENT OF LOCAL LEADERSHIP IN EDUCATION

It is only in relatively recent times that education has been clearly recognized to be a public or governmental function. Parents were at first assumed to be responsible for the upbringing of their children, and up until the time of the Protestant Reformation only those children whose parents could afford to pay for it received any formal schooling. The church assumed some educational responsibilities, but the instruction provided was in the main purely religious or directly preparatory for service in the church. Following the Reformation and the Counter-Reformation, the church began to assume an active responsibility for the general education of young people, to the end that they might learn to read the Scriptures, and thus be equipped with the knowledge necessary for the salvation of their souls. In England, for example, the education that was not provided from the resources of parents was furnished during a large part of the nineteenth century by church societies.

Education was first undertaken as a governmental function in certain of the German states. A series of benevolent rulers, wishing to improve the condition of their people and to educate them to be good citizens of the state, began to develop public schools. In this development there was no particular conflict between the interests of the church and those of the state; the established ecclesiastic organizations were directly related to the civil government, and the curriculum of the public schools could include all the instruction in religion that the church authorities deemed desirable.

In colonial America the schools were, for the most part, either maintained privately or by religious organizations. In colonial Massachusetts, however, the church and community government were intimately related and school affairs were handled in the town meeting, as was all other civil and religious business. The way in which town meetings provided for the schools is shown in the following quotations taken from a number of old town records.

Wednesday the 14 of May 1718 the Town met at the Meetinghouse according to adjornment of theire Town Meeting of the 26 of March Last ... and nextly voted to have Mr Samuell Stow for a School-master for the yeare ensuing, begining the first Day of May Currant

and to allow him 40 pound for the yeare: or proportionable for what
time he shall Serve: and to Raise the same by the Next Invoice.[1]

At a Legall meeting of the Inhabitants and freeholders of the Town
of Lunenburg assembled December the 31: 1733. . . .
    1ly.   Voted to hire a School master Three months from: the Time
the School master begins his School. —
    2ly.   Voted that the School Shall be kept at the House of Mr.
Gardners the Three months aggreed on to keep a School:
    3ly.   Voted and Chose Mr Andrew Gardner to be the School
master to keep the School the Term of Three months as afore said
in said Town or Such other as he Shall Provide therefor.[2]

At a Legal School-Meeting of the Hopland School District in Lee
on Monday the Thirtieth day of June at the red School house in said
District 1794.
Capt. Abijah Merrill Moderator.
Voted to Divide the District into Two Schools.
Voted That the District be Divided as follows (Viz)
The River shall be the Line from Mr. Pixleys Down said River to the
Bridge near the Forge from thence up the Road north to the Road
Leading from Esqr. Ingersoll's to Stockbridge thence on sd. Road
to Stockbridge Line including the Inhabitants on said Road and all
south of Said Road and the River as above Described is to be one
District.
Desolved the Meeting.[3]

With the creation in this country of a republic based on democratic principles, it was recognized that education must be as
universal as the suffrage.   The early statesmen who led in the
development of American democracy were keenly aware of the
extent to which the new type of government must rely on an
educated citizenry for its success.   The Constitution of the
United States, however, forbade the setting up of any established

[1] *The Early Records of Lancaster, Massachusetts, 1643–1725*, p. 185.   Henry
S. Nourse, editor.   Lancaster, Massachusetts: Town of Lancaster, 1884.
[2] *The Early Records of the Town of Lunenburg, Massachusetts, Including That
Part Which Is Now Fitchburg, 1719–1764*, p. 83.   Compiled by Walter A.
Davis.   Fitchburg, Massachusetts: City Council, 1896.
[3] *Records of the Town of Lee from Its Incorporation to A.D. 1801*, p. 212.   Lee,
Massachusetts, 1900.

religion, and the education necessary for the success of democracy
therefore could not well be entrusted to ecclesiastic authority.
Furthermore, there was a mixture of religious views in most parts
of America.   Obviously no one sect could, under these circumstances, be permitted to control the education that would shape
the future of American democracy.   Thus there seemed no alternative but to provide for public secular schools, and that has been
the plan followed in this country ever since the full implications
of the relationship between education and democracy began to be
realized.

It would be possible to cite many statements made by leaders
in the early national life of the United States which show how
strong was the civic motive for the organization of American
schools.   The following quotation from one of the reports of
Horace Mann, first secretary of the Board of Education of Massachusetts, is typical.

> Above all others, must the children of a Republic be fitted for
> society, as well as for themselves.   As each citizen is to participate
> in the power of governing others, it is an essential preliminary, that
> he should be imbued with a feeling for the wants, and a sense of the
> rights, of those whom he is to govern; because the power of governing
> others, if guided by no higher motive than our own gratification, is the
> distinctive attribute of oppression; — an attribute whose nature and
> whose wickedness are the same, whether exercised by one who calls
> himself a republican, or by one born an irresponsible despot.   In a
> government like ours, each individual must think of the welfare of the
> State as well as of the welfare of his own family; and therefore, of the
> children of others as well as of his own.   It becomes then, a moment-
> ous question, whether the children in our schools are educated in
> reference to themselves and their private interests only, or with a
> regard to the great social duties and prerogatives that await them in
> after-life.[1]

Certain church groups, it is to be noted, have never accepted
the principle that education is a secular function to be directed

[1] Horace Mann, "Ninth Annual Report of the Secretary of the Board of
Education," *Ninth Annual Report of the Board of Education of the Commonwealth of Massachusetts, Together with the Ninth Annual Report of the Secretary
of the Board,* p. 64.   Boston: 1846.

by the state. Such groups as the Catholics, the Lutherans, the Seventh Day Adventists, and others maintain schools[1] for their own children, at their own expense. These groups are of the opinion that religion is a vital part of education; because the public schools are not permitted to teach religion, the church groups feel impelled to provide schools of their own to furnish this necessary element in the training of youth. The state permits the maintenance of such schools, but may require them to meet its own standards. As noted in Chapter V, a recent decision of the Supreme Court of the United States held, in the Oregon Case, that the state has no power to require all children to attend public schools; thus some measure of official sanction has been given to the maintenance of non-public schools.

When it became apparent in the United States that the public-school system must provide the universal education necessary for the success of democracy, some agency for the oversight of the local school had to be created. In the early period, as was shown previously in this chapter by quotations from the minutes of town meetings, the affairs of the public school were handled by the local governmental authorities in much the same way as they handled other public business. As early as 1800, however, there began to grow up the tendency to differentiate the school business from the conduct of other public business. In New England, for example, the custom was established of appointing for school affairs a special committee, acting under the authority of the selectmen as the local governing agency. This special committee came to be known as the school committee. The following record shows the appointment of a school committee in a Massachusetts town.

At a legal meeting of the inhabitants of the Town of Fitchburg assembled on Monday the Seventh day of March AD 1808....
Voted and Chose Joseph Fox Esqr., Capt James Cowdin, Jona.

---

[1] These schools are sometimes erroneously called parochial schools. Some of them are parochial schools, i.e., maintained by a parish, but others are diocesan schools, and others are also maintained by church organizations that are neither parishes nor dioceses.

Lowe, Abraham M. Farwell, Joseph Downe, Jur Verin Daniels, Joshua Stickney, Josiah Brown, Benja. Herrick, Elias Messenger, and Amos Lawrence Jr school Committeemen ... School Committee

Voted to Chose a Committee to examine the schools the present year
Voted that the committee consist of Eleven.

Voted and chose the Rev'd Titus T. Barton, the Revd Mr Bascom, Wm. Cunningham, Joseph Fox, Joseph Richardson, Doct Snow, Deacon John Thurston, John Muzzy, Robert Allen, David Boutell, and Abraham Willard

Voted that the Committee be requested to attend the schools when they begin and at the time of closing the schools and it shall be the duty of the school Committeemen of each destrict to inform the examining committee when the schools shall begin

Voted that the school Committeemen shall the last week in August make out an exact return of the number of scholars in his destrict and present the same to the selectmen by the first monday of Sept. that an accurate approporotionment of the money may be made, that the town clerk be directed to furnish the school Committee with this vote [1]

The school committee usually included the minister of the local church since he was one of the leading intellectuals of the community. In addition, certain other public-minded citizens served. A typical record showing how this kind of committee functioned is as follows:

The committee chosen by the town to inspect the schools beg leave to report their situation and examination. ...

January 6th, 1801. Your committee visited a school kept in Reuben Richmond's house instructed by Mrs. Nabby Williams of 32 scholars. This school appeared in an uncultivated state the greater part of the scholars.

On the 26 of Feb., visited Mrs. Nabby Williams' school the second time and found that the scholars had made great proficiency in reading, spelling, writing and some in the grammar of the English language.

Nov. 10th, the committee visited and examined two Schools just opened; one kept in a school house, near Baylies works, of the number of 40 scholars, instructed by Mr. Philip Lee. This School we found

[1] *The Old Records of the Town of Fitchburg, Massachusetts*, IV: 376–78. Compiled by Walter A. Davis. Fitchburg, Massachusetts: City Council, 1901.

to have made but small proficiency in reading, spelling and writing, and to be kept only six or seven weeks; upon inquiry why it should be taught no longer, we were informed that the ratio of school money for this School was and had been usually expended in paying the Master both for his service and board, and in purchasing the fire wood which is contrary to the usual custom of the town.

The other School, visited the same day, was kept near John Reed's consisting of the number of between 30 and 40 Scholars instructed by Mr. William Reed; This School, being formed into regular classes, appeared to have made a good and pleasing proficiency in reading, spelling, writing, some in arithmetic and others in the Grammar of the English language. This School's share of school money is expended to pay the Master for his service only, so that the School will be continued three months. . . .

Feby. 26th, visited Mr. Dean's School 2 time, the Scholars were crowded into a small room, the air was exceedingly noxcious. Many children were obliged to tarry at home for want of room and though the school was kept only a few weeks they were deprived of its advantages. A want of books was the complaint. The committee were anxiously desirous that this evil might have a remedy and were of opinion it may be easily done. The Scholars appeared to increase in knowledge & claim our approbation.

March 5th, visited two schools, one kept at Mr. Aaron Pratt's of the number of 30 scholars instructed by Mr. Philip Drown. This school appeared quite unimproved and uncultivated in reading and spelling, some of them did better in writing. This uncultivated state did not appear to be from a fault in the children but, as your committee were informed, from the disadvantage of having had masters illegally qualified for their instruction; of which class is their present master unauthorized by law.[1]

One occasion on which the school committee was very likely to appear in what purported to be a formal examination of the school was the closing day of the school term. One description of such an occasion is as follows.

The Committee on Schools respectfully report that they attended the several examinations of the Public Schools of the city ordered by the Board of Education at the close of last term.

[1] Reprinted in the *Report of the School Committee of the City of Taunton, Massachusetts, for the Year Ending December 31, 1915*, pp. 68–73.

Three successive days, one for each of the school houses, were devoted to this important object, there being during this period a vacation at the schools not examined, so that members of the Board of Education, the teachers of all the schools and their pupils, citizens and others were enabled to attend all examinations.

The pupils who were examined by classes in their daily recitations, were subjected to the most severe and scrutinizing tests, to determine satisfactorily the actual proficiency of the schools, classes, and individual scholars.

In their searching examinations, teachers, citizens and the members of the board present participated in submitting problems for solution and in putting questions to pupils, of which they had had no previous intimation, thereby fairly and fully determining their respective attainments, affording also a just estimate of the qualifications and efficiency of our teachers and of the method of instruction pursued in our public schools.

Your committee recommend that a suitable prize be offered as a reward to the school which shall excel at the Annual Examination, to be bestowed with some eclat; and also that prizes be given to the best scholars in all the schools. It is believed that such inducements would excite a lively spirit of honorable rivalry among our public schools and their pupils.[1]

As the management of schools took on more importance in each community, the next step was the creation of a special trustee and in larger communities a board for the local management of the schools. The school trustee or board generally came to be an agency separate from the executive branches of government in charge of other local public affairs. By the second quarter of the nineteenth century the special school authority was fully established as in control of the education of the young people of the community. The trustee or board employed the teacher, had charge of the school building and other school properties, and dictated the program of instruction. One account which shows something of the character and mode of operation of a school trustee is as follows:

[1] Quotation from a report by the Committee of Schools, January 5, 1863. J. W. Smith, "St. Paul Schools in the Early Days," *School Bulletin of the Department of Education of the City of Saint Paul*, XI:4:8 (January, 1929).

"Want to be a school-master, do you? You? Well, what would *you* do in Flat Crick deestrick, *I'd* like to know? Why, the boys have driv off the last two, and licked the one afore them like blazes. You might teach a summer school, when nothin' but children come. But I 'low it takes a right smart *man* to be school-master in Flat Crick in the winter. They'd pitch you out of doors, sonny, neck and heels, afore Christmas."

The young man, who had walked ten miles to get the school in this district, and who had been mentally reviewing his learning at every step he took, trembling lest the committee should find that he did not know enough, was not a little taken aback at this greeting from "old Jack Means," who was the first trustee that he lighted on. The impression made by these ominous remarks was emphasized by the glances which he received from Jack Means' two sons. The older one eyed him from the top of his brawny shoulders with that amiable look which a big dog turns on a little one before shaking him. Ralph Hartsook had never thought of being measured by the standard of muscle. This notion of beating education into young savages in spite of themselves, dashed his ardor.

He had walked right to where Jack Means was at work shaving shingles in his own front yard. While Mr. Means was making the speech which we have set down above, and punctuating it with expectorations, a large brindle bull-dog had been sniffing at Ralph's heels, and a girl in a new linsey-woolsey dress, standing by the door, had nearly giggled her head off at the delightful prospect of seeing a new school-teacher eaten up by the ferocious brute.

Between the disheartening words of the old man, the immense muscles of the young man who was to be his rebellious pupil, the jaws of the ugly bull-dog, and the heartless giggle of the girl, Ralph had a delightful sense of having precipitated himself into a den of wild beasts. Faint with weariness and discouragement, and shivering with fear, he sat down on a wheelbarrow.[1]

As the final step in this process of separating the educational system from other branches of community organization there began in the 1830's the custom of appointing an executive officer of the local school board, with the title superintendent of schools. At first the functions of this officer were chiefly to care for school

[1] Edward Eggleston, *The Hoosier School-Master*, pp. 11–12. New York: Orange Judd and Company, 1871.

property and to gather statistics and make reports. The position, however, was one of strategic importance in the developing school system, and during the last half of the nineteenth century functions of a supervisory nature over the whole program of instruction have come to be the chief duties of the local superintendent of schools. Gradually this office has developed into a most important executive position, with vast potentialities for constructive leadership as the schools took on new functions and increased in their importance.

Today in most communities in the United States the superintendent of schools is one of the most important personages. In the small and medium-sized cities his salary is typically the highest of any public officer, or semi-public personage. He commands a prestige equal to that of the members of the respected older professions, such as law and medicine.

With the evolution of the office of local superintendent of schools the problems of school management have been subjected to scientific study, and much has been discovered with reference to effective methods of carrying on the business of public education. A large body of literature dealing with school management and supervision has been produced.

There has been an extensive development, in recent times, not only of the office of the local superintendent of schools, but of other executive offices within the school system. The principalship of elementary schools and that of secondary schools have become specialized services. Supervision has developed as an important field of service within the school system, engaging the talent of specialized officers associated with the superintendent. Business management, plant operation and maintenance, and research services have all been given considerable attention, and in the typical modern urban school system each of these functions is staffed with a competent specialized personnel.

AREAS FOR LOCAL SCHOOL ADMINISTRATION

One of the important problems confronting the people of the state when they set up their plan for local school administration is the geographical areas which are to be used as local school units. Shall the area be large or shall it be small? Shall its boundaries coincide with those of other local governmental units, or shall there be school districts which are not necessarily coterminous with the units for civil government? About such questions there has been much discussion, and a considerable body of literature has been produced.

The early plan in the New England area was to make the "town" the unit for school administration, as it was for the civil government. Later, however, when the unity of the old New England town began to break down and people began to scatter into outlying areas, the district became the unit for local school government in New England. The district consisted of the territory served by one school building, and thus under the district plan of school organization the unit was very small. The New England influence was strong in the states that were formed in the Middle West during the early part of the nineteenth century, and the organization for schools tended to follow the New England pattern. Thus the system that came to be followed almost everywhere in the North in the early days made the local school district the unit for school administration. The district usually consisted only of a one-room school, with from ten to forty pupils in attendance.

The inadequacies of the district as a unit for local school administration were gradually realized by educational leaders, and the tendency, after the first quarter of the nineteenth century, was to organize somewhat larger units. Horace Mann made a vigorous attack on the district system, pointing out, as shown in the following quotation, the inadequacy of a small unit of school organization.

With the exception, perhaps of a dozen towns, all the rest in the State, are divided geographically into school districts. Provision for

the territorial sub-division of our towns was first made by the statute
of 1789 — the germ of which was in the Province Law, 8 Geo. 3. ch.
309. I consider this, beyond comparison, the most pernicious law
ever passed in this Commonwealth, on the subject of schools. Other
things being equal, or, making due allowance for inequality in other
things, the schools are now invariably the best, in those towns, which
are not divided into districts, but in which the school system is administered by the town, in its corporate capacity. The reasons for
this are obvious and numerous.

In cases where the schools are maintained by the town, in its corporate capacity, it is obvious that every section of the town would be
treated substantially alike. No portion of the inhabitants would
contribute, for any length of time, to pay for benefits from whose
participation they were debarred. If only one good schoolhouse were
erected within any part of the town's jurisdiction, all other parts
would demand as good a house for themselves. Having contributed
to the erection of a good house for the favored section, an equitable
claim for one substantially as good, would vest in every other section.
This would partake of the nature of a claim for remuneration or reim-
bursement; and it would be so obviously founded in justice, that no
man regardful of his own interests could omit to make it, and no respectable man on whom it was made, could resist it. In such a case,
therefore, not only all parental and patriotic motives, but even interested ones, would array themselves on the side of advancement.
Under the present system, the erection of a new schoolhouse awaits
the imperious call of necessity, or the slow action of duty in the public
mind; and perhaps no call of necessity has ever been so loud and imperative as not to encounter opposition from more or less of the taxable inhabitants.

The same principles would come into full activity, in regard to the
length of schools, and the competency of teachers. All would insist
upon reform and become advocates for progress. Were the whole
town responsible in its corporate capacity, for the whole of the schools
within it, the inhabitants of no town would ever think of, the inhabitants of no section of any town would ever submit to, a school of only
three or four months in a year, for one part, while other parts were
enjoying a school for ten months, or for the whole year. No section
would ever accept a teacher, hired for $10 a month, and perhaps dear
at that, while others were favored with teachers richly worth $30 or
$40 a month. Each section too, would demand an equal supervision
from the school committee, and would make favoritism or predilection

as dangerous as they are unjust. So of school furniture, apparatus, libraries, and of other constituents, in the prosperity of a school. In fine, if towns, as such, were to administer the school system within their respective limits, the great principle of republican equality would have an unobstructed sphere of action, and would yield its harvest of beneficent fruits; now, selfishness has ever-renewing opportunities for interposing its mischievous obstructions to the progress of our schools. But the calamity of this system is entailed upon the State. A few towns, it is true, have abolished their district organization, and reverted to the ancient system. But we can hardly expect that their example will be generally followed, at least for a long time to come.[1]

As pointed out in the foregoing quotation, it was especially evident in urban areas that a single administration might well serve a whole city, instead of having as many administrative units or districts as there were school buildings. The history of the development of the city of Chicago in this respect is typical of that in other parts of the country. By 1853 there were seven school districts in Chicago, each managed in complete independence of the other. In that year the city council took a forward step in appointing a city superintendent of schools to unify the work of the various districts. In 1857 the legislature of Illinois abolished the separate districts in the city of Chicago, and since that date the entire municipality has formed a single unit for local school administration.

In rural areas the district unit resulting from frontier conditions has often persisted. In early days the relative isolation of the rural population and the simplicity of the educational facilities naturally encouraged the maintenance of small units of school government. The strength of tradition is revealed by the fact that while cities with thousands of children in attendance at school are now universally managed as single districts, the unit in rural regions in most northern states continues to be the area

[1] Horace Mann, "Eighth Annual Report of the Secretary of the Board of Education," *Eighth Annual Report of the Board of Education of the Commonwealth of Massachusetts, Together with the Eighth Annual Report of the Secretary of the Board*, pp. 77–79. Boston:1845.

served by a small one-room school or in some states the relatively small area of a township (usually consisting of thirty-six square miles).

The reasons which in former times led to the establishment and maintenance of small administrative districts in rural areas are no longer applicable. With the coming of good roads and with the increasing complexity of the problems of administering an effective modern school system, the rural areas can now readily be organized into larger and more efficient units. As previously stated, however, the people of the rural areas are loath to give up the small school unit. In a number of states there are more school officeholders than there are teachers, and these officeholders now represent an entrenched interest that is difficult to dislodge. Time after time, in some of the northern states, proposals to enlarge the local unit of school administration for rural areas have met defeat in the state legislature.

In the South, by contrast, the unit of local government has always been relatively large. The plantation type of agriculture lent itself to relatively large units of local government. In many of the southern states the county is the local unit for school administration. Usually in the county-unit plan the rural areas of the county are combined as a single unit for school administration, with the urban areas each set up as independent units. In Florida, however, the entire county, including both rural and urban areas, forms the unit for local school administration. In a number of northern states the county has been adopted as the unit for school supervision, even though certain areas within the county, such as the township or the school district, may be given the basic control over the organization of the schools.

It is conceivable that local units of school administration might be done away with entirely and the state made the sole unit for school administration. In effect, this has been done in one state, Delaware, and a number of states have in recent years moved rapidly in the direction of adopting the state as the unit for financing the school system. The tradition of local self-government in educational affairs, however, is very strong in the United States, and there seems little likelihood, in the near future at least, of any change that will abolish completely all local units. The problem is to find the most effective unit for local school administration.

It has been suggested that the school unit might be set up around the community into which the population is informally grouped. Practically every inhabitant recognizes his membership for purposes of shopping, entertainment, and church membership in some community which has its focus in some village or city or trading center. A community of this type would in most cases be large enough to provide a reasonably efficient unit for the local management of schools. The adoption of the community as the unit of school organization would have the disadvantage of setting up an educational unit which is not coterminous with other governmental units, but the district type of school organization is now different from the general governmental unit with which it is related, and the adoption of the community instead of the district as a local school unit would present no insurmountable problems.

The improvement of the present situation with respect to local school units is one of the important problems that must be solved in the near future if effective education is to be provided the children in the rural areas. The units of school administration in most rural areas are at present too small for effective service. Adequate leadership cannot be provided under existing conditions and the cost of education per child served is often exorbitant, especially if the deficient quality of the program is taken into consideration. The tax base is usually too small to provide effective support, the school plants in rural areas are inferior to those in the cities, and the teachers in rural schools are often inadequately prepared and relatively unsupervised. Most of these deficiencies could be remedied by enlarging the local units for school administration.

LOCAL ORGANIZATION FOR SCHOOL ADMINISTRATION

The administrative organization in well-planned local school units includes a number of different agencies. Typically a board of education is placed in general charge of the local school system. A superintendent of schools serves as the chief executive officer of the organization, with a staff to assist him. A principal is in charge of each building, with a staff of teachers each of whom is a specialist in some particular phase of education.

The Board of Education

The board of education consists of laymen who represent the citizens of the community and serve without pay or with only a small per diem for attendance at meetings. The meetings of the board may be held weekly or monthly for the transaction of necessary business. One of three methods is commonly followed in the selection of board members: selection by the city council or board of aldermen; appointment by the mayor or some other public official (often with formal confirmation by the council or aldermen); and election by the qualified voters.

The local board of education or school board has a dual responsibility, first to the local citizenry, and second to the state. The state properly holds the local board of education responsible in case the schools are not managed according to its requirements. The local citizens usually have sufficient influence to insure the selection of board members who will manage the schools in accordance with their wishes.

The general functions of the local board of education are legislative, not executive. This statement means that the board, when properly organized, is concerned with the determination of policies, not with the application of those policies to specific cases. The board members are not chosen because of their expertness in the detailed management of educational affairs, but only because they are considered competent to decide on policies in accordance with the general desires of the citizens in the community. Whenever the local board of education or any individual member of the board begins to undertake executive functions, trouble is almost certain to ensue within the school system.

The Superintendent of Schools

The superintendent of schools is typically chosen by the board of education to serve as its executive agent in the detailed management of the school system. As noted in an earlier paragraph, the office of superintendent has developed during the past half century into a position of great importance in the local community. Unusually capable men and women have been attracted to this position, and the leadership they have exerted has probably done more than any other one factor to establish the confidence of the American people in their public-school system. In recent years specific preparation for this important position has become available, and many of those entering such positions today have been prepared through a special course of training.

The superintendent of schools is properly looked upon as the head of the local educational organization. He is responsible for the planning and promoting of educational improvements as well as for the faithful carrying out of the policies agreed upon by the board. Part of this responsibility for leadership involves the continued education of members of the school board and citizens of the community with respect to the needs, accomplishments, and possibilities of improvement of the schools. In a well-managed school system, all the other employees of the board of education are made responsible to the superintendent of schools and look to him ultimately for the direction of their work and for the appraisal of the results they obtain.

The relationship between the school board and the superintendent must of necessity be close. Whenever the board of education lacks confidence in the superintendent, or whenever the superintendent feels that he cannot with good conscience carry out the adopted policies of the board, the only recourse is the resignation of the superintendent. Situations requiring the resignation of the superintendent arise occasionally in almost every community, and can at times become very distressing. It must be pointed out, however, that the board of education is chosen as the representative of the community, and the community, within the limits determined by the state legislature, should have the right to determine the policies for its school system. In a case of disagreement between the superintendent and the board of education, it must be assumed that the board represents the community until the board itself is discredited by the community.

To assist the superintendent of schools in the discharge of his duties, there is usually a staff of specialized experts. The size of the staff depends on the size of the school system. In the very smallest school systems, there may be no staff for the superintendent, but after the enrollment reaches about eight hundred pupils, there usually is at least an office clerk. From this small beginning the staff increases in the larger systems to include a business manager, a plant manager, attendance officers, assistant superintendents for the various specialized services, supervisors in the various subjects such as music, drawing, English, mathematics or in special fields such as kindergarten, primary teaching, and secondary education, and research specialists, clerks, and bookkeepers.

The Principal and Teachers

If there is more than one school building in the system, a principal is usually appointed to be in charge of each building. In a very small system, with only one building, the superintendent himself may serve as principal of the building, but typically there will be as many principals in the school system as there are building units. The principal is usually responsible directly to the superintendent of schools. The amount of authority delegated to the principal varies considerably, but especially in the larger systems the principals of buildings have a considerable degree of independent authority in the management of their schools.

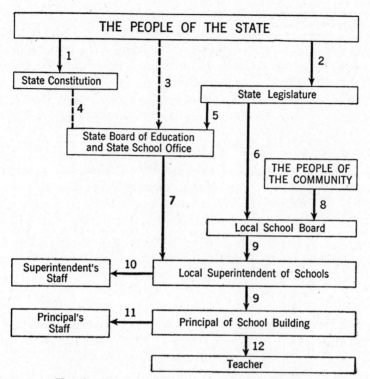

Key for Lines of Administrative Responsibility

1. Elect representatives who frame
2. Elect members of
3. In some states elect members of
4. In many states authorizes the creation of
5. Provides for organization of
6. Provides for organization of and delegates authority to
7. Exercises general supervision over and requires reports from
8. Select, either directly by election, or indirectly by appointment
9. Selects, and delegates authority to
10. Appointed by school board on recommendation of superintendent and report to him
11. Appointed by board on recommendation of superintendent and principal
12. Supervises the work of

FIGURE 3. ORGANIZATION FOR ADMINISTRATION OF SCHOOLS IN TYPICAL STATE

In the larger building units, the principal often has a staff to assist him. This staff may consist only of a clerk, or it may be extended in larger buildings to include an assistant principal and other types of specialists. In secondary schools it often includes heads of departments of instruction.

The teachers are typically responsible to the principal of their building, rather than directly to the office of the superintendent of schools or to any member of the superintendent's staff. The teachers are specialized with reference to the types of work for which they are fitted. In the elementary school, the teachers are specialists in the work of the various grade levels, such as the primary grades or the intermediate grades. In the secondary school and frequently in the upper grades of the elementary school, the teachers are specialized according to subjects, and in a well-managed system teachers are assigned only to those subjects in which they have had special preparation.

Administrative Relationships

The accompanying figure is a diagram of the organization of the state and local school systems. This chart is very much simplified, and is intended to show only the bare outlines of the organizational structure. In this chart the lines denoting the relationship between the various agencies have been numbered, and each is explained to indicate the particular type of relationship existing in the case of any two agencies.

RELATION OF EDUCATION TO OTHER LOCAL GOVERNMENTAL AGENCIES

The local public-school system is only one of the enterprises carried on by the local governmental agencies. The modern city, for example, must maintain police and fire protection; it must provide parks; it must have a department of sanitation; dozens of other services of this type might be listed to show the vast variety of activities, many of them involving large problems of management and considerable outlay of public funds, which must be carried on by any well-organized city.

A fundamental question in the American political system is that of the relationship between the educational organization and the other enterprises of local government. Shall the schools be considered an enterprise to be governed entirely separately from the police department, the fire department, the department of sanitation, and the department of parks, or shall the schools be merely one of the many branches of a centralized local government?

Educators have in the majority of cases been strongly of the opinion that the schools should not be connected with the other branches of local government, and should be organized entirely separately as a completely independent jurisdiction. Those who hold this view contend that the school system is a branch of the state government and that therefore it should be, to a certain extent, free from the influences to which other purely local functions of government are subject.

When the schools are organized separately from the local civil government, conflict is likely to arise with regard to financial support. The same group of taxpayers must provide the resources from which both the schools and the other local governmental agencies are financed. If the school system is permitted a separate taxing power, then the taxpayers may be unduly burdened. Officers of a local civil government elected on a platform of lowering taxes may, for example, find their efforts completely nullified by increases in the taxes for schools made by an independent agency of government. Typically all taxes, including those for schools, are collected by a single public officer who is a functionary of the civil government; when taxpayers complain to him regarding the size of their tax bills, he is put in an intolerable position, if the part of the governmental organization to which he belongs does not have control over the levying of taxes for the school system.

Besides this conflict in regard to finances, a separate organiza-

tion for schools entails other difficulties in co-ordinating the facilities of the various branches of local government.   For example,
both the parks and the schools maintain playgrounds.   The children who use the facilities of the two branches of local government
are the same; they use the school facilities while the school is in
session, and during the out-of-school hours and in vacations they
use the playground facilities of the parks.   The possibilities of
co-ordination in playground services, with improved facilities for
the children and lowered cost for the taxpayers, are obvious.   In
practice, such co-ordination is difficult when entirely different
agencies of local government control the two sets of facilities.
Other examples of desirable co-ordination between the schools
and the other branches of local government could readily be
cited.

Two different types of school organization are found in the
American educational system.   One type is known as the dependent system, in which the schools are organized as a branch
of local government, and are responsible ultimately to a central
direction in the same way as the department of parks, police and
fire departments, and other branches of local government.   The
other type, known as the independent system, maintains no connection whatever between the schools and the other branches of
local government, except possibly in the appointing of school
board members.   The distinction between these two types of
systems is seen most clearly in the manner in which taxes for the
schools are raised and the amount to be spent on schools is determined.   If the school board must submit its request for financial
support to the city council, board of aldermen, or some other
agency which has power to change the amounts, then the organization is a dependent one.   If the school board is given authority
to levy its taxes directly and no other agency has power to lower
the amount requested, the system is an independent one.   Each of
these plans is to be found in numerous communities in the United
States.

Sharp differences of opinion prevail with respect to the merits of the two types of system. Political scientists in general favor a unified type of local government, and thus from their point of view the dependent type of school system seems the more satisfactory. They point out that only by the centralization of responsibility can good government be achieved. To divide up the responsibility for keeping taxes low and for maintaining public services at a satisfactory level of efficiency is very likely to make it impossible for the citizens of the community to keep proper check and control over their governmental services.

Educators, as has already been noted, strongly favor the independent type of school system. The underlying motive for this attitude seems to be the fear of what is called political domination of the schools. It is obvious that the school system in a democracy must not become a tool of any political group or party. Educators maintain that only by divorcing the school system completely from the local government with its political control can the necessary services to democratic government be performed.

In addition to this argument for the independent type of school system, there is the theoretical argument, previously given, to the effect that schools are a branch of the state government, and therefore cannot be subject to the same type of local control as most of the other functions of local government. It is pointed out, for example, that if the city chooses to neglect its park service, or its fire protection service, only the citizens of that community will suffer, but if the community neglects its schools, all the state and indeed all the rest of the country suffer, for many of the children whose education is neglected will not remain in the community where they were reared. This argument is not a particularly compelling one, for there are many other services of local government, such as health, sanitation, and police protection, which, if neglected, will be detrimental to the citizens of other communities.

Thus far scientific studies have not been definitely convincing with respect to the merits of the two types of educational organization.   Examples of well-managed and effective school systems can be found under both the dependent and independent types of organization, and neither type seems to guarantee against ineffectiveness in the school system.   Perhaps the only conclusion that can be drawn at this stage is that good administration and competent personnel are more important factors than the formal organization of the school system.

BIBLIOGRAPHY

Almack, John C., editor, *Modern School Administration*, pp. 3–22, 113–213, 263–96.

Burton, William H., *Introduction to Education*, pp. 303–26.

Butterweck, Joseph S., and J. Conrad Seegers, *An Orientation Course in Education*, pp. 321–35.

Chamberlain, Leo M., and Leonard E. Meece, *The Local Unit for School Administration in the United States*, Parts I, II.   Bulletins of the Bureau of School Service, College of Education, University of Kentucky, vol. VIII, no. 3, 4 (March, June, 1936).   44 pp.; 56 pp.

Chamberlain, Leo M., *The Teacher and School Organization*, pp. 54–110, 327–55, 469–89.

Clapp, Frank L., Wayland J. Chase, and Curtis Merriman, *Introduction to Education*, pp. 173–95.

Cocking, Walter D., and Charles H. Gilmore, *Organization and Administration of Public Education*.   Staff Study no. 2, Advisory Committee on Education.

Cubberley, Ellwood P., *Public School Administration* (third edition), pp. 44–131, 149–679.

Cubberley, Ellwood P., *State School Administration*, pp. 139–269.

Douglass, Aubrey A., *The American School System*, pp. 445–55.

Educational Policies Commission, *Social Services and the Schools*.   Washington: National Education Association, 1939.   xi + 148 pp.

Educational Policies Commission, *The Structure and Administration of Education in American Democracy*.   128 pp.

Engelhardt, Fred, *Public School Organization and Administration*, pp. 1–562.

Frasier, George Willard, and Winfield D. Armentrout, *An Introduction to the Literature of Education*, pp. 383–89.

Henry, Nelson B., and Jerome G. Kerwin, *Schools and City Government: A Study of School and Municipal Relationships in Cities of 50,000 or More*

Population.   Chicago: University of Chicago Press, 1938.   xii + 104 pp.

Judd, Charles H., *Education and Social Progress*, pp. 128–51.

Judd, Charles H., *Problems of Education in the United States*, pp. 119–33.

Reeder, Ward, *A First Course in Education*, pp. 438–48.

Smith, Payson, Frank W. Wright, and Associates, *Education in the Forty-Eight States*, pp. 123–40.   Staff Study no. 1, Advisory Committee on Education.

Wilson, Lester M., and I. L. Kandel, *Introduction to the Study of American Education*, pp. 71–85.

CHAPTER VIII

Non-governmental controls
of education

THE PRECEDING CHAPTERS have described the organization of the governmental controls of education at the federal, state, and local levels in the United States. Besides the legally constituted controls, there are a number of non-governmental agencies that actively affect the program of education as carried on under public auspices. Although these non-governmental agencies are without legal authority to enforce their will, they are nevertheless able to give more or less guidance and direction to the work of schools, and no account of the American educational system would be complete without some description of the nature and methods of their operation.

Some of these non-governmental controls of education are in reality merely pressure groups formed from some minority element in the general citizenry. These pressure groups may operate either directly or through the regular legal channels for the control of education. Other agencies of the type here considered have been created deliberately within the educational system, usually to accomplish some objective overlooked by or impossible of attainment through the regular legal controls.

Controls of education of the type here referred to are sometimes designated as "extra-legal" controls. This term should not be interpreted to mean that these are illegal controls, for that is not the case. They merely operate outside the regular legal or governmental channels that have been set up for the direction of the educational system. A number of different types of these non-governmental or extra-legal controls of education will be described.

ACCREDITING AGENCIES

One of the most important extra-legal controls operating within the American educational system is exercised by the numerous associations known as accrediting agencies. The accrediting associations are voluntary organizations which admit to membership after a more or less careful investigation regarding the quality of the program maintained by the institution. Membership in an accrediting association therefore becomes a hallmark of quality — something like the mark "sterling" on silverware. Accreditation may be defined as the process of inspecting and rating educational institutions, and the granting of membership to those found to be of satisfactory quality.

The influence of the accrediting associations is limited to the giving of publicity regarding their findings. Thus it is only as other institutions, educators, and the general public give weight to the holding of membership that the accrediting associations are able to exert any measure of control and influence. In practice, however, accreditation is so eagerly sought that institutions heed carefully the standards or suggestions announced by the associations as criteria for admission to membership.

Origins of the Movement

The accrediting movement has come into prominence chiefly since the beginning of the twentieth century, although its beginnings are to be found in the last decade of the nineteenth century. The way in which the development occurred can be aptly illustrated from the field of medical education.

For a long time in this country medical education was carried on by the apprenticeship method. The first medical schools were set up to supplement rather than to supplant apprenticeship, and were organized as integral parts of institutions of higher education and directly connected with large public hospitals.   After-ward a wave of commercial exploitation swept over medical education and the schools became largely proprietary in character and their standards degenerated accordingly.   A notable report prepared in 1910 by Abraham Flexner [1] laid bare these unsatis-factory conditions in American medical education.   The members of the medical profession were aware of the conditions and wel-comed the report.   The American Medical Association stepped in at this juncture and classified all medical schools as of grades A, B, and C.   There was no legal sanction for this classification, but so important was it for a medical student to secure his diploma from a high-grade institution that medical schools of grade C disappeared quickly.   Schools of grade B continued for a while but were eliminated in the course of time.

While the effects of classification were making over the medical education of the country, many of the requirements for equip-ment and training of the staff which were dictated by the Medical Association for classification in the highest grade were enacted by the states into law.   What had originated as extra-legal con-trol thus became part of the statutory requirements in many parts of the United States.

The example of the medical profession has been followed in some measure by other professions.   Standards have been set up which make it increasingly difficult for low-grade instruction to survive, and these standards have become effective because of the prestige of the standardizing agency.

Another example of a somewhat different type of extra-legal control grew out of the long-established practice of colleges of restricting admission to those students who could pass certain examinations.   The college entrance examination was a necessity in the early days of American education because a great many boys prepared for college by tutoring.   Not infrequently in the

[1] Abraham Flexner, *Medical Education in the United States and Canada.* Bulletin 4.   New York: Carnegie Foundation for the Advancement of Teach-ing, 1910.

colonial period a bright boy would be helped by the clergyman in his community to learn enough Latin and mathematics to qualify him to enter college.   Each college set up its own requirements for admission and tested the qualifications of candidates by conducting examinations.   As the country grew larger, the individual institutions found it increasingly difficult to conduct examinations in all the centers where there were possible candidates for admission.   The colleges in the eastern part of the country therefore pooled their interests and brought into existence a board which conducts a standard examination and reports the grade of a candidate to any college to which he may apply for admission. The organization of a centralized board for administering uniform examinations is a long step toward the exercise of extra-legal control over both the colleges which accept students and the secondary schools which prepare their pupils for the examinations.

The relations between colleges and secondary schools in the newer parts of the country have been standardized in a way different from that described in the foregoing paragraph.   The history of this second method of standardizing secondary schools begins in Michigan.   When the University of Michigan was organized, it was regarded as the center of a great system of public education covering the whole state.   The secondary schools were conceived to be branches of the University, and under this conception the University was made in a sense responsible for the instruction given in the secondary schools.   The University, instead of passing on individual candidates for admission, was supposed to pass on the excellence or deficiency of the secondary school in which candidates were prepared.   From this practice there developed a system of certification.   Any secondary school adjudged to be adequate in its instruction and general administration was certified and its graduates were allowed to enter the University without further test.   In the course of time graduates of secondary schools outside of Michigan applied for admission to the University, and it became the practice for the University of

Michigan to approve secondary schools in Ohio, Indiana, and other states.

The practice of the University of Michigan was soon imitated by all the colleges and universities west of the Allegheny Mountains. Before long, however, each institution found that it was seriously burdened by the necessity of approving distant secondary schools. In 1895 the leading universities in the North Central states banded together and established an organization known as the North Central Association of Colleges and Secondary Schools. This association prepared and published a list of approved secondary schools which was used by the higher institutions in admitting students. After some years the secondary schools demanded that a list of approved colleges and universities be established, so that the schools might select as teachers only those who had had sound preparation in institutions of high quality, and so that graduates of secondary schools might be advised intelligently concerning the choice of a higher institution for their further education. The approved lists of the North Central Association soon came to have great prestige; communities, because of their desire to have their schools approved, have in some cases been practically coerced into the provision of far better equipment and facilities than they would otherwise have furnished; colleges, desiring to open opportunities for their graduates to teach in the better secondary schools, have bent every effort to meet the requirements of the accrediting association.

Levels of Education Affected

Control by accrediting associations today does not operate equally at all levels of the American educational system. The associations have no concern with elementary schools, and thus exert no control over that level of education. The secondary schools that are members of regional associations are almost all located in cities. Only a very few rural secondary schools hold regional accreditation, and most schools in rural areas have little or no hope of ever meeting the requirements for membership.

Although the accrediting process thus does not affect directly the entire group of secondary schools, the influence is wider than the membership, for the requirements set up are everywhere respected as reflecting the characteristics that should be striven for in a well-organized school.

At the college and professional-school level the accrediting process exerts an extremely powerful control. Membership in an accrediting association is almost a life-and-death matter for an institution of higher education, and the standards of the accrediting agencies are carefully heeded by almost all the colleges and universities in the country.

Types of Accreditation According to Scope of Recognition

The accrediting associations may be classified into three groups with reference to the scope of recognition accorded to membership. Certain of the associations operate on a national basis. The national associations deal only with the level of higher education, and membership in such an organization implies recognition of the college or university and its product anywhere in the country. National accreditation also involves international recognition, for the foreign universities customarily use the accredited lists of the national associations in judging the fitness of American students for courses of advanced study.

A type of recognition somewhat narrower in scope than national accreditation is afforded by the regional associations. The country is practically covered by such agencies, one for the New England states, one for the Middle states, one for the Southern states, one for the North Central states, and one for the Northwest. Accrediting by the regional association implies recognition only within the region involved, but in practice there is reciprocity between the various regions, so that membership in a regional agency actually carries with it recognition that is national in scope. The regional associations accredit both colleges and secondary schools.

In some states there have been organized state accrediting

associations, which form a third level in the accrediting process. These voluntary associations in the states deal only with colleges and universities, and are not as powerful as the regional agencies. Usually the state itself as a governmental agency also carries on an accrediting process for both secondary schools and colleges; this of course is not an extra-legal control of education but a part of the regular governmental control. This type of recognition by the state, however, is frequently referred to as accreditation.

Types of Accrediting Agencies

The agencies engaged in the accrediting of educational institutions may be classified into some half-dozen types. One kind of agency consists of associations of professional practitioners; this type provides for the accreditation of institutions preparing young men and women for the profession concerned. For example, the American Medical Association, composed of the practicing physicians and surgeons in the country, provides for the inspection and rating of all the institutions attempting to prepare young people for the M.D. degree. The American Bar Association, composed of the practicing lawyers of the country, also has set up standards which schools of law wishing its stamp of approval must meet. Inasmuch as a professional association is usually rather large, with membership composed of practitioners of the profession, the actual process of accreditation is typically carried on by a committee; the committee may come to have a powerful control over the conditions under which preparation for the profession may be offered.

A second type of accrediting agency consists of an association of professional schools. In the deliberations leading to admission to membership in such organizations, the institutions comprising the association are usually represented by their administrative officers, such as the president or dean. Thus, the American Association of Teachers Colleges, which promulgates standards regarding institutional conditions under which teachers should be prepared, is in practice operated by a group of executive officers from teachers colleges holding membership in the association. Similar associations of professional schools operate in the fields of pharmacy, journalism, business, architecture, and a number of other professions. Although this type of accreditation, as well as the type discussed in the preceding paragraph, is based merely on a recognition within the professional group concerned, the membership lists have been given the effect of legal sanction in a number of states which limit admission to the professions to those who have been prepared in the accredited institutions.

The third type of accrediting agency consists of the regional associations of secondary schools and colleges. In general, the control of these associations lies almost exclusively with the administrative officers of member institutions. The peculiar strength of the regional associations lies in the reciprocal relationship between the secondary schools and the colleges comprising the membership. Member secondary schools are required by these associations to select their teachers only from the colleges belonging to the association, and the colleges in turn are expected to give preference in admission of students to those who have graduated from accredited secondary schools. Because of this understanding, the graduate of an unaccredited college can find a teaching position only in an unaccredited school. Inasmuch as the stronger secondary schools, where the salaries are better, are nearly all accredited or are striving to be accredited, the graduate of the unaccredited college is at a serious disadvantage in finding employment in the teaching profession. The college, in turn, feels this pressure, and strives in every way to meet the standards set by the regional accrediting association.

The fourth type of accrediting association includes but a single agency, the Association of American Universities. This organization could better be designated as the association of graduate schools, for its active control lies in the hands of the deans of graduate schools in the great universities of the country. Membership in this Association is extremely limited, with only thirty-two universities holding this distinction in 1939. The Association, however, inspects colleges to determine whether they have adequate facilities for preparing students for effective graduate work; those that are deemed worthy are given a place on the approved list of the Association. This approved list, therefore, becomes a sort of nationally and internationally recognized accreditation, for the graduate of a college on the approved list of the Association of American Universities may enter any of the graduate schools of this country and of most foreign countries with full recognition of his undergraduate work.

The fifth type of accrediting agency consists of the state boards of certification, which license individuals for the practice of the various professions. As previously noted, this is not an extralegal form of control, but rather it is a part of the ordinary powers of government. The state assumes the right, in most instances, to say who shall be permitted to practice medicine, law, dentistry, and to hold a teaching position in the public schools; in enforcing such provisions, the state frequently takes into account the type of institution in which the candidate has had his preparation for the profession. Graduates of unaccredited institutions are not licensed for the professions, and thus the state may exert a definite control over professional institutions through the setting up of standards which must be met before approval is received. Inasmuch as almost all liberal arts colleges prepare teachers for the public schools, recognition by the state for the purposes of certifying teachers is sometimes referred to as accreditation in such institutions.

The sixth type of agency engaging in the accrediting of institutions is the individual university. In a number of cases the state university rates the colleges of its region and accords to graduates or transfer students from such institutions advanced standing in accordance with this rating. Thus the University of Illinois classifies institutions into groups A, B, and C, in accordance with the degree to which their work is recognized upon transfer to the University. The colleges sometimes refer to this recognition as accreditation. In some cases a college, which is unable to meet the standards of the regional accrediting association, is able to make an arrangement with a large university in its state so that its students may have certain credits accepted on transfer, thus affording them some measure of recognition for the courses they have completed.

Purposes of Accrediting

The principal purpose of the accrediting process is to aid inter-institutional relationships and to furnish information about the quality of institutions that will be valuable to the general public. For example, when a student transfers from one institution to another at any level, it is necessary, before he can be accorded any definite status, for the college or university to which the student goes to have some information about the general quality of the institution from which he comes. Prior to the development of the accrediting agencies, universities typically had their own lists of institutions from which they would accept students without discount in credit. The accrediting process is also useful to those who employ the graduates of colleges and universities, as it gives some general idea of the quality of preparation that has been had.

Students should inquire carefully concerning the accreditation of the institution which they expect to attend. Only under exceptional circumstances is it wise today for a student to attend an unaccredited college or university. Upon graduation or upon the occasion of transferring to another institution the student who has obtained his education in an unaccredited institution is almost certain to meet embarrassment and disappointment through the failure of other institutions and the various public and private employing agencies to recognize his academic credentials at face value.

Criticisms of Accrediting

The accrediting movement is a relatively new development in the history of American education. The oldest accrediting agency of general significance dates only from 1895. Publication of standards for accrediting and of lists of accredited collegiate institutions based on these standards did not begin until well along in the second decade of the twentieth century. The accrediting procedure is at present by no means perfect, but it has undergone steady improvement since the first accrediting standards were promulgated.

The improvement of educational institutions through the accrediting process has not been accomplished without opposition and criticism. Oftentimes complaints against the accrediting movement come from the executive officers in institutions that are unable to meet the standards set up, and these opinions naturally may be given little weight. Other criticisms, however, have come from thoughtful educators or interested laymen whose motives could not be questioned. The accrediting movement, for example, has tended to reduce the number of medical schools, to raise the qualifications demanded of students for admission to training in medicine, and to require a high quality of academic work for graduation from the medical course; these tendencies, it is sometimes claimed, are responsible for reducing the number of licensed physicians to a point where some communities, especially in rural regions, are not adequately supplied with medical service.

In some states members of the legislature have expressed irritation over the fact that secondary schools and colleges often seek to obtain larger appropriations or better equipment by using the argument that the regional accrediting association will bar them from the approved list unless the requested funds and equipment are supplied. The irritation has actually reached a point in some states where bills have been introduced into the legislature to forbid any publicly supported school or college from holding membership in an accrediting association. No state, however, has ever yet enacted such a law.

Frequently the accrediting process has been criticized because it has tended toward too much standardization. In fact the accrediting associations are sometimes referred to as "standardizing agencies." In the promulgation of criteria for accreditation, however, the accrediting associations are not attempting to make all institutions alike. A college or secondary school can meet the standards in every particular and still retain as much individuality as any effective institution could ever wish. The North Central Association adopted in 1934 a plan for accrediting colleges which aims to get away from the mechanical application of standards. Under the present procedure the various characteristics of a single institution are compared with the corresponding characteristics of other institutions in the Association, and membership is accorded or denied after a broad general survey of a whole list of characteristics. A similar project, looking toward the application of such methods to the accreditation of secondary schools, has recently been completed under the auspices of a national committee. Although the accrediting process has encouraged a certain amount of uniformity, this uniformity has pertained to such \necessary matters as definitions of terms and minimum essentials rather than to the characteristics that mark institutions as distinctive or outstanding.

The criticism against too much standardization sometimes takes the form of a complaint that the accrediting agencies have so dominated the operations of individual colleges as to destroy their long-cherished autonomy. Observation of the way in which these extra-legal agencies have operated, however, leads to the conclusion that the type of control exercised has been thoroughly beneficent. The accrediting associations are interested only in sound educational programs, and institutions sometimes need protection against unsound developments that may be planned by them or imposed upon them without due regard to the educational outcomes.

Effects of the Accrediting Movement

Although criticisms such as the foregoing have been noted, the accrediting movement has had a marked effect in improving the general quality of educational services in American schools and colleges. The weaker institutions have been stimulated to improve their programs, and those that have neglected or been unable to make such improvement have found survival more difficult than it would otherwise have been. The accrediting movement has particularly operated in the direction of requiring better financial support for institutions of education, and of stimulating improvement in the physical equipment and in the preparation of the teaching staff. The regional and national accrediting associations have tended toward a uniformity of understanding in educational procedures that could never have been attained under a system of state and local control. On several occasions, the accrediting associations have proved a valuable bulwark when secondary schools or higher institutions have been attacked by politically-minded spoilsmen.

The time may eventually arrive when the function of accrediting educational institutions can be taken over entirely by some governmental agency, thus changing the process from an extralegal to a legal control. A governmental control of the type now exercised by the accrediting agencies, however, would be considered undesirable by most of the privately controlled educational institutions of the country. Certainly until some method is found for setting up for the purpose a governmental agency that is free from unsound political influences, there will be an important place in the American educational system for accrediting agencies of the voluntary type to fill.

PROFESSIONAL ASSOCIATIONS OF EDUCATORS

The individual members of the teaching profession are organized into numerous associations which are entirely different from the accrediting agencies described thus far. The professional associations are of two main types: the general associations, which include in their membership teachers and school administrators without regard to their special interests; and the specialized organizations which include in their membership only those educators whose interests lie along some particular line of work.

The National Education Association, the largest of the general professional organizations, was established in 1857.   In 1939 it enrolled 201,682 members, or 21.5 per cent of the total number of persons engaged in educational service in the country.   A state teachers' association is organized in every state, and the combined membership of the state organizations amounted in 1939 to 86 per cent of the total number of teachers in this country.   The general professional organizations of educators in many instances are dominated by the group who are in administrative positions in the school system; that is, by the superintendents, principals, and college and university presidents and deans.   On the other hand, there is at times vigorous assertion of the views of classroom teachers.

Lately there has come into existence another type of professional organization modeled along the lines of the labor union, in which the rank and file of the teaching force are welcomed as members but in which the administrative group, corresponding to the management group in industry, is not given a controlling voice in the determination of policy.   Generally an educational association of this type is affiliated with a national labor organization.   The movement in this direction is as yet young, but it has already served to give teachers more influence in determination of policy.

Besides these general organizations, and frequently affiliated with them, are large numbers of special organizations representing practically every type of educational interest.   Some of these associations are organized for specialists in various subject-matter fields; others are organized according to the level at which service is rendered, such as the kindergarten or the elementary school; others are organized for various types of school administrators and specialists engaged in many different lines of educational activity such as guidance, business management, or research.

Almost all the educational associations engage more or less actively in agitation for improved school conditions.   What is known euphemistically as "legislative work," but is more truly described by the term "lobbying," is carried on vigorously by most educational associations of the general type, and by not a few of the special type of educational associations.   It is no mere coincidence, for example, that the National Education Association, the American Vocational Association, and numbers of other national associations concerned with education have their general headquarters in Washington, D.C.   Activities directed toward the creation of sentiment in favor of legislation beneficial to education is, of course, a thoroughly legitimate activity when carried on in accordance with well-recognized ethical principles.   Groups of educators in a democracy have every right through collective action to bring their points of view to the attention of the public.

To a limited extent control is exercised by associations of professional individuals of a particular type through a process of agreement.   If a large majority of the teachers of secondary-school English, for example, attend a meeting of the state teachers' association and hear some promising innovation described, they may be motivated to try the new procedure on their return to their classrooms.   The articles in a journal published by a professional association are widely read and doubtless have an effect in inducing teachers and administrators to introduce new devices and procedures.   When processes of stimulation such as these are multiplied a thousand times in many different lines, the actual course of educational procedure may be modified considerably by a professional association which is entirely outside the legal arrangements for the control of the school system.

SCHOOL-AND-HOME ASSOCIATIONS

Another type of organization that affects the program of the school is the association linking school and home.   Perhaps the most common of such organizations is the so-called parent-teacher association.   An organization of this type performs a useful service in acquainting parents with the plans, policies, and procedures of the school.   The parents of the pupils are the part of the population most intimately concerned with what goes on in schools.   Most parents recall their own school days and are somewhat disturbed to find their children being taught by new methods, or following novel curriculums, or using different texts from those with which they were familiar as pupils.   The parent-teacher association provides opportunity for discussing such matters in the friendly atmosphere of a social meeting.   Such an activity, of course, does not involve any formal control over the program.

A parent-teacher association, however, sometimes engages in activities other than educating its members.   One of the commonest activities of such associations is the raising of funds to provide special equipment needed by the school but not furnished by the regular authorities.   Such a procedure seems innocuous, especially as the funds are nearly always small; but it is axiomatic that finances and control are usually associated, and there is the probability that, having provided funds for the equipment, the parent-teacher association may want something to say about the use and disposal of this equipment, and at that point control is almost certain to be involved.   Fund-raising activities by parent-teacher associations are usually a waste of effort, for an equal amount of time and energy spent in acquainting the general public and the school authorities with the needs for better facilities would be much more productive of results in improving the service of the schools.

Occasionally an association of the parent-teacher type gets out of hand and begins to dictate policies and procedures to the regularly constituted school authorities.   Interference in matters connected with the personnel of the school system, such as the dismissal or retention of a teacher or administrative officer, has sometimes been observed in the case of such associations.

It is all too easy for parents, particularly when organized in an association, to get the idea that schools are conducted for their especial benefit and should follow their particular wishes.   In an earlier chapter the thesis has been defended that schools are social institutions, operated for the benefit of society as a whole, and not for the benefit of any limited class, not even for the personal benefit of the children or their parents.   As a rule, parents wish only the best of school conditions for their children; determination of what is best within the limits of the finances available, however, is not a matter for the parents to decide, but is the responsibility of the regularly constituted school authorities.   The parent's only rights in case of dissatisfaction are: first, those of the ordinary citizen, to carry his complaint to the proper authorities; second, to use his ballot to effect a change in policy; and third, to protest by removing his children from the school and placing them in another where conditions are more to his liking.   The school authorities, it goes without saying, should listen carefully to criticisms and advice from parents, as from other interested persons; but the school system is not organized to give parents power to dictate the program of education.

On the whole, the work of parent-teacher associations must be judged as a favorable influence in the educational system.   Associations of this type err, however, when they begin to develop any type of activity that looks toward the control of schools. The proper sphere of activity for such associations is, first, the education of their own numbers and, second, the enlightenment of the general public regarding conditions and needs of the schools.

NON-ACADEMIC ORGANIZATIONS

Many organizations not primarily concerned with educational matters seek to achieve some of their objectives through the use of the schools.   There are large numbers of organizations of this type in the United States, and a complete list of them has never been compiled.   Among them may be mentioned such well and favorably known organizations as the American Legion, the American Red Cross, chambers of commerce, community chests, labor unions, and local newspapers.   Each of these organizations, in seeking to accomplish some of its objectives, notes the influence of the schools on the lives of young people, and thereupon seeks to have included in the school program types of activities that will further the objectives of the organization.

Groups of the type here under discussion attempt to influence the school program in many different ways. One of the common methods is to ask permission to participate in the school program on certain days, particularly on days that have some special significance for the cause which the organization represents. The organization may ask that their speakers be permitted to address the school assembly. They may sponsor essay contests in the schools, thus diverting the attention of pupils and teachers from the regular curriculum. Sometimes such agencies seek to use the schools as a fund-collecting agency, and children are urged, through the medium of the schools, to bring their contributions for some cause which, in itself, may be entirely worthy. Certain commercial concerns have been exceedingly clever in insinuating advertising campaigns into the schools, disguised perhaps as a novel feature of art instruction or as a health program, but actually designed to sell more soap or more toothpaste.

Many non-academic groups have developed into strong pressure agencies for the insistence on the teaching of certain subjects. Sometimes these groups are sufficiently powerful to induce the state legislature to enact a law requiring the teaching of the subject in which they are interested. In other cases, pressure is brought on the local school board to make changes in the curriculum favorable to the point of view which the organization seeks to foster. The work of several groups of this type was described in Chapter IV.

The very nature of the agencies that seek to use the schools to further their peculiar objectives makes it difficult to deny them the entrée they seek. The respectability of such an agency as the local community chest, or of a patriotic organization, makes it both difficult and hazardous for school authorities to do anything except accede to their requests. Thus there is brought to bear upon the schools a type of control that is not contemplated in the regular legal or governmental organization.   That such pressures, even when they seem unobjectionable to certain groups, are in reality unwise and embarrassing to the schools should be readily apparent.   The schools are maintained for the education of youth for the present and future social order, not for the attainment of the objectives of any organization comprising a minority of the citizens, however worthy that organization and its objectives may be.   The schools are not maintained as a money-collecting agency, or as a means of encouraging the sale of certain commercial products, or even as a means of propagandizing for the ideals or tenets of any limited group in society.

ENDOWED FOUNDATIONS

A number of American philanthropists, wishing to give funds for the general benefit of society and realizing that they personally are incapable of determining the precise uses to which the money might best be devoted, have set up endowed foundations to administer their philanthropies.   These organizations are usually under the direction of a self-perpetuating board of trustees which determines in detail the manner in which the income, and in many cases a part of the principal of the fund, shall be expended.   Some philanthropists, in setting up foundations, have indicated that the money should be used to promote education.   The total amount of assets now held by such organizations is known to be relatively large, although no reporting system has complete information on all the funds.   Ernest V. Hollis [1] reports that a total of $233,000,534 was contributed by foundations for educational purposes during the decade 1921–30.

The endowed foundations, for the most part, have devoted their attention more to privately controlled education than to the public-school system, and to the level of collegiate, university, and professional education rather than to the elementary or secondary

[1] Ernest V. Hollis, *Philanthropic Foundations and Higher Education.*

school.   This statement does not mean to imply, however, that public education at all levels has not been influenced by the philanthropies of endowed foundations.

In almost every instance, the endowed foundations strenuously disavow any intent to control education.   Their only object is to dispense funds in such a way as to be of maximum benefit to the type of education with which they are concerned.   These foundations, however, have actually given no small degree of direction to the American educational system, and therefore they deserve consideration under the topic of extra-legal controls of the system.

The mere fact that these foundations have money to spend for certain specific purposes tends to fix attention on these objectives. For example, one of the well-known foundations has long been interested in promoting better library service.   One may question whether the present "library-mindedness" of the entire school program does not have a direct connection with the long-continued activity of this important philanthropic organization.   The worthiness of such a type of direction may be entirely unquestioned, but it is undeniably true that in certain definite respects these endowed foundations have exerted control over American education merely through the availability of their funds for special types of services.

The endowed foundations have also been active in carrying on research and in publishing educational literature.   For example, one of the foundations a few years ago made an investigation of intercollegiate athletics and published its findings; these findings aroused great general interest, and stimulated many institutions either to explain the conditions reported or, all too often without permanent results, to revise the policies and procedures that were criticized.   The report on medical education by Flexner, referred to earlier in this chapter, is another example in point, for it was made possible by a grant from one of the endowed foundations.

TRADITION AND OTHER SOCIAL INFLUENCES

A powerful control which must be catalogued as extra-legal is the influence of tradition. When a method of conducting schools or a particular subject of instruction has been long established it becomes extraordinarily difficult to dislodge. For example, the long-accepted practice of schools has been to demand a certain type of order or discipline in the classroom. When an experimental school permits pupils to move about the classroom freely and to engage in conversation with others, an observer who is familiar with traditional practices experiences a shock. Such an observer condemns the disorder, as he calls it, and thereby throws the weight of his influence against freedom in the form which the experimental school is practicing it. Similarly an established subject in the curriculum is difficult to dislodge. Parents like to have their children receive instruction in the same subjects in which they were instructed. A new subject often meets a silent but highly effective opposition, which springs from conservatism that hardly recognizes itself as conservatism.

The social influences that have been described in this chapter are far more influential than many of the explicit legislative enactments that appear in statutes. It often requires legal action to inject into the curriculum a new subject of instruction, such as a course on conservation of natural resources, while an older subject like algebra persists because of its traditional place in the curriculum. Algebra seems to be an inevitable and necessary part of the curriculum because it has long been taught in the schools. Educators clearly must follow the principle that no subject has a right to persist in the curriculum unless it can be demonstrated to have relation to some social need.

What is here said is to be recognized as a reiteration in a new form of the statement, made in earlier chapters, that the school is a social institution. There are, it is true, legal enactments which determine what the schools do. In the social order there are other subtle influences, which must be discovered by penetrating analysis, that sometimes stand in the way of progress and at other times constitute bulwarks against social change which would result in disaster.

BIBLIOGRAPHY

Butterworth, Julian Edward, *The Parent-Teacher Association and Its Work.* New York: The Macmillan Company, 1928.   x + 150 pp.

Chamberlain, Leo M., *The Teacher and School Organization*, pp. 599–624.

Co-ordination of Accrediting Activities.   American Council on Education Studies, series I, vol. III, no. 9.   Washington: American Council on Education, 1939.   v + 50 pp.

Cubberley, Ellwood P., *Public Education in the United States*, pp. 704–16.

Cubberley, Ellwood P., *State School Administration*, pp. 734–60.

Holbeck, Elmer Scott, *An Analysis of the Activities and Potentialities for Achievement of the Parent-Teacher Association.*   Teachers College Contributions to Education, no. 601.   New York: Teachers College, Columbia University, 1934.   viii + 126 pp.

Hollis, E. V., *Philanthropic Foundations and Higher Education.*   New York: Columbia University Press, 1938.   xi + 366 pp.

Keppel, Frederick Paul, *The Foundation: Its Place in American Life.*   New York: The Macmillan Company, 1930.   viii + 114 pp.

National Congress of Parents and Teachers, *The Handbook of the National Congress of Parents and Teachers.*   Washington: National Congress of Parents and Teachers, 1929.   112 pp.

Raup, Bruce, *Education and Organized Interests in America.*   New York: G. P. Putnam's Sons, 1936.   vii + 238 pp.

Wattenberg, William W., *On the Educational Front: The Reactions of Teachers Associations in New York and Chicago.*   New York: Columbia University Press, 1936.   218 pp.

Zook, G. F., and M. E. Haggerty, *Principles of Accrediting Higher Institutions.*   Chicago: University of Chicago Press, 1936.   xvii + 202 pp.

CHAPTER IX

FINANCING THE EDUCATIONAL SYSTEM

THE FINAL CONTROL of any social enterprise is almost certain to be closely associated with the source of its financial support. The preceding chapters have described the various governmental and non-governmental controls in the American system of education, but to understand fully the way in which these controls are exerted it is necessary to have a knowledge of the way in which the educational system is supported.

THE DEVELOPMENT OF THE FREE PUBLIC SCHOOL IN THE UNITED STATES

As has been indicated in the preceding chapters, the typical school in the United States is today under public control, and the public schools at the elementary and secondary level are free of charges for tuition to those who attend. The idea of a school that would be supported at public expense has developed through a number of stages in the history of education in the United States. Cubberley [1] notes the following seven stages in this development:

1. Originally education was provided only from private benevolence or religious charity or through the charging of tuition fees to those pupils whose parents could afford to pay. Sometimes schools supported by charity or tuition fees were given small grants of public funds at irregular intervals.

[1] Ellwood P. Cubberley, *Public Education in the United States*, p. 118. Boston: Houghton Mifflin Company, 1934.

2. Somewhat later financial assistance began to be granted from public sources to private or semiprivate schools or to societies which were undertaking the provision of schools, to enable them to reduce their tuition fees or to extend the term of instruction beyond that which could be provided by the ordinary resources of the school.   In numerous cases the aid was in the form of some special privilege such as permission to organize a lottery.

3. When the agitation for a form of education under direct public control became pronounced, the state tended at first to enact permissive legislation which allowed special districts the right to organize public schools and to tax themselves for this purpose.   Naturally, only the most enlightened communities took advantage of such opportunity, and even in progressive districts there were always a number of citizens who were bitterly opposed to the organization of a local public school.   As a rule such schools were at first considered to be a provision for pauper children, but later they were opened to others than paupers.

4. When the importance of education in a democratic government came to be realized, the states began to enact legislation requiring local communities to make provision for the education of children who belonged to families that could not afford to pay tuition fees in private schools.   This step usually allowed the community the option of organizing its own school or of paying for the tuition of pauper children in established private schools.

5. After state school funds were created as a result of the federal policy of making land grants for educational purposes, the states began to be concerned about the expenditure of the income from these funds.   There was a tendency among the states to enact legislation requiring local taxes or other types of payment for the maintenance of schools to supplement the grants of funds distributed by the state.   The district might still require tuition fees from pupils in partial support of its public school, but from some local source funds were required to be provided in order to supplement the grants made by the state.

6. The next step was the elimination of the tuition fee and the

assumption of the entire cost of instruction by the public. This step meant that the state or local government was supplying the educational opportunity for all children whether their parents could or could not afford to pay for education. This step marks the real establishment of a free public school. When first introduced, it was bitterly opposed in many areas and denounced as radical and socialistic.

7. The final step involved the elimination of the pauper school idea and the discontinuance of aid to private or sectarian schools. The public school was thus recognized as the common school for all the American people.

The foregoing seven stages, as has been previously indicated, were originally described by Professor Cubberley a number of years ago. During the twentieth century there has been added in effect an eighth stage in the developmental process of free American secondary and elementary education. The stages previously described, though nominally leading to a free public school, actually left many of the costs of education to be borne by the parents of the pupils. The actual instruction was free and the building was constructed, heated, lighted, and cared for at public expense, but there were numerous other costs of education at the elementary and secondary levels which were privately borne. For example, children living at a considerable distance from a school found it necessary to have transportation if they were to get the benefit of the facilities maintained for them. Many children were prevented from attending school because they could not provide their own transportation. In recent years transportation for school children has in most states been provided when needed at public expense. Textbooks and other school supplies were formerly provided privately, but now many school systems have taken the step of providing such materials at public expense. The list of services of this type which have recently begun to be assumed by the public instead of by the pupil and his parent could be extended to considerable length. Health service, dental inspection, and hot lunches are among the items now furnished pupils free of charge in many well-managed local school systems. Lately funds have been provided by the Federal Government through the National Youth Administration, which make it possible for pupils to earn enough, by performing certain socially useful and productive tasks, to pay for personal expenses which parents are unable to meet and for which communities are unable to make provision.

THE MAGNITUDE OF THE FINANCIAL PROBLEM

The financing of the educational program in the United States is a huge problem. The total amount of support for the schools of the entire country increased more or less steadily until it reached a high point, as reported by the United States Office of Education, of $3,364,872,000 in 1929–30. School budgets were reduced drastically during the economic depression of the 1930's, and the total expenditure for education in 1933–34 declined to the low point of $2,604,410,935. Since that time the amount has risen. Of the grand total expenditures for education in the United States about five-sixths is for public schools and about one-sixth is for privately controlled schools. The figures given above include education at all levels from the kindergarten through the university. According to the estimates by the Research Division of the National Education Association, the total expenditure for public schools in this country in 1930 was about $3\frac{1}{3}$ per cent of the total national income in that year; in 1934 the total expenditure for all public education was estimated to be 3.87 per cent of the total national income.

The magnitude of expenditures for public education can scarcely be realized adequately from the mere naming of a sum such as two or three billion dollars. A comparison of the amounts expended for other purposes makes somewhat clearer the amounts involved in financing education. According to the Research Division of the National Education Association, the total expenditure for schools in this country in 1930 amounted to a sum

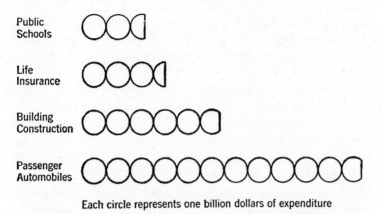

Each circle represents one billion dollars of expenditure

FIGURE 4. TOTAL ANNUAL EXPENDITURES IN 1930 FOR ALL PUBLIC SCHOOLS, FOR LIFE INSURANCE, FOR BUILDING CONSTRUCTION, AND FOR PASSENGER AUTOMOBILES

equivalent to 74 per cent of the total annual payments for life-insurance premiums, to 45 per cent of the total annual expenditures for all kinds of building construction, to 22 per cent of the total amount spent by the American people for passenger automobiles in that year.

SOURCES OF SUPPORT

Four different sources provide the major part of the funds expended for educational purposes in the United States. The principal source of support for the public schools is taxation, and the largest amounts derived from tax sources are raised by the general property tax. Philanthropy, originally the only source of support of schools for those who could not afford to pay their own tuition, is still an important source of income for private schools and to a limited extent for the public schools. Tuition fees are important sources of support for private schools and to a considerable extent for the support of all education at the collegiate and university level. Income from endowment provides support for most of the privately controlled institutions of higher education, for some of the privately controlled secondary schools, and part of the support for a number of publicly controlled universities.

Besides these important sources of support, it should be noted that borrowed funds are frequently used to finance special projects, such as building construction. Weaker institutions of the privately controlled type sometimes resort to borrowing in order to finance their current operations.

Finally, it must be pointed out that a considerable but undetermined amount of the real support of education in the United States comes from the contributed services of teachers and administrators. In some of the schools supported by religious denominations the staff is wholly or partly composed of members of teaching orders who devote their lives to this service without any remuneration other than their living expenses. In schools and colleges of other types a missionary spirit is often manifested by those who give instruction and accept salaries far below those which they could earn in other callings. It is an axiom that nobody goes into teaching in order to get rich; thus society capitalizes to some extent on the fact that those who enter the teaching profession do so in part because of their desire to render social service rather than make as much money as they possibly can. Such conditions can only mean that the teachers themselves bear part of the real cost of maintaining the educational system through their willingness to accept salaries lower than those of persons of similar qualifications in other callings.

The fact that the schools are in part financed by contributions of teachers was made strikingly evident during the economic depression of the 1930's, when teachers in many school systems stayed at their posts and taught without pay, or with pay only in the form of warrants that were not cashable at par, rather than see the schools close their doors and deny educational opportunities to young people. Teachers thus provided a pool of credit by means of which many school systems were able to continue in operation during the years of the depression.

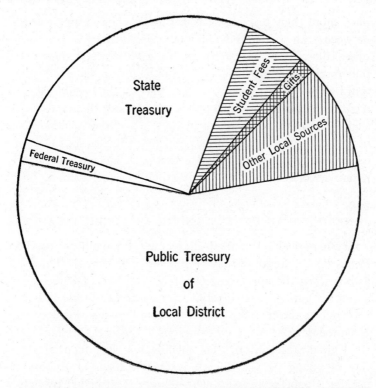

State
Treasury

Student Fees

Gifts

Federal Treasury

Other Local Sources

Public Treasury
of
Local District

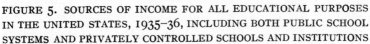

FIGURE 5. SOURCES OF INCOME FOR ALL EDUCATIONAL PURPOSES
IN THE UNITED STATES, 1935–36, INCLUDING BOTH PUBLIC SCHOOL
SYSTEMS AND PRIVATELY CONTROLLED SCHOOLS AND INSTITUTIONS

The two last-mentioned sources, the borrowing of funds and
the contributed services of teachers, are not considered in the
amounts of support normally reported for the American educational system. The four sources previously mentioned: taxes,
philanthropy, tuition fees, and endowment income, are the
sources from which the funds are secured that are reported in all
statements of expenditures for the educational system.

The income for educational purposes is not evenly distributed
among the various sources noted above. In 1935–36 the public
treasury carried 83 per cent of the total burden; student fees sup-

plied more than 5 per cent of the total; philanthropy supplied between 1 and 2 per cent; and the remainder came from other miscellaneous sources.   About 65 per cent of the income of the public schools is provided by the local government and 30 per cent by the state government.   The share of the Federal Government in the financing of the public schools is small, amounting to slightly more than 2 per cent in 1935–36.   Other minor sources of support, such as tuition fees (chiefly in institutions of higher education), philanthropy, and endowment income, provide the remainder of the funds used by the public-school system.

NEED FOR AN UNDERSTANDING OF PUBLIC FINANCE

The historical and statistical facts which have been presented in foregoing paragraphs have profound significance.   There was a time when the upbringing of a boy or girl was not recognized as an obligation requiring the vast expenditure which is now involved in the maintenance of the public educational system. Even today most of the great nations of the world are far behind the United States in providing facilities for the advanced education of young people.   The secondary schools of Europe are usually supported by tuition fees, and are attended by only a small fraction of the youthful population.   They are exclusive schools designed for the education of highly selected youth.   In general, public facilities for the education of girls in Europe are altogether inferior to those which exist for boys.   When the United States organizes and supports such an educational system as that which it now maintains for the free education of all classes of young people, the motives which prompt it to do so must be deep-seated and intimately related to the most fundamental characteristics of its unique civilization.

The support of public education is at present one of the most discussed and frequently most misunderstood issues of public administration.   Enrollments in schools, especially at the upper levels, have increased at a prodigious rate, and with the increase in enrollments has come, of course, a necessity for increase in expenditures. The public has the increase in expenditures vividly called to its attention but is not fully acquainted with the underlying conditions which compel the raising of large revenues. Each individual family is eager to take advantage of free educational opportunities for its children, but is unable to comprehend the situation which has developed in recent years in the industrial and social life of this nation.

It has been especially true in recent years when public finance has been in trouble that drastic reductions have been common in educational budgets. Furthermore, there has been an effort to transfer the tax burden from the local community to the state and from the state to the Federal Government. The student of education is compelled, if he would understand the present-day problems which confront the schools, to go far beyond the analysis of the curriculum and of the administrative organization of the schools. He must become acquainted with certain broad principles of economics and political science which must be understood if the schools are to be maintained efficiently in the years that are to come. No blindness on the part of educators is more fatal than the blindness which arises from the failure to see that the schools are inextricably related to the whole economic system of the nation. It is essential therefore that there be at this point a discussion of certain facts which are not ordinarily thought of by pupils or even by teachers in the educational system.

GOVERNMENTAL UNITS WHICH SUPPORT EDUCATION

Grave difficulties in supporting schools of satisfactory grade arise out of the variations in economic ability among the local units, which now provide more than two-thirds of all the support for public education. The tax on which local units depend for the revenues needed to conduct schools is the general property tax. The value of property available for taxation in the local units may have no relation to the number of children to be educated or to the cost of educating them. Studies in many states have shown that the amount of taxable wealth per school child is scores or even hundreds of times greater in the most able communities than in the least able. In most states many of the local school units with the lowest economic ability would be unable to support even a minimum program of schools if they were to devote to that purpose all the taxes that could possibly be raised, neglecting completely the support of other governmental functions.

Furthermore, the units in which the wealth per child is lowest typically have an unusually large number of children in their population. Such areas are also those from which migration of population is most common. The richer communities do not have an average birth rate sufficient for the maintenance of their population, and hence migration is constantly taking place from the areas of lower economic ability into the more favored areas. Thus, unless some arrangement is made for the maintenance of school services in the least favored areas by funds supplied from other than local sources, the wealthier communities will constantly suffer from an influx of poorly educated people.

To overcome the disadvantages of the great variations in economic ability among local school units, the creation of larger units for the support of schools has been urged. In most states the use of the county rather than the district or township as the unit for the support of schools would go far, but probably not far enough to smooth out inequalities of ability to support education. The reason why a larger unit of taxation is advantageous is obvious. The county seat has property values that are greater than those of a small district located in the open country. Furthermore, a town or city usually has manufacturing plants which are not to be found in rural areas. A town may also have a railroad or other corporations which it may be able to tax.

In view of the advantages which larger units have for raising tax revenues, the tendency has developed in some quarters of going beyond the county and making the state the unit for the support of public education. The state, by raising funds as a single unit and then distributing them back to the local districts in terms of the needs of those districts, can nullify the ill effects of local variations in economic ability. The poorest district, with large numbers of children to educate, will receive state funds sufficient for a minimum standard of schooling, regardless of its inability to raise from local sources the funds that are needed.

Dependence on the state as the unit for support of education has the further advantage of access to taxes other than the general property tax. There are other types of taxes, such as inheritance taxes and income taxes, which cannot well be administered by units smaller than a state.

Considerations which lead to the adoption of the state as the unit for school support have been urged in support of the contention that the Federal Government should supply funds for education in the states. As explained in Chapter V, the fact is that in certain limited branches of education federal support has already been provided. Vocational education has since 1917 been given large grants from the federal treasury. These grants were made available to the states and through the states to local communities, provided each dollar contributed by the Federal Government was matched by a dollar raised by the state or local community.

When larger units are drawn upon for school support, an important problem arises with respect to the method of distributing funds to the local districts. In general, two theories have been proposed to govern this distribution; one theory is that the funds from the large unit represent a reward for effort and that the distribution should be in the extent to which the community taxes itself and thus provides for education. This theory is generally referred to as the theory of support proportional to effort. The federal funds for vocational education, for example, are distributed within many states on this basis; a community must be willing to raise local funds for the program of vocational education, and the grants from outside funds may not exceed 50 per cent of the total amount expended for the salaries of teachers of vocational subjects.

The second and contrasting theory is that the fund from the large unit of taxation should be distributed on the basis of the need of the local community for educational service. The principle of need is recognized by educators as superior to the principle of effort as a basis for distributing funds. The greatest difficulty with the theory of effort is that in a large number of local communities economic ability is so low that even with a maximum of effort a suitable school program could not be maintained. It is clear also that a given effort, as measured, for example, in terms of tax rate, might actually mean a much more serious burden in a community with limited resources than in a community with more favorable economic conditions.

If the fund is distributed on the basis of need, the problem of measuring the need of the local community is difficult. In earlier days the distribution was made on a simple basis such as the number of children of school age. While this is a crude measure of need, it clearly is not precise. The cost of educating ten children in a sparsely settled area, for example, may be as great as the cost of educating forty or fifty children in a city. The cost of education also rises with the level of education, and thus if a large percentage of the children are in the secondary school, the need of the community for funds to support education is greater than if the percentage of children in the upper levels of the school system is relatively low.

Some states have used a combination of the methods of effort and need in distributing their school funds. The local communities under such a plan may be required to levy a certain tax rate before they become entitled to the special state aid fund. If the proceeds of this tax are insufficient to maintain an educational program of minimum standards, the state then supplies from its funds the entire balance necessary for that purpose. The justice of this system depends to a large extent on the amount which the local district must levy before the state aid becomes available.

Much study has been given in recent years to the problem of distributing state school funds. The tendency in the more recently adopted plans has been to consider the state as the unit which should supply the basic amount necessary to finance the educational program. Thus the state may furnish each local community a given amount per teacher, and the local community may then supplement this fund from its own resources to any extent it can or deems desirable, in order to maintain an educational program above the minimum quality that could be provided by the state grant. The tendency is clearly toward a much wider use of the state as a unit for the support of education, and toward improved methods of distributing state funds to local communities in terms of their needs for educational services.

The Federal Government, as has been noted previously, has only a negligible share in the financial support of education in the United States, but since the reasons given for dependence on the state as a unit for school support apply equally to dependence on the Federal Government, the desirability of federal support has been more and more vigorously urged. The variations among the states in ability to support education are wide. It was pointed out by the Advisory Committee on Education, which reported in 1938, that the application of a model tax plan uniformly in each of the states would yield for school purposes less than $14 annually per child of school age in three states but more than $125 annually in three other states. Under such conditions it is obvious that some of the states, even on a state-wide basis, are unable to support from their own resources the minimum educational program that is desirable for the country as a whole.

Another important reason for urging larger dependence on the Federal Government for support of education is the fact that wealth and income tend to accumulate in centers other than those in which they are produced. Thus the regions that produce the wealth and income may find themselves without the power to tax the economic resources they produce because those resources

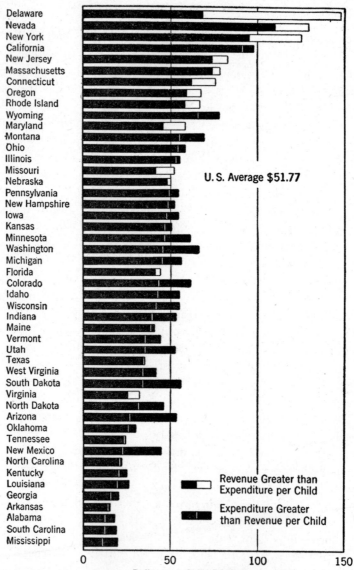

FIGURE 6. CURRENT EXPENDITURE FOR EDUCATION PER CHILD OF SCHOOL AGE IN EACH STATE, 1935–36, AND ESTIMATED REVENUE AVAILABLE FOR THE EDUCATION OF EACH CHILD IF EACH STATE MADE AVERAGE EFFORT, 1935

Data from *Report of the Advisory Committee on Education*, p. 30. Washington: Government Printing Office, 1938.

through the processes of commerce and banking are transferred elsewhere, chiefly to large cities and frequently to distant states. The
Federal Government can reach these concentrations of wealth
wherever they may be located in this country and can distribute
revenues back to the states in proportion to their requirements.

The Federal Government furthermore is an efficient tax col-
lector. States that adopt progressive systems of taxation may
find themselves temporarily at a disadvantage because taxpayers,
whose resources should support the public schools and other
governmental functions, may change their residence to other
states where the tax laws are more favorable to the holders of
wealth than to the children who should be educated. When the
taxes are levied by the Federal Government such an escape is not
possible for the taxpayer.

The *Report* of the Advisory Committee on Education discusses
thoroughly the whole question of federal support for education.
The Committee after an exhaustive inquiry came to the conclusion that a much larger use of federal funds for the support of
education is not only justified but necessary if an educational
program suitable to the needs of a modern democracy is to be
maintained in this country.

THE SYSTEM OF TAXATION

Inasmuch as the public schools are dependent on the funds
raised by taxation for support, the system of taxation adopted
by a local community, by a state, or by the nation is of vital importance to the development of the educational program. Unless
the system of taxation is sound, the schools are almost certain to
lack the revenues necessary for their support. It is important,
therefore, for everyone who is interested in effective education to
take note of the features of the tax system and to work actively
for any movement looking toward the improvement of the plan
of taxation.

Several kinds of taxes are at present used for the support of public education.   The chief dependence, as was stated earlier, is on the general property tax, which is administered by estimating the value of the property owned by each taxpayer and then levying a tax at a certain rate on all the property in the jurisdiction. Thus if the total value of taxable property in a local school district is twenty million dollars and if the school budget for that district calls for the expenditure of one hundred thousand dollars, a tax rate of fifty cents on the one hundred dollars of valuation will be required to produce the needed fund.

The general property tax was a reasonably equitable method of raising public funds in an age when practically all property was of a tangible sort.   In the pioneer period, for example, it was possible for the assessor to visit each home to see the amount and quality of land, the number of cattle, the kind of household furnishings, and all the other types of wealth possessed by the taxpayer, and to estimate their value with reasonable accuracy. Under modern conditions, however, when much of the wealth held by a taxpayer may be in intangible securities or in assets that are readily concealed, the property tax tends in practice to become a tax on real estate alone, because real estate is the only asset that cannot well be hidden from the tax assessor.

A tax which has advantages over the real estate tax is the income tax.   This is one of the main sources of revenue for the Federal Government of the United States, and this tax is also levied by many of the states.   The income tax is particularly appropriate because the amount of payment is closely related to the taxpayer's ability to pay.   All taxpayers normally pay their taxes out of income, even though the levy may be made against such capital assets as real estate.   For this important reason the income tax is a superior type of tax.

Inheritance taxes are in effect in almost all the states, and the funds produced by these taxes are in most cases used in part for the support of the state educational system.   The inheritance tax is also a source of revenue for the Federal Government.   This tax seems to be especially advisable because it is paid after the original owner's use of the assets is ended.

During the economic depression of the 1930's, when other sources of public revenues were falling off rapidly in productivity, many of the states turned to the sales tax as a method of raising revenues. In a number of states the funds raised by the sales tax are in part used for the support of public education.

Other types of taxes levied by a smaller number of states are corporation taxes and severance taxes. Severance taxes are levied on the extraction of minerals or other natural resources. They provide only a small part of the total revenue used for public education in the United States.

Students of taxation have given much thought to the question of what constitutes a sound system of taxation. It will be recognized at once that the soundness of any system of taxation will be judged differently by different people. Probably no person who has to pay large amounts of taxes under a given system considers it sound. Nevertheless, economists are able by certain objective measures of the effect of taxation to determine the relative merits of the various types of taxes under given conditions. Lutz [1] suggests seven requisites or criteria for a sound system of taxation.

The first requisite is fiscal adequacy or productivity, the ability to produce revenue over both a short time and a long period of years. It is obvious that a system of taxation, to be adequate, must produce revenue in sufficient amounts to maintain necessary governmental services.

The second criterion is economy or cheapness of collection. Some taxes, for example, cost so much to collect that they leave little net revenue for the support of governmental services. Such taxes are not desirable from the standpoint of raising revenues.

The third requisite, according to Lutz, is equity, a characteristic that must be to a great extent subjectively determined. In general, however, tax experts are of the opinion that a tax, to be equitable, must be progressive rather than regressive; that is, it

[1] Harley L. Lutz, *Public Finance*, pp. 257–71. New York: D. Appleton and Company, 1928.

must bear proportionately more heavily upon those with the greatest ability to pay than upon those with the least ability.

The fourth requisite of a sound tax system is elasticity. By this is meant the ability to respond readily to a need for changes in the amount of revenue.

The fifth criterion is simplicity. In a democratic government, at least, it is necessary that the system of taxation be sufficiently simple to be readily understood by the voters. Under any condition, the system of taxation should be simple enough so that the taxpayer can readily compute the amount he should pay.

The sixth requisite is diversity. Dependence on a single source of revenue or a single type of tax is characteristic of an unsatisfactory system of taxation.

The seventh and final characteristic of a good tax system is flexibility or modifiability. A number of the states violate this principle by having the features of their tax system written into their constitutions. If the constitution is difficult to amend, as is often the case, the system of taxation may be practically unmodifiable even when conditions clearly warrant a change.

The various types of taxes now used to produce revenue for the support of public schools differ considerably in the extent to which they meet these criteria of a sound system of taxation. It will be recalled that the chief dependence for the support of the public schools is on the general property tax. Today no recognized authority on taxation defends the use of this tax as the principal source of public revenue. Under modern conditions, the general property tax becomes grossly inequitable and difficult of administration.

The sales tax, to which politicians have turned as a source of revenue during the financial stress of the 1930's, is frowned upon by most tax experts. The sales tax has the dangerous characteristic of regressiveness; that is, it falls with a greater burden upon those with restricted resources than upon those with large incomes who do not need to spend all their income for goods subject to the sales tax.

Experts on taxation favor the net income tax as an important element in a sound system of taxation. With the rate of taxation differentiated according to size of income, the income tax can be made a progressive tax. The tax on net income also may be arranged to meet most of the other criteria for soundness.

The inheritance tax is also considered an important part of a sound system of taxation, although the amount of revenue derived from this tax may fluctuate widely from year to year. Other taxes, such as corporation taxes and severance taxes, are considered sound, but as a rule they can be depended upon for only a minor part of the revenue needed for governmental services.

The difficulties at present faced in financing the educational system are due to two important factors: first, dependence upon an entirely outmoded system of taxation; second, dependence upon the local school unit for raising the bulk of the revenues needed.

As previously noted, the property tax is the only type of tax which can be used effectively for the raising of local revenue. The other types of taxes, particularly the income, inheritance, and corporation taxes, must be administered in a unit at least as large as the state. Because of the tendency of large taxpayers to move from one locality or one state to another, these taxes can be administered on a national basis much more effectively than on even a state-wide basis. It seems clear that the schools of the United States will not obtain the revenues needed for their financial support until there has been a reform of the taxing system, shifting the burden to larger units and to types of taxes other than the general property tax.

HOW CAN THE ULTIMATELY DESIRABLE SCHOOL PROGRAM BE FINANCED?

The marked extensions of the service of the public schools and the mounting cost of education in recent decades have caused many leaders to raise a question as to whether the amount of money being spent for schools is not too large. A fair-minded view of the needs for educational services, however, and of the degree to which these needs are being met by the funds at present provided, seems to support the conclusion that present facilities fall far short of the minimum desirable provision of educational opportunities in many communities, and that only rarely can there be shown a lavishness of expenditure for education that indicates a waste of public funds. The schools of the poorer areas are so grossly inadequate as to make it obvious that a much larger total support of education than is now provided is urgently needed in this country.

One possible solution for the problem of financing the ultimately desirable educational program should be ruled out without further consideration: extension and improvement of the public-school facilities should not be financed at the expense of those who are engaged in educational service. This has happened too often in the past, when teachers, principals, supervisors, and superintendents have willingly undertaken extra burdens or have made personal financial sacrifices in order that the children in the schools might have improved or extended facilities. The staff members in many school systems have already gone further in this direction than is socially desirable, and it seems that no further extensions or improvements of the public-school facilities can reasonably be expected from that source. It is clearly undesirable as a matter of either temporary or long-time public policy to expect the personnel of the school systems to carry such a burden.

The two solutions that have been suggested in the preceding section, the reform of the tax system and the shifting of the burden to larger geographical units, such as the state or the Federal Government, offer much promise of improving the financing of an adequate educational system. The ultimate question still remains, however, as to whether modern economic society can provide the resources that are necessary to support an educational program considered entirely adequate for modern needs. It has been estimated that to provide every person with all the education which he should have in order to make him socially useful, and to provide that education through teachers suitably trained and remunerated, in buildings which are provided with all the facilities needed for a modern educational program, would require under present circumstances probably double the amount of funds now expended for education in the United States. Could the resources of this country support a school system costing some six billion dollars annually?

The question is at present, of course, purely theoretical, for no one envisions the probability that such a goal can be achieved in the immediate future. Ultimately, however, the setting up of such an objective is not only possible but inevitable.

An answer to the question of whether such a large sum can be contributed from the resources of society for the support of education seems perfectly clear. The income of the nation's producers is today expended for many purposes which are less vital to the real needs of the social order than a suitable provision of education. Whenever the citizens and voters are sufficiently convinced of the necessity for maintaining the type of school facilities that educators regard as the minimum adequate program, it will be relatively easy to divert the resources now used for non-essential goods to the support of the school system. Furthermore, since a large share of the expenditures for schools goes into wages or services these amounts are not withdrawn from the national income but actually serve to increase it, and are thus made available for expenditures for goods of all types.

The issue thus reduces to the question of the capacity of the country to produce the goods and services that are needed for modern civilization. No informed person doubts that America has the necessary capacity to produce the needed commodities. At least the years of the depression seem to have indicated a capacity to produce that has far outstripped the facilities for distribution and consumption. It seems clear that the financing of an ultimately desirable school program means only an improved adjustment in the distribution of goods and services, not a larger basic production. This is, however, by no means a simple prob-

lem.   A revision of the system of taxation and the shifting of the
burden of school support to larger governmental units are only
preliminary steps in a process that challenges the best thinking of
the coming generation.

BIBLIOGRAPHY

Almack, John C., editor, *Modern School Administration*, pp. 25–45.

Burton, William H., *Introduction to Education*, pp. 327–62.

Butterweck, Joseph S., and J. Conrad Seegers, *An Orientation Course in
  Education*, pp. 164–77.

Clapp, Frank L., Wayland J. Chase, and Curtis Merriman, *Introduction to
  Education*, pp. 196–228.

Cubberley, Ellwood P., *Public Education in the United States*, pp. 163–211,
  734–39.

Cubberley, Ellwood P., *State School Administration*, pp. 407–511.

Douglass, Aubrey A., *The American School System*, pp. 32–59.

Frasier, George Willard, and Winfield D. Armentrout, *An Introduction to
  the Literature of Education*, pp. 389–401.

Heer, Clarence, *Federal Aid and the Tax Problem.*   Staff Study no. 4,
  Advisory Committee on Education.   Washington: Government Printing Office, 1939.   x + 100 pp.

Judd, Charles H., *Education and Social Progress*, pp. 104–27.

Judd, Charles H., *Problems of Education in the United States*, pp. 138–68.

Morrison, Henry C., *The Management of the School Money.*   Chicago:
  University of Chicago Press, 1932.   xx + 522 pp.

Morrison, Henry C., *School Revenue.*   Chicago: University of Chicago
  Press, 1930.   x + 242 pp.

Mort, Paul R., and others, *State Support for Public Education.*   Washington: American Council on Education, 1933.   x + 496 pp.

Patterson S. Howard, Ernest A. Choate, and Edmund de S. Brunner,
  The School in American Society, pp. 159–89.

Rainey, Homer, *Public School Finance.*   New York: Century Company,
  1929.   xx + 386 pp.

Reeder, Ward, *A First Course in Education*, pp. 507–41.

Research Bulletins of the National Education Association: *Financing
  Public Education*, XV:1:3–54 (January, 1937); *Why Schools Cost More*,
  XVI:3:138–78 (May, 1938).

Swift, Fletcher Harper, *Federal and State Policies in Public School Finance.*
  Boston: Ginn and Company, 1931.   xviii + 472 pp.

Wilson, Lester M., and I. L. Kandel, *Introduction to the Study of American
  Education*, pp. 89–100.

CHAPTER X

The educational plant and its equipment

THE WORD "SCHOOL" is used today with two different meanings: one meaning emphasizes the building in which the instructional program is housed; the other refers to the instructional program itself. Perhaps the former of these two meanings is the one that first comes to the mind of the layman when he hears the word "school." It is a curious fact that ordinary interpretation lays such emphasis on the physical aspects of education that it is difficult to attract popular attention to the necessity of constructing a school building with due regard to the use to which the building is to be put.

HISTORICAL DEVELOPMENT OF SCHOOL ARCHITECTURE

In remote historical times the problem of schoolhouse design was unknown. The great architectural structures of antiquity were temples, palaces, tombs, and citadels. This early situation contrasts sharply with modern conditions. The archaeologist of the year 5000 A.D. who exhumes the remains of a midwestern village in what is now the United States will readily identify the schoolhouse as one of the most important and permanent of the structures in the community. One who today travels through any part of the United States is sure to be impressed by the fact that the school building in almost every community is conspicuous as one of the most substantial architectural features. Churches there are, and courthouses too, usually of fairly substantial construction, but as a rule the building which is the pride of the community is the schoolhouse. The evolution of the school building is interesting; only a brief sketch of this evolution can here be traced.

As already indicated, there were no schoolhouses in ancient times. Socrates conducted his dialogues as he walked with his disciples about the streets of Athens. A portico or a corner of the market place or the home of the master sufficed as the meeting place for the pupils of the great teachers of olden times. The words "academy" and "academic" are derived from the name of the grove, Academe, in which Plato conducted his famous dialogues. Elementary education in those days was a matter of parental care. Where it had developed beyond this stage it was individual instruction, usually given by a slave in the parental home. No school buildings were needed in that social order.

In medieval times a type of school arose that was closely associated with the church. The building was usually located on the parish grounds adjacent to the church edifice, a custom that still survives in many present-day parochial school plants. The school building naturally took on an ecclesiastical aspect, harmonizing in design with the church beside which it was located. Some authorities have pointed out that this has been an unfortunate influence in school architecture, and has led to such unnecessary and even harmful features as spires and cupolas, narrow windows, unsatisfactory height, insufficient ground space, and classroom platforms (pulpits) for the teacher. Other authorities point out that this influence has not been pronounced in the history of American schoolhouse planning, and that these unnecessary and unsatisfactory features came by an entirely different route.

In early American times little or no attention was given to the schoolhouse as a separate building. It was customary to hold the school in any convenient place, such as the meeting-house or even the home of the schoolmaster. Indeed, there are cases on record where the size of the teacher's house was an important factor in his obtaining the contract for the ensuing year. By the beginning of the nineteenth century attention was being given to the construction of separate buildings for school purposes. The buildings that were erected at that time in the frontier regions of the country were generally of log-house construction. The most favored location was a bit of waste ground at the intersection of two roads.

The schoolhouse of that time was practically always a one-room building, with an extremely simple interior arrangement. A row of benches, usually fashioned from split logs, extended around three walls of the room. The pupils sat facing the wall and worked at a rough shelf extending out from this wall. The lighting was poor and equipment was extremely meager. Toilet accommodations were completely lacking in most of these schools.

In the first quarter of the nineteenth century American education was profoundly affected by the so-called Lancastrian movement. The Lancastrian method of instruction may be briefly described as a plan whereby one schoolmaster instructed pupils in large groups, sometimes as many as several hundred. Before this time instructional methods had been almost wholly individual. The Lancastrian plan divided the school into groups of about ten pupils each, with a monitor, an older pupil, over each group. The master taught a lesson to the monitors, and they then returned to their groups and taught the same lesson to the pupils under them. The Lancastrian movement gained wide favor in this country and seems to have contributed markedly to the growing sentiment in favor of public schools, since instruction became much less expensive under this plan than it had formerly been.

Under the pre-Lancastrian plan of instruction it was necessary that schoolhouses be small one-room buildings no larger than could be supervised by one teacher; under the Lancastrian plan a large room was necessary, in which three or four hundred pupils or even more could be seated. During the second quarter of the nineteenth century large school buildings of the Lancastrian type were constructed in many cities. The floor plan was simple, consisting of nothing more than a single large room with benches for the pupils; a monitor's desk at the end of each row of benches; and a master's desk, in front of which the monitors gathered for their instruction.   Inasmuch as steel and reinforced concrete construction had not yet been invented, the Gothic type of architecture was utilized to obtain the large room that was necessary for the Lancastrian plan.

During the period of the 1840's there occurred a general awakening of interest in the problem of school housing.   Some of the earliest professional literature on education deals with this question.   Surveys of school conditions on a state-wide basis were carried on in as many as five different states.   Almost uniformly these surveys pointed out the deplorable conditions under which pupils were housed, particularly in the rural districts, where at that time most of the population lived.   Improvement of conditions was vigorously demanded.

The Lancastrian system gave way in the course of time to the graded system, the introduction of which has been described in an earlier chapter.   The first step in the process of evolution away from the large single-room type of building was the addition of one or two small rooms, sufficient to accommodate eight or a dozen pupils.   These were used as recitation rooms for small groups.   Later the large room was divided into two parts, and even later into four parts.   As the graded system developed, the building plans were generally modified to provide, as an ideal, a separate room for each grade.

A floor plan for graded school buildings which was somewhat more elaborate than that of the original four-room plan was that adopted in the so-called "box" type of building, as shown in Figure 7.   This type, many examples of which are still extant, usually provided two or three stories, with four rooms on each floor.   In the center of the building was a wide hall, frequently open up through the two or three stories.   This hall was a convenient assembling place for pupils, the lower floor and the balcony-type hall on the upper floor affording sufficient standing room for the entire school.   The box type of school building

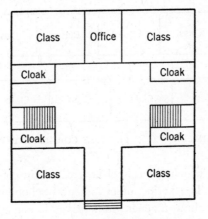

FIGURE 7. FLOOR PLAN OF BOX-TYPE BUILDING

proved to be a serious firetrap, for the wide central hall formed a veritable flue for any blaze which was once started. As all the stairways were on the inside, they were filled with smoke and flame at the very beginning of a fire. The Collinwood, Ohio, fire in 1908, in which 173 pupils and 2 teachers lost their lives, was in a building of this type.

In order to get away from several disadvantages of the box-type building, the corridor plan of construction was evolved. Under this plan the classrooms and service rooms are arranged on either side of a long central corridor, with stairways at either end (Figure 8). Newer developments have for the most part been modifications of the corridor type of building. Such typical plans as the U-type, E-type, T-type, L-type, and J-type buildings are merely examples of corridor-type buildings with the corridors arranged at right angles.

The period following the Civil War was an era in which many school buildings were constructed. During this period much attention was paid to the ornamental features of the school building, although no important improvement was made in the educational aspects of schoolhouse planning. Ornamentation of school buildings reflected current popular tastes, and affords an example

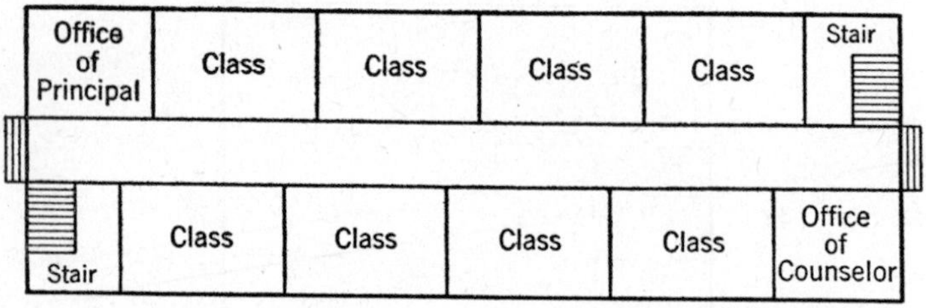

Office of Principal	Class	Class	Class	Class	Stair
Stair	Class	Class	Class	Class	Office of Counselor

FIGURE 8. SIMPLE FLOOR PLAN OF CORRIDOR-TYPE BUILDING

of the way in which the school is affected by conditions in the social order. The period of ornamental schoolhouse construction lasted for about a generation. Even in some buildings constructed within the past thirty or forty years there is evidence of the persistence of this influence. Most school buildings constructed since the beginning of the twentieth century, however, have reflected a chaste simplicity in keeping with the dignity and the everyday importance of public-school work.

In general architectural planning, one of the most significant developments of the twentieth century has been the introduction of fireproofing. Educators have been slow to realize the importance of this feature, although occasional disasters in which numbers of pupils and teachers have lost their lives have led to greater attention to the elimination of fire hazards and to the construction of buildings in such a way as to minimize the chance for panic. In spite of the great advances made on the engineering and architectural side, which now permit the construction of buildings having an almost negligible fire hazard, many schoolhouses constructed in modern times are not adequately fireproofed. Under present conditions it is difficult to justify the construction of anything other than a fire-resistive type of school building.

Perhaps the change of greatest significance in schoolhouse planning during the last generation has resulted from increased attention to the educational and hygienic aspects of building design. In the typical school building constructed today provisions are made for sanitary toilets, adequate lighting both natural and artificial, modern heating and ventilation, comfortable seating, hygienic drinking fountains, and well-designed blackboards and instructional equipment.   All these features constitute a notable advance over the buildings constructed only a generation ago.

The housing of the educational program in the United States is a problem of great magnitude.   The Advisory Committee on Education reported that the value of all public-school properties in this country in 1930 was $6,674,445,000, and that the average annual expenditure for the construction of public-school buildings during the decade ending in 1930 was approximately $370,000,000. The problem of housing the school program is important, not only in terms of the amounts of money involved, but also in terms of the effect on the lives of the children of school age.   With the lengthening of the period of schooling for the individual child, it becomes increasingly important that the time in school be spent in the best possible physical environment.

THE TEXTBOOK AS AN ITEM OF SCHOOL EQUIPMENT

In an earlier chapter it is pointed out that the American schools are peculiarly dependent on textbooks.   One reason for this dependence is the lack of training of the teachers in the earlier American schools.   Another and even more important reason is that schools were organized for the purpose of preparing pupils to become independent in their religious views by reading the Scriptures, each for himself.   As a result, the schools of America are and have been throughout their history reading schools rather than listening schools like those of Europe.

One of the earliest examples of printed material for use in the colonial schools was the hornbook.   This was a paddle-shaped piece of wood on which was pasted a small placard.   Over the placard was fixed a sheet of transparent horn.   The printed material presented on the hornbook consisted of the alphabet in several styles of type, some simple syllables for use in teaching reading, and some passages of religious character such as the Lord's Prayer, the Ten Commandments, or the apostolic benediction. Although the content was meager, the device had the advantage of durability, and in the days when printed material was scarce and costly, the hornbook rendered a great service in teaching children the rudiments of reading.

The earliest type of textbooks in use were called primers. The primer was not intended merely as a first reading book, but was expected to provide all the instructional material needed to prepare the child to read the Bible for himself. The content of the early primers consisted almost exclusively of religious material. This content strikes one today as heavily weighted with maturely worded statements intended to impress the child with the awfulness of the state of sin and misery into which he was born. In this respect, however, the primers merely reflected the prevailing theology of the time.

The forerunners of the modern textbooks began to appear about the middle of the eighteenth century. The textbooks in use prior to the Revolutionary War were imported from England. With the coming of independence, Americans began to produce their own instructional materials for the schools, instead of relying on books printed in England. One of the first products of this period was the famous blue-backed speller of Noah Webster. This textbook, one of the first to break away from the strictly religious content, contained not only spelling, but a little chronology, a little geography, and some simple arithmetic. Webster's speller was enormously successful. He was only a twenty-four-year-old school teacher when he produced it, but the book sold over 24,000,000 copies, and the royalties kept him and his family in comfort during the period while he was producing his well-known dictionary of the English language.

One of the early textbooks which exercised a profound influence on teaching throughout the nineteenth century was Warren Colburn's arithmetic, first published in 1821. Colburn's methods of teaching were patterned after those which Pestalozzi had developed in Europe. Some quotations from Colburn's writings indicate the purposes and character of his textbook. In criticism of the rule-of-thumb method which was traditional he wrote:

By the old system, the learner was presented with a rule which told him how to perform certain operations on figures, and when these were done, he would have the proper result. But no reason was given for a single step. His first application of his rule was on a set of abstract numbers, and so large that he could not reason on them, if he had been disposed to do so. And when he had got through, and obtained the result, he understood neither what it was, nor the use of it. Neither did he know that it was the proper result, but was obliged to rely wholly on the book, or more frequently on the teacher. As he began in the dark, so he continued; and the results of his calculation seemed to be obtained by some magical operation, rather than by the inductions of reason.

By the new system, the learner commences with practical examples, on which the numbers are so small that he can easily reason upon them. And the reference to sensible objects gives him an idea at once of the kind of result which he ought to produce, and suggests to him the method of proceeding necessary to obtain it. By this he is thrown immediately upon his own resources, and is compelled to exert his own powers.[1]

In describing his own methods Colburn wrote as follows:

One general maxim, which I observe with pupils of every age, is, never to tell them directly how to perform any example. If a pupil is unable to perform an example, it is generally because he does not fully comprehend the object of it. I endeavour to explain the object, and ask him some questions which will have a tendency to recall the principles necessary. If this does not succeed, his mind is not prepared for it, and he must be required to examine it more by himself, and to review some of the principles which it involves....

Several considerations induce me to think that when a principle is

---

[1] Warren Colburn, "On the Teaching of Arithmetic," *The Introductory Discourse and Lectures Delivered in Boston, before the Convention of Teachers, and Other Friends of Education, Assembled to Form the American Institute of Instruction, August, 1830,* pp. 282–83. Boston: Hilliard, Gray, Little and Wilkins, 1831.

to be taught, practical questions should first be proposed, care being taken to select such as will show the combination in the simplest manner, and that the numbers be so small, that the operation shall not be difficult.   When a proper idea is formed of the nature and use of the combination, the method of solving these questions with large numbers should be attended to.   This method, on trial, has succeeded beyond my expectations.   Practical examples not only show at once the object to be accomplished, but they greatly assist the imagination in unfolding the principle and discovering the operations requisite for the solution. . . .

This principle is made the basis of this treatise; viz. whenever a new combination is introduced, it is done with practical examples, proposed in such a manner as to show what it is, and as much as possible, how it is to be performed.   The examples are so small that the pupil may easily reason upon them, and that there will be no difficulty in the operation itself, until the combination is well understood.   In this way it is believed that the leading idea which the pupil will obtain of each combination, will be the effect which will be produced by it, rather than how to perform it, though the latter will be sufficiently well understood.[1]

The radical innovations introduced by William H. McGuffey in his readers at the end of the first third of the last century contributed to modern methods of teaching even more than did the books of Webster and Colburn.   McGuffey adopted the principle that reading materials should be interesting to pupils.   He broke away from the tradition that readers should be religious in their contents, although he retained something of the spirit of the older readers in that his stories always included a moral.   It is said that he used to call in the children of the neighborhood and read to them the stories which he had collected from all possible sources.   He included in his readers only the stories that the children reacted to as interesting.   He graded his readers according to the degree to which children of different ages manifested interest in the different stories.   The McGuffey readers are so conspicuous as landmarks in American educational history that it is not

[1] Warren Colburn, *Arithmetic; Being a Sequel to First Lessons in Arithmetic*, pp. vi–viii. Boston: Cummings and Hilliard, 1822.

out of place to quote at length from some of them.   A part of one of the stories in the Third Reader is as follows:

Lesson XIII

1. Per′-sian, a native of Persia.
   Dis-tinc′-tion, high rank or character.
2. Sum′-mons, a call to appear at any place.
   In-trust′-ing, putting in the care of any one.

4. Court, a king's palace.
   Im-ag′-in-ed, thought, supposed.
   Re-flec′-tion, attentive thought or consideration.
5. Lam-ent-a′-tions, cries of sorrow.
6. Pre-cip-i-ta′-tion, imprudent haste.

Effects of Rashness

Articulate each sound and pronounce each word correctly.

Scarce-ly, not *scurce-ly*: to′-ward, not *to-ward′*: dan-ger, not *dan-ger*: in-qui′-ry, not *in′-qui-ry*: fol-low'd, not *fol-ler'd*: ad-vent-ure, not *ad-ven-ter*, nor *ad-ven-tshure*.

Do not pronounce *a* as *u* in such words as the following: *infant*, (not *infunt*). *husband, appearance,* (not *up-pearunce*), *animal, instantly, instance, repentance, precipitance,* &c.

1. A certain Persian of distinction, had, for years, been extremely anxious that he might have a son, to inherit his estate.   His wishes were at length gratified.   A son was born, and the fond father was so anxious for the health and safety of the little stranger, that he would scarcely suffer it to be taken out of his sight, and was never so much delighted, as when he was employed in holding it.

2. One day, his wife, on going to the bath, committed the infant to her husband's care, earnestly entreating him not to quit the cradle, until she came back.   Scarcely, however, had she quitted the house, when the king sent for her husband.   To refuse, or to delay obeying the royal summons, was impossible; he, therefore, went immediately to the palace, intrusting the child to the care of a favorite dog, which had been bred in the family.

3. No sooner was the father out of sight, than a large snake made its appearance, and was crawling toward the cradle.   When the dog saw the child's life in danger, he instantly seized the snake by the back of the head, and destroyed it.

4. Soon after, the father returned from court, and the dog, as if conscious of the service he had performed, ran out to meet him.   The man saw the dog stained with blood, and imagined that he had killed the child.   Without making any further reflection or inquiry, he struck

the faithful little animal such blow with his stick, that he instantly expired.

5. When the father came into the house, and saw the child safe, and the snake lying dead by the side of the cradle, he smote his breast with grief, accusing himself of rashness and ingratitude toward the dog. While he was uttering these woeful lamentations, his wife came in, who, having learned the cause of his distress, blamed him severely for his want of reflection. He confessed his indiscretion, but begged her not to add reproaches to his distress, as reproof could now avail nothing.

6. "True," said she, "advice can be of no service in the present instance; but I wish to rouse your mind to reflection, that you may reap instruction from your misfortunes. Shame and repentance are the sure consequences of precipitation and want of reflection." [1]

That the teaching of reading in McGuffey's day was from the present-day point of view artificial is evidenced from the following extract from the Introduction to the Fifth Reader.

ANALYSIS OF THE PRINCIPLES OF ELOCUTION

Introductory Remarks

The first step to be taken by one who desires to become a good reader or speaker, is to acquire a habit of distinct articulation. Without this, the finest voice, the utmost propriety of inflection, and all the graces of articulation, fail to please.

The habit of defective articulation is generally contracted in the first stages of the learner's progress, and arises either from indolence, which produces an indistinct and drawling utterance, or from too great haste, which leads to running words together, and to clipping them by dropping unaccented words and final consonants.

Habits of this kind, frequently, indeed, *generally*, become so inveterate by the time the pupil is sufficiently advanced to use a work on rhetorical reading, or any treatise on elocution, that the most constant and unremitting attention is necessary on the part of both teacher and pupil, in order to correct them. Nothing but a resolute determination to succeed, and faithful practice upon exercises selected with especial reference to the end in view, can accomplish this

---

[1] Wm. H. McGuffey, *McGuffey's Eclectic Third Reader: Containing Lessons in Prose and Poetry*, pp. 52–55. New York: Clark, Austin and Smith, 1843.

object.   There must be added to this, a constant watchfulness against relapse, when the learner comes to lessons of a more general character.[1]

In the schools of the early nineteenth century there was no uniformity of textbooks in the class.   The pupil studied whatever book he happened to have, if indeed he was so fortunate as to have a book at all.   Instruction was individual, rather than in class groups, so no difficulty arose when a pupil studied his arithmetic out of one book while his seatmate studied out of a different text.

The modern textbook is a far cry from these earlier beginnings. The textbook business is now highly commercialized and intensely competitive.   To be successful a book has to meet modern standards that have been developed through extensive research.   By means of this research there have been discovered the ways in which instructional material can be presented most effectively through the medium of the printed page.   As a result of these investigations, the modern textbook is an especially effective aid to the instructional process.

Along with improvements in school buildings and in textbooks have come additions to the instructional equipment of schools. Wall maps are now available in abundance in well-managed schools.   So also is demonstration apparatus that is especially useful for instruction in the sciences.   Pictures decorate the walls of many school buildings, and music rooms and well-stocked libraries are commonly provided.

Entirely new devices of communication are now being developed which may ultimately have effects on education as far-reaching as the textbook.   The talking picture and the radio have both proved valuable instructional adjuncts, and undoubtedly these devices will be depended upon more and more in the

[1] Wm. H. McGuffey, *McGuffey's Rhetorical Guide: or Fifth Reader of the Eclectic Series: Containing Elegant Extracts in Prose and Poetry: with Copious Rules and Rhetorical Exercises*, pp. 13–14.   Cincinnati: Winthrop B. Smith and Company, 1844.

future. Large numbers of schools are already equipped with apparatus for projecting sound films and for radio reproduction. An increasing body of effective instructional material is being made available in talking pictures, and the technique of instruction by radio is being constantly improved.

FACTORS MODIFYING STANDARDS FOR SCHOOL BUILDINGS AND EQUIPMENT

The foregoing discussion has emphasized the fact that the modern school building and its equipment differ markedly from anything known in earlier periods. Several factors may be mentioned that have served during the past generation to modify ideas regarding what is desirable in the physical make-up of a school.

The first is the modern attention to hygiene, sanitation, and safety. This point, which has already been mentioned and need not be discussed at length, is a reflection of social attitudes. Modern advertisers are thoroughly aware of this social attitude, as is witnessed by the constant repetition of the words hygienic, sanitary, and the like, and their derivatives. Public consciousness on these questions has been thoroughly awakened, and many states have written into their laws definite requirements applying to the construction and equipment of all new school buildings. In many states the plans for every new school building must receive the approval of state authorities.

A second factor affecting schoolhouse planning has been the growth of cities and the consequent increase in size of building units in urban areas. Where formerly the eight- or twelve-room schoolhouse of the box type was the typical city school building, the large city school now provides twenty-four or more rooms for elementary pupils, and high-school plants sometimes provide accommodations for thousands of pupils.

A third factor may be mentioned as affecting the rural areas, just as the increase in density of city population has affected the urban school. The coming of good roads and automobile trans-portation has rendered the old one-room schoolhouse at the cross-roads both undesirable and unnecessary in all except the most inaccessible rural areas. In its place there has come in progressive communities the modern consolidated school, with provision for transportation of the pupils by motorbus. In the typical rural consolidated school practically all the facilities common to city schools can be and are provided. For a given quality of instruction, the cost per pupil served in consolidated schools is much less than in the old-fashioned one-room school. While some Americans of the older generation have fond memories of the one-room school and ascribe to it many educational virtues that they fail to find in modern school systems, there is little doubt in the mind of educators that the passing of the one-room building marks a real gain in educational service.

A fourth factor that has had a marked influence on schoolhouse design has been the extension of the school age, both downward and upward, with a resulting increase in school population. This extension has forced on educators considerations of economy in planning, since the provision of the necessary housing has severely taxed the resources of almost every community in the country. Special facilities of various sorts have also been made necessary to meet the needs of these new groups of pupils.

A fifth factor which may be mentioned is the increasing recognition of the educative value of play, manual arts, and motor activities in general. While the early school buildings were primarily places for pupils to sit and study their books (and not well adapted even to that end), the modern educational plant comprises playgrounds, athletic fields, gymnasiums, manual arts rooms, domestic science kitchens, and a host of other facilities that have been introduced mainly because social conditions have forced educators to recognize the fact that there are many parts of a well-rounded education that cannot be gained by reading a book and reciting a lesson. Many such educational activities that were formerly furnished by other agencies have now, owing to changed social conditions, been incorporated into the schools.

As a sixth factor, other curricular changes may be briefly mentioned as having a pronounced effect on schoolhouse planning. The coming of instruction in science has led to the inclusion of laboratories in school buildings. Emphasis on work in art and music has necessitated adaptations in building design to serve the needs of these subjects. The introduction of vocational studies has given rise to such problems as the housing of a noisy typewriting room, an automobile shop, a forge shop, a woodworking shop, and other special rooms of this sort. In Chapter IV it was shown how these curricular changes were the result of social and economic forces.

A seventh factor that may be mentioned as having an effect on school-building design is the changing conception of the ideal size of class units. It was formerly assumed that the smaller the class the greater the instructional benefit derived by each pupil. Particularly at the higher levels questions have recently been raised regarding the truth of this assumption. As a result, many secondary schools have large classes and many colleges provide some very large lecture sections, oftentimes including several hundred students. Most modern secondary-school and college buildings are being planned with a varied schedule of rooms so as to accommodate classes of different sizes. Scientific research on the question of class size has been largely responsible for this change in school-building design.

An eighth factor that has modified ideas with regard to schoolhouse design results from the changes that have occurred in the plan of school organization. Among these may be mentioned the platoon type of school. Under this plan the pupils are arranged in two or more shifts, known as platoons. While one shift is in the classrooms, a second shift may occupy the gymnasium, the vocational rooms, and the auditorium. At stated intervals during the day the platoons change places, so that each pupil has the complete round of instruction and activities. This plan of organization has been adopted in a number of American cities.

The schools of Gary, Indiana, and Detroit, Michigan, which are organized on the platoon plan, have frequently been described in educational literature.   The platoon type of organization has been advocated both because of the enriched opportunities it makes available to the pupils and because it is more economical of building space than the traditional school.   A successful platoon school, however, needs a building especially designed for the purpose.

Other changes in the type of organization that have affected building plans have been the development of the junior high school and the junior college.   Each of these organizations has building needs peculiar to itself.   Although in many communities a junior high school or a junior college organization has been developed in a former elementary- or high-school building without any more extensive remodeling than the mere changing of the sign over the door — and sometimes not even that — many authorities believe that for best results both the junior high school and the junior college need specially planned building facilities.

A ninth factor has been change in teaching methods.   For example, in Barnard's book on *School Architecture*, published in 1848, the statement is made that every schoolroom should have a raised platform for the teacher.   Such a fixture was appropriate to the *ex cathedra* type of teaching, but is utterly unsuited to the modern discussion method.   The socialized recitation demands an arrangement of furniture differing widely from the traditional plan.   Laboratory methods have increased the amount of space provision necessary for a given number of pupils.   The wider use that is being made of the library has necessitated attention to the planning of this unit.   Illustrations might be multiplied of the effect that the introduction of new instructional methods has had upon school buildings and equipment.

Finally, a tenth factor may be mentioned, the commercialization of the school-equipment business.   The professional journals having a wide circulation among school executives are filled with advertisements advocating the virtues of this brand of chalk, or this type of blackboard, or this kind of seating, or flooring, or lighting, or laboratory desk, or what not. The expenses of national conventions of educators are in large part financed by the exhibits, consisting of scores, even hundreds, of booths occupied by alert salesmen of almost every conceivable item of school furniture and equipment. In most respects the commercialization of the school-equipment business has been a fortunate development for the schools, inasmuch as new devices have been rapidly pushed into the field and utilized in the schools. To a limited extent high-pressure salesmanship has operated to foist on credulous school administrators some devices which are much less valuable than their advocates claim.

THE NATURE OF PRESENT STANDARDS FOR SCHOOL BUILDINGS AND EQUIPMENT

During the past two decades there has arisen a large body of literature dealing with school-building standards. For the most part the present standards are based on authoritative opinion, rather than on scientific experimentation. Men and women who have had opportunity to observe widely have agreed on what constitutes a satisfactory educational provision. Many of the standards, such as "The vicinity of sources of immoral influences should be avoided," are self-evident and perhaps need no experimental proof for verification. Others are generally accepted, although no experimental demonstration has proved them to be true. For example, it is generally agreed that the skyline should have an angle not more than 30 degrees from the base of the building.

A few examples may be cited, however, of standards that are based on scientific research. Southerland,[1] by an actual count of the number of hours of sunshine interference, showed that the

[1] F. B. Dresslar, *American School Buildings*, p. 43. United States Bureau of Education Bulletin, 1924, no. 17. Washington: Government Printing Office, 1925.

preferable directions for the lighting of classrooms are the west and the east. Reeves and Ganders [1] showed the advantages of vacuum cleaning over the ordinary brush sweeping by a series of studies, including the weighing of the dirt and dust collected and a semi-objective scoring of the quality of the cleaning work. A ventilation inquiry in New York carried on experiments with children under varying types of ventilation. Experiments of this type are unfortunately all too rare in the field of school planning and building management.

There is a real need for further research on building standards. The great majority of the accepted standards for school buildings still await experimental verification. The field of schoolhouse planning, however, is not an easy one in which to do experimental work. The basic techniques of investigation are now somewhat limited, and there is real need for the development of new techniques, as well as the application of research methods that are already familiar to students of education. Experimental techniques in this field have the disadvantage of being expensive; they are also difficult to apply without placing some of the experimental groups of children in undue jeopardy. For example, it might be a questionable practice deliberately to seat a large group of children for right-hand lighting, with the hope of being able to detect some larger degree of eyesight failure among such a group than is normally found with children occupying rooms seated for left-hand lighting.

The necessity of research for determining standards for school buildings and equipment is illustrated by some of the standards formerly held on good authority which have now been discarded. Attention has already been called to Henry Barnard's suggestion in 1848 that every classroom ought to have a platform for the teacher. Examples from more recent years are fairly numerous. There was a time not long ago when experts advocated north

[1] Charles E. Reeves and Harry S. Ganders, *School Building Management*, pp. 59–64. New York: Bureau of Publications, Teachers College, Columbia University, 1928.

light as the ideal for a schoolroom; now it is generally recognized that such light in northern latitudes in winter months is too weak. Basements were formerly thought a highly desirable, almost necessary adjunct of a sanitary building, in order to protect the inmates from the "ground air." The standards still insist on fire escapes as necessary on every building, and some state laws or regulations refuse to approve a school building, even though of fireproof construction, unless it is decorated with exterior fire escapes. Many authorities now point out that a fire escape of the ordinary type is usually a source of additional hazard in case of fire or panic, and that if the interior stairways are adequate in number, properly located, carefully fireproofed, and separated from the remainder of the building, there is no need for exterior fire escapes.

The question of ventilation has in recent years been the subject of a controversy among the authorities and experts. Recent research has discredited the former demands with respect to adequacy of ventilation, and has shown that the increase of carbon dioxide content is not a significant factor in judging air conditions. Other investigations have shown that mechanical ventilating equipment, installed at great expense in public-school buildings, stands idle a large part of the time and in many cases is never operated at all. The ventilation inquiry referred to earlier seemed to indicate that old-fashioned window ventilation is the most satisfactory type, judging from the effect on the health of the pupils. Thus, while the former standards for ventilation had an excellent theoretical basis, the results of research studies have raised grave questions regarding the validity of these standards. It is only fair to say that possibly the last word has not yet been said on the subject of ventilation, and that additional research will undoubtedly be forthcoming.

This discussion of the nature of present school-building standards should not be interpreted as advice to disregard them. The school administrator must accept authoritative opinion until more completely validated standards are developed. Although many of the standards still await experimental proof, in the practical situation the administrator who proceeds with the construction of a new building in violation of any of the commonly accepted standards lays himself open to severe criticism.

GENERAL CHARACTERISTICS OF A SATISFACTORY SCHOOL BUILDING

A few of the general standards that a satisfactory school building should meet will be briefly discussed.

The first standard is that the building should be aesthetically pleasing. This is not a simple matter, since it involves not only the architectural outlines of the building itself, but also adjustment to environmental factors of landscape, near-by buildings, type of residential district, section of the country, and the general trend of the fashions of the times. The achievement of this goal is essentially a problem for the architect.

The second standard is that the building should be structurally firm, safe, and enduring. Shoddy construction cannot be tolerated in a school building. Extra precautions must be taken in a structure occupied principally by young children to avoid every possible source of harm or danger. This involves such technical matters as the figuring of floor loads with an ample safety factor, the calculation of wind stresses, the avoidance of fire hazards, and similar items. This principle carries through even to such small details as the placing of snow guards on the roof, the covering of exterior steps, and the avoidance of the use of winders in stair treads. The schoolhouse is to the general public the most visible and tangible part of the educational system, and the community usually has a great measure of pride in its new school building. If, within a few years after its construction, defects in the construction begin to appear, the community is likely to lose faith in those who were originally responsible for the building.

The third standard that should be met by a new school building is flexibility. Educational adjustments are coming so rapidly these days that it is difficult to foresee what may be the demands for space only a few years hence. Under such conditions there is need for the planning of buildings so that they will easily lend themselves to modification. During the last two or three decades it became almost an axiom that no new building should be constructed which does not definitely plan for exterior expansions. At the same time there is need for interior flexibility. This means, for example, that partitions between classrooms should be easily removable, and that heat and water pipes, ventilation ducts, and the like should be carried in the corridor walls, rather than in partition walls.

A fourth general standard for a satisfactory school building requires planning for the correlation of the various functions to be served. The instructional rooms within a given department should be located near each other; the physics lecture room should not be on the third floor if the laboratory for that science is on the first floor. The principle of correlation applies not only within departments, but also to the grouping of whole departments. Certain departments are noisy, for example those which provide instruction in music, typewriting, and shopwork, and must be isolated in some way. The chemistry department should be so located that fumes will not penetrate to the rooms occupied by other departments. The administrative offices involve a special problem in correlation; they should be centrally located, so that the visitor unfamiliar with the building will naturally drift into the office on first entering, instead of aimlessly wandering around and interrupting the exercises in rooms where classwork is being conducted.

A fifth general standard, one which is closely related to the principle of correlation, requires an arrangement for economical circulation of pupils. The location of general service rooms, such as the auditorium, library, study halls, toilets, cafeteria, can be planned so as to cut down the amount of travel by students and relieve corridor congestion at busy periods.

A sixth general standard, one which is increasingly important in these times, is that the building must be reasonable in cost. There are no adequate standards of what constitutes a reasonable cost. Local conditions, such as the accessibility to building materials and rates of wages paid unskilled and semi-skilled labor, the speed with which construction must proceed, the time of year, and numerous other factors influence the cost of construction. It is essential that the cost of every feature be carefully studied, with a view to determining whether its inclusion is worth while. Features that do not contribute in some important and direct way to an efficient educational program should be seriously questioned if they add to the cost of the building.

Finally, and most important of all, the building must be adequate to meet the existing educational needs. This means that it must be large enough to accommodate the pupil groups to be served, and that it must provide in a satisfactory manner all the needed modern educational facilities. In all the multitudinous details of educational service the new building should provide the very latest equipment. Staff members who are responsible for the planning of a new school should make a wide and critical study of other buildings in order to make certain that proposed plans are satisfactory on all points.

BIBLIOGRAPHY

Almack, John C., editor, *Modern School Administration*, pp. 77–110.

Ayres, Leonard P., and May Ayres, *School Buildings and Equipment*. Cleveland Education Survey, VIII. Cleveland: Survey Committee of the Cleveland Foundation, 1916. 118 pp.

Burton, William H., *Introduction to Education*, pp. 381–90.

Chamberlain, Leo M., *The Teacher and School Organization*, pp. 413–39, 559–96.

Clapp, Frank L., Wayland J. Chase, and Curtis Merriman, *Introduction to Education*, pp. 398–408.

Cubberley, Ellwood P., *State School Administration*, pp. 515–81.

Harrison, Margaret, *Radio in the Classroom*, pp. 141–57. New York: Prentice Hall, 1937.

Judd, Charles H., *Education and Social Progress*, pp. 83–103.

National Society for the Study of Education, *The Textbook in American Education*. *Thirtieth Yearbook*, Part II.   Bloomington, Illinois: Public School Publishing Company, 1931.   viii + 364 pp.

Reeder, Ward, *A First Course in Education*, pp. 178–226, 484–506.

Reeves, Charles Everand, and Harry Stanley Ganders, *School Building Management*.   New York: Teachers College, Columbia University, 1928.   xiv + 396 pp.

Smith, Payson, Frank W. Wright, and Associates, *Education in the Forty-Eight States*, pp. 76–86, 108–22.   Staff Study no. 1, Advisory Committee on Education.

Spain, Charles L., *The Platoon School*.   New York: The Macmillan Company, 1924.   xviii + 262 pp.

Strayer, George D., and N. L. Engelhardt, *School Building Problems*. New York: Teachers College, Columbia University, 1927.   xiv + 698 pp.

CHAPTER XI

THE ARTICULATION OF THE SCHOOL PROGRAM

THE PROGRAM of education in the United States is arranged in a number of separate units such as the kindergarten, elementary school, secondary school, and college. In general, pupils are assigned to these units in accordance with their maturity and the stage of their intellectual achievements. The arrangement of these units is in ladder form; the completion of any one unit leads directly to the next unit.

It is the purpose of this chapter to discuss the articulation of the various units of the American school system, and the degree to which the ideal of uninterrupted progress is actually achieved in the present arrangement in this country. The terms articulation and co-ordination, which are often used interchangeably, should first be defined.

The Department of Superintendence of the National Education Association (now the American Association of School Administrators) devoted its *Seventh Yearbook* (1929) to the subject of the articulation of the units of the American educational system. In that report articulation is defined as "that adequate relation of part to part which makes for continuous forward movement." This is an excellent definition. It should be noted, however, that the continuous forward movement may be considered either in terms of the progress of the child through the formal units of the school system, or in terms of his progress as a learner in the various disciplines and skills taught in the schools. Under ideal conditions these two types of progress would be identical, but in practice it often happens on the one hand that a child progresses through the units of the school system without making continuous forward progress in his learning, and on the other hand that a child makes progress in learning that is not adequately recognized in his advancement through the units of the system.

The desirability of effective articulation between the units of the school system is evident for two reasons. The first is that economy in the educational process can be secured only in this way. If there are periods when continuous forward progress is not being made, the system cannot be said to be efficiently organized. The second and more basic reason is the need for effective articulation which arises from the fundamental concept of a democratically organized society. One of the ideals of social organization in the United States is that the way ahead for each individual must be kept open, so that he is allowed to progress to the extent of his capabilities. If there are points in the school organization or features of an educational program that block the continuous forward progress of some pupils and do not permit them to accomplish all that they are capable of accomplishing, then the system fails to meet the ideals of democratically organized society. It is important therefore to examine the American educational system to determine the degree to which articulation is achieved.

STAGES IN THE DEVELOPMENT OF AN ARTICULATED SCHOOL SYSTEM

The constitutions that were adopted in the new states of the Middle West during the early part of the nineteenth century exhibit a definite vision regarding an arrangement for an articulated school system. The statement in the 1816 Constitution of Indiana, which has been quoted in context in an earlier chapter, is typical:

Article IX. Section 2. It shall be the duty of the General Assembly, as soon as circumstances will permit, to provide by law for a general system of education, ascending in a regular gradation from township schools to a State University, wherein tuition shall be gratis and equally open to all.

Although this ideal of an articulated school system with regular gradation was present at least this early, the objective was not realized in any substantial way in any of the states until after the Civil War, and then more often in theory than in actuality. Even a moderate degree of articulation between the units of the school system was not achieved until relatively late in the nineteenth century.

The school system in the United States has passed through several stages with respect to articulation. At the beginning of the nineteenth century there were a number of school units in existence, none of which articulated with the others. The dame school, for example, was customarily kept for very small children and provided instruction only in the rudiments of reading and writing. There were reading schools and writing schools maintained in parallel organization and with no particular provisions for articulation between them or with the dame school which many of the children might have attended before entering the reading and writing schools. The academy was an important type of secondary school at that time, but it accepted pupils without reference to their previous accomplishments in any particular school unit, and those who completed its course found themselves without opportunity for "continuous forward movement" into any other educational unit. The Latin grammar school served principally to prepare boys for college, but the boys who completed its course could enter college only through demonstration of competence in a series of examinations.

Some of the stages in the development of an articulated educational program which has been aimed at during the past generation are portrayed graphically in Figure 9. Accurate data are not at hand from which the degree of articulation or lack of articulation between educational units in early times can be ascertained, so the relationships shown in the diagram are to be considered as only approximations.

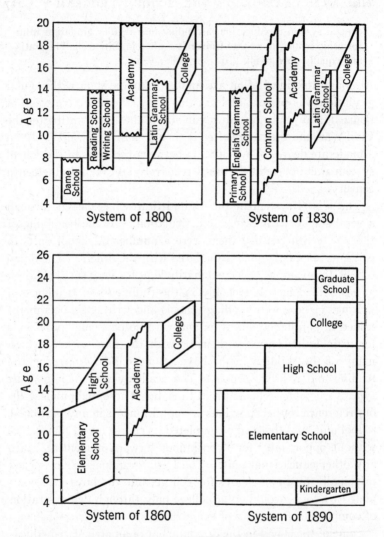

FIGURE 9. CROSS-SECTION VIEWS OF ORGANIZATION OF NON-PRO-
FESSIONAL AMERICAN EDUCATION AT THIRTY-YEAR INTERVALS
DURING THE NINETEENTH CENTURY, SHOWING AGE LEVELS NOR-
MALLY SERVED BY EACH UNIT

It will be observed that by 1860 there was some articulation between the elementary school and the high school. The high school was beginning to replace the academy as the institution for secondary education. The bringing of the high school into articulation with the college, and the addition of the kindergarten at one end and the graduate school at the other end of the educational system, were accomplishments of the last quarter of the nineteenth century.

The American school system as it now exists and as shown in the final diagram in Figure 9 is in theory a completely articulated system of education. A child may enter the kindergarten or the first grade; and as he completes each unit of the school system, the next is more or less automatically opened to him. He may continue his educational progress, in theory, just as far as his ability and efforts will allow him to go. Despite the achievement of this theoretical articulation, however, at present the co-ordination is far from perfect. Many circumstances arise which block the continued forward movement of pupils.

EXAMPLES OF INCO-ORDINATION

Instances in which faulty articulation in the school system is exhibited are abundant. Sooner or later, the problem of lack of co-ordination comes to the attention of almost everyone who has anything to do with the educational process. Most students who have progressed as far as the college or the graduate school can look back on their own careers and readily discover points at which continuous forward movement was impeded or entirely obstructed. A number of examples can be given to illustrate some of the typical failures to achieve articulation.

Uneven Progress in Subjects

The data presented in the Cleveland Survey, with regard to the results of tests in handwriting in the four upper grades of various elementary schools of that city, illustrate how articulation is often

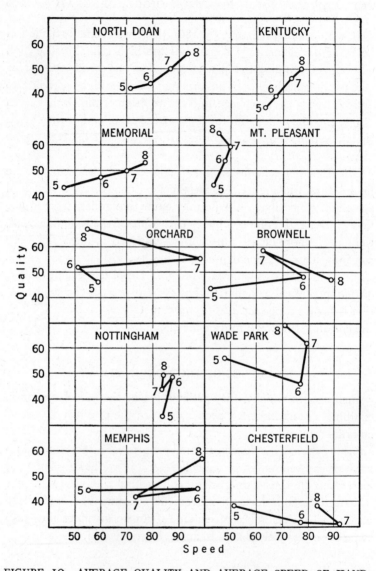

FIGURE 10. AVERAGE QUALITY AND AVERAGE SPEED OF HAND-WRITING OF PUPILS IN GRADES 5, 6, 7, AND 8 IN TEN SCHOOLS

Charles H. Judd, *Measuring the Work of the Public Schools* (Cleveland, Ohio: The Survey Committee of the Cleveland Foundation, 1916), p. 76.

absent in a given subject because of the different emphases given by teachers to phases of pupil activity.   If continued forward movement had taken place in handwriting, children in each grade would, on the average, have done better on tests of handwriting than children in the preceding grade.   The tests given in the Cleveland Survey permitted an analysis of achievements in the two factors in handwriting, speed and quality.   Figure 10 shows the results of these tests in ten elementary schools.

In a few of these schools, the average scores of the pupils on speed and quality of handwriting indicate substantial forward progress from grade to grade in each characteristic.   A number of the schools, however, exhibit a curious pattern of wholly irregular movement from one grade to the next in speed and quality in handwriting.   In some of these schools, speed is obviously emphasized in certain grades, while in other schools in certain grades quality is emphasized at the expense of speed.   The result is a failure to achieve a well-balanced forward progress in these two important phases of handwriting.   It is apparent from the results of these tests that the teachers do not have a common understanding with respect to the goals to be sought in teaching.

Overlapping of Subjects

A second evidence of faulty articulation in the school system appears when there is overlapping of subject-matter content at various levels.   One of the studies which shows inco-ordination of this type is that by W. J. Osburn.[1]   His investigation sought to determine the extent to which the subject matter at one level of the educational system is the same as that at another level.   His results show that 17 per cent of the course in high-school physics is repeated in college.   One-fifth of the high-school English course is presented earlier in the elementary school, and one-tenth of it is presented over again in the college unit.   Almost 20 per cent of the content of high-school history was found to have been

[1] W. J. Osburn, *Overlapping and Omissions in Our Courses of Study.*   Bloomington, Illinois: Public School Publishing Company, 1928.

taught in the elementary grades, and almost 23 per cent of it is taught again in college.

Another student of the problem has reported that the children in one of the large city school systems of the country come into contact some thirty-nine times during their twelve years in the elementary and secondary school with the discovery of America by Christopher Columbus. A candidate for the Bachelor's degree in college who has specialized in English will probably have studied Shakespeare's "Julius Caesar" some four times during his school program in the elementary grades, high school, and college. Examples of this type of overlapping can readily be multiplied.

It must be recognized that not all overlapping of subject matter is bad or indicative of faulty articulation. Some repetition of topics is necessary for review and for effective mastery of a subject. Oftentimes it is necessary to repeat items in establishing new inter-relationships among topics and subjects. Repetition, where necessary for the purposes mentioned, should be carefully planned and kept to the minimum if the learner is to make continuous and effective forward progress.

Gaps in Subject Matter

A third type of faulty articulation arises from the exact opposite of overlapping of subject matter. The educational achievements of many pupils give evidence of serious gaps or deficiencies in their educational programs. Tests given groups of college freshmen, for example, usually show some who have progressed that far in the educational system without effective command of reading techniques, or with deficient achievements in the field of arithmetic, although both reading and arithmetic are normally expected to be mastered at the level of the elementary school. Graduate students, in all too many cases, approach the writing of a Master's or even a Doctor's thesis without having mastered the rudiments of spelling, grammar, and English composition. Events of the past decade have clearly shown that the schools at all levels have failed to provide adequate preparation in the field of the social sciences.   Even the individuals comprising the well-educated part of the citizenry of this country are, with few exceptions, economic illiterates.   That a deficiency of this kind exists is a serious criticism of the school system in which the present generation received its preparation.

Critical Attitudes of Teachers

Another evidence of faulty articulation is found in the attitudes of teachers toward the work of the schools at levels below that in which they are engaged.   The professor in the graduate school is often heard to complain that his students must have had poor training in the undergraduate colleges which they attended.   The college instructor frequently exhibits dissatisfaction with the preparation which his students have had in the secondary school. The secondary-school teacher blames the elementary school for having sent on a horde of inadequately prepared pupils.   The teacher in the upper grades of the elementary school finds fault with the teaching done in the primary grades because the children have not been properly taught to read and write.   The teacher of the primary grades and the teacher of the kindergarten probably tend to lay the responsibility for the shortcomings of their pupils on the home.   The fact that criticisms of this type are widespread among the personnel of the educational system indicates clearly a lack of understanding of the difficulties which are encountered by teachers at each level of the educational system in achieving what is expected of them.

Some years ago the members of the department of English at one of the midwestern state universities decided to do something more than merely complain to each other about the inadequate preparation in English which students entering as freshmen in the university often exhibited.   The freshman students in one year who exhibited marked deficiency in ability to write English were listed by this department in accordance with the high schools in which they were prepared; a sharply worded letter was drafted and sent to each of these high schools, naming its graduates who had been found deficient in English, and suggesting pointedly that the school should improve its work in that field. The university department was greatly embarrassed to receive a number of replies from high-school principals to whom their letters had been addressed, thanking them for their information, but stating that the teacher of English in the school had been prepared and recommended to the position he or she now occupied by the university department of English. The letters from the principals indicated further that, if freshmen with better preparation in English were desired, the university department might obtain them by turning out teachers of English who were able to supply satisfactory instruction.

The incident illustrates the fact that responsibility for failure to prepare students adequately cannot always be assigned definitely to a single unit of the educational system. Furthermore, the question is not so much one of assigning blame as that of remedying the difficulty wherever it is found. Usually each unit must assume responsibility for overcoming the deficiencies of pupils as they are discovered.

Breaks Between the Units of the System

Although pupils can pass from a lower unit to a higher in the American educational system without serious difficulty, it is true that marked changes between practices of the various units often cause students to fail. There are pronounced breaks between the elementary school and the secondary school, and between the secondary school and the college. The curriculums of these units are separately determined, and the lack of continuity in the program arises in part from this fact. Methods of instruction also are different in each of these units, and this fact introduces a handicap to the continued forward progress of many pupils. The degree of individual responsibility expected of pupils differs at the various levels. In the elementary school, for example, the teacher customarily maintains a close personal contact with the pupils, and closely supervises their work. In the secondary school, far greater responsibility is laid on the pupil for budgeting his own time and preparing his assigned lessons. At the college level, the student is expected to be largely self-directing in his choices of methods and times of work. When changes of these types come upon pupils without adequate warning, as they tend to do at the points of juncture between the units of the school system, some disruption of the learner's forward progress is likely to result.

College Entrance Requirements

Perhaps one of the most striking examples of inco-ordination between the units of the American educational system appears in the fact that admission to college depends on compliance with certain entrance requirements imposed by particular institutions. Originally, as was shown in Figure 9, the college was not closely co-ordinated with the other units of the educational system. Each college determined its own requirements for admission, and these were in each instance described in terms of examinations set by the college.

In order to overcome some of the difficulties in making the transition from secondary school to college, as was explained in a preceding chapter, arrangements were made to accept certificates of graduation from the secondary school in lieu of examinations. This arrangement, however, was hedged by many prescriptions with respect to the types of subjects to be studied in the secondary school by the prospective college student, and with respect to other conditions surrounding the secondary-school program. Administrators of secondary schools have charged, often justly, that the programs of their schools have been dominated too much by the college. The colleges, on the other hand, have contended that their requirements have been the means of compelling secondary schools to maintain high standards.

With the expansion of the secondary-school enrollments and the registration of large numbers of youth who have no expectation of going on to college, the maintenance of a secondary-school curriculum determined by college entrance requirements has become an absurdity. The secondary school was forced to expand its offerings to take care of the newer types of children enrolled, and the college in turn has shown a disposition to accept for entrance many types of secondary-school studies that were not a part of the traditional entrance requirements. Some objective investigations have shown, moreover, that the type of subjects studied in the secondary school, other factors being held constant, has no relationship to the success of the student in college. In other words, pupils of equal degrees of ability who have studied different subjects in the secondary school do equally well in college.

These various factors have contributed toward a marked relaxation of the subject-matter prescriptions for college entrance during the past two decades. To some extent, secondary-school administrators still justly complain about the domination of their programs by the colleges, but the difficulty is now much less than it formerly was.

Transfer Between Normal School and College

Faulty articulation in the American educational system, of a type somewhat different from any discussed thus far, is occasioned by the historical aloofness of the institutions established for the preparation of teachers from the other institutions of higher education. It is to be noted that the normal schools were not shown in Figure 9; their inclusion would have complicated the chart too much. Transfer from the normal school to the liberal arts college or to the graduate school has in the past been difficult, and usually could be accomplished only with considerable loss of credit by the student.

The reason for this lack of articulation lies in the separate origin of the institutions of the normal-school type. In an earlier chapter it was explained that the first normal schools were distinctly not on the collegiate level. As these institutions increased their requirements for admission and graduation until they became equivalent to those of the liberal arts colleges, it has been only natural for the students and graduates of the normal schools to claim a status equivalent to that granted students from liberal arts colleges on transfer to the university or graduate school. The graduate schools and the deans of the liberal arts colleges, however, have been slow to recognize this changed status of the normal schools and teachers colleges, and as a result students from such institutions have found some impediment in their continued forward educational progress.

Articulation Between Home and School

Finally, it may be pointed out that arrangements for securing the best co-ordination between the home and the school are not effectively provided in most American school systems. As has been pointed out in an earlier connection, much of the education of a child goes on in the home rather than in the school. Unless these two agencies are working toward a common goal, each with an understanding of the other, they are likely to be at cross purposes and to tend to nullify the educational efforts of each other, so far as the child is concerned. If, for example, the school tries to inculcate certain standards of English usage but the home maintains no such standards, the child is likely to follow the pattern of usage established in the home rather than that which the school attempts to teach. In many respects there is opportunity for better co-ordination than now exists between the home and the school in carrying on the educational process.

DISADVANTAGES OF FAULTY ARTICULATION

The handicaps imposed upon the pupil by faulty articulation in the school system are many and important. Failure to make satisfactory progress, discouragement and discontentment with school work, and ultimately elimination from the school system are the direct result of inco-ordination. While shortcomings of the schools other than faulty articulation are sometimes responsible for like unfortunate results, the share of the difficulty to be charged to the lack of effective co-ordination in the educational program is large.   Because of the graded organization of the schools, progress tends to be measured in the child's mind in terms of promotion from one grade level to the next, and promotion rather than actual progress in learning becomes the goal of his endeavors.

The vigorous American ideal of an open road ahead for everyone is likely to triumph in the end over any arbitrary obstacle that may temporarily be set up to block its attainment.   The school system cannot long stand in the way of this ideal without being called sharply to task for its failure to serve the demands of the social order.

Observers have pointed out that the American pupil requires longer to reach a given stage of educational attainment than the pupil in European schools.   It is variously estimated that the American boy or girl requires to reach the level of completion of the junior college about two more years of schooling than is required to attain approximately this same level by pupils who go through secondary schools in Europe.   A comparison of this sort cannot be exact, for there are no common measures that can be applied to systems which differ so largely in their curriculums and in their objectives.   It may be pointed out, furthermore, that some of the superior progress of the European schools may be attributable to the better preparation of teachers and to the higher motivation of pupils.   It seems obvious, however, that the American pupil could be saved much time in reaching a given degree of educational attainment if a better articulation of the school program were arranged.

The facts are that large numbers of American citizens are dissatisfied with the present organization and service of the public schools.   As laymen, they are not able to diagnose the difficulty exactly, but there is a widespread feeling that the public schools are not at present making the maximum use of their opportunity to serve the social order.   Some of this criticism, on analysis, seems readily attributable to the failure to achieve a better articulation and co-ordination within the school system. This is a problem to which educators can well afford to devote their attention and effort. Much has already been accomplished, but the task is by no means complete. It seems desirable, before looking at efforts to improve articulation in the American educational system, to analyze first some of the causes of faulty articulation.

REASONS FOR LACK OF ARTICULATION

The causes of inco-ordination within the school system are many and varied. Some of them can readily be remedied, but others are more or less inherent in the nature of the educational system; it may not be possible to remedy or remove this latter type, but steps can be taken to reduce to a minimum the difficulties that these unavoidable causes place in the way of pupils.

Historical Origins of the Different Units

It can be pointed out in the first place that a basic cause for inco-ordination between the units of the American educational system is the separate historical origin of these units. The kindergarten, for example, was developed first in Germany, and was introduced into the United States from that country and from England. The elementary school, as has been shown in an earlier connection, was developed on the basis of a Prussian model. The high school is a unique American product. The college was originally an English institution. The graduate school was imported from Germany. An educational system made up of units so derived may well be expected to suffer from inco-ordinations between its units, at least until effective efforts have been made to bridge over the junctures.

Aims of the Different Levels

In the second place, it seems inevitable that the aims of the various levels in the educational system will not be exactly the same. The points where changes occur in the aims become manifest to the pupil, and these are likely to be points at which articulation is apparently lacking. For example, the aim of selection is not recognized to any degree at the level of the elementary school. All normal children, regardless of their ability, are expected to progress through the elementary school; exceptions are classified as abnormal in one or more respects. At the level of professional education, quite by contrast, selection becomes an important purpose of the educational program. Society clearly does not want persons prepared for service as physicians and surgeons whose native abilities are low or undeveloped, so the medical school has an obligation to select as its students only those who give promise of being successful practitioners.

Institutions for the preparation of teachers have in the past been entirely too lenient in the admission of students, and have allowed too many persons to make preparation for teaching whose only important qualification for that service was a desire to enter quickly upon some respectable and remunerative employment. The educational system would undoubtedly be stronger today if institutions preparing teachers had exercised more rigid standards of admission in terms of personal characteristics needed for effective service. A system of selective admission to the teaching profession would, of course, need to be based on valid criteria, and it is significant that those engaged in the preparation of teachers have, up to this time, developed few measures of any great value for prognosis of future success in teaching. In other professions, however, the function of selection is considered a necessary part of the process of preparation, and the aims of the educational institutions serving such professions definitely recognize this function.

It is obvious, then, that at the point in the educational progress of the person where selection must occur, there is likely to be imposed an important impediment to the continued forward movement of many who might wish to prepare themselves for service in a particular profession. Other instances in changes of objectives at various levels in the system could be pointed out, but sufficient illustration has been given to indicate how this factor may operate as a handicap to ready progress through the educational system.

Specialization of the Teaching Staff

A third reason for faulty articulation within the school system is the failure of teachers to understand the total educational process.   As has been stated earlier, the teachers in the American educational system are specialists in one grade level of the elementary school, or in one subject-matter field in the secondary school or college.   Most teachers have little or no professional knowledge about the problems of education at levels or in subjects other than those with which they are directly concerned.   It would be a useful experience for teachers occasionally to do some teaching in unaccustomed areas if this could be done without endangering the effectiveness of the instruction received by the children.   It would certainly be useful for the teacher in the secondary school to become intimately acquainted with some of the problems of the teacher in the elementary grades, and in turn the teacher in the elementary grades might obtain a better idea of what she should be doing if she were to have intimate contact with the problems of teachers in the secondary school.   The high degree of specialization in the preparation and service of teachers at the various levels and in the various subjects tends to introduce inco-ordinations in the educational program of the pupil, who must obtain his instruction from these specialists, most of whom have little knowledge of what instruction the same pupil has received, is receiving, or will receive from other teacher-specialists during his educational career.

Institutional Preparation of Teachers

Another cause of faulty articulation, more pronounced in the past than at present, is closely related to the specialization of the teaching staff.   The teachers for the various levels of the school system have been prepared largely in different types of institutions. The task of the normal school in the past has been the preparation of elementary-school teachers. Universities and liberal arts colleges have been most active in preparing teachers for the secondary school. The graduate schools have been the exclusive agencies preparing teachers for the colleges. This specialization of institutional functions has not tended to foster among the teachers at various levels an effective understanding of each other's problems. To some extent, the recent development of teachers colleges has broken down this institutional classification in the preparation of teachers, for these institutions are now also preparing secondary-school teachers in large numbers. The graduate schools also are now giving some of the advanced preparation required for secondary-school teachers as well as that for college instructors. As the institutions of higher education develop programs that are more nearly uniform, the inco-ordinations due to the different kinds of institutions preparing teachers are likely to become less and less.

Standards of Promotion

Another cause of inco-ordination arises from the fact that standards of promotion and advancement from one grade level to the next are frequently vague and not well understood by teachers and pupils. The teacher who promotes a pupil to the next grade frequently holds an idea of the attainment necessary for that promotion somewhat different from that held by the teacher of the grade to which the pupil is advanced. Tests and examinations of the standardized type, by which the attainment of the pupil can be tested objectively, have been available only in recent years, and even with the help of such devices it is not always possible to describe accurately the degree of attainment necessary for the advancement of a pupil from one level of the educational system to the next. This difficulty is heightened at the points of juncture between the various units of the educational system, for it is somewhat difficult to get a common understanding between the teachers in the highest levels of one unit and those in the lowest levels of the next unit, when these are under separate administrative jurisdiction.

Areas Served by Schools

A situation which gives rise to an important difficulty of articulation in school programs relates to the variation in the geographical range that may be served by units dealing with children at different age levels. The child in the primary grades must attend a school near his home unless special transportation is furnished.

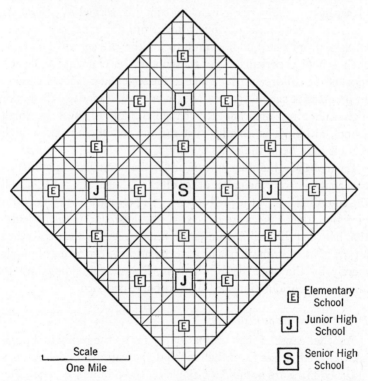

FIGURE 11. IDEAL PLAN FOR LOCATION OF SCHOOLS IN A CITY, SHOWING AREA SERVED BY ONE SENIOR HIGH SCHOOL, FOUR JUNIOR HIGH SCHOOLS, AND SIXTEEN ELEMENTARY SCHOOLS

Vertical and horizontal lines represent streets drawn at intervals of one-eighth mile. Light diagonal lines are boundaries of elementary-school attendance districts. Heavy diagonal lines are boundaries of junior-high-school attendance districts.

As a rule, the travel distance for children in the lower grades should not exceed a half-mile.   The child in the upper grades of the elementary school or at the junior high-school level can be expected to walk as far as a mile to reach his school.   The high school can serve a much larger area, a radius of two miles not being at all unreasonable.   At the college level, there is almost no limit to the territory that can be served, for college students travel from one end of the country to the other to reach the institution of their choice.

Because of the varying areas that may be served by schools at different levels, it is obviously necessary for most children to transfer from one building unit to another at certain points in their school experience.   At the end of the elementary school, most of the children must change to the secondary-school building. In progressive school systems the change is first made to the junior high school and then another change is made to the senior high school, although in smaller systems the junior and senior high schools may be in the same building.

Each of these building units is under the immediate administrative control of a principal or other officer.   Regardless of how well the co-ordination of the program may be provided through central direction, the chances are large that in some respects the articulation between the building units will not be easy for the pupil; thus a type of inco-ordination is introduced into the programs of pupils merely by the necessity of changing from one building unit to another at various times in their school experience.

Decentralized Administration

Another cause of inco-ordination, so far as the individual pupil is concerned, arises from the fact that the various school systems in the country are not under a single central administration.   The system of each state is independent of that of each other state, and most of the states allow their local school units a large degree of independence in setting up their programs.   If each child had his entire school experience in a single local school system, his program could be a reasonably well co-ordinated one, but when, as is the actual case with large numbers of children, the pupil attends two or more different systems during his school experience, the opportunities for inco-ordination are evident. As was previously pointed out, the population of the United States is mobile and large numbers of children complete their school work in different local systems from those in which they started.

It might be suggested that this lack of co-ordination in the program of the individual pupil arising from differences in the various local systems could be overcome by a high degree of central control over the school program. A remedy of this sort would probably be worse than the condition it seeks to relieve. Communities vary somewhat in their local needs and one of the important problems of curriculum construction involves the making of the necessary adjustments to meet the peculiar needs of the locality. It seems almost inevitable, therefore, that mobility of population and the local control of school systems will entail a certain amount of inco-ordination in the programs of individual children, particularly if the provisions in the local community are well adapted and adjusted to the local needs.

Record System

Usually the record system for the individual pupil lacks continuity throughout his experience in the school system and a certain amount of inarticulation arises from this cause. In many school systems it is customary for the record of the elementary-school pupil to remain in that school and not to accompany the child when he progresses to the secondary school. In relatively few cases does the complete record of the child accompany him when he moves from one community to another. Attempts to improve the co-ordination of the program for the individual child must necessarily be based on reasonably complete records. This lack of continuity in the record system is one of the handicaps to the improvement of co-ordination within the program of the individual child.

EFFORTS TO IMPROVE CO-ORDINATION

For more than a generation educators have been aware of the faulty articulation that exists at many points in the American educational system, and additional evidence regarding the existence of these inco-ordinations is constantly being accumulated. Vigorous efforts have been carried on to overcome the difficulties arising from faulty articulation. Some four or five major types of efforts in this direction may be briefly reviewed.

Junctures at New Points

Previously in this chapter it has been shown that a large amount of faulty articulation arises at the points of juncture between the institutional units of which the school system is composed. One of the remedies that has been applied consists in making the junctures at new points in the system. Thus instead of having a kindergarten and an elementary school as separate units, there has been created in many school systems a kindergarten-primary unit. The junior high school has been developed in many cities to include the upper grades of the elementary school and the lowest grade or grades of the high school, thus making a single institution that bridges the traditional gap between the elementary school and the secondary school. In some progressive communities the junior college has been established on a four-year basis, including the two upper years of high school as well as the two years of the junior college.

The reconstruction of the units of the American educational system offers much promise for improved articulation, and a regrouping would doubtless result in other educational advantages as well. Several different patterns of reorganization have been proposed, and many of these newer arrangements are in actual operation in certain school systems. Even with this reconstruction, however, the danger remains that the new units, after they have become well established, will show as much lack of articulation with each other as is now shown in the system composed of the traditional units.

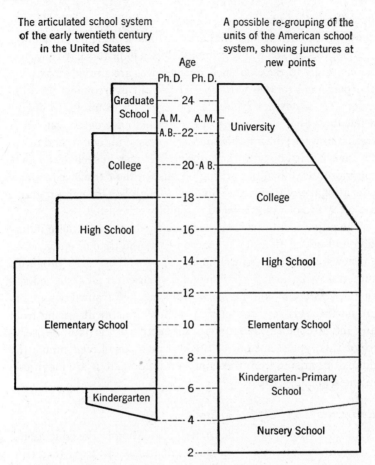

FIGURE 12. THE TRADITIONAL UNITS OF THE AMERICAN EDUCA-
TIONAL SYSTEM, AND A POSSIBLE REGROUPING OF THE UNITS

Personnel Services

If it be accepted that some inco-ordination is inevitable because
of unchangeable conditions which give rise to faulty articulation,
it becomes necessary to set up within the system arrangements
for counteracting the unfortunate effects of faulty articulation.
The development of guidance programs and personnel services

has afforded an opportunity for such arrangements. Pupils who show signs of deficiencies that are due to lack of articulation in the school program, or whose school histories indicate that they may be expected to develop such deficiencies, are provided through the personnel service with special help in overcoming the difficulty. It is customary now in colleges, for example, to devote a few days at the beginning of each year to a program known as freshman week; during this time a process of induction and orientation is carried on with the entering freshmen in such a way as to minimize the difficulties arising because of their transfer to a new educational environment. Similar, though less formal, programs are a feature of well-managed secondary schools.

The adjustment service goes much further than a mere induction and orientation of the newcomer at the time of entrance to the new institution. In well-managed personnel service programs the student is furnished advice and counsel on all of his educational, vocational, and personal problems, and trained counselors are on the alert to discover signs of maladjustment arising from any and all conditions that affect the success of the pupil. A service of this type seems one of the best methods of overcoming the difficulties arising from those inco-ordinations that are inevitable in the school system.

Reorganization of Subject Matter

Another effort to provide better articulation in the educational program consists in the reorganization of subject matter of instruction so that it will contribute better to the continued progress of the learner. One of these modifications is found in the survey courses. These courses deal comprehensively with an extensive body of subject matter, and introduce students to a large field rather than to a single narrow phase of a particular field. For example, the secondary schools formerly taught each of the sciences as separate subjects. The high-school pupil could normally include only one or two sciences within his four-year program and thus he would not be instructed in other scientific fields which would have contributed to his understanding of the world about him.   Today a widely adopted practice is the introduction of a course called "general science," in which important concepts from each of the fields of science are presented without developing in detail the content of any one of the fields.

In a similar manner survey courses have been developed at the college level.   In colleges which do not give survey courses the only opportunity afforded students to learn about such a subject as American history, economics, or physiology, is through an introductory course limited to that topic.   The number of introductory courses suitable for a beginner in each field of study is commonly greater than can be taken by any one student during his entire four-year program, even if he were to devote his full time to such courses.   The result is that the student is denied the opportunity to become acquainted with large areas of human knowledge during his four-year college course.   To overcome this difficulty survey courses introducing the student to broad areas of knowledge, such as the social sciences, the humanities, or the physical or biological sciences, have been widely developed and are given during the early years of the college program.

The Gary Plan of Co-ordination

The widely publicized plan of school organization instituted by the late Superintendent William Wirt of the Gary, Indiana, public schools has as one of its less conspicuous features an arrangement designed to overcome the difficulties that arise from administrative inco-ordination within the local school system.   The Gary plan is based on the principle of housing the children of all grades from the kindergarten through the high school in a single building unit or at least under a single administrative principal.   By this plan the school avoids the administrative inco-ordinations that arise because of the transfer of pupils from one building to another upon the completion of a lower unit.

Formal and Informal Dissemination of Ideas

A factor which strongly tends to overcome lack of articulation between and among school systems is the facility with which ideas and information are disseminated throughout the educational profession. Educators at frequent intervals are accustomed to attend conferences in which they hear described the plans, policies, and procedures of school systems other than their own. Teachers visit other systems and confer regarding practices and procedures. Educational journals carry articles describing innovations. Books written by experts in the various phases of educational service carry authoritative recommendations.

Because of these influences, and despite the possibility of dissimilarity arising from local control, there is a marked tendency toward a general uniformity in the pattern of schools in the United States. Some schools, of course, are at any given time pioneering in developing new practices. Others are lagging far behind the van of progress. In general, however, similarities in pattern tend to develop through interchange of ideas.

BIBLIOGRAPHY

Ayres, Leonard P., *Laggards in Our Schools: A Study of Retardation and Elimination in City School Systems.* New York: Charities Publication Committee, 1909. xvi + 236 pp.

Burton, William H., *Introduction to Education*, pp. 187–93, 241–93.

Butterweck, Joseph S., and J. Conrad Seegers, *An Orientation Course in Education*, pp. 1–24, 340–58.

Chamberlain, Leo M., *The Teacher and School Organization*, pp. 490–555.

Judd, Charles H., *Education and Social Progress*, pp. 152–80.

Judd, Charles H., *The Evolution of a Democratic School System*, pp. 71–114.

Judd, Charles H., *Problems of Education in the United States*, pp. 36–67.

Osburn, Worth James, *Overlappings and Omissions in Our Courses of Study.* Bloomington, Illinois: Public School Publishing Company, 1928. iv + 168 pp.

Reeder, Ward, *A First Course in Education*, pp. 323–64, 468–83.

Wilson, Lester M., and I. L. Kandel, *Introduction to the Study of American Education*, pp. 103–24.

CHAPTER XII

THE ELEMENTARY SCHOOL

THE FIRST SCHOOL attended by the majority of American boys and girls is known as the elementary school. In preceding discussions of other topics some of the characteristics of the American elementary school have already been referred to; these need not be given extended treatment at this point. Such features will first be briefly reviewed and the remainder of this chapter will be reserved for a discussion of the characteristics and problems of the elementary school which have not been treated in previous chapters.

It has already been pointed out that the schools of the United States are for the most part public schools. This is particularly true of the elementary grades, for 90 per cent of all elementary-school pupils are enrolled in public schools.

The elementary schools in the United States, unlike the schools at similar levels in many other countries, are secular schools and do not teach religion. The secular character of American schools is a necessary corollary of public control in the United States for, under a government in which there can be no established church, the sectarian tenets of any denomination cannot be a part of the teaching of the public schools. The question of what constitutes religious teaching, however, has not been fully decided, and the states differ in their legislation on this subject. In some cases, the reading of the Bible is forbidden in the public schools; in other states, only limited sections of the Bible may be read; in some states the reading of the Bible in the public schools is required. The wearing of religious garb by teachers in the public schools is forbidden by statute or court decision in many states; in some, however, members of the religious orders are permitted to teach in the public schools.

The whole question of religious teaching has been the subject of a minor, though bitter, controversy. Many of the citizens of the United States, particularly those belonging to certain faiths, are of the opinion that religion is the only basis of morality and knowledge, and they therefore maintain a complete educational system under church auspices and support, in order that their children may not be deprived of what is judged to be a part of a well-rounded education.

The typical elementary school in the United States, as has been previously indicated, is a free school; it does not charge tuition fees. Every state has recognized its duty to educate its future citizens and to support the educational program at public expense. As has been previously pointed out, the concept of what constitutes a free education is an evolving one, and today children at the elementary level are usually provided not only with free tuition but also with transportation, textbooks, health inspection, and other types of service which are considered necessary to make the educational program effective.

AGE-SPAN COVERED

The elementary school typically begins its work with pupils at about the time they reach the age of six years. In this respect the schools of the United States are much like those of other countries, for all over the world children start their formal schooling at about their sixth year, or at least within a range no greater than from their fifth to their seventh year.

The reasons for fixing the age of six as the time for entrance to the elementary school are two. In the first place, by that time the child has normally acquired a command of his muscular processes which permits him to be comparatively independent in his behavior. He is ready, therefore, to begin attendance on an institution. In the second place, a child by the age of six usually has a sufficient command of the vernacular to permit the beginning of instruction in reading and related subjects.

In recent years methods have been developed for testing the readiness of the pupil for beginning the study of reading. These tests show that children differ somewhat in the age at which reading readiness appears, but that on the average this stage of development is attained at an age of about six or six and one-half years. Scientific studies thus confirm the well-established practice of beginning regular school education at about the age of six.

The typical elementary school in the United States covers a period of eight years, and the pupils thus complete this unit of the school normally at about the age of fourteen. In an earlier connection the reasons for the eight-year curriculum in the elementary school of the United States have been discussed. The influence of the Prussian *Volksschule* seems clearly to be an underlying cause. The eight-year elementary school, however, is by no means universal in the United States; three principal exceptions to this arrangement may be noted.

In certain areas, particularly in the southern states and in one well-known city school system, that of Kansas City, Missouri, a seven-year elementary school is maintained. During the seven-year program the pupils are given all the learning experiences that are commonly provided in the traditional eight-year school. A careful study made a number of years ago indicates that the seven-year elementary school obtains a level of achievement from its pupils similar to that obtained in other systems during the eight-year program. In other words, the children at the end of a carefully prepared seven-year program may be as far advanced in subject-matter fields as those who have followed the eight-year curriculum of the traditional American elementary school. Superintendent James M. Greenwood, who was a staunch defender of the seven-year elementary school of Kansas City, reported on this school in 1903 as follows:

A seven-year course for ward schools is not a recent discovery in Kansas City. The schools were organized on this basis in 1867, and

THE ELEMENTARY SCHOOL

have been operated on it ever since. Therefore I speak with confidence, strengthened by convictions as deeply and clearly fixed as
anyone can possibly have after watching and directing this work for
twenty-nine years. Had I found after going to Kansas City that the
children required eight years to do the work satisfactorily, I should
have asked the board of education to change from seven to eight
years; but I have never found it necessary, or even desirable, to suggest a change. Beginning under the seven-year course, and not feeling sure at first as to results, I watched carefully and cautiously the
entire work over which the pupils passed, and I made it a point to test
our seven-year pupils with all kinds of questions used by the eight-
year pupils in the best schools of this country; and our seven-year
pupils stood as high as the highest, whether the questions were from
Brooklyn, the "Regents' Examination Questions" of New York,
Civil Service or West Point preliminary questions, or those prepared
by city or state superintendents. The tests were chiefly on English
grammar and composition, arithmetic, geography, and United States
history. We have always emphasized reading, spelling, writing, and
the four branches previously mentioned, and not neglected vocal
music, drawing, and calisthenics.[1]

In the New England states many local school systems maintained in the past a nine-year elementary school. This type of
school still persists in some districts. Sometimes the pupils enter
at a slightly earlier age than in the typical eight-year system, and
approximately two years instead of one are spent in the work
that in the eight-year elementary school is given in the first
grade.

The chief deviation from the eight-year elementary school has
arisen during recent years in the six-year school. This type of
development has occurred wherever the junior high school has
been introduced, the upper two years of the former eight-year
program of the elementary school having been transferred to the
new junior-high-school unit. Because of the increased efficiency

[1] James M. Greenwood, "Seven-Year Course of Study for Ward-School
Pupils," *Proceedings of the Department of Superintendence of the National Educa-
tional Association at the Annual Meeting, February, 1903*, pp. 114–15. Also
Journal of Proceedings and Addresses of the National Education Association,
XLII:248–49 (1903).

of the instructional process, a pupil can now be given much more education in the first six years of the elementary school than formerly. Reorganization to eliminate the reviews to which much time was devoted in the upper years of the traditional elementary school also tends to make possible the completion of the elementary-school program in six years instead of eight. Such reorganization permits pupils to begin secondary education two years earlier than formerly.

The development in the direction of establishing a six-year period for elementary education has been looked upon with favor by educators, and is now rapidly becoming typical in the more progressive school systems. It seems clear that the elementary schools in the United States in the future will cover a six-year period rather than the traditional eight-year period.

The movement toward a general adoption of the six-year elementary school was greatly accelerated by the findings of a commission which prepared and published in 1927 a report on the length of elementary education. The following passages quoted from that report summarize the findings.

> The report presented in the foregoing chapters shows in a very impressive way that rudimentary studies are, in fact, characteristic of the first six grades and that, in spite of all the conservatism which opposes the reconstruction of the educational system, secondary education is beginning in the seventh grade. . . .
>
> That an earlier beginning of secondary education grows naturally out of the expansion of American education will be readily understood when it is remembered that the elementary school is today working under conditions which are favorable to more rapid advancement of pupils than was formerly possible. Formerly, pupils made slow progress because the school year was short, teachers were little trained, and textbooks were less attractive than they are now and less well adapted to the needs of pupils. Improvement along all these lines has brought as its direct results both a more highly differentiated curriculum in the upper grades and increasing disposition to detach the seventh and eighth grades from the elementary school. . . .
>
> [The] definition of elementary education should not be determined by the prevailing notion that the elementary school is the limit of popular

education.   The essentials of elementary training are certain defina-
ble degrees of intellectual and social maturity.   If these can be properly attained in less time than formerly, there is no justification
for setting a period of eight years and insisting that this period be
filled with rudimentary subjects.[1]

GRADE GROUPING IN THE ELEMENTARY SCHOOL

The elementary school in the United States is a graded school,
with a curriculum in which subject matter is allocated to the various grade levels, and in which pupils are classified into grades in
accordance with their advancement in the curriculum.   To one
who has been educated in the typical American elementary
school the graded organization may seem entirely natural, but
as a matter of fact the plan of grouping children by grades for
instructional purposes is a relatively recent innovation in educational procedure.

The instruction in many of the early schools of this country
was organized on the plan of individual teaching.   Each pupil
recited individually to the teacher and made progress in his subjects in accordance with his ability and industry.   Where pupils
did not recite singly they were grouped together so as to make it
possible for the teacher to instruct several at the same time, but
the groups were not the same in the different subjects.   Group
teaching was ungraded in the sense that a pupil advanced according to his attainment in particular subjects.   A pupil might
recite in reading with a group that had made little progress in
learning to read, while in arithmetic he might work with a group
well advanced in that subject.   Ungraded classes are to be contrasted with individual instruction, but both of these types of
organization differ from the plan commonly followed in present-
day elementary schools.

It may be pointed out that the elementary school is the only

---

[1] *Report of the Commission on Length of Elementary Education.*   Supplementary Educational Monographs, no. 34, pp. 131–34.   The University of Chicago,
1927.

part of the American educational system where pupils are graded. In the secondary school, for example, promotion is by subjects. The pupil who fails in his freshman algebra is required to repeat only the subject he has failed and he goes ahead with the second year of work in the subjects in which he has made passing marks. In the elementary school, by contrast, the pupil who fails in fifth-grade arithmetic is commonly required to repeat the entire work of that grade, even though he may have passed in all other subjects, for there are in general no provisions for his taking one subject over again apart from the grade group in which it is regularly given.

In addition to providing an economical arrangement for the education of large numbers of children, the plan of grouping by grades has the important advantage of preventing too early and too limited a specialization on the part of a pupil. Many children manifest early a specialized interest in some subject of study and would, if left to their own choice, neglect the other phases of a well-rounded development. For example, some children would do nothing but read and would fail to make progress in handwriting, arithmetic, or other essential subjects. Cases are on record in which a child has developed a specialized interest in mathematics to such an extent that he was able to find the correct answer to difficult arithmetical problems almost instantly and without the use of paper and pencil, but at the same time was unable to read fluently or to write legibly. Under the graded system the child with a specialized interest is required to bring up his competence in all the subjects to at least the minimum level required for promotion to the next grade before he is permitted to proceed in the school with the study of the subject of his special interest.

Difficulties Introduced by the Graded System

The graded system has to be adjusted in many ways to take account of the fundamental psychological fact that pupils do not progress intellectually in the same way or at the same rate and consequently any group that starts together at the beginning of the school year tends to become heterogeneous as the year progresses. An early example of the recognition of this fact is afforded by the school system of St. Louis where, under the superintendency of William T. Harris, a plan of promotion was adopted which is described by him as follows:

In St. Louis there is no attempt to bring all classes within the same grade to one standard of advancement, so that, *e.g.*, in January, all pupils within a given grade shall have arrived at just the same point in a study. At all times there are new classes just beginning the work of a grade, or year's work, in some one of our schools. The classes are not separated by intervals of one year in their work, but by irregular intervals varying from six weeks to twenty. It is considered desirable to have these intervals small, so that reclassification may be more easily managed. Pupils who fall behind their class for any reason (such as absence, lack of physical strength or of mental ability) may be reclassified with the next lower class without falling back a year, and thereby becoming discouraged. Pupils who are unusually bright or mature, may be promoted to the class above, or form new classes with the slower pupils of the class above, who need to review their work. Thus it happens that in a district school, there is a continual process going on, the elements of which are as follows: (1) The older and more advanced pupils are leaving school for business or other causes. This depletes the classes of the most skillful and best paid teachers who are usually placed in charge of the most advanced pupils. Again, there is at all times of the year an influx, into the lower grades, of pupils who have just completed their sixth or seventh year and are now anxious to begin their school career. Thus the pupils in the primary rooms of our schools tend continually to be overcrowded. (2) To correct this continued tendency which overcrowds the rooms of the least skillful and poorest paid teachers and gives small quotas of pupils to the most skillful and best paid teachers, from time to time (usually once in ten weeks, but oftener in some schools), each class is sifted, and its most promising pupils united with what remains of the next higher class; (*i.e.*, with the not-promising portion of it — those who for absence, or dull intellect, or weak wills, fail to keep up with the best). (3) To make room for this transfer, a portion of the highest class is sent to the Branch High Schools. (4) The number changed from class to class is usually small. The disturbance in classes is very slight, compared with the advantages gained by the teacher in being relieved of the necessity to drive the laggards, and drill and cram them to make them keep up with the average of the class. The teacher was once obliged to spend most of her time upon the dull ones in the useless endeavor to force them to make up lost time, or to equal the strides of the more mature, more regular, or more brilliantly gifted pupils, and, of course, these latter pupils lost proportionately, and the net result of the process was to overwork the incompetent, and to hold back the competent ones. The teacher, in the vain effort to hold together the extremes of her class, separating more widely every day till the end of the year, became cross and petulant, and sank continually into the abyss of drill-machine pedagogy.

Under our present system we can make room when needed in the lower grades, and fill up the classes of our skillful and high-priced teachers.[1]

The plan adopted by Superintendent Harris proved to be too complicated to be administered in the form in which he organized it and it gradually gave place to less elaborate methods of meeting the needs of individual pupils.

While difficulties in keeping a group of pupils together are readily apparent in those cases in which some pupils drop behind the class, it is perhaps true that the consequences of rigid grading are in fact most disastrous in the cases of bright pupils. All too often adjustments are thought to be unnecessary for the pupil who has superior ability and who could move more rapidly in the curriculum than is normally expected. The bright child is thus allowed to remain idle after he has met the requirements of the day for his class. The result is that he cultivates habits of laziness, and finding that he is not challenged to use his abilities to their fullest extent he frequently becomes a source of disciplinary problems in the classroom.

When an adjustment for the superior child is attempted, it sometimes takes the form of skipping a grade. In theory this would seem to be an unfortunate practice, for if the curriculum is

[1] W. T. Harris, "Annual Report of the Superintendent," *Twenty-First Annual Report of the Board of Directors of the St. Louis Public Schools, for the Year Ending August 1, 1875*, pp. 28–29.

carefully organized, the child who omits any one of the grades misses contact with important units of instruction. There is also the difficulty of fitting the child into a social situation in which he is younger than his classmates. Studies of the effects of accelerated progress on the subsequent educational and social adjustment of the child seem, however, to indicate that harmful effects are not often found. One of the most recent studies, after an exhaustive inquiry following accelerated pupils through the high school, through the college, and beyond the school for several years, concludes that acceleration makes for better adjustments, both social and intellectual, and might well be practiced more widely than at present. Findings of this sort may be interpreted either as evidence of the laxness with which the curriculum is organized or as evidence of the repair powers of the intellectual mechanism of the superior pupil.

The difficulties of fitting the graded system to pupils whose rates of progress vary enormously from individual to individual began to receive study late in the nineteenth century. In 1904 Superintendent Maxwell of New York City reported an extensive investigation regarding the effects of non-promotion. An extract from his report is as follows:

These tables [age-grade tables for the elementary schools] are presented this year for the first time in the City Superintendent's Annual Report. Inquiry develops the truth that the condition of affairs described has existed for many years; it is now brought to light for the first time. For a proper understanding of the facts, it is necessary to bear in mind that the normal ages of children in the several grades, if they enter at six years or six years and a half, and are not retarded during their course, are as follows:

First year grades........	6 to 8 years
Second year grades......	7 to 9 years
Third year grades.......	8 to 10 years
Fourth year grades......	9 to 11 years
Fifth year grades........	10 to 12 years
Sixth year grades.......	11 to 13 years
Seventh year grades.....	12 to 14 years
Eighth year grades......	13 to 15 years

The next table shows the number in each year grade above the normal age, and the percentage of this number on the whole number of children in the grade:

Grades	Number of Pupils	Number Above Normal Age	Per Cent of Whole Number
First year...........	87,676	20,392	23.2
Second year.........	84,254	32,141	38.1
Third year..........	82,959	37,414	45.0
Fourth year.........	73,617	36,275	49.2
Fifth year...........	61,666	30,226	49.0
Sixth year..........	45,341	19,069	42.0
Seventh year........	31,941	10,493	32.8
Eighth year.........	24,220	6,133	25.3
	491,674	192,143	39.0

Why, it will be asked, is there such an enormous number of children above the normal age in each grade? Many causes doubtless contribute to this most unfortunate result, among which may be mentioned the following:

1. In well-to-do families there is a constant and, I am convinced, a mistaken tendency to keep children from school until they are seven or eight years of age.

2. The large size of our classes, particularly in the lower grades, prevents that attention on the part of teachers to individual pupils, which is necessary to normal progress as well as to individual development, and hence pupils are not promoted as rapidly as their best interests demand.

3. The teaching in the part-time classes is necessarily less effective than in full-time classes, and this fact operates to retard the promotion of pupils.

4. The great influx of non-English-speaking foreigners every week into our schools, introduces into the lower grades thousands of children who as a rule are beyond the normal age of American children in these grades. . . .

The most important problem of the day in school administration is, how to get the older pupils who are cumbering the lower grades into the higher grades. Their presence in the lower grades is detrimental to the younger children, because they take much of the teachers' time and attention that belong to the children of normal age. Their presence in the lower grades is detrimental to themselves, because, by their position in the school, they do not enjoy the associations or re-ceive the instruction their years demand, and because, in the majority of cases, they are precluded, at the age of fourteen, from qualifying for the Health Department certificates which the law exacts as a pre-liminary to employment. To the solution of this problem, the Board of Superintendents, the District Superintendents, and the Principals must devote their best efforts.[1]

The facts to which Superintendent Maxwell called attention were recognized by school administrators and students of educa-tion as of great importance. Following the example set by his report, school systems began extensive studies. These resulted in the tabulation of the ages of pupils in the various grades in a form shown in Table 6. This type of table is known as an age-grade table, because it shows the number of pupils of each age in each grade. The squares indicating the normal age for each grade are outlined heavily so that one may see at a glance the extent to which pupils are older or younger than is considered normal for the grade in which they are placed. It will be noted that in the school system from which the data of Table 6 were obtained relatively few pupils are younger than is normal for their grade.

The pupils shown in an age-grade table above the diagonal of the chart, who are older than normal for the grade in which they are placed, are said to be "over-age"; those who are younger than normal for their grade are said to be "under-age"; all others are said to be "at-age" or of "normal-age."

Table 7 is known as a grade-progress chart because it deals with the number of years which the children in each grade have been in school. This is not the same as the age-grade distribution, for children enter school at different ages and sometimes a child is held out of school for a year or two because of his health or for other reasons. The pupil who has not been in school as long as is normal for his grade is said to be accelerated; the pupil who has

[1] William H. Maxwell, *Sixth Annual Report of the City Superintendent of Schools to the Board of Education of the City of New York for the Year Ending July 31, 1904*, pp. 47–49.

TABLE 6. DISTRIBUTION OF PUPILS BY GRADES AND CHRONOLOGICAL AGE — AN AGE-GRADE TABLE *

Age	Grade 1		Grade 2		Grade 3		Grade 4		Grade 5		Grade 6		All Grades Total
	B	A	B	A	B	A	B	A	B	A	B	A	
15–9 to 16–2..												1	1
15–3 to 15–8..							1	2		1	1	1	6
14–9 to 15–2..									2			4	6
14–3 to 14–8..									1	2	3	1	7
13–9 to 14–2..						1		3		3	7	7	21
13–3 to 13–8..				1				1		2	2	2	8
12–9 to 13–2..	1			1			3	1		2		2	10
12–3 to 12–8..					1	3	1		4	3	2	3	17
11–9 to 12–2..				1	3	3	3	2	7	5	5	3	32
11–3 to 11–8..		1	2		1		3	4	7	13	8	3	42
10–9 to 11–2..		1	1			1	1	3	4	7		2	20
10–3 to 10–8..			4	1	3	3	4	7	4	10		1	37
9–9 to 10–2..				3	3	3	8	7	4	4			32
9–3 to 9–8..	1	2	3	4	8	5	7	7		1			38
8–9 to 9–2..	3	2	5	4	6	7	6	1					34
8–3 to 8–8..	4	3	8	3	9	5	2						34
7–9 to 8–2..	4	6	7	10	9								36
7–3 to 7–8..	10	10	11	3									34
6–9 to 7–2..	21	13	5										39
6–3 to 6–8..	24	8											32
5–9 to 6–2..	30												30
5–3 to 5–8..	5												5
Total........	103	46	46	31	43	31	40	37	37	49	28	30	521
Number over-age....	44	25	30	18	25	19	25	22	29	27	20	21	305
Number normal-age.	54	21	16	13	18	12	13	14	8	17	8	6	200
Number under-age...	5						2	1		5		3	16

* Report of a Survey of the Public Schools of Shelbyville, Kentucky, p. 176. Bulletin of the Bureau of School Service, vol. I, no. 1. Lexington, Kentucky: University of Kentucky, 1928.

TABLE 7. DISTRIBUTION OF PUPILS BY GRADES AND BY YEARS IN SCHOOL — A GRADE-PROGRESS CHART *

Years in School	Grades												Total
	1 B	1 A	2 B	2 A	3 B	3 A	4 B	4 A	5 B	5 A	6 B	6 A	
Under ½	62												62
½	2	10											12
1	6	20	29	1									56
1½	1	5	2	9	1								18
2	2	1	14	8	23								48
2½		1		2	1	10							14
3			5		8	19	11	15	2				60
3½				2		1	3	13					19
4	1			3	3	8	9	8	11	17			60
4½						1	2	1					4
5	1		2	2			3	4	9	5	10	4	40
5½									2	1	5	1	9
6				1		3	5	2	11	7	11	8	48
6½											1		1
7						1	1		2	5	2	10	21
7½							1				1		2
8						1	1	1	2	2	3	1	11
8½													0
9								1			1		2
9½													0
10												1	1
Total	75	37	52	28	36	44	36	45	39	37	34	25	488
Number accelerated				1	1			15	2	17		4	40
Number normal progress	62	10	29	9	23	10	11	13	11		10	1	189
Number retarded	13	27	23	18	12	34	25	17	26	20	24	20	259

* Report of a Survey of the Public Schools of Shelbyville, Kentucky, p. 177. Bulletin of the Bureau of School Service, vol. I, no. 1. Lexington, Kentucky: University of Kentucky, 1928.

been in school longer than is normal for his grade is said to be retarded; the others are said to be making normal progress.

Plans for Overcoming Difficulties of the Graded System

A teacher must deal, under modern school conditions, with groups of pupils and for that reason the graded system cannot be abandoned. Economy demands that there be brought together in a single classroom sometimes as many as forty pupils. This number precludes attention in any intimate way to individual differences. The effort is therefore made to reduce the number of pupils in a class or to find some other way of overcoming the maladjustments that result from grouping and grading. Some of the devices which have been tried, in addition to the St. Louis plan described earlier, may be considered and commented on with respect to their success or limitations.

The semester plan of promotion. If the school is organized on the basis of grade groups, each representing one year's progress for the child, the failure of the pupil to be promoted means that he must repeat the work of an entire year. A device that has been employed in large numbers of American school systems to provide greater flexibility in the promotional arrangement is the division of the school year into two semesters, with promotions at the end of each semester. The curriculum is then organized on a semester basis, and thus the pupil who fails is under the necessity of repeating the work of only the half year instead of that of the entire year.

The semester plan of promotion is feasible only where the number of children is large enough to provide groups of economical size for instructional purposes. The semester organization is common in city school systems, but in rural regions, where sparseness of population results in relatively small classes, the semester plan is not generally used.

Some investigations indicate that the semester plan does not result in any real economy for pupils, particularly for those who go from the elementary school into the secondary school at mid-year. The curriculum opportunities in the secondary school are almost always more restricted for the pupils entering at the beginning of the second semester of the year than for those entering at the first semester. Entrance to college is also somewhat awkward at any point other than at the beginning of the academic year. Thus the pupil who is either accelerated or retarded in the elementary school by an odd number of semesters is likely to find considerable inconvenience in arranging his program in the secondary school and college.

The assistant-teacher plan. A plan for overcoming the difficulties of the graded system, developed at Batavia, New York, calls for the assignment of an assistant teacher to each class group. The classes are composed of from 25 to 35 per cent more pupils than usual, and the assistant teacher devotes her time to helping the slow pupils keep up with the work of the class. This plan aims to eliminate failure and to move all the pupils along regularly from grade to grade each year.

The Batavia plan seems to rest on the theory that slowness of a pupil in learning can be overcome by increased attention on the part of the teacher. There is room for considerable doubt as to the soundness of this theory. It will be observed, furthermore, that the plan makes no provision for the bright pupil, but requires him to move along at the average pace.

The parallel curriculum plan. Another plan provides for the progress of pupils along two parallel tracks, one requiring eight years for completion and the other six, each covering the same content. A plan of this type, developed at Cambridge, Massachusetts, provides for three promotion periods yearly. The pupils are assigned to the fast-moving or to the slow-moving group in accordance with their ability. Transfers can readily be arranged at certain points for pupils who are found to be able to move either more or less rapidly than the group to which they are assigned.

This plan makes a better provision for the bright pupils than for the dull ones. Although adjustments for individuals are more readily possible when there are two rates of progress available than when there is only one rate for all, the fact still remains that numerous children are not suited exactly to the rates of progress required in either of the two programs.

Individual progress plan.   A plan providing for a high degree of flexibility in the progress of pupils was developed at Pueblo, Colorado, and later extended to a few other cities.   This plan provides individual progress for each pupil at his own rate, with promotion to the next grade at any time during the school year when the work of one grade is completed.   At the beginning of each school year the pupil simply starts at the point where he left off at the end of the preceding year.

The plan requires the abandonment of the recitation as such and the substitution of individual or laboratory methods.   Some of the pupils within the grade group may work together in a small section at some time if they happen to be at the same point of development, but such groups are not stable and each pupil is expected to progress at his own rate.   The teacher spends her time passing from desk to desk directing and assisting the work of the pupils and determining their readiness for progress to the next unit.   Promotions are based entirely on the ability to do the work that is expected to be covered.

The Pueblo plan, it will be observed, is a compromise between the older form of individual instruction and the necessity of supervision of a group by a single teacher.   In a few centers, notably the San Francisco Teachers College and the Winnetka, Illinois, school system, the plan of individual instruction has been experimented with further.

Differentiated course plan.   A plan which has been tried out in a number of city school systems provides for differentiation of the requirements for promotion of pupils in accordance with their ability.   The pupils of average ability are expected to complete the normal course of study.   The bright pupils are given an enriched curriculum and are expected to cover much more than the normal amount of material at their grade level in order to be promoted to the next grade. The pupils of low ability are given a curriculum containing only the bare essentials. Thus, while the average pupil might read five or six books in his first-grade reading experience, the slow pupil might read only one, and the bright pupil might read ten or more.

It is important to note that under this plan the bright pupil does not undertake work beyond the level of the grade to which he is assigned; the additional books which he reads in the first grade are of a difficulty suited to the first grade, not to the second grade. The plan thus enriches the program for the bright pupil at the grade level corresponding to his chronological age and does not provide for his completion of the elementary school at an age earlier than is normal.

The differentiated curriculum plan has the great advantage of adapting the work to the pace of practically any pupil, except possibly those of the very lowest mental ability. The superior pupil is encouraged to work to the limit of his capacity and the amount of material covered in the enriched curriculum for the bright group may vary considerably from pupil to pupil. Assignment of a pupil to one of the three groups may be changed at any time without interfering with his progress through the grades. The plan can best be followed where the number of children is large enough to permit several class groups in each grade; some schools, however, have found it possible to vary the curriculum in this manner within any one grade group, thus adapting the plan to systems enrolling only a small number of pupils.

Ability grouping. Another plan sets up different rates of progress for dull and bright pupils without changing the kind or amount of subject matter covered. By means of intelligence tests or other measures of ability pupils are assigned to instructional sections that are relatively homogeneous, with the expectation that the rate of progress of the pupils within each group will then be approximately the same.

The plan of ability grouping is feasible only in city systems where a considerable number of children are housed in a single building. Usually three groups are differentiated, known in some systems as the X, Y, and Z groups, respectively. Under normal conditions the number of groups from the average ability level is two or three times the number at either the low or the high ability level.

Evidence that favors the plan appears in certain careful studies of the results obtained by homogeneous grouping of pupils, but the evidence with respect to the relative merits of various bases of groupings is conflicting and inclusive. It appears from the studies made that homogeneous grouping is of greatest benefit to dull children, and of least benefit to bright children; in fact, the bright children frequently do not make as satisfactory progress under the plan of ability grouping as under the plan of heterogeneous grouping.

The ungraded room. Another plan that has been adopted in a number of city school systems sets up in each elementary school a room not designated for any grade level, where the instruction is individual. The pupil who is falling behind in his work in one of the regular grade groups can be assigned to the ungraded room for a time; here he may progress at his own rate and may then transfer back to a regular grade whenever a class reaches the point at which he is working. Thus a pupil, who during the year is found to be unable to keep up with the work of his class, may be assigned to the ungraded room; at the end of some months he may have made up his deficiency and progressed sufficiently to enable him either to fit into the regular work of the class from which he was temporarily withdrawn or to join some other regular class group. The ungraded room, because of its individualized instruction, may have a much smaller number of pupils per teacher than is normal for the regular classes.

The plan, in theory, also cares for the needs of bright pupils by permitting them to cover certain work more rapidly than is normal, thus allowing the superior pupils to skip a grade with no loss of curriculum content. In actual practice, however, it seldom proves feasible to assign many bright pupils to the ungraded room, and hence the organization has served chiefly the dull pupils. Under such circumstances the ungraded room almost inevitably becomes stigmatized as a "dumbbell" room and the pupils who are assigned to it develop an unfortunate attitude towards the organization.

Conclusion. This brief review of several types of reorganization that have been or are being tried in an endeavor to adjust the curriculum of the schools to the individual differences of pupils indicates a vigorous movement away from the formal lockstep imposed by a rigid graded system. Varying degrees of satisfaction have been found in the use of these plans; none of them, with the exception of the plan of semester promotion, has been adopted extensively. It is evident that removal of the handicaps arising from the graded system is still far from being accomplished in the American educational system.

Major Sections in the Graded School

Besides the grouping into the grades representing a year's progress for the normal pupil, the elementary school is divided into larger sections that are more or less generally recognized. Three sections are commonly distinguished in the eight-year elementary school: the primary, the intermediate, and the grammar grades. In the six-year elementary school the last of these sections becomes a part of the junior high school rather than of the elementary school. Teachers are somewhat specialized with respect to each of the levels of the elementary school and in some states a distinct certificate, based on a differentiated curriculum of preparation, is required for teaching in each of the different levels of the elementary school.

In the primary grades, which are usually considered to comprise the first three years of the elementary school, the relationship between pupils and teacher is close and personal. This grade level provides for most children the transition stage from the home to the institutionalized form of schooling, and the teacher must serve as a sort of foster mother to the children during at least the first part of the primary period.

In the intermediate grades, usually comprising the fourth, fifth, and sixth years of the program, the pupils have acquired a measure of independence and are busy perfecting themselves in tool subjects such as reading and arithmetic. They are also studying such content subjects as geography and history. In schools in which the curriculum has been enriched they study also the rudiments of natural science and social studies other than history.

The grammar grades are essentially a part of secondary education, whether set up as parts of a junior high school or not. In a well-managed eight-year elementary school it is customary for the teaching in the grammar grades to be departmentalized, so that one teacher instructs in arithmetic, another in history, another in literature, and so throughout the whole list of subjects.

THE CURRICULUM OF THE ELEMENTARY SCHOOL

The elementary school has a curriculum that deals with rudimentary subjects. It is concerned with general education, with the types of educational experience that everyone needs in order to be reasonably effective as a member of modern society. From the negative point of view it may be noted that the curriculum of the elementary school does not stress subjects such as foreign languages and advanced mathematics.

The elementary school is concerned, furthermore, with the task of providing pupils with the intellectual tools necessary for their further education. It is during this period that skill in reading is developed, a skill that is essential to further progress in any line of educational endeavor. The pupil must be thoroughly grounded in the fundamentals of arithmetic in the elementary school, so that both in life situations and in his further educational experience he will be able to use arithmetic effectively as a tool. Handwriting, spelling, and correct use of the mother tongue are other subjects that are studied, in part, at least, as tools for effective further progress in education.

The schools of the United States today exhibit a high degree of uniformity in the curriculum of the first six grades. Diversity in curriculum among school systems becomes apparent after the sixth year. There are minor differences in the content of the curriculum of the first six years or in the grade placement of subjects, but the educational experiences that are considered appropriate to this period are similar in all the systems of the United States.

The elementary school was originally conceived as the final limit of education for the great majority of pupils. Today the American educational system has far outgrown this limitation and, as noted in an earlier connection, the secondary school is now enrolling a substantial majority of all the pupils of the appropriate age group. This fact means that the function of general education, which was once exclusively the field of the elementary school, has today moved up into the secondary school and indeed occupies much of the attention even at the college level. With this lengthened period for general education, the American educational system now has an opportunity, such as was never before available, for the thorough preparation of the young people of the oncoming generation for their responsibilities as citizens and members of the social order.

One of the most important developments in the history of elementary education was the report of the Committee of Fifteen. This committee of the National Education Association under the leadership of William H. Maxwell was appointed in 1893 and made its report in 1895. The need for a study of the elementary school was brought into the foreground by the appointment one year earlier of the Committee of Ten for the study of the secondary school.

The report of the Committee of Fifteen raised vigorous question about the limitations of the elementary-school curriculum as it then existed, and recommended an enrichment of the program by the addition of many subjects that would be interesting and profitable to pupils. A time allotment was also suggested for the various subjects of the elementary-school curriculum.

Those who know the elementary-school curriculum only as it has existed in the better managed school systems of the country during the twentieth century can scarcely realize the meagerness of the content of the curriculum in earlier times. The reading material, for example, was extremely limited. Originally it consisted exclusively of religious materials; inasmuch as the only important purpose of the instruction in reading was to prepare for reading the Bible, the beginner was required to read Biblical material at as early a stage as possible. Later some non-religious reading material was introduced into the curriculum of the elementary school but the selections always showed "a good moral tendency." Arithmetic until relatively recent times consisted mainly of drill on the fundamentals and memorization of rules. Such subjects as geography and history, if presented at all, were taught by a catechetical method and pupils were expected to learn their lessons by memorizing pages of the text, to be repeated verbatim to the teacher in proof that the lesson had been correctly learned. To facilitate memorization, the text was sometimes put into rhymed-verse form.

Perhaps the most effective way in which one can obtain a realization of the barrenness of the curriculum content of the earlier elementary schools is by examining some of the old school books. The first quotation which follows illustrates the catechetical method of presenting subject matter. The quotation consists of selected questions and answers from Nathaniel Dwight's *Short but Comprehensive System of the Geography of the World*, published in Hartford in 1795 (quotations are from the Philadelphia edition of 1802):

Q. What is the situation and extent of Scotland?
A. It is situated between 54 and 59 degrees of north latitude, and between 1 and 6 degrees of west longitude; it is 300 miles long, and 190 broad.

Q. How is Scotland bounded?

A. It is bounded on the north, east and west, by the Atlantic Ocean; and on the south by England; and contains 27,794 square miles.

Q What is the air of Scotland?

A. It is in general cold for about nine months in the year; but near the sea it is more temperate than in the interior parts of the country, being warmed by the sea breezes.

Q. What is the soil of Scotland?

A. It is not so fertile as England, nor so well adapted to agriculture; though some are very productive.

Q Is the water in Scotland good?

A. It is said to be better than in most other countries.

Q. Are there any lakes in Scotland?

A. There are many, which the inhabitants call Lochs, well supplied with fish; but two are very remarkable: One near Lochness is on the top of a hill almost two miles high. This lake is small, but it has never been sounded, nor does it ever freeze. About seventeen miles distant is another lake which is frozen all the year.

Q. What are the diversions of the Scots?

A. They are all of the vigorous athletic kind; such as dancing, *goff* and *curling*. The goff is a species of ball playing performed with a bat and a ball, the extremity of the bat being loaded with lead, and the party which strikes the ball with fewest strokes into a hole prepared for the purpose wins the game.

.   .   .   .

Q. What are the characteristics of the Irish?

A. They are impatient of injuries, implacable in their resentments, and vehement in all their affections. They are of quick apprehension; courteous to strangers, and patient of fatigue. The higher classes, and some of the lower, are well educated, and as respectable as their neighbours in the like circumstances.

Q. What are the customs and diversions of the Irish?

A. There are a few customs existing in Ireland peculiar to this country. These are the funeral howlings and presenting their corpses in the streets to excite the charity of strangers, their convivial meetings on Sunday, and dancing to bag-pipes, which are usually attended with quarreling. They are attached to the music of the bag-pipe, and their tunes are plaintive and melancholy.

.   .   .   .

Q. What are the customs of the Spanish?

A. The ladies paint themselves very much. Both sexes live very temperately, drinking but little wine. They usually drink coffee and

chocolate, morning and evening, and eat flesh at noon.   Both men
and women commonly sleep after eating.

Q. What are their diversions?

A. They consist chiefly in dancing, serenading and bull-baiting,
which last is a very barbarous practice.

.   .   .   .

Q. What is the temper of the New-England people?

A. They are frank and open, not easily irritated, but easily pacified.
They are at the same time bold and enterprising.   The women are
educated to house-wifery, excellent companions and house-keepers;
spending their liesure time in reading books of useful information, and
rendering themselves not only useful, but amiable and pleasing.

The following quotation from *The Progressive Reader or Juvenile Monitor*,[1] Concord, New Hampshire, 1830, illustrates the use
of rhymed verse in the early textbooks.

STORY OF AMERICA IN VERSE

Columbus was a sailor brave,
The first that crossed th' Atlantic wave.
In fourteen hundred and ninety-two,
He came far o'er the ocean blue,
Where ne'er a ship had sailed before,
And found a wild and savage shore,
Where naked men in forests prowled,
And bears and panthers roamed and howled.

At length, when years had passed away,
Some English came to Virginia;
'Twas sixteen hundred seven; be sure
You let this in your mind endure;
For 'twas the first bold colony
Planted in North America;
The first that laid the deep foundation,
On which has since been built a nation.
Well, here they raised a far-famed Town
On James' river, called Jamestown.
They struggled hard 'gainst many sorrows,
Sickness and want, and Indian arrows;

---

[1] Clifton Johnson, *Old-Time Schools and School-Books*, pp. 252-53.   New
York: The Macmillan Company, 1917.

But bold and strong at length they grew,
And were a brave and manly crew.

'Twas eight years after this, — I mean
The year sixteen hundred fifteen, —
Some Dutch, from Holland, settled pat on
An Island which they called Manhattan,
And straight they sat themselves to work,
And built the city of New-York.
Now let the laughing wags and jokers
Say that the Dutch are stupid smokers;
We only tell, that, dull or witty,
They founded famous New-York city;
The largest city in the west,
For trade and commerce quite the best.

The modern curriculum of the elementary school is far in advance of these meager materials. The following statement showing the expansion of the curriculum in the school system of Newton, Massachusetts, illustrates what has been going on in many other school systems in all parts of the country.

Criticism is often voiced against modern educational practices and objectives as a consequence of the large number of subjects taught. Some of these are derided as "fads and frills" by those who believe that the old and narrow curriculum was not only adequate for all pupils but that it resulted in a better and more thorough training. It is true that the number of school subjects has greatly increased since the establishment of public education, and the end has probably not yet been reached.

Whether or not all these larger opportunities are necessary or justifiable, neither the schools nor the teachers are responsible for them. For the most part, they have resulted from legislation inspired by people who have visioned the need of a broader education and a better preparation for citizenship in this modern and complex civilization.

It is undeniably true that these larger opportunities have added materially to the cost of education and for that reason more than any other, the teaching of these subjects has been criticized. Special teachers must be employed and extra equipment and accommodations provided. This situation, however, is not quite so expensive as it might appear, for all pupils are not required or expected to pursue all of the subjects.... Only by discontinuing subjects requiring special teachers can any appreciable saving be made, and all these subjects are required by law.

After this statement a chart is exhibited showing in outline the changes that have taken place in the curriculum of the elementary schools of Newton.

EXPANSION OF ELEMENTARY SCHOOL CURRICULUM — 1775 TO 1925

1775[1]

Spelling	Writing	Arithmetic
Reading		

1850

Grammar	Reading	Arithmetic
Geography	Writing	Good behavior
Spelling		

1875

Physiology and hygiene	Spelling	Good behavior
Drawing	Reading	Music
Grammar	Writing	History
Geography	Arithmetic	Agriculture

1900

Manual training	Geography	Music
Sewing	Spelling	History of the United States
Physiology and hygiene	Reading	Elements of Science
Drawing	Writing	Agriculture
English, grammar and language	Arithmetic	
	Good behavior	

1925

Duties of citizenship	English, grammar and language	Music
Manual training	Geography	History and Constitution of the United States
Physical education	Spelling	Nature study
Homemaking	Reading	Literature
Physiology and hygiene	Writing	Civics
Art and handwork	Arithmetic	
	Good behavior	

[1] *Annual Report of the School Department, Newton, Mass.*, XCII:17–19 (1931).

One sometimes hears a comment to the effect that the elementary school of today is failing in its functions because it no longer sticks to the meager curriculum of the three R's. Some have even stated that the elementary school is neglecting the fundamentals, and is turning out children who cannot read or write or compute correctly. Such people have not examined the evidence carefully, for there is no doubt whatever that instruction in these rudimentary and fundamental subjects is today far more successful than ever before in the history of education. The enrichment of the program by the new subjects has not been at the expense of sound and thorough preparation in the older subjects. The new subjects have been attacked as wasteful of the taxpayers' money, but it must not be forgotten that these subjects, in addition to their obvious utility for both the social and the individual development of the child, have been responsible for transforming the elementary school from a dreary routine to an enjoyable experience. The curriculum of the elementary school is today for pupils not merely a preparation for life — it is life. Universal education cannot succeed on any other basis.

BIBLIOGRAPHY

Burton, William H., *Introduction to Education*, pp. 194–211.

Clapp, Frank L., Wayland J. Chase, and Curtis Merriman, *Introduction to Education*, pp. 229–57.

Dougherty, James Henry, Frank Hermon Gorman, and Claude Anderson Phillips, *Elementary School Organization and Management*. New York: The Macmillan Company, 1936. xx + 453 pp.

Douglass, Aubrey A., *The American School System*, pp. 115–25, 130–55.

Hockett, J. A., and E. W. Jacobson, *Modern Practices in the Elementary School*. Boston: Ginn and Company, 1938. v + 346 pp.

Lane, Robert H., *The Progressive Elementary School*. Boston: Houghton Mifflin Company, 1938. ix + 198 + xi pp.

Otto, Henry J., *Elementary School Organization and Administration*. New York: D. Appleton-Century Company, 1934. xviii + 652 pp.

Parker, Samuel Chester, *A Textbook in the History of Modern Elementary Education*. Boston: Ginn and Company, 1912. xxiv + 506 pp.

Patterson, S. Howard, Ernest A. Choate, and Edmund de S. Brunner, *The School in American Society*, pp. 196–200.

Reavis, William C., Paul R. Pierce, and Edward H. Stullken. *The Elementary School:* Its Organization and Administration. Chicago: University of Chicago Press, 1931. x + 572 pp.

Reeder, Ward, *A First Course in Education*, pp. 449–53.

Report of the Commission on Length of Elementary Education. Supplementary Educational Monographs, no. 34. Chicago: Department of Education, University of Chicago, 1927. xii + 168 pp.

Smith, Payson, Frank W. Wright, and Associates, *Education in the Forty-Eight States*, pp. 19–26, 149–55. Staff Study no. 1, Advisory Committee on Education.

Wilson, Lester M., and I. L. Kandel, *Introduction to the Study of American Education*, pp. 125–58.

CHAPTER XIII

THE SECONDARY SCHOOL

THE TERM "secondary education" suggests immediately to the average American the institution known as the
"high school." The term "high school," however, should be
avoided in a general discussion for, as has been pointed out in
previous connections, there have been in the historical development of American education at least three different types of
secondary schools: the Latin grammar school, the academy, and
the high school. Furthermore, in European practice the term
"high school, *Hochschule, école supérieure*," means an institution
of university or college grade. For these reasons, it seems best
to use the term "secondary education" rather than the more
familiar institutional designation, in referring to the school that
follows the elementary school and precedes the college.

The secondary school originally was clearly defined in terms of
its function of preparing for entrance to the college, for the Latin
grammar school had no other function. For many decades, however, it has been apparent that this definition is no longer suitable
for secondary education in the United States; large numbers of
pupils who attended the academy did not intend to go on to college, and a large majority of those who attend the modern high
school do not continue into an institution of higher education.

Perhaps the best way in which the secondary school can be
defined is by reference to the age group served. It is generally
recognized that the secondary school ministers to the needs of
pupils in the early years of adolescence. The age at which
adolescence begins and the age at which it ends varies from person
to person, but the period can be roughly defined as the span from

about age twelve to age eighteen. It will be sufficient for the purposes of the present chapter to define the secondary school as the institution serving the needs of young people of approximately those ages.

The organizational units of the American educational system which should be classed as secondary education are not fully agreed upon. The present-day high school based on the completion of the eight grades of the elementary school, and the junior high school based on the completion of six years of elementary education, are universally recognized as institutions of secondary education in this country. The junior college, which carries the student two years beyond the end of the four-year high school, is by many regarded as appropriately a part of secondary education, although some authorities classify the junior college as a part of higher education. Less frequently one meets the suggestion that the intermediate grades of the elementary school are in reality a part of secondary education, and some would classify all instruction in the colleges and universities below the graduate level as a part of secondary education. For the purposes of this discussion, secondary education will be considered to include the present institutions known as the junior high school, the high school, and the junior college.

THE STANDARDIZATION OF THE AMERICAN HIGH SCHOOL

The public high school in the United States developed in the period following the Civil War, but the communities establishing such schools found no model on which to base the organization and program. For the most part the high school tended to copy the curriculums of both the Latin grammar school and the academy, but there was no universally accepted agreement regarding the length of the program, the nature of the courses to be offered, and the arrangement of the subjects.

The statistics reported by the United States Commissioner of

Education did not even recognize the public high school as a distinct classification until 1890. In the years prior to that the data given for secondary schools seem to relate only to the privately controlled or proprietary academy. In some of the Commissioner's reports during the 1880's there is evidence of the confusion prevailing among educators with respect to the definition of the high school. Local communities apparently differed considerably in the types of high schools maintained, some providing only a two or three year course, others a four year or even a longer program.

Educators began to be aware of this confusion and, as a result of agitation over the question,[1] the National Education Association in 1892 appointed a Committee of Ten to study the problem of secondary education. With President Charles W. Eliot of Harvard as its chairman, the Committee of Ten completed its work and published its report the next year. The pronouncements of the Committee had a most important effect on the program of American secondary education during at least a generation thereafter, for this was the first official statement regarding the nature of the program that should be offered in the public high schools. Progressively minded educators proceeded to introduce the recommendations of the Committee into their high schools, and the secondary-school program which has been followed by the majority of the educated persons of the present adult generation was the direct result of the pronouncements of the Committee of Ten. The importance of the effects produced by the work of the Committee warrant a fairly full treatment of the nature of its organization and procedure.

In order to carry on its work the Committee of Ten appointed nine subcommittees, or conferences as they were called, to deal

[1] Charles W. Eliot, "The Gap between the Elementary Schools and the Colleges." *Journal of Proceedings* of the National Educational Association, 1890, pp. 522–33.

J. H. Baker, "Uniformity in Requirements for Admission to College." Report of Committee on Secondary Education. *Journal of Proceedings* of the National Educational Association, 1891, pp. 306–16.

with the following specific subject-matter fields: Latin, Greek, English, other modern languages, mathematics, physical sciences, biological sciences, history and other social studies, and geography. Ten specialists in the subjects concerned were appointed to each of these conferences. Those appointed were for the most part college professors in the respective subject-matter fields; there was in addition some representation from the privately controlled academies, and some, but relatively few, persons in the conferences who came from service in the public high school.

The conference group in each field met and prepared a report concerning the place of its subject-matter specialty in the program. The Committee of Ten drafted a set of questions to guide the work of the conferences in preparing their reports. Each subcommittee or conference was asked to deal with questions such as the following: (1) How much instruction is needed in this subject, especially in the four years of high school? (2) At what level should the study first be introduced? (3) Should the subject be accepted for college entrance? (4) Should the subject be treated differently for pupils going to college and for those not going to college?

All the conference reports were in agreement on the last two of these questions. Without exception each of the groups of subject-matter specialists concluded that their subject should be accepted for college entrance and each of the groups was of the opinion that there should be no differentiation in the organization or treatment of the subject for pupils who were going on to college and for those who did not intend to go to college. The conference reports differed somewhat in their responses to the second question, regarding the level at which the subject should be introduced. Some of the groups of specialists suggested that their subject should be introduced in the elementary school and carried through the high school; most of the reports recommended the introduction of the subjects in the first year of high school.

The greatest difficulty arose because of the answers regarding the amount of study that should be offered in each subject during the high-school period. Many of the conference groups con-cluded that the amount of time devoted to their subject should be increased over that which was then provided in the secondary schools, and practically all of the conferences outlined a program of at least four years of work in their subjects during the high-school period.

The report on history and other social studies, for example, looked at the then current offering of history in the secondary schools and found it entirely unsatisfactory. Most of the high schools that were offering any history at all were providing a one-year course simply labeled "history," in which everything was covered from the Garden of Eden to the present. This, the subject-matter specialists agreed, was very bad. They proposed instead a four-year program of courses in history, arranged in a chronological organization to include Greek and Roman history in the first year, medieval history in the second year, English history in the third year, and American history in the fourth year. Such a series of courses, they said, would represent a scholarly organization of the subject matter and would give the pupil a comprehensive grasp of history.

The difficulties entailed by the series of such recommendations are now obvious. When the Committee of Ten added up the total of the suggested offerings, it found far more than could be included in four years or even in a much longer period. Another difficulty, apparently not foreseen by the Committee of Ten, is also illustrated by the conference report on history and other social studies. Elimination of many pupils had always taken place during the four years of the high school; a large percentage of those who entered did not stay for the second year and further elimination had marked each successively higher level of the pro-gram. The report of the conference, it will be noted, places American history in the fourth year, at a point in the curriculum which a great majority of the young people never reached. Be-cause of the widespread adoption of the recommendations of the

Committee of Ten, many adults of the present generation have been introduced as first-year high-school pupils to the history of Greece and Rome, while only a small number have had opportunity at the secondary level to study the history of their own country.

To take care of the overcrowding that obviously would result in the high-school curriculum if the reports of the conference sub-committees were to be adopted, the Committee of Ten made certain recommendations regarding the organization of the high-school curriculum. One suggestion was to the effect that type curriculums might be set up with some differentiation in the subject matter of each. Thus there might be: a classical curriculum, which would lay emphasis on the ancient languages; a modern language curriculum, which would emphasize English and other modern foreign languages; a scientific curriculum, which would stress mathematics and the physical and biological sciences.

A second suggestion was that the elective system might be introduced into the high school. Under the elective system the school would be expected to offer a variety of subjects, including all those called for in the report, but each pupil would choose for himself the subjects of study that would be of most value to him. Both the type-curriculum plan and the elective system had earlier been adopted in the colleges, and the idea of introducing these plans into the high school was therefore based on the experience with similar plans at the college level.

The third suggestion made by the Committee of Ten was for the extension of the high-school program downward to include the seventh and eighth grades, thus providing in the high school a six-year curriculum. The addition of two years' time in the high-school curriculum, it was believed, would afford the opportunity to include a large amount of the material demanded by the conference reports. This suggestion was at first viewed with considerable suspicion by those interested in the elementary school, and a short time later the report of the Committee of Fifteen, which dealt with the problem of the elementary-school curriculum, suggested that the only high-school subjects that should be considered for introduction as early as the seventh grade were algebra and Latin.

Although the suggestion was made for taking over the seventh and eighth grades as a part of the high school, the recommendations of the Committee of Ten tended to standardize the high-school program at a length of four years.

The Committee of Ten made the further suggestion that the units of instruction in the secondary school be defined in terms of the number of recitation periods per week in a given subject. It was suggested that the normal program for a high-school pupil should consist of four subjects, in each of which there would be five recitations per week. The Committee strongly recommended against the inclusion of any courses to which less than four periods per week were devoted.

The suggestion with respect to the organization of offerings and the number of subjects to be studied by the pupil each year had a most important effect on the arrangement of the secondary-school curriculum, for this recommendation was widely accepted. A decade or more later the organization of subject matter into these standard units was still further solidified by the action of one of the endowed foundations. The Carnegie Foundation for the Advancement of Teaching, which undertook to provide retirement allowances for college and university professors, found itself under the necessity of defining the types of higher institutions in which staff members would be eligible for participation in the retirement plan. In defining the institutions of higher education for this purpose the Foundation introduced a prescription stating that only those colleges and universities would be considered which required for entrance at least fifteen units of secondary school subject matter. For a description of the units the Foundation referred to the earlier definition of the Committee of Ten, and because of this connection, the course unit came to be known as the "Carnegie Unit." Even today the plan of organizing the subject matter in secondary schools is in terms of the so-called

"Carnegie Units"; a curriculum cast in any other mold is in danger of not being considered academically respectable.

Another important feature of the report of the Committee of Ten was its recommendation with respect to the scope of subject matter to be offered in the secondary school. The Committee recommended that high-school offerings cover some twenty-five specified subjects and stated emphatically that other subjects should be offered only at the option of local authorities and not in substitution for any of the preferred subjects. The organization of the conference subcommittees, as listed previously, gives a clue to the subjects considered essential by the Committee. No subcommittees were set up for the fine arts or the vocational subjects; these subjects, perhaps for that reason, were not included as a part of the necessary offering in the secondary school.

Although the report of the Committee of Ten had great influence on the organization of American secondary education, another factor was also at work. Social forces, which were either neglected by educators or were only dimly understood, began to compel the introduction of new subjects that had not obtained the approval of the Committee of Ten. In any case where a conservative attitude of educators is opposed to important social forces one can readily foresee which side will be victorious. Secondary schools, quite contrary to the recommendations of the Committee of Ten, were soon forced to expand their offerings, particularly in those fields of the fine arts and the vocational subjects that had been completely neglected by the academicians of the Committee of Ten.

The extent of the expansion of the secondary-school curriculum may be realized by comparing information given in a speech made by Charles W. Eliot in 1892 with that given in the National Survey of Secondary Education in 1932. Mr. Eliot reported that a total of thirty different subjects were found in the offerings of the secondary schools of the country in 1892. Forty years later the National Survey of Secondary Education reported a study, based on offerings in 148 cities of medium size, in which a total of 419 different courses were found.

Although it is true that in respect to the scope of offerings the report of the Committee of Ten has not been followed in the American secondary schools, in other respects the recommendations of the Committee have had a most important effect on the program. Even the new subjects that were introduced were made to conform to the pattern of the subject-matter units recommended by the Committee. The length of the program, as suggested by the Committee, has been regarded as formally fixed, and it is only with the greatest difficulty and against the opposition of many established interests that communities have been able to extend their secondary-school programs downward into the junior high school or upward into the junior college period beyond the level contemplated by the report of the Committee of Ten. Even with the expansion in the scope of offerings there has tended to persist a distinction between the respectable subjects recommended by the Committee and the new subjects that have been introduced because of social demands. The report of the Committee of Ten can quite properly be regarded as the authority under which the present pattern of American secondary education was determined.

SUBJECT-MATTER OFFERINGS OF THE SECONDARY SCHOOL

The most impressive characteristic of the modern American secondary school is the diversity of its subject-matter offerings. As pointed out previously, the survey of 148 medium-sized cities revealed more than four hundred different courses offered in public secondary schools. Another study reported in the National Survey of Secondary Education traced the history of the offerings in typical secondary schools from the period of the Civil War. Up to 1895 the average offerings were slightly less than twenty units, or possibly as many courses as one pupil could have taken

in a five-year period.   In 1930, by contrast, the average offerings
were sixty-seven units, enough to have occupied the attention of
a single pupil for almost seventeen years.   During the more recent
years covered by the investigation, units of subject matter were
being added to the programs of secondary schools at the rate of
about two each year.

The nature of the offering may be examined in each of the
broad subject-matter groupings that are generally recognized.

English

The only subject required of all pupils in present-day secondary
schools is English.   At least three years of study in English are
required in most secondary schools and the opportunity for a
fourth year is generally provided and is commonly accepted by
the majority of pupils in such schools.   This subject is a relatively
new one in the secondary school; it had no prominence until after
the Civil War.   Two purposes are aimed at in English courses: the
development of the pupil's ability to express himself effectively
in writing and speaking the mother tongue; and the cultivation
of knowledge about and appreciation of literature in the English
language.   In some schools courses are offered in allied subjects
such as journalism, creative writing, debating, and dramatics.

Foreign Languages

A notable shift has taken place in the relative emphasis on the
various foreign languages in the secondary-school program.
When the Committee of Ten made its report, Greek was listed as
one of the nine important fields of study; today Greek has practically disappeared from the secondary-school curriculum.   Latin
has also experienced a marked decline in relative popularity; enrollments in this subject have fallen behind the general rate of
increase in the secondary-school enrollment.   The modern foreign
languages have experienced a growth in enrollment, French at
present being the most popular subject in this field.   Prior to the
first World War, German was the most widely taught of the

modern foreign languages but the circumstances of the war caused
the teaching of German to be discontinued in most American
secondary schools and it has come back only slowly in the years
since 1920.   Spanish is taught widely in the secondary schools
of the southwest part of the country but is offered for the most
part only in the larger schools of the other regions of the country.
Scandinavian languages are taught in some schools in the west
north-central region.

The language group as a whole shows a relative decline in importance since 1890, so far as the percentage of pupils enrolled is
concerned.   It is commonly recognized that knowledge of foreign
languages is not as essential as certain other subjects for pupils
who do not go on to college, and even the entrance requirements
of many higher institutions now permit the admission of students
who have had no preparation in foreign languages in the secondary school.

The traditional organization of instruction in the foreign languages in the secondary school devotes the first year to instruction in grammar and composition and to the building of a reading
vocabulary.   Later years are then devoted to the reading of
literature in the foreign language and to the perfecting of the
pupil's knowledge of grammar and the extension of his reading,
writing, and speaking vocabulary.   Relatively few pupils who
take a foreign language in the secondary school study it for more
than two years.   As a result most pupils never attain any permanent facility in the use of the language or in the understanding
of its literature.   In recent times there has been an attempt to
reorganize the methods of teaching languages; pupils in some
progressive schools begin with the development of reading skills,
leaving the more formal aspects of grammar to later stages of the
program.

The Sciences

Important shifts have taken place in the science subjects offered in secondary schools.   Physical geography was widely

taught in the schools of a generation ago, but now is offered much less frequently. Botany and zoology, as separate subjects, are now replaced by biology. Smaller percentages of pupils are now studying physics and chemistry. There has been wide acceptance of a plan providing for a general science course, usually taught in the early years of the secondary-school program. The science courses offered in the secondary school usually make provision for some laboratory experience on the part of the pupils.

Social Studies

The field in which perhaps the most important development has taken place in the secondary-school curriculum is that of the social studies. As has already been pointed out, the report of the Committee of Ten encouraged a considerable expansion in the offerings in history, although this report made little or no mention of the other social studies. The standard offering in history during the years following the report of the Committee of Ten consisted of four years of history, and while the average pupil was not able to find a place for more than two units in his four-year curriculum, even this amount represents a marked increase over that provided by the typical secondary-school curriculum of earlier times.

The other social studies have been slowly developed in the secondary-school curriculum. Some secondary schools during the nineteenth century introduced the study of the United States constitution, and near the beginning of the present century there was a growing tendency to offer a course in civil government. During the second decade of the present century courses in civics, variously known as community civics or American government, became the standard offering. The courses in community civics were, for the most part, designed for the early years of the secondary-school period; those in American government were reserved for the later years. Courses in economics and sociology have been given somewhat infrequently in secondary schools and when offered are usually reserved for pupils in the senior year,

The Fine Arts

Although the report of the Committee of Ten neglected the fine arts as subjects of instruction in the secondary school, these subjects have been widely developed in recent years. Music is generally a required subject in the junior high-school period, but is usually made an elective in the curriculum of the senior high school. The instruction in music is directed toward both vocational and avocational ends, and distinct efforts are made to develop a fundamental basis for appreciation of music. The opportunity offered pupils to develop their musical interests through participation in bands, glee clubs, choruses, and orchestras is an outstanding feature of the instruction in music in the American secondary school.

The graphic arts were first introduced into the schools because of their industrial applications. The petition presented in 1869 to the legislature of Massachusetts by a group of citizens who were interested in having the subject of drawing added to the curriculum has already been quoted in Chapter IV. It will be recalled that the argument in that petition for the introduction of art rested chiefly on the advantages that such training would give to American manufacturers and industrialists.

Today the emphasis in the secondary-school program is largely on appreciation of the products of the graphic arts and on the development of creative ability. Like music, drawing and painting are offered as required subjects in the junior high-school period but are usually electives in the program of the senior high school.

Vocational Subjects

The largest expansion in numbers of subjects has taken place in recent years in the area of vocational preparation. Manual training was first introduced following the Centennial Exposition of 1876, when it was realized, after the distribution of prizes, that American craftsmen could not compete on equal terms with those from Europe. The agitation for a type of instruction which

would prepare young people for craftsmanship fitted in neatly
with the ideas of educators who were beginning to realize the
need for a broadened curriculum in the schools. The early efforts
in this direction naturally cast the training in the forms of the
older established subjects, and manual training became a somewhat formal, abstract, and disciplinary study, rather than a specific preparation for a skilled vocation.

A trend toward trade training developed after the turn of the
century. Trade courses were organized for the express purpose
of providing training in skills more or less specifically related to
the work in which the pupil was later to engage. Vocational
education, as this type of preparation has been called, was first
established in Massachusetts in the early 1900's and later in other
states. The movement soon gained national support, and in
1917 Congress enacted the Smith-Hughes Act which provided
funds for a program of vocational education in every state.

One of the fields in which vocational preparation was early
introduced, even before trade courses were organized, was that
of the commercial subjects, such as bookkeeping, stenography,
and typing. To a large extent instruction in these commercial
subjects was given at first in private and proprietary schools,
often known as business colleges. In 1911 a survey in the city
of Chicago found that the tuition fees paid for instruction in
commercial subjects in private schools were in the aggregate equal
to the total annual public expenditures for secondary education
in that city. As a result of such findings, commercial subjects
were added to the curriculum of the public secondary schools.

The federal subsidies which were provided through the Smith-
Hughes and subsequent Acts for vocational education in agriculture, trades and industries, and home economics, together with
the direct promotional efforts of agents paid from federal and
state funds, have been most important factors in developing vocational education. Today a wide variety of subjects is offered
in the field of vocational education, and courses are provided for
almost every conceivable type of vocation open to secondary-

school graduates. Opportunities have been broadened, not only in the all-day program of secondary schools, but also in evening classes and part-time schools.

Today every well-equipped secondary school provides some opportunity in vocational education for its pupils. In rural areas agriculture and home economics are the usual subjects offered, although in schools located near larger centers of population the commercial subjects are sometimes offered in the rural high schools. The secondary schools in urban areas, being larger than those in rural areas, can offer a wider variety of opportunities, and courses in the commercial subjects, trades and industries, distributive occupations, home economics, and related subjects are widely offered.

Teacher Training in the High School

By the second quarter of the nineteenth century the academy had begun to develop as an important institution for the preparation of teachers for the elementary schools. The secondary schools were the main centers for the preparation of elementary-school teachers for almost a hundred years, although as early as 1839 a state normal school had been organized, and as the years passed a few additional schools of this type developed. The early normal schools were distinctly of the secondary level. It was not until well into the twentieth century that the states began to require preparation beyond the secondary school for certification for elementary-school teaching. The courses offered in the early days in academies and high schools as well as in normal schools were courses in methods of teaching, school law, and in some cases psychology. Today such subjects are offered in the secondary schools of only a few states where certification laws have not yet recognized the desirability of preparation at the college level for all teachers. It seems clear that subjects designed to prepare teachers will soon be eliminated from the programs of secondary schools.

THE INSTITUTIONAL ORGANIZATION OF
SECONDARY EDUCATION

The introduction of the technical and vocational subjects raised a serious question regarding the institutional form of secondary education. These subjects, it must be remembered, were introduced into the schools because of social pressures, and educators as a group were not cordial toward the newcomers. The vocational subjects were obviously of a different type from the traditional academic offerings of the secondary school, and their incorporation into the curriculum disturbed many established practices.

In some cities facilities for vocational education were first provided by the establishment of separate schools in which such subjects could be offered. By this means, it was believed, the traditional program of the existing secondary schools could be saved from contamination and the needs of the nonacademically minded pupils could be served. These separate vocational schools were frequently designated as manual-training high schools, technical high schools, commercial high schools, or vocational high schools.

When the pupils interested in technical and vocational subjects were segregated in the separate institutions, however, it was quickly discovered that they demanded opportunities to study not only the strictly vocational subjects but all the subjects of the traditional secondary-school curriculum as well. Thus the technical and vocational high schools were forced to add to their programs of offerings practically all the academic subjects usually taught in secondary schools. As a result the technical high schools evolved into what are today known as "cosmopolitan" schools, offering a wide variety of subjects of both the cultural and the vocational types.

The establishment of separate vocational schools was naturally possible only in the larger cities where the number of pupils was large enough to provide enrollments for two or more secondary

schools.   In the smaller cities the organization of separate schools
was not feasible and as a result vocational subjects were added
to the program of the existing schools.   The additions of the vocational subjects were usually made gradually and in time the
schools in the smaller cities thus came also to be of the cosmopolitan type.

The question of the type of institution for secondary education
is not yet entirely settled, but the trend is clearly at present in
the direction of the cosmopolitan school.   Although the specialized vocational school is still found in the larger cities and is still
advocated, particularly by those especially interested in vocational education, the program of such schools is actually that
of the cosmopolitan school.   Even in the large cities there are
few strictly academic schools without some vocational subjects
in their programs of instruction.

Some attempts have been made to promote the idea that segregation of the young people destined to enter employment on the
completion of their school work from those who will go on to
college is desirable from an educational standpoint.   Many educators are of the opinion, however, that segregation results in an
undemocratic form of organization and savors too strongly of the
European ideal of a dual system of schools for a two-class society.
It may confidently be stated that the cosmopolitan secondary
school, serving all the children of all the people, is one of the great
triumphs of educational democracy.   If social and economic
stratification is to be avoided, the indication is clear that the cosmopolitan school must remain the dominant institutional form of
secondary education in the United States.

The vocational school has certain limitations.   Only rarely can
it give a pupil the opportunities for complete training that will
prepare him fully for a trade.   The equipment of a school shop
cannot keep pace with the progress of equipment in industrial
establishments.   Furthermore, there are in almost every vocation large numbers of workers for whom an elaborate training,
especially a four-year specialized unit-trade training, is wholly

inappropriate. The great majority of the workers in modern industrial plants are semi-skilled routine workers. The highly specialized trade training offered in the typical separate vocational school is as far removed from the needs of the ordinary pupil, prior to his entry on employment, as is the program of the strictly traditional school which offers only an academic curriculum.

In general it may be said that the secondary schools have outgrown the purposes which they were originally organized to serve. The Latin schools of earlier times were organized and conducted as preprofessional schools designed to educate prospective clergymen and lawyers. The academies introduced some popular subjects. The academies were "people's colleges" far more than were the Latin schools. The modern secondary school has been forced by the demands of its pupils to take on a character much broader than that of its predecessors. A modern cosmopolitan school must provide the literary-mathematical courses which will prepare the pupils who are destined to enter the professions. There is equal need for unit-trade courses which afford basic preparation leading into the highly skilled occupations.

The curriculums which are designed to meet specialized needs have been deficient in their provisions for training pupils for the common duties and responsibilities of the citizen. A new type of curriculum, which can be described as one providing general rather than specialized education, is coming to be recognized. Since practically all young people of the present day continue their education beyond the elementary level, the demand for general education that does not lead into the professions and does not aim at cultivating the higher skills needed in special trades is urgently called for. The great majority of workers in modern industry and agriculture are semi-skilled. They are not specialists. Particularly at the time of entry on first employment the young worker today in most lines of industry does not need to have developed a high degree of technical skill in some occupation. Industry expects to give its workers the necessary specific training after they enter employment.

CURRICULUM ORGANIZATION IN SECONDARY SCHOOLS

The introduction of the technical and vocational subjects and the expansions of offerings in the other fields of secondary-school instruction have made necessary certain changes in the organization of the curriculum.

Plans of Curriculum Organization

Originally the high school offered only a single curriculum, every study being prescribed and all students taking the same subjects in their four-year course. This type of curriculum organization has now disappeared in all except the smallest schools in rural areas.

A later development was the pure multiple type of curriculum. Under this plan the pupil was permitted to choose which of several type curriculums he would follow, but when once the decision was made no choice of courses, or only very limited election, was allowed within the program. The Committee of Ten recommended this type of curriculum organization. Although it was widely followed in the latter part of the nineteenth century, few secondary schools organize their curriculums on this plan today.

Another type of curriculum organization provides certain subjects which are constant and must be carried by all pupils, the remainder of the program being subject to the pupil's election under guidance. The "constants with variables" plan of curriculum organization, as this arrangement is called, thus provides for a core of subjects that are common to the programs of all pupils in the school, but at the same time permits adaptation to individual needs by allowing choice of a variety of electives. This plan of curriculum organization was popular in the early years of the twentieth century, but in recent times has been followed by a decreasing number of schools.

The fourth plan of curriculum organization, which may be designated as the "multiple curriculum with variables," is a combination of the two last-mentioned plans. Type curriculums are set up, each of which has a fairly large core of prescribed subjects; the remainder of the program in each of the curriculums is chosen by the pupil, with the guidance of counselors, from a wide list of electives. Usually the electives must be chosen so as to develop certain blocks or sequences of subject matter, known as majors and minors, in the pupil's program. This plan of the multiple curriculum with variables seems to be the most popular one at present, and the number of schools employing it is steadily increasing.

College Entrance Requirements

As has been indicated in an earlier connection, the requirements for entrance to college have long exercised an important influence on the program of studies and the arrangement of the curriculum in secondary schools. Although the new subjects introduced during the past forty years were not originally on the list of those required for entrance to college, these subjects have proved popular with pupils and large numbers of those who wish to enter college also wish to have the advantage of studying these new subjects. The pressure on the college from these sources has been too great to be withstood and gradually the institutions of higher education have relaxed the subject-matter prescriptions in their entrance requirements.

The National Survey of Secondary Education, published in 1932, presented data showing that the entrance requirements for colleges of liberal arts prescribe specifically some ten of the fifteen high-school units in eastern colleges and about eight in midwestern institutions. The trend at present seems to be distinctly in the direction of less prescription of subjects for entrance to college; colleges have been increasingly liberal in their willingness to accept all types of subjects when taken as part of a pupil's elective program.

Careful investigations show that no subject has unique value in preparing for college. It is true that some subjects seem to be more effective than others in weeding out pupils with low intelligence. If, however, selection on the basis of intelligence is to be the only purpose of requiring certain subjects in secondary schools, the selection could be made more economically through the administration of intelligence tests than through the prescription of subjects in the secondary-school curriculum. Investigations have clearly shown that when intelligence and other factors affecting success in college are held constant, pupils who have studied any given subject in the secondary school do not succeed any better in college than those who have not studied it. This finding throws doubt on the wisdom of prescribing any particular secondary-school subjects for college entrance, other than those that have a demonstrated relationship to the advanced studies of the curriculum which the college student is expected to follow.

Enrollments in the Various Subjects

A realistic method of studying the curriculum is to investigate the actual distribution of subjects in the programs of those who have graduated from the secondary school. Sometimes a study of this type reveals that the programs of pupils have been quite different from the prescriptions which have been set forth in some official statement regarding the organization of the curriculum. Table 8 presents data adapted from the National Survey of Secondary Education, showing the percentage distribution of the

TABLE 8. MEAN PERCENTAGE DISTRIBUTIONS OF WORK TAKEN BY
GRADUATES OF SIX HIGH SCHOOLS, 1890, 1900, 1910, 1920, 1930 *

Year	Percentage of Total Work in Each Field					
	English	Social Studies	Foreign Languages	Mathematics	Science	Non-Academic
1890....	13.1	10.9	38.7	16.0	17.7	3.6
1900....	12.2	11.8	31.4	15.5	13.0	16.0
1910....	15.6	10.7	29.2	14.5	13.3	16.7
1920....	19.9	13.2	20.7	13.9	11.2	21.2
1930....	21.3	16.3	17.6	13.5	10.1	21.2

* A. K. Loomis, Edwin S. Lide, and B. Lamar Johnson, *The Program of Studies*, p. 246. Office of Education Bulletin, 1932, no. 17, Monograph no. 19.

work taken by graduates of six high schools at ten-year intervals from 1890 to 1930.

It will be observed from this tabulation that the amount of English taken by the average high-school graduate increased by more than 50 per cent from 1890 to 1930, and the amount of work in social studies increased in almost the same proportion. The percentage of time devoted to foreign languages, on the contrary, was in 1930 considerably less than half what it had been in 1890. The relative emphasis on the sciences also showed a sharp decline. Mathematics has steadily declined in relative importance, but the total decrease over the forty-year period is not large in this subject.

Perhaps the most striking figures in this tabulation are those relating to the non-academic subjects, which include the fine arts, physical education, and the vocational subjects. This field of study was almost completely omitted from the programs of secondary-school graduates of 1890, but in 1930 it comprised more than one-fifth of the total program of the average graduate.

The data presented in Table 8 relate only to the programs of graduates. These figures do not tell the complete story with respect to the distribution of emphasis in the secondary-school programs because of the elimination which takes place in enrollments during the successive years of secondary schooling. Considerably more than one-fourth of the pupils of secondary schools have always been enrolled in the first year, and considerably less than one-fourth in the senior or final year. For that reason the subjects that are given in the lower years of the curriculum have been studied by more pupils than those given in the upper years.

An important method of studying the relative emphasis on subjects, therefore, is afforded by data concerning the number or percentage of all secondary-school pupils enrolled in the various subjects. The United States Commissioner of Education has from time to time collected and published information of this type. Table 9 presents data showing the percentage of the total pupils in public secondary schools who were enrolled in the various subjects in 1890, 1905, 1922, 1928, and 1934.

TABLE 9. PERCENTAGE OF TOTAL PUBLIC HIGH SCHOOL PUPILS
ENROLLED IN CERTAIN SUBJECTS IN 1890, 1905, 1922, 1928, AND 1934 *

Subject	Percentage of Pupils Enrolled In				
	1890	1905	1922	1928	1934
English	..	97.9	78.6	93.1	90.5
Latin	34.7	50.2	27.5	22.0	16.0
French	5.8	9.1	15.5	14.0	10.9
German	10.5	20.3	0.7	1.8	2.4
Spanish	..	..	11.3	9.4	6.2
Italian	..	..	0.0	0.1	0.2
Algebra	45.4	57.5	40.2	35.2	30.4
Geometry	21.3	28.2	22.7	19.8	17.1
Arithmetic	..	..	10.5	2.4	2.3
Trigonometry	..	1.7	1.5	1.3	1.3
Astronomy	..	1.2	0.1	0.1	0.1
Physics	22.2	15.7	8.9	6.9	6.3
Chemistry	10.1	6.8	7.4	7.1	7.6
Physical geography	..	21.5	4.3	2.7	1.6
Zoology	..	..	1.5	0.8	0.6
Botany	..	..	3.8	1.6	0.9
Biology	..	..	8.8	13.6	14.6
Geology	..	2.3	0.2	0.1	0.1
Physiology	..	22.0	5.1	2.7	1.8
Hygiene and sanitation	..	..	6.1	7.8	6.5
General science	..	..	18.3	17.5	17.8
History	27.3	40.9	50.7	46.5	42.7
Government	..	18.0	19.3	20.0	16.3
Sociology	..	..	2.4	2.7	2.5
Economics	..	..	4.8	5.1	4.9
Problems of democracy	..	..	..	1.0	3.5
Agriculture	..	..	5.1	3.7	3.6
Home economics	..	..	14.3	16.5	16.7
Industrial subjects	..	..	11.3	13.3	14.0
Bookkeeping	..	..	12.6	10.7	9.9
Shorthand	..	..	8.9	8.7	9.0
Typewriting	..	..	13.1	15.2	16.7
Commercial arithmetic	..	..	1.5	7.0	4.9
Commercial law	..	..	0.9	2.6	3.2
Commercial geography	..	..	1.7	4.8	4.0
Commercial history	..	..	0.4	0.2	0.2
Penmanship	..	..	1.7	0.8	0.3
Office practice	..	..	0.4	1.4	1.6
Elementary business training	..	..	..	3.0	6.1
Drawing and art	..	..	14.8	18.6	15.3
Music	..	..	25.3	26.0	25.5
Physical education	..	..	5.7	15.0	50.7

* In 1922, 1928, and 1934 the percentages of pupils are based upon the number of students in the schools reporting studies. In 1890 and 1905 the percentages are based upon the total number of students in the schools. Data adapted from *Offerings and Registrations in High-School Subjects*, 1933–34, pp. 28–29. Office of Education Bulletin, 1938, no. 6. Washington: Government Printing Office, 1938.

Caution must be exercised in interpreting these data, and one who would use them critically should refer to the limitations which are explicitly set forth in the Bulletin of the Office of Education in which the original data are given. The accuracy of the reporting has undoubtedly increased during the period covered by these data, and one cannot estimate exactly what effect this increased accuracy may have on the apparent distribution of enrollments in the various subjects. Some subjects which were certainly offered in a number of public high schools in 1890 are missing from the tabulation for that year. The list of subjects given for 1934 represents a categorization of some 206 subjects as actually reported. With these qualifications in mind, certain generalizations may be attempted from the data of Table 9.

The table indicates that with relatively few exceptions all pupils enrolled in the public high school in the most recent period studied English. Half the pupils were enrolled in physical education. History was studied in 1934 by less than half as many pupils as English. Algebra, with 30.4 per cent of the pupils enrolled, and music with 25.5 per cent, are the only other subjects which in 1934 had more than one-fourth of the pupils enrolled. The trends over the years in the various subjects are interesting but the reader can pick these out without specific attention being drawn to them. Especially noteworthy are the vocational subjects and the fine arts, now included in the list, which were not even reported until recent decades.

Extra-Curriculum Activities

Not only have great changes and expansions taken place in the curriculum of secondary schools, but the program of extra-curriculum activities or allied activities, as they are sometimes called, has also undergone a similar expansion. In any well-managed secondary school the educational values arising from extra-curriculum activities are today fully recognized and every effort is made to stimulate and promote the development of sound and effective programs in this area. Teachers are sought and put in charge who are especially qualified and equipped to give leadership along these lines. In many schools definite periods in the daily schedule are set aside for clubs and other non-curricular activities. Important studies have been made regarding the methods of managing such activities to the end that they may be most fruitful in serving the objectives of secondary education.

No attempt will be made here to present a complete catalogue of the kinds of activities carried on as a part of a well-managed extra-curriculum program. They include specifically such activities and organizations as athletics; debate; dramatics; departmental clubs; publishing of school newspapers, annuals, and literary magazines; self-government associations; hobby clubs; and musical organizations.

One of the purposes of a program of extra-curriculum activities is to provide experiences in social organization based on democratic principles. An ever-present tendency which must be guarded against in the management of secondary-school pupils is the formation of cliques and small groups with essentially selfish interests. This tendency reaches perhaps its worst form in a secondary-school fraternity. Membership in such fraternities is now forbidden by law to public school pupils in a number of states and is frowned upon everywhere by observing schoolmen. The program of extra-curriculum activities must be continually guarded to preserve it from the undemocratic influences that tend to appear.

At the opposite extreme there is need for avoidance of paternalism in managing the program of extra-curriculum activities. These enterprises should provide opportunity for self-expression on the part of the pupils, and too much control or direction by teachers and members of the school administrative staff is almost certain to destroy the interest of pupils. Much wisdom is required on the part of a school administrator to provide exactly the right amount and kind of direction, so as to avoid the two extremes: failure to attain objectives because of lack of control, and destruction of pupil interest because of an over-paternalistic control.

THE JUNIOR COLLEGE

In an earlier chapter, in which the co-ordination of the American educational system was discussed, attention was called to the development of new units of school organization, such as the junior college. It must not be thought that the junior college represents merely a different way of marking off points of division in the educational system, for this new unit has tended to develop important distinctive features of its own. Both publicly and privately controlled junior colleges are to be found, and the publicly controlled institution of this type is rapidly increasing both in numbers and in enrollments. W. C. Eells [1] reported that in 1940 there were 575 junior colleges in the United States, with a total enrollment of 197,710 students. The junior-college enrollments almost tripled between 1930 and 1940. The junior college is almost wholly a product of the twentieth century, and yet during the brief period of its development the number of junior colleges has reached almost half the number of four-year colleges, a type that has been in existence for more than three centuries in America.

The most common type of junior college is a two-year institution based on the completion of the 12th grade of the high school. A number of communities, however, have established a junior college as a four-year unit, beginning at the 11th grade of the school system. The four-year junior college has many advantages and seems destined ultimately to become the prevailing type.

For the most part the publicly controlled junior college is operated by the local school system, and is rightfully considered as an extension of the period of secondary education. The curriculum of the junior college has been to a considerable extent under the domination of state universities and other four-year institutions, for many of the young people who complete the

[1] Walter C. Eells, "Status of the Junior College in the United States, 1939–40," *School and Society*, LI: 219–21 (February 17, 1940).

junior college expect later to attend some institution granting the Bachelor's degree. The influence of the universities over the junior-college curriculum is lessening as it becomes evident that the junior college can best serve its community by offering a much broader program than the preparatory studies common to the first two years of degree-granting institutions. Terminal curriculums, providing opportunities in vocational lines and in semi-professional subjects, are now a feature of well-organized junior colleges.

Only the more populous communities are able to maintain junior colleges effectively, for it is only in such centers that a sufficient number of students can be gathered together to provide an efficient operating unit. The area served by a junior college may be relatively large, however, for young people of junior-college age may be expected to commute for a considerable distance. Even with the wider area that may be served, the provision of junior-college facilities in sparsely settled districts is at present a difficult problem.

The junior college is a relatively expensive addition to the local school system; teachers at this level usually are required to have high qualifications, and extensive apparatus and equipment are necessary for effective instruction. In practice it has proved possible to maintain satisfactory junior-college facilities only in communities having a favorable economic situation, although in some states special grants from state funds are used to assist local districts in maintaining junior colleges. Little doubt remains, however, as to the desirability of the wider spread of this new unit, and there is every probability that at some time in the future junior-college facilities will be as available to American boys and girls as high-school facilities now are.

STRESS WITHIN SECONDARY SCHOOLS DURING THE EXPANSION PERIOD

The expansion that has taken place in the secondary school during the past half century has produced tremendous stresses and strains within that organization. The difficulties that have beset the development of the program have been many and varied, and the fact that the organization has survived at all is impressive evidence of the basic soundness of the modern secondary school as a social institution appropriate to American civilization.

In earlier connections, two of the important difficulties arising from the expansion of the high school have been commented upon. Enrollments have increased so rapidly that plant space could not be provided to house the programs adequately. The cost of education per pupil at the level of secondary education is considerably greater than the cost at the level of the elementary school, and the fact that increases in enrollment have been so large at the most expensive level has given rise to a great difficulty in financing the current budget for the educational program. Besides these two important difficulties of housing and financing, certain other problems arising from the expansion of the secondary-school program, that have not been discussed in earlier connections, may be briefly treated.

Supply of Teachers

The rapid expansion of enrollments has required an ever-increasing supply of teachers for the secondary schools. College enrollments have not increased as rapidly as enrollments at the secondary level and consequently at some periods there has been a shortage of teachers for the regular academic subjects of secondary schools. Accompanying the expansion of the services of the secondary schools has been a steady insistence on higher and higher qualifications for teachers, so that the supply of well-qualified teachers has almost always been insufficient to meet the demands. Under such circumstances it has been difficult to maintain standards for certification of teachers and thousands of persons have been certified, in many cases being granted teachers' certificates valid for life, who are not at all well qualified for the positions they hold.

The difficulty of obtaining a sufficient supply of well-qualified teachers of the academic subjects has been great, but a much greater difficulty has been experienced in obtaining teachers for the new subjects. In many instances no recognized facilities have been available for the preparation of teachers of these new subjects. Lack of well-qualified teachers has been particularly true of the vocational subjects, especially in the field of trades and industries. What qualifications or preparation, for example, would be desirable for a teacher of plumbing? Obviously such a person should have a vocational competence equal at least to the status of a journeyman in the trade he is teaching; but journey-men in the skilled trades do not ordinarily have a background of professional and academic preparation sufficient to qualify them for effective service in teaching. In most secondary schools, therefore, the arrangements for recruiting teachers of these new subjects have left much to be desired. The only feasible arrange-ment has been to locate a well-qualified journeyman who has had somewhat more than average education and to persuade him to accept the salary available for a teacher, in the hope that he will be able to increase his professional qualifications by an in-service type of preparation.

The expansion in extra-curriculum activities has also laid new demands on the teaching staff, and in the selection of teachers attention must now be given to the special abilities of the per-sonnel for directing these activities. The staff of the secondary school must include persons competent to coach athletic teams, to train debaters, to direct dramatics, to conduct musical organi-zations, to provide leadership in hobby clubs, and to guide wisely each of the large numbers of extra-curriculum activities now main-tained. To locate available teachers with such abilities, together with the desired academic and professional qualifications, is not an easy task.

Heterogeneity of the Program and Staff

The wide variety of interests served by secondary schools has introduced such heterogeneity into the composition of the staff that it has been difficult to hold the organization together for the accomplishment of common purposes. The specialization of teachers in the various subject-matter fields has tended to develop a lack of understanding of the general problems of secondary education. This has been particularly true because of the introduction of new subjects, for the teachers of such subjects obviously have been of a type considerably different from the teachers of the older academic subjects. The teachers of the new subjects have usually been in the minority in the cosmopolitan secondary school, and the teachers of the older subjects have not always been cordial in welcoming these newcomers to the academic society. Consideration of problems of general interest in a teach‧ers' meeting has frequently resulted in a one-sided discussion and in a decision in which the various points of view represented by the members of the teaching staff have not had adequate attention.

Lack of thorough and common understanding of many phases of the secondary-school program has been characteristic not only of teachers but also of the school administrative group. For the most part members of the present generation of school administrators have been drawn from among those who have been prepared for, and experienced in, teaching the regular academic subjects. Frequently they have not been hospitable toward the expansion of the non-academic fields. In the case of the vocational subjects this condition has resulted in considerable central dictation regarding the program, particularly in those subjects supported by federal grants under the Smith-Hughes Act and subsequent acts. This dictation of local school policies by a central agency in vocational education has been necessary in order to establish the kinds of facilities considered proper in these fields, but it has unfortunately led to more or less confusion and friction in the organization of secondary schools.

To weld together into a smoothly functioning organization the wide variety of diverse personalities and interests now represented in the secondary-school program is a task demanding a high level of educational statesmanship, both on the part of the administrative staff and the teachers. Those who are engaged in educational service at the secondary level need a comprehensive grasp of the problems involved in the entire area of secondary education, and an understanding of the nature of the social pressures that have been important in molding the American secondary school.

Competition Among Subjects

In an earlier connection it was pointed out that two types of curriculum organization are at present common in secondary schools, the "constant with variables" type, and the "multiple curriculum with variables" type. In each of these types of curriculum organization considerable election is permitted pupils in arranging their programs. The introduction of the plan of permitting pupils to choose some of the subjects they will take has tended to introduce competition among the subjects and to multiply the difficulties of obtaining unbiased consideration of curriculum problems by members of the teaching staff.

Under the plan of a fixed curriculum, characteristic of the secondary-school program of an earlier day, there could be no competition among subjects because all pupils studied all the subjects that were offered. Even the teachers of this earlier time were not specialized in their respective subject-matter fields, for any teacher was presumed to be competent to give instruction in any or all of the subjects included in the secondary-school curriculum. Under such circumstances it was not difficult to obtain well-balanced consideration of all problems affecting the curriculum by members of the instructional staff. In sharp contrast to this earlier situation, teachers are now specialized in their respective subjects and they realize vividly that their vested interests are affected by the choices which pupils make in selecting their programs of study and by the favored position given prescribed subjects in the curriculum. The data presented in Tables 8 and 9, for example, are disturbing in some cases and encouraging in others to teachers in the various subject-matter fields.

The formulation of a sound program under present circumstances in secondary schools seems especially difficult because of the impossibility of obtaining unbiased consideration of curriculum problems by members of the teaching staff. National organizations of teachers have been formed in each of the subject-matter fields and an important function of such associations seems to be advocacy and maintenance of the given field of study in the secondary-school curriculum. Even some of the so-called scientific investigations that have been carried on by certain of these national organizations, in an effort to study the place that should be given the subjects in the secondary-school curriculum, are not above suspicion of bias or prejudice. Collectively and individually, teachers have tended to view changes in the curriculum in the light of the probable effects on their special teaching subjects, a procedure that seems unlikely to result in an effectively planned curriculum.

Protests and Questions

The expansions in secondary schools have not taken place without important repercussions both inside and outside the school system. The lay public has generally been critical of the service rendered in the schools, and citizens, without knowing precisely what features of the program should be specifically criticized, have voiced dissatisfaction with the general quality of the product of secondary schools. College professors have deplored the fact that students coming to the institutions of higher education seem to be less well prepared now than formerly. Objective facts are lacking for the support of such a conclusion regarding the preparation of students but many college officers have a distinct subjective impression that this is true. Within secondary schools many conservative members of teaching and administrative staffs have resisted changes. Groups which may be considered representative of the intellectual aristocracy have protested against what they consider the futile attempt to provide a universal education at the secondary level.

Regardless of these questions and protests, the fact remains that most young people today are not able to enter industry or other types of gainful employment before age eighteen, and in many cases not before age twenty. The best method of occupying the time of such young people is an important problem, and the solution of this problem by requiring an extended educational period, regardless of the immediate value of the education as such, may be socially wise.

The situation presents a notable challenge to all engaged in educational service, to demonstrate that the program of the schools can be adapted to serve the needs and capabilities of the entire population of the appropriate ages. The traditional curriculum of the classical type obviously will serve the needs of only a select few. Vocational education has not proved to be a satisfactory substitute for the traditional curriculum, for vocational education is often quite as special as was the older curriculum. Vocational education has the additional disadvantage of being susceptible to overproduction in an economic society. Education for citizenship, for worthy home membership, and for effective use of leisure time, seem to be areas in which proper emphasis has been lacking and in which overemphasis is impossible. Along the lines suggested in this comment probably lies the solution for the possible employment of the time of young people prior to their entry on gainful occupation. In all probability instruction will have to be cast in a new mold, disregarding the traditions of the older academic subjects and also of specialized vocational education before the types of education which are socially most desirable can be made of sufficient interest to appeal to most young people in this country.

If the secondary schools are to continue to deserve the support of society, their programs must be adapted to meet the new social demands that are created by modern conditions and by the enrollment of the great numbers of pupils who now attend these schools.

BIBLIOGRAPHY

Briggs, Thomas H., *Secondary Education.*   New York: The Macmillan
Company, 1933.   x + 578 pp.

Burton, William H., *Introduction to Education,* pp. 212–24.

Cardinal Principles of Secondary Education.   A report of the Commission
on the Reorganization of Secondary Education, appointed by the
National Education Association.   Bureau of Education Bulletin, 1918,
no. 35.   Washington: Government Printing Office, 1918.   32 pp.

Chamberlain, Leo M., *The Teacher and School Organization,* pp. 440–66.

Clapp, Frank L., Wayland J. Chase, and Curtis Merriman, *Introduction to
Education,* pp. 258–323.

Cubberley, Ellwood P., *Public Education in the United States,* pp. 627–50.

Cubberley, Ellwood P., *State School Administration,* pp. 384–403.

Douglass, Aubrey A., *The American School System,* pp. 156–85, 395–
413.

Douglass, Aubrey A., *Modern Secondary Education, Principles and Practices.*   New York: Houghton Mifflin Company, 1938.

Douglass, Harl R., *Secondary Education for Youth in Modern America.*
Report to the American Youth Commission of the American Council on
Education.   Washington: American Council on Education, 1937.
x + 138 pp.

Espy, Herbert G., *The Public Secondary School.*   Boston: Houghton
Mifflin Company, 1939.   xii + 596 pp.

Frasier, George Willard, and Winfield D. Armentrout, *An Introduction to
the Literature of Education,* pp. 321–37.

Judd, Charles H., *The Unique Character of American Secondary Education.*
The Inglis Lecture, 1928.   Cambridge, Massachusetts: Harvard University Press, 1928.   64 pp.

Kandel, I. L., *History of Secondary Education.*   Boston: Houghton Mifflin
Company, 1930.   xvii + 578 pp.

Koos, Leonard V., James M. Hughes, Percival W. Hutson, and William
C. Reavis, *Administering the Secondary School.*   New York: American
Book Company, 1940.   xii + 678 pp.

Koos, Leonard V., *The American Secondary School.*   Boston: Ginn and
Company, 1927.   xii + 756 pp.

Koos, Leonard V., *The Junior-College Movement.*   Boston: Ginn and
Company, 1925.   xii + 436 pp.

Koos, Leonard V., *The Junior High School.*   Boston: Ginn and Company,
1927.   xiv + 506 pp.

Koos, Leonard V., *et al., National Survey of Secondary Education,* Monograph no. 1, *Summary*. Office of Education Bulletin, 1932, no. 17. Washington: Government Printing Office, 1934. ix + 232 pp.

Patterson, S. Howard, Ernest A. Choate, and Edmund de S. Brunner, *The School in American Society*, pp. 200–11.

Reeder, Ward, *A First Course in Education*, pp. 453–63.

Russell, John Dale, *et al.*, *Vocational Education*. Staff Study no. 8, Advisory Committee on Education. Washington: Government Printing Office, 1938. x + 326 pp.

Smith, Payson, Frank W. Wright, and Associates, *Education in the Forty-Eight States*, pp. 27–48, 155–60. Staff Study no. 1, Advisory Committee on Education.

Wilson, Lester M., and I. L. Kandel, *Introduction to the Study of American Education*, pp. 161–93.

CHAPTER XIV

Higher education

THE THIRD AND FINAL level of education, that which
is carried on in institutions of higher learning, lies beyond the completion of the secondary school. A precise definition of higher
education is difficult because of the wide variety of activities at
this level. In the preceding chapter the statement has been
made that the terminal point for secondary education is not accurately fixed; this fact is one of the reasons why a satisfactory
definition of higher education becomes difficult. Simply to say
that higher education is the highest level of the educational system obviously requires a more fundamental consideration of the
bases on which a definition of higher education rests.

Higher education may be defined in terms of the institutions
customarily recognized as rendering service at this level. At
present, general acceptance would be given to the classification of
universities, and liberal arts colleges, and probably of teachers
colleges, as institutions of higher education. Certain other
types of institutions, such as normal schools and technical institutes, would today be accepted by most authorities as within
the field of higher education, though a few decades ago such institutions were not so classified. The junior college, as was noted
in the preceding chapter, probably belongs to the field of secondary education; yet by many it is still classed as an institution of
higher education.

The name by which an institution is known is not always a reliable index of the level at which it renders service. Many institutions bearing the title of college have in the past been nothing
more than secondary schools, and even today one should not

take at face value the designation given an institution in its charter. Institutional designations, moreover, do not have the same meanings in different times and places, so that in other countries and in other periods in history the definition formulated in terms of present-day American institutions would have little validity.

Perhaps the simplest method of defining higher education in institutional terms is that adopted in the first paragraph of this chapter, in which the definition was suggested in terms of institutions which accept as students those who have completed the secondary school. From a historical standpoint this definition is an anachronism, for higher education developed first and the secondary school was established afterward to prepare boys for the university. One might appropriately at one time have defined the secondary school as the institution in which boys are prepared for the university, but to define higher education in terms of the completion of the secondary school would have been meaningless at that time. Furthermore, as was pointed out in the preceding chapter, the definition of secondary education is by no means agreed upon, and there is little gain in defining higher education in terms of an institution which is itself only vaguely defined.

Another basis for the definition of higher education is in terms of objectives. When the objectives of the various levels of education are analyzed, however, it is quickly found that the overlapping is so great as to lead to little discrimination. The objectives of higher education do not differ significantly in most instances from those of secondary education. The only unique function or objective of higher education, research, characterizes such a small part of the total process that the entire level cannot be defined by reference to this single and unique objective.

A definition of higher education in terms of methods of instruction or methods of study is sometimes useful. Again it must be noted, however, that higher education does not differ sharply in these respects from the other levels of education. The intellectually exacting character of the work, for example, is a relative matter; it varies gradually with the individual learner as he proceeds from the lowest to the highest levels of education, and thus it provides no valid basis for institutional definition. The ability of students in higher institutions to carry on their studies independently is sometimes pointed out as a distinguishing characteristic; but on the one hand every well-managed secondary school attempts to develop independence in its pupils, and on the other hand one who views the situation realistically cannot speak with much confidence regarding the actual degree of independence displayed by the majority of college and university students.

A definition of higher education in terms of subject matter offers a tempting approach, but here again investigation discovers little of a determinative character. The subject matter taught in institutions of higher education overlaps to a surprising degree that taught in the secondary school. Whole areas, such as the teaching of foreign languages, are duplicated in the two levels of education. Careful studies have shown, as was pointed out in Chapter XI, that in the content of such subjects as physics, history, and English, the actual overlapping of secondary-school and college curriculums is large.

A definition in terms of subject-matter content would lack universal validity, for subjects have shown an amazing tendency to move up and down, mostly down, in the curriculum. Almost every academic subject now studied in the secondary school was at one time a part of the college curriculum. A few subjects now limited almost exclusively to the curriculum of the college were at one time widely taught in secondary schools. A definition in terms of subject matter, therefore, offers little promise of supplying an accurate and universal description of higher education.

Another basis for defining higher education is sometimes sought in a description of the characteristics of the students who are served. The reader will recall that secondary education was defined in Chapter XIII as the level of the school system suitable to the needs of pupils in their adolescent years. Higher education might similarly be defined as the level at which service is rendered to young people in the period of late adolescence and early postadolescence. This definition has considerable validity, particularly if emphasis is placed on the intellectual maturity of the students rather than on their chronological or physiological ages. In these terms higher education might be defined as that form of the institutionalized educational process suited to the needs of young people whose intellectual maturity is that of the normal person in the late adolescent or early postadolescent years.

The acceptance of the foregoing definition, however, would lead to the inclusion of some types of instructional activities that by many authorities would now not be recognized as strictly within the limits of higher education. For example, is advanced instruction in music or art, carried on in some high-grade conservatory, a form of higher education? Questions of this type concern only a relatively small part of what would be clearly marked out as the field of higher education. Perhaps it is necessary to admit that no exact definition is at present possible, and to leave these border areas somewhat indeterminate.

In spite of the difficulty of finding a satisfactory definition of higher education in America there are a number of characteristics that distinguish this level from other levels of education in this country, or from education of the same level in other countries. It is the purpose of this chapter to review some of these characteristics.

CONTROL AND SUPPORT

American higher education is to a considerable extent privately controlled. Of the 1628 institutions reporting in 1935–36 to the United States Commissioner of Education, 1051 were under private control and 577 were under public control. The average size of the privately controlled institutions is much smaller than that of the publicly controlled colleges and universities. Total enrollments of 1,208,227 students in higher institutions were reported in 1935–36; of these 614,131 were in publicly controlled colleges and universities and 594,096 in privately controlled. It will be remembered that only about 10 per cent of the pupils at the elementary and secondary levels are enrolled in privately controlled schools.

The enrollments of college students, now almost equally balanced between public and private institutions, are slowly tending towards the public institution, and it seems probable that in the future the publicly controlled institution may become the dominant form of higher education in this country. Publicly controlled institutions of higher education began to develop chiefly after the Civil War. The types of institutions at present growing most rapidly, the junior colleges attached to public-school systems and the teachers colleges, are both under public control.

A number of authorities have pointed out the desirability of maintaining approximately an even balance between publicly and privately controlled education at the college and university level in this country. Each type of institution acts as a stimulant to the other. If on the one hand the private institutions settle into a rut and become unprogressive, the public institutions are likely to forge ahead and to pave the way for new advances. On the other hand, if the publicly controlled institutions fall into the hands of political spoilsmen, the programs of the private institutions are unaffected and remain as the standard to guide the publicly controlled institutions in their return to effective service.

During the depression of the 1930's the availability of federal funds for expenditures in the construction of buildings afforded an important advantage to the publicly controlled universities and colleges. These grants, which were provided for the purpose of furnishing employment to persons on relief, were not available to privately controlled institutions. Because of the difficulty of obtaining funds from their usual sources of support, the privately controlled institutions during the depression have made relatively few extensions or improvements to their physical plants, while the publicly controlled institutions with the use of these public funds have in almost all states benefited greatly by the construction of needed new plant facilities.

The support of American higher education differs sharply from that of elementary and secondary education in the extent to which it is derived from students' fees. Even the publicly controlled institutions are in most instances dependent to some extent on student fees as a source of support, and the privately controlled institutions typically obtain more than half of their income from this source.

Because fees must be paid, students in institutions of higher education tend to be selected to a considerable extent on an economic basis. Although some assistance is available in the form of scholarships and other types of financial aid, large numbers of capable young people are at present denied the opportunity for higher education because of their economic circumstances. The democratic character of the public-school system, therefore, is not fully maintained as students pass from the level of secondary to that of higher education.

Although the fees charged in publicly controlled institutions tend to be considerably less than those in privately controlled colleges and universities, students of limited resources find it difficult to meet the fee requirements of even the publicly controlled institutions. Furthermore, attendance at institutions of higher education entails expenses other than fees because many students have to take up residence away from home, a serious handicap on a large number of capable young people.

A recent report published by the National Resources Committee [1] states:

> On the basis of the rather slight data available it seems probable that while about 30 per cent of the youth of college age among the people in the upper three deciles of economic ability go to college, less than 1 per cent of those in the lowest three deciles enter college.

---

[1] *Research — A National Resource. I. Relation of the Federal Government to Research.* Report of the Science Committee to the National Resources Committee, November, 1938, p. 184. Washington: Government Printing Office, 1938.

A careful follow-up study of the high-school graduates of superior mental ability in one American community, in which attendance or non-attendance at college was studied in relation to the economic status of the family, resulted in the following conclusion:

> Our educational ladder is not freely and equally open to all. The battle for free education has not been won. At present many of our schools are, only in theory, open to all equally. Every person cannot have an unlimited amount of schooling, for securing it is contingent on the possession of a considerable amount of money. There is little justification for saying that schools are free while some parents must make extreme sacrifices in order to send their children to college. Higher educational advantages are entirely denied to many mentally superior and ambitious young persons because their families cannot afford to give them the additional schooling.[1]

The public junior college is rapidly developing as a corrective of the undemocratic nature of the older types of higher institutions, but in many areas the junior college too has followed the custom of charging tuition fees. One might prophesy that, as the social demands come more and more to require higher education, the desirability of providing it at public expense will be recognized. The parallel with the historic struggle to obtain a tuition-free elementary and secondary school comes to mind. Current trends, it must be confessed, are exactly in the opposite direction, for fees are steadily being increased and there is no indication at present that institutions of higher education intend to abandon their dependence on student fees as sources of support.

INSTITUTIONAL AUTONOMY

Higher education in the United States is conducted in separate, autonomous institutions, which for the most part have no authoritative organizational relationship with one another. In fact, it is scarcely correct to speak of a system of higher education

[1] Helen B. Goetsch, "Relation of Parental Income to College Opportunity," *School Review*, XLVIII: 26–33 (January, 1940).

in this country in the same sense in which one speaks of a system of elementary and secondary schools in a state, for in almost all the states the institutions of higher education are unco-ordinated and self-determining in all respects. In a few states the publicly controlled institutions of higher education are under the direction of some central agency which has power to co-ordinate programs. Even in such instances the degree of co-ordination actually developed is typically not large and the individual institutions are permitted to work out their own programs without important limitations.

The privately controlled institutions are not subject to general direction in any state, although some of the states exercise varying amounts of control over limited phases of institutional organization and activity. In general, no power exists in any state to compel the existing privately controlled institutions to organize their programs in such a way as to maintain a co-ordinated system of higher education.

The autonomy of institutions of higher education in this country is in sharp contrast to the public control of the elementary and secondary schools. Individual elementary or high schools exist only as a part of the school system and, although there are large elements of local control at this level, both the general nature and many of the details of the program are determined by state authorities. For example, in most states the local elementary and secondary schools can employ as teachers only persons who hold a teaching certificate issued by the state. The colleges and universities, by contrast, can employ instructors without reference to credentials issued by any superior controlling body.

Extra-legal controls, particularly those provided through the accrediting associations which were discussed in Chapter VIII, do provide an important measure of direction and restraint on the programs and activities of higher institutions. The regional associations, however, are purely voluntary organizations that have no legal status, and it is only as other institutions and the general public accord significance to membership that the accrediting associations are able to exercise any control over the autonomous institutions of higher education.

Several reasons may be suggested for the institutional autonomy which is characteristic of American higher education. It may be pointed out that the higher institutions in this country were modeled directly on those of Europe, and the European universities which developed in the late middle ages were of an autonomous type. The traditions on which the British universities had grown up allowed practically complete institutional autonomy to Oxford and Cambridge, a policy which has been maintained in the founding of other British universities. The influence of the British tradition was strong in the formative period of American higher education and doubtless had much to do in establishing the principle of institutional autonomy.

A second influence tending toward institutional autonomy was denominationalism. With few exceptions all the early American institutions of higher education were founded under the auspices of religious denominations for the purpose of training ministers of the gospel. Each of the religious sects was jealous and suspicious of all the others, and particularly in the preparation of ministers and other religious leaders was it considered necessary to maintain complete independence from the heterodox influence of institutions under the auspices of other denominations. This policy probably carried over into the state-controlled institutions, merely because the tradition of institutional autonomy had become firmly established by almost two hundred years of private and denominational control before the state universities began their development.

A third factor in the situation making for institutional autonomy was the nature of the financing of the early colleges and universities. In practically every instance the institutions of higher education were supported from gifts, endowments, and fees of students. These sources of support were independent of public control and it was natural for the college so financed to be self-determinative with respect to its own program.

Whatever the reasons for the development of the tradition of autonomy and independent institutional organization, the fact remains that this idea is still strongly entrenched in all types of colleges and universities. Any movement that looks toward breaking down the power of the individual institution to determine its own program is certain to meet both passive and active opposition. It must be said that higher education today in the United States suffers in no small measure because of this condition. Duplication of service, intense competition for students, unsuitable locations, and failure to serve the needs of large sections of the population, are some of the important consequences of the tradition of institutional autonomy.

Undoubtedly if an intelligent dictator could be given complete centralized power over higher education in the United States, he could arrange institutional programs and services so as to obtain a much larger educational return for the present expenditure of funds. Such a reform, however, is only an idle dream at present, for there is little evidence that colleges and universities, even under circumstances of a major economic depression, are relinquishing their well-established traditional autonomy.

THE LIBERAL ARTS COLLEGE

The liberal arts colleges are more numerous than any other type of institution of higher education in the United States. A liberal arts college is typically an institution offering the Bachelor's degree on the basis of a four-year program beyond the completion of the secondary school; a few of the stronger liberal arts colleges also offer a fifth year of work leading to the Master's degree in some subject-matter fields.

The distinction between the liberal arts college and the university is not always clear. The university always includes a liberal arts college as a part of its organization but it also maintains a graduate school, offering Master's and Doctor's degrees, and usually includes several professional schools. Some of the separate liberal arts colleges have one or two professional schools, music being the field most commonly represented by a special school or conservatory attached to the liberal arts college. Custom generally decrees that an institution shall be called a university only after it has developed a graduate school and at least three professional schools in addition to the core of the liberal arts college. There are in reality therefore two different types of liberal arts colleges in America: (a) one which is a part of a university; and (b) one which is detached and separate, offering only the liberal arts program or including possibly one or two professional schools.

The separate college of liberal arts, widely distributed in the United States, is peculiar to this country. European practice knows the liberal arts college only as a constituent part of a university. To find the liberal arts college maintained as an institution entirely apart from a university affiliation seems very odd to a European visitor, as odd as it would be for an American to find in some small town a collegiate department of English or history independent of any connection with a university or college.

The development of the separate college of liberal arts in America seems to have been one of the accidents of history. Harvard, the first American college, founded in 1636, was based on an English model, for the leaders of the Puritan movement had been educated at Emmanuel College of Cambridge University. At that period of history the college was the dominant form of organization within the British university. The British university itself was merely a hollow shell; all the important activities of the educational program were conducted in the separate colleges. Afterwards the university in Great Britain recovered some of its power as a central agency, but at the time of the founding of the new institutions in America the college in the British universities existed as a highly independent unit. So in this country colleges, rather than universities, were founded.

Another factor causing the development of liberal arts colleges, rather than universities, was the influence of denominationalism in the United States. The various sects, as has already been pointed out, were jealous of one another and wished to have the training of their ministers carried on in separate institutions. Numerous separate colleges of liberal arts served this end better than a few large collections of colleges in university centers.

The sparseness of the population during the period when the colleges were being founded in this country was probably another factor leading to the establishment of separate liberal arts colleges. Particularly throughout the Middle West the founding of colleges followed closely on the establishment of comparatively isolated settlements. Because of the difficulties of travel it was deemed better to have a number of widely scattered educational institutions than to have a few centers where the resources for higher education were concentrated. Many of the colleges founded prior to the Civil War were expected ultimately to grow up and develop into large and important universities; a few of them did, but most of them never got beyond the nucleus of the liberal arts college program and large numbers of them, not being able to maintain this bare necessity, have perished.

Whatever causes may be assigned, the fact remains that today higher education is carried on in a large number of separate liberal arts colleges in the United States. Typically these institutions are small; few of them enroll more than one thousand students and half of them probably enroll fewer than five hundred full-time students. They have been the stronghold of cultural education and have emphasized the traditional type of liberal training with less attention to vocational purposes than most of the other kinds of higher institutions. A few of them have achieved real distinction and are noted for progressive innovations and for the high quality of their work. Many of them, however, represent a certain scholarly gentility, but provide educational services on a level below that available in the better institutions of the country.

The liberal arts college has in recent years been caught between two forces which seem to threaten its very existence. On the one hand, the rapid development of the public junior college has drawn away large numbers of students who, it is presumed, would otherwise have enrolled in the liberal arts college. If the tendency toward expansion of the junior college continues, the day may come when that institution will care for practically all students up to the end of the second college year, and the liberal arts college will then be forced to begin its program at the third-year level. On the other hand, the graduate professional schools are extending their organization downward and are developing integrated programs of liberal arts and professional work beginning with the present third year of college. If the two upper years of the present liberal arts college are absorbed by the graduate professional schools while the two lower years are taken over by the public junior colleges, what will be left for the liberal arts college?

It must be remembered that these are only tendencies, not accomplished facts, and the liberal arts college will have a considerable life ahead of it, even if the present tendencies continue at their present rate. The situation, however, has caused anxious thought among those who are devoted to the traditions of the liberal arts college.

The development of the junior college is progressing rapidly and the prophecy has been made that the time is not far distant when the liberal arts colleges will find it desirable to begin their programs at the present third-year level, and will carry through to the Master's degree with a three-year instead of the present four-year program. This solution will be possible only in the stronger of the present liberal arts colleges, for education at the level of the Master's degree is expensive and relatively large resources will be necessary to support an institution which maintains such a program. The weaker institutions will then probably be discontinued or in some instances they may provide a nucleus for a local junior college. The services of higher education would suffer no loss in either of these outcomes.

HIGHER EDUCATION FOR WOMEN

One area in which the United States has led the world is the higher education of women. The traditions of Europe were for centuries opposed to the admission of girls to secondary schools, and it is only in the most recent times that European universities have admitted women.

Agitation for facilities for the higher education of women began to be pronounced in the United States about the beginning of the second quarter of the nineteenth century. Certain institutions, which were called female seminaries, were founded to provide a type of higher education for women. For the most part the programs of these institutions for women in the early days did not attempt to provide the same subjects as were studied in the colleges for men, for it was widely believed that women were not capable of intellectual efforts of that type.

Oberlin College in 1837 introduced the experiment of coeducation, considered a most rash and daring experiment in that day — so rash in fact that no other college dared organize on a co-educational basis for more than twenty years. Following the Civil War, however, a number of public and private institutions of collegiate grade began to open their doors to women, although they were acting against the earnest protests of physicians, theologians, and other supposedly intelligent leaders of the time. The protests gradually died out during the last decade of the nineteenth century, and today women in the United States are admitted to higher education on a par with men.

Some idea of the struggle which was necessary to achieve the present facilities for higher education of women may be obtained from a few quotations which refer to conditions at about the beginning of the last quarter of the nineteenth century. The first quotation is from a book by Dr. Edward H. Clarke which denounced the idea of higher education for women from the medical point of view. The book, *Sex in Education*, was especially popular in the 1870's and quickly ran through several editions; it was undoubtedly influential in retarding the development of higher education for women.

The delicate bloom, early but rapidly fading beauty, and singular pallor of American girls and women have almost passed into a proverb. The first observation of a European that lands upon our shores is, that our women are a feeble race; and, if he is a physiological observer, he is sure to add, They will give birth to a feeble race, not of women only, but of men as well. "I never saw before so many pretty girls together," said Lady Amberley to the writer, after a visit to the public schools of Boston; and then added, "They all looked sick." Circumstances have repeatedly carried me to Europe, where I am always surprised by the red blood that fills and colors the faces of ladies and peasant girls, reminding one of the canvas of Rubens and Murillo; and am always equally surprised on my return, by crowds of pale, bloodless female faces, that suggest consumption, scrofula, anemia, and neuralgia. To a large extent, our present system of educating girls is the cause of this pallor and weakness. How our schools, through their methods of education, contribute to this unfortunate result, and how our colleges that have undertaken to educate girls like boys, that is, in the same way, have succeeded in intensifying the evils of the schools, will be pointed out in another place.[1]

The next quotation was written by a minister, and reflects the opposition to the opening of colleges to women on a coeducational basis.

I see the question is entertained by some of our grave New England Colleges, whether they shall not admit women within their walls. (I dare not say "females," — because one of our lady-writers protests that this is an indelicate word, and may mean a feminine dog or horse — as well!)

Shall our colleges be opened to receive women?... I want very modestly to ask a few questions. I fear I shall put them too bluntly, but I will try to be gentle.

1. Is it certain that the normal structure, the physiology, the diseases, the tastes, the sensibilities, the nerves, the habit of thought and feeling, the physical endurance, the strength and weaknesses of the two sexes, are so nearly alike, that it is wise to shut them up in a college, to be educated together?

[1] Edward H. Clarke, M.D., *Sex in Education*, pp. 21–22. Boston: James R. Osgood and Company, 1873.

2. Is it necessary for women? We have just about us the Mount Holyoke Seminary, are to have one at Northampton costing $400,000, have Vassar College, and I know not how many more seminaries of a high order — one in almost every town — all for females. (I beg the lady's pardon.) Do we need to multiply facilities for their education?

3. A rule should work well both ways. Will these lady colleges, such as Vassar — open their doors for young men? Sauce that is good for the goose, must be good for the gander. If the sexes had better be educated together, then hasten to invite us in. Are they prepared to do that?

4. If ladies enter our colleges and compete in the long course, with the other sex, they must do it by sacrificing the female accomplishments — the piano, cultivated singing, and attractive dress. Why must they? Simply because they can't compete with the young men without using all their time and exhausting all their strength.

5. Is it certain that the delicate, nervous, physical organization of woman is such — (I admit all you ask as to her quickness of mind, and fine mental attributes,) that she can endure the physical strain requisite for a regular, old-fashioned, college course? I am informed that in institutions where the experiment has been tried, of 100 young men who are fitted for college, sixty-six go through the course. Out of 100 females, *only six* go through the course. Exceptions there may be but as a general thing, can the female constitution bear the long strain?

6. Are we prepared to change the whole organic plan of our colleges — introducing the accomplishments which are as natural to woman as her breath, which accomplishments the Bible recognizes — "that our daughters may be polished after the similitude of a palace" — shaping the course of study so that she will not sink under the strain — (for an army *must* grade its march to the feeblest battalion) — having women on the Board of Trustees and in the Faculty — for it must come to that — throwing aside the experience of the ages in the hope that our new experiment is to advance human improvement? The whole system of dormitories and boarding must be altered. The girls must go out evenings and debate in the societies. Shall they join the secret societies? If not, do they have all the rights of the young men? Where will you begin to tear down and fit the dormitories? I only ask the question.

7. Provided you say that woman can bear the wear and strain of the College course, and you want her to be educated like men and with

men, what about the gymnasium — is she to perform there? What about the boat club, is she to be shut out of the delightful training and struggling in the boat-race? I only ask in my ignorance; for if you try to make her a college student, I can't see why she must not be one! Is she any way inferior to her brother? May she not smoke the cigar in the street as well as he? Why not?

Once more. For the widely separated duties of life — which, by laws unalterable, *must* be separated — is it certain, or even probable, that it will be any advantage to either sex to change the whole organic structure of our colleges in order that this experiment may be made? It does not meet the case to cite the experience of childhood. We all agree that in childhood, in the nursery, so long as they are under the mother's eye, they should be educated together, but the question is, when the days of flirtation have arrived — when the thoughts of the young naturally and strongly flow towards one point — when the passions are strong and the will weak, and the judgment inexperienced, is it wise to bring the two sexes together in the college?

The institution that does that must take a wide departure from its own organization and become "lob-sided" — or am I mistaken? [1]

The third quotation consists of a series of excerpts from an article written by Dr. Martha Carey Thomas in 1908, describing her experiences in the 1870's and 1880's in obtaining her education and in developing Bryn Mawr College, of which she was an early president.

It was not to be wondered at that we were uncertain in those old days as to the ultimate result of women's education. Before I myself went to college I had never seen but one college woman. I had heard that such a woman was staying at the house of an acquaintance. I went to see her with fear. Even if she had appeared in hoofs and horns I was determined to go to college all the same. But it was a relief to find this Vassar graduate tall and handsome and dressed like other women. When, five years later, I went to Leipzig to study after I had been graduated from Cornell, my mother used to write me that my name was never mentioned to her by the women of her acquaintance. I was thought by them to be as much of a disgrace to my family as if I had eloped with the coachman....

[1] Quoted from an article by the Reverend John Todd, D.D., in the *Congregationalist* (August 31, 1871), by James Orton, *The Liberal Education of Women*, pp. 178–82. New York: A. S. Barnes and Company, 1873.

I think I can best tell you in a concrete way what has been accomplished in women's education by describing to you the condition of affairs which I found in 1884, when I returned from Germany, and set about planning the academic organization of Bryn Mawr. The outlook was discouraging except for the delight women were beginning to show in going to college. No one knew at all how things were going to turn out. The present achievement was small; the students were immature and badly trained; the scientific attainments of the professors teaching in colleges for women, with a few shining exceptions, were practically *nil*. Women were teaching in Wellesley, Mount Holyoke, and Smith without even the elementary training of a college course behind them. Men in general, including highly intelligent presidents of colleges for women, as well as highly intelligent presidents of colleges for men, held in good faith absurd opinions on women's education. When I protested to the president of the most advanced college for women in regard to this lack of training, he told me that we could never run Bryn Mawr if we insisted on the same scholarly attainments in women professors. He — and I think he will forgive me for quoting his opinion in those early days, because I am sure that he has since changed it — and the president of perhaps the greatest university for men in the United States, both told me that there was an intuitive something in ladies of birth and position, which enabled them to do without college training, and to make on the whole better professors for women college students than if they had themselves been to college....

We did not know when we began whether women's health could stand the strain of college education. We were haunted in those early days by the clanging chains of that gloomy little specter, Dr. Edward H. Clarke's *Sex in Education*. With trepidation of spirit I made my mother read it, and was much cheered by her remark that, as neither she, nor any of the women she knew, had ever seen girls or women of the kind described in Dr. Clarke's book, we might as well act as if they did not exist. Still, we did not *know* whether colleges might not produce a crop of just such invalids. Doctors insisted that they would. We women could not be sure until we had tried the experiment....

We did not really know anything about even the ordinary everyday intellectual capacity of women when we began to educate them. We were not even sure that they inherited their intellects from their fathers as well as from their mothers. We were told that their brains were too light, their foreheads too small, their reasoning powers too defective, their emotions too easily worked upon to make good students. None of these things has proved true.[1]

Today no one questions the desirability of providing higher education for women, and women now comprise more than 40 per cent of the entire enrollment in higher education in the United States. Differences of opinion and policy still exist with reference to the institutional plans for women's education. In the East and to some extent in the South the practice of separating the sexes for higher education is followed by many of the stronger institutions. Throughout the Middle West and West the dominant plan provides for the education of both sexes in a single institution. Under the circumstances of the economic depression of the 1930's a number of colleges of the single sex type began to admit students of the other sex, in order to increase their enrollments and enable them to operate on a more efficient basis.

ADMINISTRATIVE ORGANIZATION

The administrative organization of colleges and universities differs in many important respects from the organization for public-school systems, which was described in an earlier chapter. Even the titles of the administrative officers in colleges and universities are different from those with corresponding functions in the public-school system. The organization and administration of higher education in this country also differ in certain respects from that of the European institutions. A few of these distinctive features of administrative organization will be briefly reviewed.

Board of Control

The common pattern of institutional organization for higher education in the United States assigns the ultimate and final control to a lay board, usually known as the board of trustees, less

[1] M. Carey Thomas, "Present Tendencies in Women's Education," *Educational Review*, XXXV:66–70 (January, 1908).

frequently as the board of regents or board of directors. The principal exceptions to this plan of control are the institutions maintained by the Catholic Church and its religious orders, in which the ultimate control is usually vested in the religious hierarchy rather than in a board.

The board of trustees of the typical American institution is a noncampus body elected in most instances by the constituency of the institution or by representatives of the constituency, and in some cases elected by the members of the board itself. The board is responsible only to the constituency, and as its ties with the constituency are typically rather loose, the lay board ultimately becomes responsible chiefly to its own interpretation of social needs and pressures.

Institutional control by a lay board is in sharp contrast to the arrangement for the control of European universities. Until the coming of the totalitarian states practically all the European universities vested their final control either in an officer of the state or in the faculty of the institution. In all European institutions the control of policies has always been in the hands of the faculty. As implied in the foregoing paragraph, traditional practices have changed with the rise of totalitarian states. Universities in such countries are now directing their energies, on the domination of the authorities of these states, to dictated activities such as research leading to the solution of practical governmental and industrial problems and instruction in conformity with the accepted ideology of the régime.

Some critics of American higher education have objected to the vesting of control in a lay board of trustees. It has been pointed out that the members of college boards are usually drawn almost exclusively from the higher economic levels and from among professional specialists, especially the ministry, and that under such circumstances institutions of higher education are in danger of becoming instruments for the protection of class advantages. This may actually have happened in a few instances, but in the main it must be recognized that college and university trustees have accepted their responsibilities with a broad-minded social outlook and with a sincere desire to render the largest possible service for the good of society as a whole.

Some effective agency seems absolutely necessary for keeping institutions of higher education in touch with social demands. Considerable doubt might be expressed as to whether the faculty, if given the final control of an institution, would be as responsive to social demands as the members of lay boards of trustees have been. The "ivory-tower" ideal of educational service is consciously or unconsciously followed by many college professors, and it is to be doubted whether institutions of higher education would be as mindful of social pressures under faculty control as they are at present under the control of boards composed of laymen.

The Faculty

Despite the fact that the ultimate control of the American institution of higher education is usually lodged in lay boards of trustees, the immediate control over most educational affairs is generally delegated to the faculty. In such matters as the curriculum, standards for admission of students, and requirements for graduation, tradition strongly favors the lodgment of control in the hands of the faculty. Higher education in this respect contrasts sharply with other levels of education in the American system. The degree of control exercised over educational policies by the teaching staff is much greater in the colleges and universities than in the secondary school or in the elementary school.

The control of the collegiate faculty over the educational program is doubtless a survival of the medieval influence under which the universities developed. It will be recalled that in the Middle Ages, when the universities were established, the guild was the dominant form of social and economic organization. The universities were first formed as guilds of scholars, and it was only natural that the members of the guild should control the conditions for admission to apprenticeship, the course of training, and acceptance into the status of journeyman or master.   The guild of scholars insisted upon these rights and today, therefore, control of academic requirements is in the main a prerogative of the college faculty.

In practice, therefore, the effective control of an institution of higher education is divided between two different agencies. Legally, the board of trustees has the final and responsible power over the entire institution.   Practically, the control of educational affairs is in every well-managed institution delegated to the faculty.   The president serves as the chief executive officer, administering the policies determined both by the board of trustees and by the faculty.

In some institutions the president assumes a dictatorial position and either fails to consult the faculty as a group on educational matters or coerces the individual members into an acceptance of his policies through his power of recommending to the board the appointment, promotion, and dismissal of staff members.   In many institutions also the president occupies a dominant position over the members of the board of trustees.   It is not at all uncommon for the president of an institution to have an active part in the initial selection of board members, and in some cases a president has been known to insist on the selection of only those persons as board members who will acquiesce in the development of the policies proposed by him.   Thus while in theory the ultimate control of a higher institution is lodged in the board of trustees and while also under sound theory the faculty is given a very large control over academic matters, in actual practice the president frequently becomes the strategic center for the more or less complete direction of the affairs of the institution.

The College President

Unusual prestige attaches to the chief executive officer of the college or university.   The president, or chancellor as this officer is called in a few institutions, outranks in popular esteem practically every other type of personnel in the educational system. Institutions, in recounting the great services they have rendered society, are certain to list the number of their graduates who have become college or university presidents, and this category seems much more important than all other types of social or public service into which graduates enter. As a matter of fact, the office of the president of a small college is a much less significant position than the superintendency of a city school system or even the principalship of a city high school; yet the deference paid to the president of a collegiate institution is unmistakably greater than that paid to any of the other executives in the educational system.

The reasons for this unusual prestige of the college presidency probably are to be found in the traditional place which higher education has held in popular esteem. A cynic might point to the institutions of higher education as the only places in the school system where democracy is openly flouted in the selection of students, the only place where admission is still based in considerable part upon economic ability. As a surviving remnant of an aristocratic social order the college, and its symbol the president, receive the deference which the common people have long been expected to pay their superiors in social status. If this cynical explanation is correct, one may expect to see the presidency of higher institutions lose its prestige if and when democracy compels the opening of the doors of opportunity to all regardless of economic circumstances.

Perhaps a truer explanation lies in the fact that the college is the oldest of the institutions of education in America. The three-hundredth anniversary of the founding of the first college was celebrated a few years ago and a number of institutions of the collegiate type have persisted from early colonial times to the present under the same names and in the same locations. The typical secondary school, by contrast, is relatively new, and few local public-school systems, in their present organization, date their beginnings back as far as a century ago.

Furthermore, it may be pointed out that some institutions of higher education have exercised a notable influence on the development of America through the training of leaders. The president of the college and university, as a leader of those who train leaders, naturally is looked upon as an important personage.

CURRICULUM AND DEGREES

Extent of Subject-Matter Offerings

The institution of higher education typically has a widely diversified group of offerings. Earlier in this discussion the expansions in the offerings of the secondary school were pointed out, but the expansions at that level have been modest indeed, compared to what has taken place at the level of higher education.

Data published in 1932 from a study of thirty-five colleges of liberal arts show an average of 801 semester hours of different offerings per institution. If it be considered that thirty semester hours is the normal load for a student for one academic year, the average college in this group offers enough different courses to keep one student busy between twenty-six and twenty-seven years. Three of the larger colleges in the group offered between 1200 and 1500 semester hours, enough to keep a single student busy for forty or fifty years. This tabulation includes only liberal arts colleges offering a four-year program of undergraduate work, although in a few cases the Master's degree was offered in some fields. If the offerings of universities in graduate courses and in professional subjects should be considered, the total would be stupendous. At the University of Chicago, for example, a survey in 1928–29 found a total of 2708 different courses offered in the one year. The normal load for a student was nine courses per year, so this institution was offering a sufficient number of different courses to keep a student busy, if he should take them all, for more than three hundred years.

The extensiveness of the offerings in higher institutions is a matter of relatively recent development. The expansion has been influenced by a number of factors, perhaps the most important of which has been the increasing knowledge about the universe which has developed in modern times. So much more knowledge is available now than was available only a few decades ago that the mere problem of transmitting this knowledge to the oncoming generation assumes breath-taking proportions. The programs of the elementary and the secondary school have been greatly enriched because of this new knowledge; but the number of years available for schooling at those levels has been more or less fixed so the only area in which unlimited expansion has seemed possible is in colleges and universities.

A second factor in the situation has been the increased variety of interests served by institutions of higher education. Originally established chiefly for the purpose of preparing boys for the ministry, the colleges and universities have come to recognize much broader purposes, and are today serving the interests of an extremely diversified student body. The adaptation of the program of the college to the needs of individual students has necessitated wide diversification of subject-matter offerings.

In the third place the new knowledge that has developed has proved especially valuable and absolutely necessary in many cases for the effective conduct of the affairs of society. A single example will serve to illustrate this fact. In the field of medicine great advances have been made in the knowledge of diseases and how to treat them. Adequate medical care must be based on a thorough preparation of young people in the knowledge of these scientific discoveries; the amount of learning which the young person must acquire before he can be considered qualified as a physician is greatly increased over that which was necessary only a generation or two ago. Society depends upon its institutions of higher education to give candidates for admission to the profession of medicine the preparation which they require, and institutions have no alternative but to increase their subject-matter offerings so that they may include all the equipment necessary for the various specialized lines of service. The same statement can be made with regard to all professions and also with regard to many new and developing nonprofessional aspects of citizenship and daily living. In consequence of these demands colleges and universities have expanded their offerings to an almost unbelievable extent.

Obviously no individual can afford to take the time which would be necessary to obtain all the knowledge represented even by what would be considered a modest offering of courses in the undergraduate college, to say nothing of the infinite variety of specialized courses at the graduate and professional level. Specialization is characteristic of all advanced education. Each person in society chooses a limited branch of service and attempts to perfect himself or herself in that branch of human activity. Thus one who prepares to be a teacher is not expected to obtain the types of knowledge that are indispensable for a physician or a lawyer. Even among teachers, as in other professions, there is a considerable degree of specialization; some obtain only the preparation needed for service at the level of the primary school, others for a particular subject in the secondary school, and still others for a narrow field of specialization at the college or university level.

The institutions of higher education are under the necessity of providing specialized preparation for all of these varied types of specialized services. Most institutions definitely limit the kinds of preparation which they will give. Some, for example, do not offer preparation for medicine. Others do not give the training necessary for engineers, or for lawyers, or for other specialized activities. The institution which accepts students who are preparing for a variety of specialized services is under moral obligation to provide the best possible programs of preparation, and hence must multiply its course offerings to correspond to the variety in the objectives of the students who are accepted.

The liberal arts college often describes itself as concerned with general education or with types of education suitable to the needs of all without reference to the various specialized activities in which they will later engage. This institution does not, however, escape the trend toward specialization. It typically prepares its students for teaching and provides also some of the preprofessional preparation for a number of different types of service. Because of the relative limitations in terms of interests served, the liberal arts college can manage with a smaller total offering than the university.

Curriculum Organization

The enormous expansion of offerings at the college level has resulted in serious problems of curriculum organization. In an earlier day it was possible to offer a single curriculum with all subjects definitely prescribed, because the group of students was homogeneous with respect to vocational and cultural purposes, and the amount of knowledge needed for these purposes was not beyond the bounds of a four-year program. Expansions in subject matter were first made by establishing new and parallel curriculums, the student being offered a choice from two or more of these curriculums. Thus the student might choose the classical curriculum, which stressed ancient languages and philosophy, or he might choose the scientific curriculum which stressed mathematics and science.

The device of parallel curriculums served for a while, but it was later found to be too narrow a structure in which to confine all the rapidly expanding knowledge that was being produced. The next plan followed was that of the elective curriculum, which was advocated and effectively developed by President Charles W. Eliot of Harvard in the period after the Civil War. The example of Harvard was followed by most other colleges. Under the elective system the colleges multiplied their offerings of courses and threw on the students the burden of selecting those courses which would be of most worth to them personally. Graduate programs were added during this same period to care for the increased specialization of subject matter.

The elective system was soon found to result in many cases in unintelligent selection and arrangement of studies by individual students. Certain devices were introduced as a curb on free and unguided election. A plan widely followed since the beginning of the twentieth century requires the student to concentrate from one-fifth to one-third of his total program in a single department of study, known as a major, and to present another similar block of subject matter, smaller in extent, in a closely related field, known as a minor. In this way students are held for a substantial degree of penetration into at least one or two fields of subject matter during their four-year program.

Another restriction, introduced at about the same time as the major-and-minor system, requires the student to distribute his program of courses over the recognized fields of subject matter. The various departmental offerings are arranged into from four to seven broad groups, representing such basic areas as the social sciences, the humanities, the natural sciences, and so on, and students are required to present for graduation some courses in each of these broad fields.

The tendency at present is distinctly toward a greater amount of prescription in the student's program and toward the provision of better advisory service for guiding him in the choice of his type of curriculum and his elective subjects. The theory behind increased prescription of courses is that mature scholars in a field know better than the immature student knows what will be advantageous for his intellectual development. The institution, therefore, has an obligation to its students to set up the most economical and effective program of study, so that the student's time will be used advantageously.

The tendency to separate general education from special education has resulted in a corresponding division both of the college curriculum and of the advisory services. Agreement is reasonably common on the allocation of the first two years of the college program to the function of general education; the function of specialized training becomes dominant in the student's program after the first two years. Thus the colleges in many instances have seen fit to divide their curriculums into two major sections, one comprising the first two years, and the other the remainder of the program. In numerous instances institutions have set up admission requirements for the upper divisional level as well as entrance requirements for admission to the lower level from the secondary school. The students typically are under the guidance of one set of counselors during their first two years and of a different set of counselors after they have chosen their fields of specialization and have advanced into the upper division.

In order to accomplish the purposes of general education a number of institutions have experimented with new organization of the fields of subject matter. One plan widely followed provides for the organization of survey courses, in which the attempt is made to present an integrated view of broad fields of subject matter instead of a narrow and specialized view. Another prominent innovation consists of the complete abandonment of the traditional subject-matter fields and the organization, for purposes of general education, of courses built along such lines as the reading of great books or the detailed examination of some particular civilization such as that of Ancient Greece. Still another plan involves the organization of courses along functional lines rather than along the lines of the traditional academic classifications. The field of general education is at present one of the livest areas of curriculum experimentation, and it is probable that out of the efforts now going on there may ultimately appear and be accepted a drastic revision of the traditional grouping of subject-matter courses.

Degrees

The institution of higher education offers degrees as evidence of the completion of its curriculums. The degree is so intimately associated in popular thinking with institutions of higher education that its special and unique character as a factor in the educational system is often overlooked. At no other level of the educational program is a degree offered. The secondary schools and

even the elementary schools now imitate the college commencement program and grant diplomas, but those who complete the
programs of these other levels are not awarded a degree. The
present custom is to award the Bachelor's degree at the end of
the four-year program of study beyond the completion of the
secondary school; to give the Master's degree for usually one, or
sometimes two years of study beyond the Bachelor's degree; and
the Doctor's degree for a minimum of three years of study beyond the Bachelor's degree.

The custom of granting degrees arose with the establishment
of the universities in the late Middle Ages. As has already been
pointed out, the institutions of higher education first appeared
at a time when the guild was the important form of social organization, and the universities were originally organized as guilds
of scholars. In the guild, three classes or grades of membership
were recognized: the apprentice who was learning the craft; the
journeyman who was competent to practice it; and the master
who was competent to take an apprentice and to teach him the
craft. One progressed from the grade of apprentice to the grade
of journeyman by serving a specified time of training. One could
achieve the grade of master only by proving himself an exceptionally competent workman. The master was usually required
to prove his competency by the production of a masterpiece.

Inasmuch as the universities were established for the purpose
of teaching apprentices the craft of scholarship, those who were
the teachers were known as masters and the designation "master" was granted originally as a degree to those who had completed the course of apprenticeship. Because the craft of scholarship was associated with the liberal arts, the completion of
apprenticeship was signalized by granting the Master of Arts,
just as one at a similar level in the goldsmith's guild would be a
master goldsmith. Somewhat later the Bachelor's degree was
introduced in the system of higher education to indicate the stage
of apprenticeship at which the student could begin some practice
in teaching under supervision, a stage now known in all well-

managed institutions preparing teachers as apprentice teaching or practice teaching.

The Doctor's degree was originally synonymous with the Master's, for both words mean "teacher." Later, however, the Master's degree came to be reserved for the teachers of liberal arts; the teachers of the professional subjects such as law, medicine, and theology, were known as Doctors.

The practice of granting degrees, established in the medieval university, has continued into modern time. Much of the ceremony of the modern college commencement program traces its origin to the medieval university. For example, when the president today confers upon the graduates the respective degrees "with all the rights and privileges appertaining thereunto," one perhaps may wonder what these rights and privileges now are, other than the right to hunt a job in an unreceptive world. But in the medieval period, the rights and privileges granted to one who obtained the scholarly degree were those of membership in a guild, an all-important possession in the society of that day.

The introduction of new fields of subject matter was a disturbing influence in the curriculum of the college, for the question was immediately raised as to the degree that would be appropriate for one who had studied these new subjects. The guardians of the older disciplines were almost always in the majority on the faculties of the colleges, and they felt it their duty to protect the traditional degrees, Bachelor of Arts and Master of Arts, against debasement or change of pattern. The compromise came in the form of a new degree. Thus when science insisted on its place in the curriculum, faculties agreed to award the degree, Bachelor of Science, instead of the Bachelor of Arts which had long been based on the classical subjects.

Later, other fields of study were added and the process of multiplying degrees began. No tabulation has ever been reported showing the number of different degrees that have been offered and conferred in American colleges and universities, but the number is undoubtedly large. The custom of granting Bachelor's degrees with designation of special fields has been widely followed, as Bachelor of Music, or Bachelor of Education, or Bachelor of Oratory. Sometimes a designation such as Bachelor of Science in Business Administration or Bachelor of Science in Home Economics, has been used.

The multiplicity of degrees has caused confusion. The necessity for this varied array of degrees arises, it will be observed, because of the inflexible attitude of the faculties representing the established disciplines toward new subjects of study. In recent years the tendency has been distinctly away from the varied assortment of degrees and toward a return to the simpler plan of granting only a single degree, the Bachelor of Arts, for the completion of any four-year curriculum. At present this is only a tendency, however, and many institutions still follow the practice of granting a number of different degrees.

LIBRARIES

An important feature of every well-equipped institution of higher education is the library. The maintenance of an adequate library is one of the responses to the vast increases in knowledge that have occurred in recent decades. Even with the multiplication of courses in the curriculum it has not been possible to teach more than a small fraction of the total knowledge available concerning the universe. In order that this knowledge may not be lost and in order that it may be made available to the occasional student who wishes to refer to it, institutions have developed libraries in which are stored thousands, or in some cases even millions of books and other documents.

The library has served not only as a storehouse of knowledge but also as an increasingly important adjunct to the instructional program. In an earlier period the method of instruction was largely of the question-and-answer type, with dependence on a single authoritative source of information by the student in the preparation of his lessons. Later the lecture method came into

prominence in the college, although the students were still expected to use textbooks in their study.   The recent tendencies
have been in the direction of expanding the amount of source
material with which the student is expected to be familiar.   Instead of or in addition to a single text, the student now is usually
asked to read from a wide variety of sources on the topics covered
in the course.

This change in instructional method has thrown stress on the
library services of colleges and universities.   Readings required
of students in large classes must be available in many copies, and
a system of reserved books with limited circulation has been
evolved to assist in caring for these demands.   Students are expected, more and more, to be able to look up the answers to their
questions in the library, and to assist in this process it has been
necessary to develop a reference service within the library.

The growth of human knowledge has complicated tremen-
dously the storing and classification of books.   The typical experience in almost every college that has constructed a new library building in recent decades is to find that the capacity of the
building is exhausted within a short time after its construction is
completed.   Extensive systems of classification have been devised
in order that the books on a given subject may be shelved together.   In a large library the process of ordering, cataloguing, and
making a book ready for use by readers is both slow and costly;
in some universities the expense involved in such services aver-
ages from one-fourth to one-half the purchase price of the
book.

The complications of the task of managing a library have led
to the development of specialized library services.   Originally
when the college libraries began to develop it was the custom to
appoint some member of the faculty as the custodian of the
books.   The responsibilities of the librarianship soon outgrew
this simple procedure and today in every well-managed college
and university the library is in charge of a professionally trained,
highly skilled expert.   In a large library there is a corps of staff

members, each of whom is an expert in one of the various specialized lines of library service. The cost of maintaining library service is no small item in the budget of institutions of higher education, averaging in the neighborhood of 4 to 5 per cent of the total expenditures for all current educational purposes.

Today higher education is characteristically said to be library-minded. The adoption of the library method of instruction has marked a significant development in the instructional methods for higher education. Perhaps the end has not yet been reached, for some have suggested that ultimately all the instructional services of a nonlaboratory type may be carried on in the library. Instead of professors lecturing to classes, the staff of the college may consist of specialized reference librarians who spend their time guiding the reading of students along the lines prescribed by the curriculum or dictated by the student's special interests.

PUBLIC SERVICE

Institutions of higher education in the United States are customarily called upon to render various types of public service and to release their staff members for such service when demand arises. The staff of the university or college includes experts in many varied lines of human interests and activity. These experts are frequently asked to give advice on problems of public or private interest, and to conduct studies for agencies outside the institution of higher education. For example, if a state or city has a tax problem that seems difficult of solution, an expert on taxation from the university may be called in to advise and to develop an improved program. If a disease breaks out in some agricultural crop, a plant pathologist from the university may be called in to diagnose the difficulty and to prescribe appropriate remedies. If a local school system needs guidance in improving its services, a professor of education may be called in to make a survey of the situation.

The rendering of public service has had an important reflex

influence on the institution of higher education. Nothing serves better to keep the instructional service of the institution closely in touch with practical realities than an occasional trip into the field by members of the teaching staff. The professor who lacks such contacts may easily fall into the habit of armchair philosophizing about his subject. In general, the instructional services of institutions are undoubtedly improved by the public service that is rendered by members of the faculty.

One other type of public service which is expected from colleges and universities today deserves some comment. The preceding discussion has related to the services by members of the faculty; the public also seems to expect some types of service from the students. These demands take the form of insistence upon certain types of exhibitions or entertainments, and in some of these areas the public demand is so insistent as to dominate entirely the college program.

Perhaps the outstanding example of this type of public demand is in the field of intercollegiate athletics. The games, originally introduced as a sport for the entertainment of student athletes and other members of the student body, have attracted large numbers of spectators from outside the institution. The whole enterprise has become commercialized and the program of athletics in many institutions is now conducted much more with an eye to the profits to be derived from the sale of admissions to the public than with an eye to the benefit of the athletes or other members of the student body.

Naturally, as the colleges and universities have come to cater to the public taste in athletics, the public has more and more insisted on a voice concerning the management of the enterprise. Today in many important educational institutions the policies regarding athletics are decided not by the regularly constituted authorities of the institution, but by a group of outsiders who are interested only in athletics as public entertainment. The abuses that have crept into the management of intercollegiate athletics were vigorously pointed out in a report by one of the foundations published in 1929.[1]   Although no complete study of the situation has been made since that time, there is reason to believe that abuses are now more common than they were formerly.

The question of the management of athletics is not one that can be easily dismissed.   Inasmuch as the public has been taught to look to the colleges and universities for this type of entertainment, it is to be expected that some type of control will be exercised from the outside.   Much of the difficulty arises from the dependence of the institutions on gate receipts for the financing of the athletic program.   Many colleges and universities, furthermore, have gone deeply into debt in order to build athletic plants, and the maintenance of an athletic program that will attract large gate receipts is necessary to retire this indebtedness.

Perhaps the error was made in ever encouraging the public to look to the college and university for this type of entertainment. That mistake has already been made and it is not easily rectified. No clearer example could be found of a situation in which social demands are modifying the program of an educational institution.   It will be granted in this instance that the social demands are perhaps unwise; nevertheless, the institutions that have encouraged the public to make such demands must now choose either to satisfy them or to undergo criticism.   The best way out of the situation, perhaps, would be for the colleges and universities to assist in developing other means of satisfying the public demand for entertainment.   It is thought by many that the corrective may come from the development of professional football and basketball teams, which seem to be giving some promise of ultimately relieving the pressure on colleges for the maintenance of unsound athletic programs.

[1] Howard J. Savage and Others, *American College Athletics*.   Carnegie Foundation for the Advancement of Teaching Bulletin XXIII.   New York: Carnegie Foundation for the Advancement of Teaching, 1929.

RESEARCH

Institutions of higher education are expected not only to preserve and disseminate the existing store of knowledge but to add to that store. In the educational system the extension of knowledge by the process of research has come to be recognized as a major function of universities.

Society is not solely dependent on institutions of higher education for extensions of knowledge by research. Both in industry and in government, particularly in the Federal Government, research has been pursued in an indefatigable spirit. A recent study suggests that probably not more than 20 per cent of the total research carried on in this country is done in institutions of higher education.

Research carried on in industry must necessarily be more or less related to practical problems and must look ultimately toward greater profit for the enterprise. Research under governmental auspices also tends to be largely of the type that results in immediately usable results although it is less severely restricted in this respect than research carried on in industrial establishments. In institutions of higher education, by contrast, there is a large opportunity for carrying on what is called "pure" or "fundamental" research, that is, research directed merely toward the discovery of new knowledge without any particular regard to the use which is or may be made of that knowledge. It is not to be overlooked in this connection that in many cases pure research ultimately proves to be of practical utility, because through such research entirely new principles are sometimes discovered which later find important practical application.

Research is carried on in the universities by two different means. In all well-managed universities qualified staff members are allowed a certain amount of time for research and are given a correspondingly light teaching load in order that they may devote themselves to the discovery of new knowledge. These institutions also accept advanced students and require them, as part of their preparation for higher degrees, to demonstrate their competence by the production of research which results in a Master's thesis or Doctor's dissertation. The whole program of preparation for the highest degree, the Doctor of Philosophy or the Doctor of Science, is customarily centered chiefly around the training in research. Certain practitioners' degrees such as the doctorate degree in medicine and the new degree, Doctor of Education, intended for the training of educational specialists of various types, do not emphasize research.

UNSETTLED PROBLEMS

The whole field of higher education is at present in a state of flux, and it is entirely probable that the next few decades will witness important changes in the program at this level. Many problems remain yet to be solved. Perhaps none is more important than the question of the extent to which wider provision of higher education should be made for an increasing number of the population. The occupations for which college preparation is important are increasing, and the services of the college in general education are needed by many future citizens. Entrance upon first employment is coming at an increasingly later stage, as has previously been pointed out, and the provision of suitable opportunities for education at the college level may thus be necessary for a much larger percentage of the population than ever before. The way in which the programs of colleges and universities should be modified in order to adapt them to this larger percentage of the population is a challenging question.

Another pressing problem arises from the enormous rate at which new knowledge is being added to the cultural heritage. The curriculum has already been overloaded by the addition of new knowledge and yet more and more is discovered every year that must at some time be brought into the curriculum. Some thinkers have advocated the view that institutions should cease to attempt the teaching of all this new knowledge, and should instead return to a simpler curriculum of an earlier day, with philosophy and metaphysics as the only subjects of instruction and with a few of the classics as the only books to be studied. Others feel that this solution is entirely too simple and suggest that a generation so instructed would not be well fitted for modern life. The attempts at survey courses and at a functional organization of studies have been mentioned earlier; these also represent promising attacks on the problem.

Certainly as long as the attempt is to teach in more or less specific terms the knowledge that is or will be useful to the student and future citizen, a continued effort is necessary for the reformulation of subject matter, so that the useless may be deleted and all that is useful in the new knowledge may be added. The process of curriculum making in the higher institutions thus becomes a continuing task, one that deserves the best efforts of subject-matter specialists and experts in the field of educational methods.

The problem of financing the expanding program of higher education is a grave one. Particularly during the economic depression of the 1930's higher education has been crippled by reduction of income from endowment, by restrictions on legislative appropriations, and by the falling off of philanthropic gifts. Higher education must continually justify itself in terms of social service if it is to expect to obtain the funds necessary for its future support.

BIBLIOGRAPHY

Burton, William H., *Introduction to Education*, pp. 225–40.
Cubberley, Ellwood P., *Public Education in the United States*, pp. 651–62.
Cubberley, Ellwood P., *State School Administration*, pp. 336–60.
Douglass, Aubrey A., *The American School System*, pp. 186–213.
Flexner, Abraham, *Universities, American, English, German.* New York: Oxford University Press, 1930. ix + 382 pp.
Hutchins, Robert M., *The Higher Learning in America.* New Haven: Yale University Press, 1936. iv + 120 pp.

Judd, Charles H., *Education and Social Progress*, pp. 181–208.

Judd, Charles H., *Problems of Education in the United States*, pp. 133–37.

Kelly, Robert L., editor, *The Effective College*. New York: Association of American Colleges, 1928. xii + 302 pp.

Kent, Raymond, editor, *Higher Education in America*. New York: Ginn and Company, 1930. x + 690 pp.

National Society for the Study of Education, *General Education in the American College*. *Thirty-Eighth Yearbook*, Part II. Bloomington, Illinois: Public School Publishing Company, 1939. xii + 382 pp.

Reeder, Ward, *A First Course in Education*, pp. 463–68.

Reeves, Floyd W., John Dale Russell, H. C. Gregg, A. J. Brumbaugh, and L. E. Blauch, *The Liberal Arts College*. Chicago: University of Chicago Press, 1932. xxxvi + 716 pp.

Smith, Payson, Frank W. Wright, and Associates, *Education in the Forty-Eight States*, pp. 161–74. Staff Study no. 1, Advisory Committee on Education.

Wilson, Lester M., and I. L. Kandel, *Introduction to the Study of American Education*, pp. 233–52.

Works, George A., and Barton Morgan, *The Land-Grant Colleges*. Staff Study no. 10, Advisory Committee on Education. Washington: Government Printing Office, 1939. x + 142 pp.

CHAPTER XV

New and Variant Forms

of Educational Service

THE CONVENTIONAL UNITS of the American educational system are organized to care for the needs of young people from about the age of six up to age twenty or twenty-five. In earlier chapters it has been shown that the elementary school, the secondary school, the college, and the graduate and professional schools are expected to provide an articulated system through which every person may progress regularly to the limit of his capabilities. The nature of these conventional units of the American educational system has also been described in considerable detail.

A number of forms of educational service maintained in the United States are not comprehended in the regular features of the elementary school, secondary school, college, and university. Some of these types of education are recognized more or less definitely as responsibilities of the school system; others are carried on by agencies outside the schools. Some of these services are only remotely related to educational objectives; others are a vital part of any well-rounded conception of educational service. The discussion in this chapter will treat ten of these variant forms of educational service. The arrangement is roughly in order of the age groups served by each unit.

THE NURSERY SCHOOL

The institutionalized form of educational service serving the youngest age group is the nursery school, which usually accepts children between the ages of two and four. The nursery school is a relatively new organization and facilities of this type are by no means widespread throughout the country.

There are two justifications for an institution to serve the needs of very young children. In the first place, industrial organization is employing the services of an increasing number of women. Many of these women workers are mothers of young children of preschool age, and some custodial arrangement for the care of such children is necessary if the mothers are to carry on their employment outside the home. In the second place, psychological studies have shown that many mental disorders which appear in adults have their origins in unfortunate environmental conditions or experiences during the first few years of childhood. By means of an institutional organization such as the nursery school undesirable tendencies can often be discovered early and plans worked out for their correction.

It is important to note, therefore, that the nursery school is a product of two different forces: the demands of modern social and economic organization, and the knowledge produced by scientific study of child development. These two forces have been frequently pointed out in earlier chapters as important influences affecting the American educational system; it is interesting to find them uniting in creating a strong demand for a new type of educational institution, the nursery school. These demands were recognized explicitly in the White House Conference on Child Health and Protection which met in 1930. One of the reports presented to that Conference called attention to the nursery school as a significant development in modern educational procedure.

In the program of the nursery school the emphasis, so far as the child is concerned, is chiefly on the development of good health habits and on social training. No attempt is usually made to lay any groundwork of intellectual instruction, but great care is taken to teach the young child to work and play amicably with the other children in the school. The physical and mental health of the child is carefully watched, and the daily schedule requires periods of rest and gives attention to the development of other health habits.

Almost equally important with the care and training given the child in the nursery school is the instruction given the parents whose children are in attendance.   The school at best can influence the lives of children for only a small part of the day and the responsibility for making effective much of the training that is given lies with the home.   Many of the nursery schools are organized on a co-operative basis; under this plan the mother is required each week to spend some time in the school, ostensibly for the purpose of helping with the work, but also for the usually unexpressed purpose of providing an opportunity for parent education.   Other more direct methods are frequently used by the nursery schools to instruct parents regarding the proper care of their young children, such as individual conferences and group meetings at which child problems are discussed.   A plan sometimes followed involves the keeping of a complete record of everything said by each child during a given period; the parents may then be informed of the psychological significance of the child's reactions.

The nursery school has developed principally outside the regular school system.   The public-school organization has not generally accepted this new institution; educational authorities have been loath to take on the added burden of providing nursery-school services for young children.   The statement is commonly made that the funds provided for maintaining the regular school system are not sufficient and that to take some of these funds for the provision of a new service, the value of which has not been proved by years of experience, is unwise.   The personnel of the public-school system, furthermore, is not well equipped by training or experience to conduct the kinds of service demanded in the nursery school.   For these, and possibly for other reasons, relatively few nursery schools have thus far been incorporated as a regular feature of the public-school system.

Most nursery schools are at present carried on as private or philanthropic enterprises. During the depression of the 1930's the Federal Government undertook the provision of nursery-school services as a part of its relief program. The nursery school was a particularly effective relief project because qualified nurses and attendants could usually be found on the relief rolls, and because children from relief families were especially in need of the services of such an institution. Furthermore, the Federal Government had on hand surplus commodities that could be used, and equipment and other needed materials could be made with relief labor. The stimulation afforded by the federal emergency educational program has thus far been the most important factor affecting the development of the nursery school in the United States. It remains to be seen whether the fostering of this development under the auspices of the federal emergency educational program will ultimately have the effect of inducing local school systems to take on the nursery school as a part of their regular service.

THE KINDERGARTEN

The institution for children of the ages immediately preceding entrance to the elementary school is known as the kindergarten. For the most part the program of the kindergarten is one year in length, admitting children at the age of five years and sending them to the first grade of the elementary school at six years. In some cases a kindergarten program of two years is maintained, admitting children at age four.

Frederick Froebel, a German philosopher, was the originator of the kindergarten. He developed the idea about 1837, and devoted the remainder of his life to the founding of kindergartens in Germany. The idea of this new type of institution was not widely accepted in Germany, although a few of the leading thinkers favored the organization of such an addition to the educational system. Kindergartens were first established in the

United States shortly before the Civil War by German-Americans who had become acquainted with the institutions in Europe. In Wisconsin and in several American cities where considerable numbers of German-speaking people lived, kindergartens were established on a private basis. In 1860 Miss Elizabeth Peabody, who had become acquainted with the kindergarten as it was developed in England, set up the first English kindergarten in Boston.

St. Louis in 1873 was the first public-school system in the United States to add the kindergarten to its facilities. The movement did not progress rapidly, and by 1890 there were only a few cities which included the kindergarten as a part of their public-school systems. Exhibitions at the Centennial Exposition in 1876 and the Columbian Exposition in 1893 did much to stimulate interest in this new educational enterprise. During the twentieth century there has been an increase in the number of school systems maintaining kindergartens, but this facility is still found almost exclusively in the cities, and exists in only a minority of them.

During the depression of the 1930's there was a tendency as an economy measure to discontinue the kindergarten in many cities. The total reported enrollment in kindergartens decreased 18 per cent between 1930 and 1934; an increase of less than 1 per cent occurred between 1934 and 1936. A small part of the decrease in enrollments since 1930 may be accounted for by the decline in birth rate rather than by the discontinuance of kindergarten facilities. Calculation from data published by the United States Office of Education indicates that approximately one child in four attended a kindergarten in 1936. Statistics of enrollment for this level of education are probably incomplete, for many small private kindergartens are maintained which commonly do not report data to any central agency.

As originally developed by Froebel, the kindergarten procedure was filled with symbolism. For example, the children sat or stood in a circle in order that they might absorb the mystic sense of unity; an elaborate series of what Froebel called "gifts" was a part of the procedure. Under modern conditions most of this formality and mystic symbolism has been dropped and the procedures have been based on scientific analyses of child psychology.

Studies of the effect of the kindergarten experience on individual children are somewhat disappointing, for measurable outcomes in terms of beneficial effect on later scholastic attainment are not found. When children of equal ability are paired with reference to having attended or not attended a kindergarten, little or no difference is found in the scholastic attainments of the two groups in their later school years. It is entirely probable that the correct conclusion to be drawn from such investigations is that the kindergarten provides an enriched experience for the child rather than preparation for the studies of the later school years.

The kindergarten has undoubtedly had a notable effect on the elementary school through the insistence on beauty as a desirable feature of the school environment. The elementary-school classroom of the 1890's, according to contemporary accounts, was a dreary place without decorations of any sort and with no attempt to present an attractive environment for the pupils or teachers. The kindergarten, by contrast, has insisted from the outset that the schoolroom and its surroundings and equipment are to be as beautiful as possible. Green plants are arranged where they may receive sunlight. Decorative curtains are hung at the windows. Blocks and other equipment are painted in bright colors. A fireplace is often provided, and the furniture is designed to interest and attract the young child. Elementary schools have not taken over this entire scheme of decoration, but dreary dungeonlike classrooms have been transformed into inviting and attractive places for work and study. Perhaps the kindergarten has not been the sole factor that has affected the transformation in the elementary school, but the influence has undoubtedly been an effective one.

In another respect also the kindergarten has had a marked

effect on the program of the later school years.   The program of
the kindergarten has been free from the usual academic traditions
and has been able to develop around the concept of the educative
value of motor activity.   The activity movement, at present
widely discussed as a desirable feature of a progressive school
organization, probably traces its origin to the kindergarten.
Thus, the kindergarten may be considered to have affected to
a notable extent the entire program of the elementary school.

CONTINUATION SCHOOLS

In order to provide opportunities of both cultural and vocational types on a part-time basis for young people who have left
school for employment, an organization known as the continuation school has been developed.   Such institutions have had
extensive development in European countries, but have not
proved widely popular in the United States.   The continuation
school in this country has been associated chiefly with the fur-
therance of education after the boy or girl has reached the end of
compulsory school attendance period and has entered employment.   In some states the compulsory school attendance laws
permit discontinuance of attendance at the full-time school at
age sixteen, for those who are able to find employment, but only
on condition that the employed youth attends the continuation
school for a further period of one or two years.   The continuation schooling required is generally three or four hours per week
or a total of approximately 144 hours per year.   The program is
usually administered in connection with some established secondary school.

The continuation-school movement was stimulated to some
extent by the Smith-Hughes Act which provided grants of
federal funds for assisting the payment of teachers' salaries in,
many types of vocational education, including the continuation
school.   The continuation school movement, however, seems
destined to be absorbed in the larger program of adult education.

The only distinctions at present between the continuation school and adult education are the tradition of relating the continuation school program to the needs of boys and girls who have only recently left school, and the connection between the continuation school and the compulsory attendance laws.   Neither of these distinctions warrants the maintenance of a program of continuation schools separate from other facilities for adult education.

AGENCIES FOR THE PREVENTION OF JUVENILE DELINQUENCY

Under a broad definition of education the juvenile courts and the agencies for the prevention of juvenile delinquency should be considered as rendering educational service.   The realization of the need for extraordinary measures for dealing with juvenile offenders has come only recently.   The common law holds that one who has committed an offense can be punished only when he is a responsible person.   Gradually it has become clear that children cannot be considered responsible because they lack the mature judgment of the adult, and hence special devices are necessary in administering justice in the case of juvenile offenders.

The plan that is widely followed calls for the establishment of a separate court, known as the juvenile court, in which young offenders are tried.   A separate vocabulary has been developed in dealing with such cases; the offense, for example, is known as a delinquency rather than as a crime, as it would be called if it were committed by an adult.   The juvenile court is given a large measure of discretion in dealing with individual cases of delinquency.   The usual procedure is to place a first offender on probation in charge of some responsible person or agency in the community, which will look after his welfare and advise and guide him away from the antisocial attitudes and practices on which he has entered.

To deal with the juvenile delinquent after he has committed an offense is not enough; measures for the prevention of delinquency are of first importance. Studies made of the geographical pattern of juvenile delinquency reveal a surprising concentration in certain neighborhoods in the large cities. The only conclusion that can be drawn from this fact of the localization of juvenile delinquency in certain urban areas is that the society which permits such areas to exist must assume the responsibility for overcoming these unfortunate environmental influences. Acting on this principle, public-spirited citizens have established neighborhood clubs and services of various types in which recreational, social, and educational activities are provided under wholesome surroundings with the purpose of counteracting the antisocial influences of the general community environment.

The public school has done little or nothing to develop neighborhood centers for the prevention of juvenile delinquency. The schools in neighborhoods in which the rate of delinquency is high usually maintain a program almost identical with that in other neighborhoods throughout the city; it seems difficult for the school system to adjust its program to the special needs of problem areas. Under private auspices, however, much has been done to demonstrate the wisdom of promoting special facilities in such areas. The Y.M.C.A. has accomplished much in this direction and various local agencies in many cities have carried on programs designed to prevent delinquency. The public park service in some cities has also been able to provide social and recreational facilities of a type that foster desirable rather than undesirable development in the young people of the urban problem areas.

The development of neighborhood clubs, while new, represents a challenging attack on the problem of juvenile delinquency. It seems evident that educational services cannot be considered to be limited to the formal instruction in academic subjects, but must also provide some counterbalance to the antisocial influences that exist to a greater or less degree in almost every community. The social and recreational activities that have an important part to play in attaining these objectives may seem a radical departure from the academic tradition, but conditions in modern urban society clearly forecast the necessity for such a broadening of the concept of what constitutes an effective and well-rounded educational service.

THE CIVILIAN CONSERVATION CORPS

Reference was made in Chapter V to the development of the Civilian Conservation Corps as one of the measures introduced by the Federal Government for relief during the depression of the 1930's. To a considerable extent the educational aspects of the camps of the Civilian Conservation Corps, commonly known as the C.C.C. camps, have been submerged by the work program, by the relief problem, and by the fact that the organization has been administered through the Army. The enrollees of the camps work eight hours a day on various types of conservation projects such as forestation, road building, soil conservation, and similar public works. Increasingly, however, the educational possibilities of the enterprise have been recognized and Congress in its legislation on the subject in June, 1937, specifically set forth the desirability of an educational program.

The C.C.C. camps are limited to young men between the ages of sixteen and twenty-five. Almost half of the enrollees are of age eighteen or younger. The enrollees are selected from among young men who are unemployed and needy, although the requirements in the latter respect are now somewhat more flexible than formerly. Enrollees in the C.C.C. camps, it will be observed, are of the customary ages for attendance in the upper secondary-school and college levels of education. These young men are not attending the regular educational institutions for one or both of two reasons: first, because they lack the necessary economic resources; and second, because they are dissatisfied with, or incapable of pursuing, the traditional academic program.

The general administration of the Civilian Conservation Corps was originally in charge of the United States Army, but in 1939 it was transferred to the newly created Federal Security Agency. Each camp is in charge of a commander who is a reserve officer of the United States Army. On the staff of each camp is also an educational adviser who is responsible for organizing facilities and maintaining educational services suitable to the needs and interests of the enrollees. The educational program is centralized through an educational officer in each Army corps area headquarters, and the educational adviser of the entire C.C.C. organization is on the staff of the United States Office of Education.

Inasmuch as the work program assumes predominant importance in the management of the C.C.C. camps, the educational opportunities can be made available only during the leisure hours of the enrollees. This imposes a serious handicap, but in spite of the fact that the educational program is secondary in the management of most camps, much has been accomplished. Opportunities for vocational education, for the study of cultural subjects, for citizenship training, for the improvement of general education, for instruction in avocational or recreational pursuits of the hobby type, and for reading in libraries have been widely developed and have proved to be effective in rehabilitating the group of young men who might otherwise have developed anti-social habits and attitudes.

The whole C.C.C. program is still in an experimental stage. It gives promise, however, of developing into an important phase of the educational service offered American youth.

THE NATIONAL YOUTH ADMINISTRATION

The C.C.C. camps were organized in 1933. After they had been in operation for two years it became apparent that they were not altogether adequate for the solution of the problems of young people for three reasons. First, they did not provide for young women; second, by taking young men away from their home communities, the C.C.C. camps made it difficult in many

cases for the young men to re-establish their social connections
after leaving the camps; and third, the limited programs in the
camps could not serve all the specialized educational needs of
young men as well as these needs are served in the regular schools
and colleges. Accordingly in 1935 the Federal Government organized a second agency, the National Youth Administration.
This agency provides for the needs of young women as well as
young men; the program is operated along lines which are directed
toward the maintenance of the community relations of the young
people; and the arrangements permit the fullest utilization of
the extensive educational resources of the regular secondary
schools and higher institutions.

The National Youth Administration, like the C.C.C. camps,
provides some employment for its enrollees. This work is defined
by the requirement that it must be socially useful. It may consist in conservation projects, in assistance in public libraries and
hospitals, in the performance of clerical duties in public offices,
or in construction of various kinds which will contribute to the
public good. These services are organized along two different
lines: first, within secondary schools and colleges; and second,
on so-called "work projects" for young people who are out of
school and unemployed. The program in educational institutions is administered by the institutions; the work projects are
under the supervision of decentralized state staffs subsidized by
the Federal Government.

Both the C.C.C. camps and the N.Y.A. supplement the school
program of the nation in the important respect that they pay a
wage to young people who are unable under modern industrial
conditions to find employment in private business and agriculture. The payment of a wage contributes to the economic adjustment of young people. The full social process of inducting
young people into adulthood has two aspects, one educational in
the ordinary interpretation of that word and the other economic.
The experimentation with economic adjustment in which the
country is engaged through the Civilian Conservation Corps and

the National Youth Administration promises to modify radically the conception of public service to young people.

THE CHAUTAUQUA MOVEMENT

An educational activity of considerable importance in a previous generation, but now largely absorbed into more general forms of adult education, is the chautauqua movement. The institution grew out of the old camp meetings, and took its name from the parent foundation located at Lake Chautauqua in New York. Many organizations in imitation of the original pattern grew up, and the program was extended to include various kinds of cultural and educational facilities. By means of traveling companies the facilities of the chautauqua were brought to large numbers of American communities.

The traveling chautauqua provided a highly organized program usually lasting one week. All kinds of talent were utilized, the programs including both entertainment and education in the form of lectures, concerts, and exhibitions of various kinds. Each performer or group of performers remained for one day in a given center and moved on the next day to the next center. By means of this organization, facilities of an educational sort were brought into large numbers of communities that had limited educational and entertainment opportunities.

The waning of the chautauqua is probably due to several circumstances. The radio and the movies have made available a similar or even superior supply of talent for almost every community in the nation. Good roads and automobile transportation have made it convenient for persons in isolated communities to go to urban centers where facilities for entertainment and education are relatively easy to obtain. For these and possibly other reasons the chautauqua, which was once a flourishing institution, has now all but disappeared.

UNIVERSITY EXTENSION

Since the beginning of the twentieth century, universities have come increasingly to recognize a responsibility for the education of persons who cannot come to the institution for regular residence instruction.   In order to accommodate persons of this type, extension divisions have been established in many of the universities of the country, designed to carry the facilities of the institution to those who cannot attend instruction on the campus. Three distinct types of services may be recognized: home-study or correspondence courses; extension classes and short courses; and alumni educational activities.   Some universities have organized, as a part of their extension programs, the general public services that were described in Chapter XIV as a feature of American higher education.   Other minor activities carried on in university extension include package library service, distribution of visual education materials, provision of booking facilities for lectures, and leadership in various kinds of state-wide academic contests.

Correspondence Study

The earliest development of facilities for study by correspondence was on a commercial basis.   A number of proprietary concerns during the last quarter of the nineteenth century began to offer opportunities for instruction by the correspondence method. Facilities of this type were also developed by Illinois Wesleyan University and by the Chautauqua College in New York.   The first large and well-recognized institution of higher education to make correspondence study a part of its program was the University of Chicago, which under the leadership of its first president, William Rainey Harper, announced at the time of its founding in 1891 a Home-Study Department as one of its important features.   The success of the Home-Study Department of the University of Chicago led other institutions to introduce this method of study, and today correspondence instruction is a well-recognized means of obtaining an education. Credits earned by this method are accepted in partial fulfillment of requirements for degrees by the great majority of American colleges and universities.

Opportunities for study by correspondence are at present widely offered by reputable educational institutions. A large number of proprietary organizations also offer instruction of this type. Some of these proprietary organizations, investigation reveals, are not operated on acceptable ethical principles. The proprietary organizations engaged in correspondence study are subject to almost no regulation by recognized educational agencies, and the rule of *caveat emptor* — let the buyer beware — seems to be the practice of some of them in their dealings with students. Although some of the proprietary correspondence schools provide effective instructional opportunities, the prospective student who wishes to take a course by correspondence can be safely advised to obtain the instruction from a reputable university rather than from most proprietary organizations.

Extension Classes

The teaching of extension classes was another one of President William Rainey Harper's new ideas when he came to the University of Chicago in 1891. The extension class has proved popular and service of this type is now maintained by many of the state universities and by some privately controlled institutions of higher education. Under the plan of extension class teaching, a university sends out one of its regular faculty members for the teaching of a class at some center away from the campus, wherever a group can be assembled large enough to warrant the formation of a class.

Smith-Lever Extension Services

As was explained in Chapter V, Congress in 1914 passed the Smith-Lever Act providing federal funds for the support of agricultural extension services. This action proved a valuable stimulant to the general movement for the development of extension facilities. The federally supported program has developed chiefly in the direction of providing short courses and maintaining expert counseling services in local rural areas. The program is administered through the land-grant college in each state. In each county which is willing to co-operate by providing a part of the cost, a county agricultural agent is maintained to advise the farmers on their problems. Provision is also made, though less extensively, for home demonstration agents in counties to assist in problems of household management. The widely known program of Four-H clubs for young people is maintained as a part of the agricultural extension services.

Alumni Education

Another type of extension service, alumni educational activities, is a relatively new development. Colleges and universities have been led to undertake this service because of the realization that the education of students should not end with their formal graduation and the granting of diplomas and degrees. The alumni education program is frequently administered by the alumni office rather than by the extension division of the university.

The movement for alumni education takes many different forms. In some institutions book lists are prepared and the alumni are provided opportunities for reading new and important publications. In other institutions the annual homecoming of the alumni is turned into a week-long educational program, during which the most stimulating lecturers on the faculty discuss the latest developments in their respective fields of academic endeavor. In other institutions alumni magazines, carrying articles of distinctly educational content, are published.

Evaluation

Studies that have been made of the results of correspondence study and extension class teaching indicate that the student may effectively carry on his education by these methods. In institutions where the work is carefully conducted and where suitable standards of performance are maintained, the students can accomplish as much through extension classes or home study as through the regular campus classes.

The extension movement in colleges and universities is being affected somewhat by the development of local junior colleges. As facilities of the junior-college type become widely available in local communities, the need for extension classes or correspondence study courses at this level disappears. The junior college, however, is not yet sufficiently widely distributed to do away with the need for extension services at that level, and education above the junior-college level still affords an important field of service for extension activities of established universities.

ADULT EDUCATION

A group of educational activities which differ considerably from the ordinary services of the conventional school system are commonly referred to as adult education. The term "adult education" is at present only loosely defined and the exact scope of activities comprehended under the program of adult education is not described in the same way by all who have written on the subject. Some, for example, would include as adult education the university extension services, the work of the continuation schools, and the service of the public library. Others would narrow the meaning of the term to the more or less formally organized class activities under various auspices for the benefit of persons whose connection with the regular school system is discontinued. Programs of adult education are based on a recognition of the fact that education is a continuous process throughout life, that the individual does not obtain in school all the intellectual equipment needed for a successful career, and that more or less conscious efforts must be made to continue the process of education after formal schooling ends.

The movement for adult education was greatly accelerated by the findings of a stimulating investigation made by Professor Edward L. Thorndike with respect to the ability of adults to learn. It has long been mistakenly assumed by most people that the ability to learn diminishes rapidly after adolescence, and that the adult would always find great difficulty in undertaking a program of study. The attitude that has long prevailed on this point is epitomized in the adage, "You can't teach an old dog new tricks." Thorndike and others have shown, quite contrary to the general assumption, that the ability to learn does not decrease with adulthood, that it probably reaches its peak at about age twenty-five or thirty, and that the decline thereafter is at a slow rate, probably not more than 1 per cent a year. These investigations indicate that, so far as capacity is concerned, the average adult is probably more able to learn than the average child in the elementary school. Such findings have served to stimulate greatly the whole program of adult education and to encourage many adults to undertake programs of study.

As at present carried on, adult education includes a wide variety of instructional opportunities along vocational, cultural, citizenship, and recreational lines. Programs are organized to apply to persons of all levels of educational attainment. One of the extensive projects in adult education deals with the removal of illiteracy and much progress has been made in teaching illiterate adults to read and write. Americanization for the foreign born has also been an important type of activity in adult education. Other programs have been developed for the benefit of those who have only a limited general education and who wish to supplement it by further study at the elementary and secondary-school level. There has been a widespread development of instruction in leisure-time activities and pursuits of the avocational and recreational type. Upgrading vocational education, whereby the worker is prepared for a position demanding increased technical knowledge or skill in the line in which he is employed, is a feature of many programs of adult education. Considerable interest has developed in programs of adult education designed to present information and to develop wholesome attitudes on general problems of civic, social, and economic interest.   Noteworthy in this connection has been the series of community forums developed under the leadership of Commissioner John W. Studebaker of the United States Office of Education.

The public schools have shown only a mild interest in programs of adult education, and in general only the larger cities have developed facilities of this type in their public-school systems. Even in such cases, the program has frequently been meager and poorly supported.   Facilities for adult education may be provided economically in the public-school system, however, because the classes are usually held in the evening hours when the regular day school is not in session.

Some difficulty has been encountered in maintaining programs of adult education under the auspices of the public-school system because of the tendency to use teachers of regular day-classes for adult classes.   Particularly when the teachers are given extra pay to take on an evening class as an extra burden, there is a tendency to overload the most capable teachers to the detriment of both the regular and the adult classes.   Furthermore, many teachers who are successful in teaching children are unsuccessful with adult groups, and vice versa.

Much of the development in adult education has come through private agencies; organizations such as the Y.M.C.A., the Y.W.C.A., and progressively minded church groups, have fostered programs of adult education.   Some of the labor organizations, notable among them the International Ladies' Garment Workers' Union, have developed extensive educational programs for the benefit of their members.   So-called "workers' education" has been successfully carried on in many centers.

Programs of adult education are most likely to reach the group for which they are intended when they are conducted by an association or organization with which the adult is normally associated or with which he comes in contact during his usual

activities. This fact has led to the development of adult education under a wide diversity of agencies. Some duplication of
service and failure to co-ordinate facilities has resulted from the
variety of independent and unrelated agencies which carry on
work in adult education. Arrangements for careful co-ordination
of facilities through councils on adult education have been worked
out in some centers, and efforts in this direction may be expected
to improve the services available without adding to their cost.

The most important single agency in the recent development of
programs of adult education has been the Federal Government.
As explained in Chapter V, the development of facilities for adult
education proved to be an exceptionally good method of furnishing relief during the economic depression of the 1930's, because
qualified persons on the relief rolls could be put to work teaching
classes of adults who were clamoring for instruction along many
lines. The teaching under such circumstances proved to be
surprisingly effective; the teacher was assured of employment only
so long as he could hold his class, and when he failed to maintain
the interest and attendance of his class group, he was judged
a failure at that type of work and was put into some other kind of
relief employment. Doubtless there would be better instruction
in the regular classes of the school system if the teaching could be
so effectively motivated. The magnitude of the emergency educational program maintained by the Works Progress Administration is indicated by data presented by the Advisory Committee on
Education; 44,000 unemployed teachers have been put to work in
classes, and enrollments have been in excess of 1,725,000 persons.

Although the services of adult education are relatively new,
much interest is manifest at present in this field. A national association has been formed with the aid of the Carnegie Corporation for the study and promotion of adult education and a journal
devoted to the problems of adult education is published. A considerable volume of literature has appeared on the subject. Much
of the literature is of the promotional or propagandistic type, as
is usual in the beginning of any such movement, but critical

analyses are now beginning to appear. Courses on adult education are being added to the programs of graduate schools, for the preparation of those who will engage in this type of educational service. The Advisory Committee on Education recommended a special federal grant, reaching ultimately $15,000,000 annually, to be distributed to the states for use in programs of adult education. The future will undoubtedly see considerable expansion of the educational services for adults.

THE PUBLIC LIBRARY

The public library usually has little or no administrative connection with the local public-school system, but it cannot be ignored as an important type of educational service. The public library, unlike the school system, is almost everywhere a local institution and is typically managed without central supervision from state sources. Many communities have been stimulated to provide public libraries by philanthropic gifts, and particularly in some of the larger cities libraries with notable collections are maintained.

At present, library service is available for public use in most urban areas of the United States, but the rural areas are only meagerly provided with such facilities. The Advisory Committee on Education estimated that the rural population lacking library services amounted to 39,500,000 persons, more than seven times the number of residents in cities who are without public library service. To overcome this difficulty, the Advisory Committee recommended a series of federal grants for the extension of library service to rural areas.

The public libraries are increasingly being placed under the direction of administrators specifically trained for the task. The professionalization of the librarian's position is a development from which important results in the direction of improved service may be expected. The well-prepared librarians are increasingly looking upon their task as an educational problem and are organizing their services to meet an educational objective. As a group, the librarians are unusually co-operative, and as individuals they are typically glad to assist schools and other educational agencies to the full extent of their resources.

The question of the location of the control of the library has not been finally determined. Some have urged that the library be set up as a part of the public-school system and administered through the regular school officials. The form of organization thus advocated has been adopted in a few cities. The librarians as a group, however, have resisted this type of organization and prefer their present independent status. The fact that the school people have done so little to promote the development of public libraries seems to suggest that the schools should not be given the responsibility for library management after facilities have once been developed under other auspices. Furthermore, the administrators of public schools at present have usually not been trained in theory of public library service and management. Some leaders have urged that the library is the logical agency in which to centralize the control and management of the adult-education program for the community.

THE FINANCING OF DESIRABLE EDUCATIONAL INNOVATIONS

The foregoing review of some of the unconventional units of educational service now being developed in the United States leads in a surprising number of instances to the conclusion that these innovations should be encouraged and extended. The question will immediately be raised as to whether these desirable developments, including nursery schools, kindergartens, neighborhood centers for the prevention of juvenile delinquency, the Civilian Conservation Corps, the National Youth Administration, university extension services, adult education, and public libraries, can be financed by the already overburdened taxpayers.

Educators would insist that the financing of these new projects should not be achieved by reducing the support of the present established educational system. The conventional school in most communities is at present all too meagerly financed and it would seem impossible to spare from its slender resources funds sufficient for undertaking all these new and desirable tasks. Many of these innovations have been financed in the past from private or philanthropic sources, but this type of support is probably not possible or desirable as a permanent method of maintaining the activities. Private or philanthropic support is usually available during the period when the usefulness of a project is being tested, but after the desirability of an innovation is assured, public support seems necessary for its effective continuance.

The financing of these desirable additions to the educational services of the country will depend in the last analysis on the desire of the public. It can well be prophesied that if the voters are convinced of the value of these services, support for them will be forthcoming. Possibly federal aid for many of these desirable services, as suggested by the Advisory Committee on Education, will prove to be the method which will be resorted to by the nation.

BIBLIOGRAPHY

Bittner, Walton S., and Hervey F. Mallory, *University Teaching by Mail.* New York: The Macmillan Company, 1933. xvi + 356 pp.

Blatz, William E., Dorothy Millichamp, and Margaret Fletcher, *Nursery Education: Theory and Practice.* New York: William Morrow and Company, 1935. xv + 366 pp.

Bryson, Lyman, *Adult Education.* New York: American Book Company, 1936. v + 208 pp.

Cartwright, Morse Adams, *Ten Years of Adult Education.* New York: The Macmillan Company, 1935. xiv + 220 pp.

Cubberley, Ellwood P., *Public Education in the United States,* pp. 563–626.

Cubberley, Ellwood P., *State School Administration,* pp. 361–83.

Davis, Mary D., and Rowna Hansen, *Nursery Schools: Their Development and Current Practices in the United States.* Office of Education Bulletin, 1932, no. 9. Washington: Government Printing Office, 1933.

Douglass, Aubrey A., *The American School System*, pp. 93–113, 303–71.

Ely, Mary L., editor, *Adult Education in Action*. New York: American Association for Adult Education, 1936.   xix + 480 pp.

Foster, Josephine C., and Naith E. Headley, *Education in the Kindergarten*. New York: American Book Company, 1936.   xii + 368 pp.

Frasier, George Willard, and Winfield D. Armentrout, *An Introduction to the Literature of Education*, pp. 295–320.

Hill, Frank Ernest, *The School in the Camps*.   New York: American Association for Adult Education, 1935.   84 pp.

Judd, Charles H., *Education and Social Progress*, pp. 252–76.

Judd, Charles H., *Problems of Education in the United States*, pp. 169–77.

Meyer, Adolph E., *The Development of Education in the Twentieth Century*, pp. 192–214.   New York: Prentice-Hall, 1939.

Noffsinger, John Samuel, *Correspondence Schools, Lyceums, Chautauquas*. New York: The Macmillan Company, 1926.   vi + 146 pp.

Patterson, S. Howard, Ernest A. Choate, and Edmund de S. Brunner, *The School in American Society*, pp. 325–57.

Reeves, F. W., T. Fansler, and C. O. Houle, *Adult Education*.   Regents' Inquiry into the Character and Cost of Public Education in the State of New York.   New York: McGraw-Hill Book Company, 1938.   xvi + 172 pp.

Smith, Payson, Frank W. Wright, and Associates, *Education in the Forty-Eight States*, pp. 141–48, 175–91.   Staff Study no. 1, Advisory Committee on Education.

Updegraff, Ruth, *et al.*, *Practice in Preschool Education*.   New York: McGraw-Hill Book Company, 1938.   xvi + 408 pp.

Vandewalker, Nina Catherine, *The Kindergarten in American Education*. New York: The Macmillan Company, 1908.   xiv + 274 pp.

White House Conference on Child Health and Protection, *White House Conference, 1930*.   New York: Century Company, 1931.   xii + 40 pp.

Wilson, Lester M., and I. L. Kandel, *Introduction to the Study of American Education*, pp. 277–92.

CHAPTER XVI

TEACHERS

IN SPITE of the great interest which parents have in the education of their children they soon recognize that it requires more patience and skill than they have to give the instruction necessary for the mastery of even the most rudimentary subjects. Teaching a child to read, for example, is a long, arduous task. If parents attempted to perform this task they would interfere with their other activities to such a degree that they would find their children to be great burdens. Above the levels of the most primitive societies, therefore, parents have customarily delegated the teaching of children to someone whom they employ to do what they are unable to do themselves.

SOCIAL STATUS OF THE TEACHER

In Greek and Roman civilization the teaching of children was done chiefly by slaves in the parental home. The Greeks designated a teacher as Παιδαγωγός, pedagogue — "A leader or guide for the boy." Although the teachers of older youth in classical times, such as Socrates and Plato, were public leaders and distinguished members of society, there is no evidence that the teachers of boys were given any recognition above that of servants or slaves. The education of girls was extremely limited and was almost entirely directed to preparation for domestic life.

In the early days in America teachers were scarcely more than attendants charged with the care of children during a part of the day when parents were engaged in duties which made it desirable for them to be free from the responsibility of watching their off-

spring. Almost anyone who could be secured for the duty was
employed as a teacher. The following extract from an autobiog-
raphy written by Reverend Heman Humphrey in 1863 gives an
illuminating picture of the schools and teachers of early days in
the United States.

> The first school I remember was kept a few weeks by a maiden lady,
> called Miss Faithy, in a barn. I was very young, as were most of the
> children. What I learned then, if any thing, I have forgotten. This
> was in the summer, of course. The next was a school, so called, kept
> a month or two by a neighbor of ours, who was the best *trout fisher*,
> with his horse-hair line, in all those parts. He wrote a fair hand, as
> I remember, on birch bark. What he taught us, but to say *tue* and
> *due*, has escaped my recollection. We had no school-house then in our
> district, and we met as much for play as any thing, where we could
> find shelter. The next winter, another neighbor took us a few weeks
> into one of the rooms of his own house, where every thing but learning
> was going on. His speech bewrayed him of Rhode Island origin, and
> whatever he knew, he certainly could never have had much if any
> chance of being whipped in school when he was a boy. I remember
> his tremendous *stamp* when we got noisy in school-time, and that is
> all. This, however, is not a fair sample of school accommodations in
> my boyhood; and I had a better chance for two or three winters
> afterward.
>
> Most of the other districts in the town had school-houses, but not
> all. The first winter that I kept school myself, was in a room next
> to the kitchen in a small private house. Some of the school-houses
> were better than others; but none of them in that or the adjoining
> towns were convenient or even comfortable. They were rather
> *juvenile penitentiaries*, than attractive accommodations for study.
> They were too small, and low from the ceiling to the floor, and the
> calculation of the builders seemed to have been, to decide into how
> small a space the children could be crowded, from the fireplace till
> the room was well packed. Not unfrequently sixty or seventy scholars
> were daily shut up six hours, where there was hardly room for thirty.[1]

The teachers in schools of the type thus described did not command great public prestige; in fact they were often laughing-
stocks. The literary accounts of the teachers of a century and

[1] "Schools as They Were Sixty Years Ago," *American Journal of Education*,
XIII: 125–26 (March, 1863).

a half ago reflect the popular disesteem of the pedagogue. One of the most widely read of these literary accounts contains the following paragraphs.

In this by-place of nature [Sleepy Hollow], there abode, in a remote period of American history, that is to say, some thirty years since, a worthy wight of the name of Ichabod Crane; who sojourned, or, as he expressed it, "tarried," in Sleepy Hollow, for the purpose of instructing the children of the vicinity. He was a native of Connecticut; a State which supplies the Union with pioneers for the mind as well as for the forest, and sends forth yearly its legions of frontier woodsmen and country schoolmasters. The cognomen of Crane was not inapplicable to his person. He was tall, but exceedingly lank, with narrow shoulders, long arms and legs, hands that dangled a mile out of his sleeves, feet that might have served for shovels, and his whole frame most loosely hung together. His head was small, and flat at top, with huge ears, large green glassy eyes, and a long snipe nose, so that it looked like a weathercock perched upon his spindle neck, to tell which way the wind blew. To see him striding along the profile of a hill on a windy day with his clothes bagging and fluttering about him, one might have mistaken him for the genius of famine descending upon the earth, or some scarecrow eloped from a cornfield.

(Two paragraphs follow, which describe the school)

When school-hours were over he was even the companion and playmate of the larger boys; and on holiday afternoons would convoy some of the smaller ones home, who happened to have pretty sisters, or good housewives for mothers, noted for the comforts of the cupboard. Indeed it behooved him to keep on good terms with his pupils. The revenue arising from his school was small, and would have been scarcely sufficient to furnish him with daily bread, for he was a huge feeder, and though lank, had the dilating powers of an anaconda; but to help out his maintenance, he was, according to country custom in those parts, boarded and lodged at the houses of the farmers, whose children he instructed. With these he lived successively a week at a time; thus going the rounds of the neighborhood with all his worldly effects tied up in a cotton handkerchief.[1]

Teachers of earlier days were paid very low wages, and as indicated in the quotation above, a part of their compensation

[1] Washington Irving's "The Legend of Sleepy Hollow," from *The Sketch Book of Geoffrey Crayon Gent*", pp. 356–58. New York: Thomas Y. Crowell Company, 1848.

was often board and lodging with some family whose children
were their pupils. The equipment of the homes, as well as of the
schools, was meager and at times the experience of "boarding
around" became almost or quite unendurable. The following
extract from a teacher's diary was published in *The American
Journal of Education* in 1867. The date of the diary is not given,
but it might be from almost any period from colonial times up
to the Civil War.

Diary of a Teacher

"boarding round" in Vermont

We make the following extract from a little pamphlet, illustrative
of the life of a country schoolmaster in Vermont, when "boarding
round" was practiced.

Monday. — Went to board at Mr. B——'s; had a baked gander for
dinner; suppose from its size, the thickness of the skin and other
venerable appearances, to have been one of the first settlers of Vermont; made a slight impression on the patriarch's breast. Supper —
cold gander and potatoes; ... went to bed, and dreamed of having
eaten a quantity of stone wall.

Tuesday. — Cold gander for breakfast, swamp tea and some nut
cake — the latter some consolation. Dinner — the legs, etc., of the
gander, done up warm — one nearly dispatched. Supper — the other
leg, etc., cold; went to bed ... dreamed I was a mud turtle, and got on
my back and could not get over again.

Wednesday. — Cold gander for breakfast; complained of sickness,
and could eat nothing. Dinner — wings, etc., of the gander warmed
up; did my best to destroy them, for fear they should be left for supper;
did not succeed; dreaded supper all the afternoon. Supper — hot
Johnny cakes; felt greatly revived; thought I had got clear of the
gander, and went to bed for a good night's rest; disappointed; very
cool night, and couldn't keep warm in bed; got up and stopped the
broken window with my coat and vest; no use; froze the tip of my
nose and one ear before morning.

Thursday. — Cold gander again; felt much discouraged to see the
gander not half gone; went visiting for dinner and supper; slept abroad,
and had pleasant dreams.

Friday. — Breakfast abroad. Dinner at Mr. B——'s; cold gander
and hot potatoes — the latter very good; ate three, and went to school

quite contented.   Supper — cold gander and no potatoes, bread
heavy and dry; had the headache and couldn't eat; ...

Saturday. — Cold gander and hot Indian Johnny cake; did very
well, glad to come off so.   Dinner — cold gander again; didn't keep
school this afternoon; weighed and found I had lost six pounds the
last week; grew alarmed; had a talk with Mr. B——, and concluded
I had boarded out his share.[1]

A serious statement showing the American attitude toward
teachers at about the middle of the eighteenth century in America
is given in a prospectus issued by Benjamin Franklin in behalf of
his proposal for an academy and charitable school.   This institution, founded by Franklin, has generally been considered the
first academy in the United States.   One section of Franklin's
prospectus, which sought funds and students for the proposed
institution, reads as follows:

The benefits expected from this institution are:
1. That the youth of Pennsylvania may have an opportunity of
receiving a good education at home, and be under no necessity of going
abroad for it, whereby not only considerable expense may be saved to
the country, but a stricter eye may be had over their morals by their
friends and relations.
2. That a number of our natives will hereby be qualified to bear
magistracies, and execute other public offices of trust, with reputation
to themselves and country, there being at present great want of persons so qualified in the several counties of this Province; and this is
the more necessary now to be provided for by the English here, as vast
numbers of foreigners are yearly imported among us, totally ignorant
of our laws, customs and language.
3. That a number of the poorer sort will hereby be qualified to
act as schoolmasters in the country, to teach children reading, writing,
arithmetic and the grammar of their mother tongue, and being of good
morals and known character, may be recommended from the Academy
to country schools for that purpose — the country suffering very
much at present for want of good schoolmasters, and obliged frequently to employ in their schools vicious imported servants or concealed Papists, who by their bad examples and instructions often

---

[1] *The American Journal of Education*, XVII:186–87.   Edited by Henry
Barnard, LL.D.   Hartford, Conn.: D. N. Camp, 1867.

deprave the morals or corrupt the principles of the children under their care.[1]

The statements quoted in the foregoing pages could readily be extended to make clear the lowly beginnings from which the teaching profession has gradually been rising to a level where it commands far more public respect than it enjoyed in early times. The change in social status of teachers is the result of training, which is now recognized as indispensable to admission to the teaching profession. As was explained in Chapter II, during the first half of the nineteenth century a number of influential citizens of Massachusetts urged the establishment of special schools, later known as normal schools, for the preparation of teachers. The following extract is from the writing of one of the men who took an active and effective part in the establishment of normal schools:

> The teachers of the primary summer schools have rarely had any education beyond what they have acquired in the very schools where they begin to teach. Their attainments, therefore, to say the least, are usually *very moderate*. But this is not the worst of it. They are often very young, they are constantly changing their employment, and consequently can have but little experience; and what is worse than all, they never have had any direct preparation for their profession. This is the only service, in which we venture to employ young, and often, ignorant persons, without some previous instruction in their appropriate duties. We require experience in all those, whom we employ to perform the slightest mechanical labour for us. We would not buy a coat or a hat of one, who should undertake to make them without a previous apprenticeship. Nor would any one have the hardihood to offer to us the result of his first essay in manufacturing either of these articles. We do not even send an old shoe to be mended, except it be to a workman of whose skill we have had ample proof. Yet we commit our children to be educated to those, who know nothing, absolutely nothing, of the complicated and difficult duties assigned to them. Shall we trust the development of the delicate bodies, the susceptible hearts, and the tender minds of our little children to those who have no knowledge of their nature? Can they, can these rude hands finish the workmanship of the Almighty? No lan-

---

[1] James Pyle Wickersham, *A History of Education in Pennsylvania*, p. 60. Lancaster, Pennsylvania: Inquirer Publishing Company, 1885.

guage can express the astonishment, which a moment's reflection on this subject excites in me.

But I must return to the examination of the qualifications of the female teachers of the primary summer schools, from which purpose I have unconsciously a little departed to indulge in a general remark. They are a class of teachers unknown in our laws regulating the schools unless it be by some latitude of construction. No standard of attainments is fixed, at which they must arrive before they assume the business of instruction. So that any one *keeps school*, which is a very different thing from *teaching school*, who wishes to do it, and can persuade, by herself, or her friends, a small district to employ her. And this is not a very difficult matter, especially when the remuneration for the employment is so very trifling. The farce of an examination and a certificate from the minister of the town, for it is a perfect farce, amounts to no efficient check upon the obtrusions of ignorance and inexperience. As no standard is fixed by law, each minister makes a standard for himself, and alters it as often as the peculiar circumstances of the case require. And there will always be enough of peculiar circumstances to render a refusal inexpedient. . . .

The faults of the primary summer schools, then, are, a want of adequate acquirements, a want of experience, and a total want of any direct preparation of their teachers for their employment. These must be acknowledged to be great faults; and they have affected and will continue to affect, essentially, the usefulness of the schools. Neither reason, observation, nor experience leaves reflecting men any consoling probability, that these defects will be remedied, or the condition of the schools be essentially improved, under their present organization. . . .

Many of the above remarks upon the character and qualifications of the teachers of the summer schools apply with equal force to the young men, who undertake the instruction of the primary winter schools, which now constitute the highest class of schools, to which the whole population of the state have free access.[1]

Vigorous discussions of the type quoted in the foregoing paragraphs led to the establishment of state-supported institutions for the preparation of teachers and to the transfer of authority

---

[1] James G. Carter, "Faults of the Free Schools," *Essays upon Popular Education, Containing a Particular Examination of the Schools of Massachusetts, and an Outline of an Institution for the Education of Teachers*, pp. 36–39. Boston: Bowles and Dearborn, 1826.

for the licensing of teachers from local authorities to state departments of education. The central state authorities developed rapidly after 1837 and though the state-supported normal schools, the first of which was opened in 1839, did not flourish until after the Civil War, the general principle gradually received popular acceptance that no one should be employed as a teacher unless he or she were well educated and supplied with some professional training. The acceptance of this principle marked the beginning of the trend toward professionalization of teaching. Today teaching is something more than an occupation. It is to be classified as one of the higher callings and its prestige is steadily growing. To be sure, there are still qualifications that must be made to the statement that teaching is a profession in all cases and in all school districts, but the trend is established.

One of the obstructions which today stand in the way of a full and satisfactory recognition of teaching as a profession is the unreasonable restrictions sometimes imposed on teachers by those who employ them. The following quotation is taken from a recent article.

Many school boards, especially in the small towns, restrict the recreational and social life of their teachers. In the larger cities there are few restrictions put upon teachers' activities outside of school, but in certain districts card-playing, dancing, smoking, and any social intercourse outside of church affairs are taboo. Smoking is forbidden Tennessee teachers by state law. The following is given as an example of an extremely restrictive local contract signed by certain North Carolina teachers:

"I promise to take a vital interest in all phases of Sunday School work, donating of my time, service, and money without stint, for the benefit and uplift of the community.

"I promise to abstain from all dancing, immodest dressing, and any other conduct unbecoming a teacher and a lady.

"I promise not to go out with any young men except insofar as it may be necessary to stimulate Sunday School work.

"I promise not to fall in love, to become engaged, or secretly married..."

Many other schools have regulations which are very nearly as restrictive. Ewing tells of a male teacher in a Missouri school district who was asked to sign a resignation with his contract, the resignation becoming effective, and all salary due forfeited, if at any time or at any place during the period of the contract he should smoke a cigarette, pipe, or cigar. An Alabama school board forbids teachers to "have company or go automobile riding" on school nights. An Ohio school board forbids teachers to "go with other teachers." A Mississippi contract reads:

"It is further understood and agreed by the parties hereto that no teacher will play society to the detriment of the school or unnecessarily frolic on school nights or indulge excessively in any sort of socials during school nights, the superintendent to be the judge in these matters and to warn teachers, and should they persist in violating this regulation, it shall be deemed sufficient cause for dismissal." [1]

A criticism which has often been made of the teaching profession is that it does not attract men as much as it should. The data given in Table 10 show that from 1880 to 1920 there was a steady decrease in the percentage of teachers who were men. Since 1915 the teaching staff has been more than 80 per cent feminine, although the percentage of men increased between 1920 and 1934.

TABLE 10. PERCENTAGE OF TEACHERS THAT ARE MEN, IN THE UNITED STATES FROM 1880 TO 1934 *

Year	Total Number of Teachers	Percentage That Are Men
1880......	286,593	42.8
1890......	363,922	34.5
1900......	423,062	29.9
1905......	460,269	24.0
1910......	523,210	21.1
1915......	604,301	19.6
1920......	679,533	14.1
1925......	777,945	16.9
1930......	854,263	16.5
1934......	847,120	19.1

* Data from Leo M. Chamberlain and Leonard E. Meece, *Women and Men in the Teaching Profession*, Bulletin of the Bureau of School Service, University of Kentucky, Lexington, IX:3:12 (March, 1937).

[1] "Unreasonable Restrictions on Teachers' Activities," *Elementary School Journal*, XXXVII:92–96 (October, 1936).

Table 11 shows that the percentage of women teachers is largest in the lowest levels of the school system and smallest in the senior high school.

TABLE 11. SEX AND MARITAL STATUS OF TEACHERS IN VARIOUS TYPES
OF SCHOOLS *

	Percentage of Total Teaching Staff in Each Type School			
	Elementary 1 and 2 Teacher Schools	All Other Elementary Schools (City and Consolidated Rural)	Junior High School	Senior High School
Women, single (including divorced and widows).......	69.2	79.2	65.8	57.9
Women, married..	18.6	16.5	10.0	7.2
Men............	12.2	4.3	24.2	34.9

* Data from *National Survey of the Education of Teachers*, vol. II, pp. 22–25.   Office of Education Bulletin, 1933, no. 10.   Washington: Government Printing Office, 1935.

The feminization of the schools has been discussed pro and con by many writers.   Some have viewed the condition with great alarm and have pointed out that it is probably unfortunate for both boys and girls in the schools to be so exclusively under the influence of women teachers in their early years.   There is, however, little or no objective evidence that can be adduced to support such a contention.

The feminization of the teaching profession is not a condition for which the schools are responsible; it reflects a general social movement.   Ever since the Civil War period women have been entering more and more into gainful employment, and teaching is merely one of the vocations readily available to women.   A change in the sex distribution of the teaching profession, if there need to be any change, will probably come only from some modification in the social and economic world rather than through deliberate action within the school system itself.

CONTROL OF TEACHER SELECTION

The practice almost universally accepted throughout the United States is to leave the choice of the persons who are to be employed as teachers in public schools to the authorities representing the people of the local community. The only curb that has been introduced on the choice by the local community is state certification. Under the plan of state certification the selection by the local community is limited to teachers who hold the appropriate certificate.

The present status of teacher certification has evolved through several stages, although some type of control over the right to teach is relatively old. In medieval times the church rigidly controlled the licensing of those who taught in the schools. Certification of the school teacher was often a function of the local minister in colonial America. The secularization of the schools required that the certification of teachers be conducted by the government rather than by the church authorities. Because of the local control that characterized the early American schools, it was only natural that the local community was given complete freedom to select its teachers according to any plan it wished.

The first limitation on the power of the local community in the selection of its teachers came in the form of a requirement that an examination must be given, and that only those who passed the examination would be permitted to teach. As indicated earlier, the character of this examination was at first left entirely to some local authority, but in a later stage the examination was prepared centrally, either by the county authorities or by the state department, even though the rating of candidates was left to the local authority. In the third stage the examination was both set and graded by the central state authority, and only those who were given passing marks by the central authority could be employed as teachers in the local community. In the fourth and most recent stage of development, certification for teaching has been based on credits and degrees obtained from recognized institutions, rather than on special examinations; all the states now issue some certificates based solely on academic attainments, and only twenty states now issue any certificates based on examinations.

The certification of teachers in this country is now largely centralized on a state-wide basis. In 1937 there were forty-one states which issued all teacher certificates except those in the largest cities and those issued by institutions of higher education. Massachusetts was the only state giving full power to local school authorities to issue teacher certificates, and in Massachusetts the state issued the certificates for teachers in some thirty state-aided high schools. In some states the evaluation of the credits earned is made in the state office and the teaching certificate is issued by the state Department of Education. In other states collegiate institutions are approved by the state department and given authority directly to issue teaching credentials to students who meet the specified requirements.

Certification of teachers is a device which is useful only in preventing the employment of the most poorly qualified persons. Even when it is well administered, the system of certification seems powerless to assure that the best qualified persons, rather than the ones whose qualifications are merely above the acceptable minimum, will be employed in any given position. Certification thus presents an interesting contrast to the type of civil-service selection which is characteristic of the recruitment of employees in the Federal Government and also in many progressive state governments. In the civil-service examination the objective is to limit the selection to the best qualified persons among a large field of available applicants. Teacher certification merely eliminates from the list of applicants the persons whose qualifications are intolerably low.

An important criticism of the plan for certification of teachers is the fact that the qualifications relate almost exclusively to academic attainments. Sometimes a health certificate is required but other important personal qualifications are usually entirely overlooked in granting state certificates to teachers. The certification process thus fails to bar from the profession many persons who are temperamentally unfit to become teachers.

The present plans of teacher certification also are subject to criticism in most instances because of the common practice of issuing permanent or life certificates after only a limited period of service. In 1937 thirty-five of the states were issuing some form of permanent or life certificate to teachers. Because such a policy as that described has been extensively followed for many years, hundreds of thousands of teachers who are not qualified for teaching certificates on present standards are now employed on the basis of permanent credentials issued at a time when standards were much lower than at present. Furthermore, nothing is usually done to investigate the possible deterioration of the teacher's qualifications after the permanent certificate is issued. For example, while a health certificate may be required at the time the permanent teaching credential is issued, the teacher may later contract some disease which should disqualify him or her from teaching; the teacher-certification plan usually makes no provision for the discovery of such conditions.

It will thus be seen that state certification affords only a slight curb on the range of choice permitted local communities in the selection of their teachers. Especially in the area of personal characteristics is local preference permitted to have full sway. This fact leads to some absurd local requirements in the employment of teachers. For example, for a long time after women had begun to wear bobbed hair large numbers of communities discriminated against any candidate for a teaching position who adopted this style of hairdressing. It can hardly be believed that the method of wearing the hair has any important relationship to effectiveness in teaching. Political connections, religious affiliations, and local residence, are also frequently made the basis for selection of teachers in the local community.

Evidence indicates that in some instances school board members make the selection of a teacher without having interviewed or

even seen the candidate.   An attractive photograph submitted
with a letter of application is often sufficient to turn the scale in
favor of the successful candidate.   The only conclusion that can
be drawn is that the selection of teachers by local authorities is
frequently quite unintelligent.   The only effective remedy for
this condition is to lodge the authority for the selection of teachers
in a professionally qualified local superintendent of schools.

THE PREPARATION OF TEACHERS

The development of a professional attitude among teachers and
of a demand on the part of the public for thoroughly prepared
candidates for teaching positions was a slow process.   After state-
supported normal schools were established the better school districts began to employ their graduates, but the curriculums of the
early normal schools were meager and there was little of what may
be called professional spirit among teachers.

The Oswego Normal School was one of the early centers for the
dissemination of a new spirit and attitude toward teaching.   The
head of the institution in the days of its greatest influence was
Edward A. Sheldon.   In the 1850's Sheldon, the superintendent
of the public schools in Oswego, New York, became greatly interested in the improvement of the teaching process.   He visited
Europe, and while there became acquainted with the work of the
Pestalozzian schools, in which a new plan of teaching, based upon
the so-called "object method," had been developed.   Upon his
return to his position in Oswego, Sheldon called the teachers of
the city together for a series of meetings in which he explained to
them the Pestalozzian method.

The method was tried in the schools by the teachers and proved
unusually successful.   It attracted wide attention over the country, and teachers from other cities requested the privilege of
visiting the schools in Oswego.   A series of lectures was started
to inform these visitors regarding the basic principles of the
method.   From this beginning, in 1861, there grew up the normal

school in Oswego. Sheldon as the head of this school sent his graduates and members of his staff to many other institutions devoted to the preparation of teachers. In the period following the Civil War the normal schools that were opened in many parts of the United States were staffed chiefly by persons who had studied in Oswego under Sheldon. The Oswego movement was important in calling attention to the needs for effective preparation in methods, especially for teachers in elementary schools.

By 1870 the preparation of teachers in the entire United States entailed expenditures of $200,000. This indicates a substantial interest in professional preparation for that date, although the amount seems small when compared with present expenditures for this purpose, which were $37,000,000 in 1930.

Since the beginning of the twentieth century the normal schools have rapidly raised the level of their programs. Originally the curriculum was carried on at the level of secondary education and required only the completion of an elementary-school program for entrance. As the number of qualified candidates increased, the requirements for admission were raised to the equivalent of graduation from the secondary school. The curriculum, which had originally been only one year in length, was also increased until four years of preparation beyond the secondary school were offered. With the attainment of this stage, the normal schools began to be known as teachers colleges and began to grant academic degrees.

For a long time the professional preparation for teachers was offered only for the benefit of those who were intending to serve in elementary schools. In the late years of the nineteenth century and early part of the twentieth, demands began to be more and more insistent for professional qualifications in candidates for positions as secondary-school teachers. Today such qualifications are recognized as essential in the public schools of every state.

Up to the present there has been no general recognition of a need to require professional preparation on the part of those who are teaching in colleges and universities. The coming of the junior college, however, has resulted in some states in an insistence on professional qualifications at this level of teaching, and in those states special certificates, based on the accomplishment of certain required preparation, are issued for teachers in junior colleges.   Some leaders have suggested that college and university teachers should also be professionally qualified for their positions.   Little is now being done in this direction, but some development toward more definite professional qualifications for teachers at the college and university level may be expected in the future.   Requirements on the strictly academic side for college teachers have been insisted upon by many of the accrediting associations.   The possession of the degree of Doctor of Philosophy is now generally recognized as desirable in all candidates for positions on college faculties.

Types of Institutions Preparing Teachers

Teachers are at present prepared in many different types of institutions in the United States.   As was explained in Chapter XIII, very little specific preparation for teaching is now given in the secondary schools of the country, although formerly the academies, and later the public high schools, did offer facilities of that type.   At present in only a few states are teachers given certificates without having had some preparation at the college level, and hence there is no longer any need for offering teacher preparation at the secondary-school level.

In some sections of the country junior colleges offer curriculums for the preparation of teachers for the elementary school.   In general, this tendency is not encouraged, for the junior college is expected to devote most of its energy to the completion of general education rather than to specific preparation for a profession such as teaching.   Furthermore, there is a tendency to require more preparation for the teaching certificate than is available in the junior college.   Consequently, it does not seem probable that the junior college will ever become an important agency for the preparation of teachers.

The normal school was the institution which provided preparation for teaching during the nineteenth century. This institution, as previously explained, is declining in numbers and is now less important than formerly in the preparation of teachers. The normal school has always devoted its principal energies to the preparation of teachers for the elementary school. Almost all the normal schools are publicly controlled institutions, although a few private ones still exist. The publicly controlled normal schools fall into three types: those supported by the state, those maintained by cities, and those maintained by counties. The last two types are diminishing in importance, and it is generally recognized that the state, rather than any of its subdivisions, should be the unit for the operation of institutions for the preparation of teachers.

On the foundations of many of the older normal schools have arisen the modern teachers colleges. The teachers colleges are increasing in numbers and in enrollments and are taking a leading position at present in the preparation, not only of elementary teachers, but also of secondary-school teachers and school administrators. In the program of preparation for secondary-school teachers and for school administrators, a number of the stronger teachers colleges have introduced a fifth year of work and are offering curriculums leading to the Master's degree. Like the normal schools of which they are outgrowths, the teachers colleges are chiefly state-supported institutions.

The liberal arts college is at present one of the important types of institutions engaged in the preparation of teachers. The arts colleges were founded originally, for the most part, by religious denominations for the purpose of preparing ministers of the gospel. Later they began to offer facilities for the preparation of candidates for other professions and today approximately 45 per cent of the graduates of the liberal arts colleges enter the teaching profession. Recognition of the special needs of graduates who are to enter teaching has led to marked changes in the traditional curriculum of the liberal arts colleges. Most of these colleges prepare their graduates for secondary-school teaching, but a number of them also offer curriculums for the preparation of elementary-school teachers. The liberal arts college is, as pointed out earlier, typically a privately controlled institution, although in a few southern states publicly controlled institutions of this type for women are maintained.

Finally, among the types of higher institutions maintaining facilities for the preparation of teachers may be mentioned the university. In many cases a division or school of education is organized within the university on a basis similar to that of other professional schools such as law, medicine, or engineering. In such cases students usually obtain their subject-matter preparation in the liberal arts division of the university and come to the school of education for their professional courses only. In some universities, however, the college of education has its own content departments and controls the entire curriculum of those who are preparing to teach.

The University of Chicago has a unique organization for the preparation of teachers, based on the idea that such preparation is a concern of the whole institution rather than of a single professional department or school. A Committee on the Preparation of Teachers, representative of all the departments which have any concern with subjects taught in the lower schools, is in general charge of the program. The Department of Education is organized to give the few professional courses that are required on a service basis, and devotes itself primarily to the advanced courses necessary for the preparation of administrators and college teachers of education, and to research for the improvement of educational organization and procedure.

Harvard University, like a few other institutions, has recognized teacher preparation as a function of many departments by developing a plan of co-operation wherein the School of Education serves as only one factor. Other divisions of the University, such as the departments of mathematics and English, take a responsible part in preparing secondary-school teachers.

This review of the various types of institutions engaged in the preparation of teachers indicates that almost every kind of institution of higher education in the country undertakes this function. Technical institutes, particularly those devoted to engineering and other similar specialized fields, usually do not offer opportunities for the preparation of teachers, but these are among the few exceptions to the general rule that in the United States practically every institution of higher education beyond the secondary-school level offers some facilities for the preparation of teachers.

Standards of Preparation

During the twentieth century there has been a notable raising of the standards required for admission to the teaching profession. The states still differ considerably in their standards for certification but there is evidence that the movement for the raising of standards will not slacken until all states have reached a relatively high level of requirements.

The minimum desirable standard for teaching in the elementary school is now commonly recognized to be four years of preparation beyond the secondary school. Five states in 1937 issued no certificates for elementary-school teaching to any one with less than four years of college preparation. Half the states, however, had in 1937 some form of certification, based either on credits or examinations, which permitted one to begin teaching with less than two years of preparation beyond the secondary school. In all but six states the standards for teaching in the senior high school in 1937 required four years or more of preparation beyond the completion of the secondary school. Three states required five years of collegiate preparation for the certificate to teach in the high school, and other states plan shortly to make such a requirement.

The requirements generally recognized as desirable in the preparation of teachers include three types of subject matter: (1) a broad general education, such as is needed by any well-educated person; (2) some concentration in the subject or subjects to be taught; (3) professional preparation in educational psychology, a knowledge of the American educational system, methods of teaching, practice teaching, and similar subjects. These requirements have been determined by school administrators in the field whose duty it is to select teachers and supervise their work.

There has been a disposition in some quarters to criticize the requirement for professional preparation. Sometimes the complaint is made that the introduction of the professional courses has limited severely the amount of work the prospective teacher can take in the content fields. This is not the case, for the amount of professional study required is relatively small and it need never interfere with the obtaining of a sound general education or sufficient special preparation in content fields.

Misunderstanding has arisen also with regard to the sources of the pressure which has led to the requirement of professional courses for teacher certification. The idea of requiring such preparation did not originate with teachers colleges or with the college instructors in educational subjects, but came rather from administrators in the field who employ the product of the institutions preparing teachers. The administrators who are employers of teachers recognized the fact that many persons who are thoroughly familiar with the content of a subject lack the ability to teach it. Most beginners tend to teach as they have been taught, a practice which obviously offers little hope for improvement. Professional courses undertake to give the prospective teacher an objective view of the teaching process and to provide some actual experience in teaching under careful supervision. Evidence indicates that the most valuable professional preparation is the course in supervised teaching, or practice teaching as it is sometimes called.

As previously noted, although the standards for admission to the teaching profession have been raised materially in recent years, many teachers at present in service were certificated under earlier requirements and hence have qualifications far below those now in effect. Even if all teachers in the United States met the minimum standards that are now required for certification, their qualifications would still be lower than those of teachers in some European countries. The fact is that the rapid expansion of enrollments in the secondary schools of this country has created a demand for teachers which has made it extremely difficult to maintain standards of preparation. European countries have drastically limited admission to the secondary school and have as a result been able to apply much more rigid standards of selection for teachers than it has been possible to enforce in this country.

Even the most advanced standards now required for teacher certification in the more progressive states of the United States compare unfavorably with the program of preparation and the requirements in many European countries. In pre-war Germany a candidate for a teaching position in a secondary school had first to be a graduate of a secondary school. After his graduation he attended a university where his course of study continued for some four to six years, leading to the Ph.D. degree. Following the receipt of the Ph.D. degree, the candidate spent two years engaging in seminar work at a selected secondary school, during which time he studied professional problems of teaching and was given an opportunity to do some practice teaching under careful supervision. Throughout this course of preparation the candidate was subjected to a series of critical ratings and examinations and was eliminated if his qualifications were judged to be less than satisfactory. Upon the completion of this program the candidate was placed on the waiting list ready for assignment to a teaching position in a secondary school.

The preparation of school administrators of various types has recently been recognized as an important special task in the United States. A number of states now require certification for educational administrative positions as well as for teaching. For the most part the requirements for administrative positions call for a year of graduate work beyond the usual preparation for a teaching position. The year of graduate work includes specialized courses in the various aspects that relate to educational administration.

The curriculum for teacher preparation is by no means a settled issue in this country. Perhaps the most important problem concerns the time when a candidate shall take professional courses. In some institutions these courses are scattered throughout the curriculum; in others they are concentrated near the end of the curriculum or after the completion of preparation in the content subject.

The development of the normal-school program from a two-year to a four-year curriculum has also created difficulties. In the two-year curriculum for the preparation of elementary teachers the greater part of the emphasis was necessarily on methods of teaching. In some institutions the change to the four-year curriculum was accomplished by merely adding two years of subject-matter content to the existing first two years of professional subjects. This produced an organization of courses in which the usual freshman and sophomore subjects of the college of liberal arts were given in the junior and senior years of the four-year normal-school curriculum. With the stabilization of the four-year teachers-college curriculum, however, these difficulties are being corrected and a soundly arranged program, including both general education and specialized professional courses, is being developed.

TENURE AND ACADEMIC FREEDOM

A perennial problem relates to the protection of the tenure and academic freedom of the teacher. Tenure is sometimes jeopardized by the fact that a clash of opinions arises between teachers and the lay authorities in control of schools. Teachers may regard it as essential to teach lessons to which the lay authorities object. The teachers in such cases insist that freedom of speech for the citizen is a fundamental concept of democracy and that effective preparation for citizenship on the part of pupils in the school requires that they be equipped to form sound and independent judgments on matters of social and civic importance. Teachers hold that the schools should not be interfered with in their teaching.

To protect the competent teacher against unwarranted interference with the teaching of the truth, assurance of tenure seems desirable. Certainly there would be agreement that the competent teacher should not be dismissed because of political or religious views not affecting the competency of teaching, even when these views differ from those of the authorities in control of the school. On the other side it is contended that teachers have no right to use their positions as public servants to teach views that are not acceptable to communities.

If complete protection of tenure is given it frequently operates to protect the incompetent and injudicious teachers as well as those who are competent. Under conditions of assured tenure it becomes extremely difficult to rid the school system of an incompetent teacher or one who disregards the proprieties — whatever these are — in his or her teaching.

In a number of states, laws to protect the tenure of teachers have been enacted, but in several conspicuous cases this method has not been found satisfactory and some of the laws have been repealed. It seems that the greatest protection to the tenure of teachers lies ultimately in the education of the public conscience to an understanding that assured tenure is the accepted and customary practice for competent members of the teaching profession.

Academic freedom, or the right of teachers to teach the truth, is subject to severe restriction in many American communities. In two states, for example, the laws prescribe that no teacher may teach the doctrine of biological evolution. The content that may be acceptably taught concerning the history of the United States during the Civil War period differs sharply in certain parts of the country. The Federal Congress recently enacted an appropriation bill for the schools of the District of Columbia carrying the famous "red rider" which forbade any teacher to teach communism; by administrative interpretation this was construed to forbid even the mentioning of communism in the classrooms of the capital city. Fortunately this congressional action was afterwards repealed.

The nation can preserve its democracy only so long as its children are permitted to learn the truth. Any limitation of academic freedom is a blow at democracy itself, for such practices savor of dictatorship and special privilege. At the same time the conscientious teacher will be careful in his instruction and personal life not to offend the good taste of the community or to teach doctrines that depart too radically from the accepted standards of the locality. Teaching should be as unbiased as possible; the function of the teacher should be to present the facts and to give fairly both sides of every issue rather than indoctrinate for any particular point of view.

SALARIES OF TEACHERS

Salaries of teachers are in general lower than those of other groups of workers with comparable preparation.[1] The fact that teaching is a socialized occupation, the chief employer being the public, perhaps makes for a lower salary rate than would obtain if teaching were carried on under purely private auspices. Also the fact that preparation for teaching in most states is relatively easy to obtain and is less expensive than preparation for other professions also accounts for lower salaries. There is no deliberate limitation of the supply of beginning teachers, and with a relatively large supply, particularly in times of economic depression, the basic salary tends to approach the minimum subsistence level.

[1] Harold F. Clark, in his *Life Earnings in Selected Occupations* (New York: Harper and Brothers, 1937), shows that the present value of the life earnings of a public-school teacher in the United States is only about 30 per cent as large as the present value of the life earnings of a doctor, lawyer, dentist, or engineer.

Population
of City
High-School Teachers

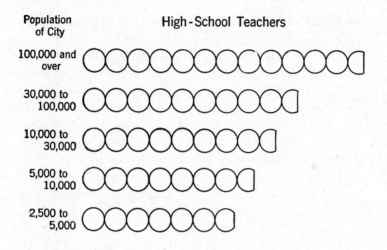

100,000 and over

30,000 to 100,000

10,000 to 30,000

5,000 to 10,000

2,500 to 5,000

Population
of City
Elementary-School Teachers

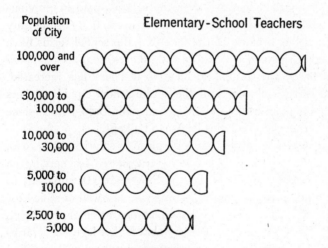

100,000 and over

30,000 to 100,000

10,000 to 30,000

5,000 to 10,000

2,500 to 5,000

Each circle represents $200 in annual salary

FIGURE 13. MEDIAN ANNUAL SALARIES PAID HIGH-SCHOOL AND
ELEMENTARY-SCHOOL TEACHERS IN CITIES OF VARIOUS SIZES IN
THE UNITED STATES, 1936–37

Data from *Salaries of School Employees, 1936–37*, Research Bulletin of the National Education Association, XV:2:68, 69, March, 1937.

In general, salaries are highest in the large cities and lowest in the rural areas. The average salary varies directly with the size of the city for practically all types of school positions. Elementary-school teachers are reported [1] in 1936–37 to have an average annual salary of $2045 in school systems in cities over 100,000 population, while in cities of 2500 to 5000 population the average annual salary was only $1008. The average annual salaries for elementary-school teachers in rural districts in nineteen states out of thirty-three reporting were below $800 in 1936–37. Teachers' salaries were reduced sharply during the early years of the economic depression in the 1930's; in many communities salaries were restored during the later years of that decade, though often not to the full level of 1929 or 1930.

Although the salaries paid in 1930 seem relatively low, they represent a marked increase over the salaries paid in previous periods. Not only has there been an increase in daily or monthly rate of pay, but because of the fact that the school terms have lengthened during recent decades, and salaries are often paid on a monthly basis, the annual income of teachers has increased. Both the real wage value and the actual amount paid teachers was much higher in 1930 than it had ever been before since statistics on teachers' salaries began to be kept.

In spite of the increases that took place in salaries up to 1930, it seems clear that the salaries at present offered teachers in the typical school system of the United States are not sufficient to attract an adequate supply of persons who are well qualified for teaching. With the increased level of preparation that is being required, it seems urgently necessary that higher levels of salaries be provided in order to insure an adequate supply of well-qualified teachers.

In the past the relationship between the supply of and demand for teachers has fluctuated considerably. In the period of the 1920's, immediately after the first World War, while the second-

---

[1] *Salaries of School Employees, 1936–37*, Research Bulletin of the National Education Association, vol. XV, no. 2, March, 1937.

ary schools were increasing in enrollments at a rapid rate, there was a serious shortage of teachers. The publicity given this shortage induced large numbers of persons to prepare for teaching and even before 1929 there was reported an oversupply of certified teachers. This oversupply continued during the depression of the 1930's, but at the present writing the supply seems to have been reduced somewhat and not to be greatly in excess of the current demand.

Although the apparent supply has been larger than the demand in recent years, the facts are that there has never been an oversupply of well-qualified teachers. In the supply figures are included large numbers of persons holding substandard certificates and others holding permanent certificates whose personal qualifications and preparation do not in reality qualify them for certification. Many other persons holding certificates are actually not in the market for teaching positions but are occupied in other vocations or have married and do not intend to teach any longer. Consequently the reported figures on the supply of teachers tend to overestimate the number actually available. It may be safely concluded that for some time there will be no oversupply of thoroughly qualified teachers, even though some teachers who are well qualified may find difficulty in locating positions because the available positions are held by persons who are not well qualified.

THE PROFESSIONALIZATION OF TEACHING

Throughout the discussion emphasis has been laid on the importance of raising teaching to the level of a profession. Some would question whether teaching can yet claim to be a true profession, and certainly it will be admitted that teaching lacks some of the characteristics of the older professions such as law and medicine.

Factors tending toward the improved recognition of the professional status of the teacher are the increased amounts of prepa-

ration now being required for certification and the improved
salary status.   Both within and without the ranks of teachers
there seems to be a growing desire and willingness to consider
teaching as one of the important and recognized professions.   On
the other side of the question may be cited the tendency of some
teachers to engage in undignified and unworthy methods of obtaining positions and the failure to follow an acceptable code of
ethics.   The lack of cohesion within the group of teachers is also
evidence of lack of professional status.

The question of preparation of teachers has been the center of
lively interest in recent years.   The National Survey of the
Education of Teachers, completed in 1933 under the leadership
of the United States Office of Education, presented much valuable
information on the subject.   An extensive study of the education
of teachers, begun in 1938, is being carried on under the auspices
of the American Council on Education by means of a grant from
one of the endowed foundations.   It is confidently expected and
hoped that from these extensive studies of the problem there will
emerge effective plans for improving and professionalizing the
personnel of the teaching and administrative staffs of the American
educational system.

BIBLIOGRAPHY

Alexander, Thomas, editor, *The Education of Teachers*.   *Twenty-Third Yearbook* of the National Society of College Teachers of Education. Chicago: University of Chicago Press, 1935.   240 pp.

Almack, John C., editor, *Modern School Administration*, pp. 49–74, 327–45.

Bachman, Frank P., *Education and Certification of Elementary Teachers*. Field Study no. 5, Division of Surveys and Field Studies, George Peabody College for Teachers.   Nashville, Tennessee: George Peabody College for Teachers, 1933.   x + 224 pp.

Beale, Howard K., *Are American Teachers Free?*   American Historical Association, Report of the Commission on the Social Studies, Part XII. New York: Charles Scribner's Sons, 1936.   xxiv + 856 pp.

Burton, William H., *Introduction to Education*, pp. 645–817.

Butterweck, Joseph S., and J. Conrad Seegers, *An Orientation Course in Education*, pp. 359–84.

Chamberlain, Leo M., and Leonard E. Meece, *Women and Men in the Teaching Profession.* Bulletin of the Bureau of School Service, University of Kentucky, vol. IX, no. 3 (March, 1937).   62 pp.

Chamberlain, Leo M., *The Teacher and School Organization*, pp. 113–323, 356–86, 625–44.

Clapp, Frank L., Wayland J. Chase, and Curtis Merriman, *Introduction to Education*, pp. 324–80, 527–57.

Cooke, Dennis H., *Problems of the Teaching Personnel.*   New York: Longmans, Green and Company, 1933.   xv + 384 pp.

Cubberley, Ellwood P., *State School Administration*, pp. 585–682.

Douglass, Aubrey A., *The American School System*, pp. 413–44.

Elsbree, Willard S., *The American Teacher.*   New York: American Book Company, 1939.   ix + 566 pp.

Evenden, E. S., *National Survey of the Education of Teachers:* vol. VI, *Summary and Interpretation.*   Office of Education Bulletin, 1933, no. 10. Washington: Government Printing Office, 1935.   xiii + 254 pp.

Frasier, George Willard, and Winfield D. Armentrout, *An Introduction to the Literature of Education*, pp. 437–550.

Judd, Charles H., *Preparation of School Personnel.*   Regents' Inquiry into the Character and Cost of Public Education in the State of New York. New York: McGraw-Hill Book Company, 1938.   xi + 152 pp.

Kilpatrick, William H., editor, *The Teacher and Society.*   First Yearbook of the John Dewey Society.   New York: D. Appleton-Century Company, 1937.   vii + 360 pp.

Reeder, Ward, *A First Course in Education*, pp. 545–720.

Research Bulletins of the National Education Association:
   The Teacher's Economic Position, XIII:4:165–267 (September, 1935).
   A Handbook on Teacher Tenure, XIV:4:167–94 (September, 1936).
   Teacher Retirement Systems and Social Security, XV:3:91–151 (May, 1937).
   Statutory Status of Six Professions, XVI:4:183–234 (September, 1938).
   The Rural Teacher's Economic Status, XVII:1:5–61 (January, 1939).
   Salaries of School Employees, 1938–39, XVII:2:67–95 (March, 1939).

Smith, Payson, Frank W. Wright, and Associates, *Education in the Forty-Eight States*, pp. 87–107.   Staff Study no. 1, Advisory Committee on Education.

Wilson, Lester M., and I. L. Kandel, *Introduction to the Study of American Education*, pp. 219–30.

CHAPTER XVII

Methods of Teaching

Throughout the preceding chapters of this book it has been shown that the organization and administration of schools in the United States, the subjects taught in these schools, the institutional forms that appear in the educational system, and the characteristics of the teaching and administrative personnel all reflect the unique type of civilization that has evolved in this country. The discussion has now reached the point where a brief treatment must be undertaken of what is happening in the classrooms of American schools. It is here that teachers in direct contact with pupils carry on the processes of instruction for which society has prepared the externals and for which the whole organization of schools is maintained. In the classrooms of schools the curriculum is administered, the preparation of teachers is applied, the requirements of the individual careers of pupils are more or less satisfactorily met; in short, the purposes of education are realized.

One might be disposed to expect that the close relationship between teachers and pupils in the classroom would result in an endless variety of instructional procedures, in which social influences would be far less determining than anywhere else in the educational system. The expectation is, indeed, partly realized when one observes the way in which teachers carry on their class instruction. Some teachers are poised and quiet; others are so energetic that they distract their pupils. Some are voluble and consume the major part of the class period talking to the pupils; others draw out their pupils and themselves recede into the background. Some ask leading questions that call for only obvious

and superficial answers; others know how to stimulate thinking
on the part of pupils with well-formulated, discriminating questions. In spite of the idiosyncrasies of teachers and their purely
personal methods of conducting class exercises, however, there
are certain fundamental aspects of teaching procedures that
can be traced to social causes which affect even the highly per-
sonalized activities of the classroom.

THE CHANGE FROM THE AUTHORITARIAN METHOD

For a long time instruction in the schools of this country was
characterized by what may be called an authoritarian method of
presentation. The essence of this method is that the subject
matter or content to be learned is considered all important; the
learner is expected to absorb this content, as set forth in the authoritative source, without change.

The emphasis on the authoritarian method of teaching originated in the fact that the content taught in the early schools was
based chiefly on religious materials. In the teaching of religion
the authoritarian method is naturally followed because of the
necessity of maintaining orthodoxy. Any deviation from the
accepted formulation of religious doctrines may change the meaning somewhat and thus becomes a heresy. Consequently, the
pupil is expected to learn the content of religious dogma exactly
as it is formulated by recognized authority. Frequently this
formulation is set forth in a catechism in which the answers are
given to important theological questions; these answers are to be
learned verbatim by the pupil and only when he can repeat the
answers without making a mistake is he deemed to have learned
his lesson. Whether he understands what the words mean may
even be regarded as irrelevant. The important duty of the pupil
is to repeat the words exactly as they are found in the authoritative source. No originality is expected of the pupil in learning
the catechism, for originality would undoubtedly lead to dangerous and unorthodox modification of the authoritative statement.

The word "recitation," which is commonly used to refer to the classroom exercise, originally expressed precisely this concept of the authoritative type of teaching. The pupil was to "re-cite" or say back again to the teacher the words which he had memorized as the authoritative answer to some set question.

Anyone acquainted with the early colonial history of New England, in the course of which many of the practices of the educational system of this country originated, will have no difficulty in tracing the authoritative method of teaching to its source. The Puritan insistence on orthodoxy was one of the outstanding characteristics of early American life. A second social effect which came from the same source is the emphasis on reading as the most important aspect of primary and elementary education. As previously pointed out, the schools of Europe depend far more than the schools of this country on oral instruction. In such a subject as geography, for example, pupils in European schools are taught, not from a textbook, but from a wall map in the classroom on which the teacher describes the various parts of the world. The New England colonies were settled by emigrants who had come because they wanted liberty to read the Scriptures each for himself. They taught their children to read because they looked on the ability to read as the surest guarantee for escape from dependence on clerical interpretation of the Bible. By teaching reading they established the custom of instruction from textbooks.

Throughout the history of this country textbooks have been the source of knowledge. Even teachers who had little knowledge could hear recitations. The independence that the early settlers sought through cultivation of ability to read, reinforced by the demand for orthodoxy, thus determined the pattern of teaching in the first schools and in the schools of later times. Tradition has handed down many an account of the formalism of the teaching of earlier times. A recitation under the old formal authoritarian method was scarcely more than a test of the type which in present-day terminology is known as a "completion test." The teacher of a lesson in geography, for example, would begin to read from a text somewhat as follows: "Pennsylvania is bounded on the east by..." Here there was a pause in the teacher's reading and some pupil was selected to complete the sentence. If the completion was correct, the teacher continued the reading. If the completion was incorrect, a sharp reprimand was administered and another pupil was called on to complete the sentence. Conformity to the exact wording of the text was the strict requirement.

Even in colleges the recitation method of instruction obtained in most classes until after the middle of the nineteenth century. The influence which changed the practices of American colleges from holding strictly to recitations from textbooks to the method of lecturing was the example of European universities. During the latter half of the nineteenth century a great many students went to Europe to take courses beyond those offered in American colleges. These students found the professors in the European universities delivering lectures in which they reported the results of their own researches or summarized the research results of others.

The lecture method had its historical origin in the fact that in earlier times books had been rare. Only the professor possessed a copy of the book with which students were to be made acquainted. He read from his text to the assembled students, making from time to time comments on what he read. In the course of years, as books became more common so that students could secure copies, the professor's instruction was reduced to comments rather than the reading of the text; and finally comments on the writings of authorities gave way to statements of the lecturer's personal views and contributions to knowledge. Today the lecture method has so largely superseded the recitation method in colleges and universities that students would think it strange and indefensibly formal if they were asked to repeat verbatim the statements found in a book.

The spirit of scholarship which led to the abandonment of

recitations in colleges is today effective in the lower schools also. A teacher who in this day and age should conduct an old-fashioned recitation based on memorization of a text would be condemned as guilty of an offense against the intelligence of pupils.

Reference was made in the preceding chapter to the stimulating influence of the Oswego Normal School under the leadership of Sheldon in breaking up the formalism of school instruction. There were others to whom credit must be given for the inauguration of a movement for a new type of teaching. One of these innovators was William H. McGuffey, who compiled for the schools a series of readers containing interesting stories. These stories were graded by a strictly empirical method which McGuffey apparently invented. After finding what seemed to be a suitable story or article, he read it to children of different ages. By watching carefully the reactions of children of various age levels to the selections, he found that he could determine within a narrow limit the ages to which any particular story or article seemed to appeal. By this method he was able to publish a set of readers graded according to the age levels to which the materials could be expected to appeal.

The McGuffey readers had a great vogue for a long time and were widely imitated. They are still fondly remembered by many people of the passing generation because of the strong moral flavor of their stories. In that respect, however, the McGuffey readers did not differ from other reading materials used in the schools of the period. McGuffey's important contribution was in the selection of attractive stories and the grading of the reading materials to suit the interests and capacities of pupils at different levels.

It is difficult to attribute the intellectual awakening of the schools of a century ago to any particular person or influences. A similar awakening was taking place in England, France, and Germany. American leaders were visiting schools on the other side of the Atlantic and were bringing back stimulating suggestions for educational reforms which reinforced the tendencies

developing in this country. Reference was made in the preceding
chapter to the influence of the Pestalozzian movement on the
development of the Oswego Normal School. A brief description
of the reform in educational methods which was initiated by
Pestalozzi will serve to illustrate the transition from the older,
more formal type of teaching, to the newer methods which recognize the interests and capacities of the pupils.

Johann Heinrich Pestalozzi, a Swiss who lived from 1747 to
1827, demonstrated his ideas on methods of teaching in a school
which he founded for that purpose. In 1781 he wrote a book
entitled *Leonard and Gertrude* in which he dramatized his views
on education in a story of a poor Swiss family. In the story the
mother, Gertrude, reformed her ne'er-do-well husband and ultimately the whole village in which she lived by giving her children
a new type of practical education. The following description
shows how Pestalozzi was gradually breaking away from the
formal education of the earlier type, in which children were expected to do much memorizing, and was advocating the training
of pupils in activities which were at once useful and educative.
The scene is laid in Gertrude's home and is being observed by
visitors, including the pastor of the parish.

> The children all helped wash the dishes, and then seated themselves
> in their customary places before their work. The gentlemen begged
> Gertrude to let everything go on as usual, and after the first half hour,
> during which she was a little embarrassed, all proceeded as if no
> stranger were present. First the children sang their morning hymns,
> and then Gertrude read a chapter of the Bible aloud, which they re-
> peated after her while they were spinning, rehearsing the most in-
> structive passages until they knew them by heart. In the mean time,
> the oldest girl had been making the children's beds in the adjoining
> room, and the visitors noticed through the open door that she silently
> repeated what the others were reciting. When this task was com-
> pleted, she went into the garden and returned with vegetables for
> dinner, which she cleaned while repeating Bible-verses with the rest.
> It was something new for the children to see three gentlemen in the
> room, and they often looked up from their spinning toward the corner
> where the strangers sat. Gertrude noticed this, and said to them:

"Seems to me you look more at these gentlemen than at your yarn."
But Harry answered: "No, indeed! We are working hard, and you'll
have finer yarn today than usual."

Whenever Gertrude saw that anything was amiss with the wheels
or cotton, she rose from her work, and put it in order. The smallest
children, who were not old enough to spin, picked over the cotton for
carding, with a skill which excited the admiration of the visitors.

Although Gertrude thus exerted herself to develop very early the
manual dexterity of her children, she was in no haste for them to learn
to read and write. But she took pains to teach them early how to
speak; for, as she said, "of what use is it for a person to be able to read
and write, if he cannot speak? — since reading and writing are only
an artificial sort of speech." To this end she used to make the children
pronounce syllables after her in regular succession, taking them from
an old A–B–C book she had. This exercise in correct and distinct
articulation was, however, only a subordinate object in her whole
scheme of education, which embraced a true comprehension of life
itself. Yet she never adopted the tone of instructor toward her
children; she did not say to them: "Child, this is your head, your nose,
your hand, your finger;" or "Where is your eye, your ear?" — but
instead, she would say: "Come here, child, I will wash your little
hands," "I will comb your hair," or: "I will cut your finger-nails."
Her verbal instruction seemed to vanish in the spirit of her real activity, in which it always had its source. The result of her system was
that each child was skilful, intelligent and active to the full extent
that its age and development allowed.

The instruction she gave them in the rudiments of arithmetic was
intimately connected with the realities of life. She taught them to
count the number of steps from one end of the room to the other, and
two of the rows of five panes each, in one of the windows, gave her an
opportunity to unfold the decimal relations of numbers. She also
made them count their threads while spinning, and the number of
turns on the reel, when they wound the yarn into skeins. Above all,
in every occupation of life she taught them an accurate and intelligent
observation of common objects and the forces of nature.

All that Gertrude's children knew, they knew so thoroughly that
they were able to teach it to the younger ones; and this they often
begged permission to do. On this day, while the visitors were present,
Jonas sat with each arm around the neck of a smaller child, and made
the little ones pronounce the syllables of the A–B–C book after him;
while Lizzie placed herself with her wheel between two of the others,

and while all three spun, taught them the words of a hymn with the utmost patience.[1]

This is not the place for a complete history of the efforts that have been made during the past century to banish formalism from the schools. Especially during the past four or five decades the numerous experiments that have been tried in classroom procedure give one an almost bewildering impression of instability and chaotic uncertainty. The teaching profession has been appealed to by innovators on every side. Temporary fashions in teaching have been widely adopted and quickly abandoned in favor of new methods which have been advocated by vociferous reformers. Underlying all the kaleidoscopic changes that have taken place is one fundamental purpose: the stimulation of pupils to think independently and to face the world with the ability to analyze situations and work out for themselves solutions of the problems which they encounter in their personal lives. It requires a long series of critical discussions to evaluate all the new methods that have been suggested and adopted. The only attempt which will be made here is to review some of the outstanding methods that are now widely employed in the better schools.

TEACHING OF READING

From the beginning of literary instruction the method of teaching reading has constituted an important problem. Roman educators worked out a method, based on logical principles, that was standard for many centuries. They observed that the smallest unit of reading material was the letter; therefore, they reasoned, one who would learn to read must first of all become acquainted with all the letters of the alphabet. The next simplest unit of reading material is the combination of two or three letters into a syllable; so on logical grounds it was thought that the next

[1] Pestalozzi's *Leonard and Gertrude*, pp. 129–31. Translated and abridged by Eva Channing. Boston: Ginn, Heath and Company, 1885.

task of the pupil must be to learn all the possible combinations of vowels and consonants as syllables. After the syllables have been mastered, the pupil can begin to learn words. Later, he may reach the stage where he can read short sentences, and then finally he can be introduced to longer units of connected reading material.

This method of teaching reading, founded on logical principles, persisted until well into the nineteenth century and indeed it is still found today in some backward schools. In the early part of the nineteenth century, however, some observers began to question the basis of the alphabet system of teaching reading, and to suggest that words rather than letters are the primary units of recognition in the act of reading. Horace Mann, in Massachusetts, was one of the leaders who early advocated the adoption of the word method of teaching reading.

Much later the psychologists were able, by studying the movements of the eyes in reading, to show that a grouping of words is seen as a unit during a single fixation of the eyes, without necessarily distinguishing either the letters or the words that make up the phrase included in a single eye-span. This discovery has led to marked modifications in the methods of teaching reading. Flash cards, each presenting a phrase approximately the length of a single eye-span, are used early in the reading program, and the child is thus taught to recognize a phrase unit, such as "the good boy" before he learns the separate words and long before he is acquainted with the names of the letters of which words are composed. Children taught by these modern methods are able to read much more effectively and require a shorter period to learn to read than has ever before been true in educational history.

In earlier times one of the important purposes of learning to read was to be able to read aloud. The necessity for effective oral reading dated from a time when most people could not read; hence, any person who was able to read was often called upon to read aloud to others. Long after the knowledge of reading became widely distributed among the population the older notion persisted; children were still taught to read aloud and great stress in the teaching of reading was placed on proper expression, enunciation, and other elocutionary arts.

In modern times, by contrast, most reading must be done silently. One who must read aloud to get the meaning of printed material is greatly handicapped and is more or less of a nuisance to his neighbors. While a few people, such as radio announcers, have need for effective oral reading, most reading today is done silently. Studies have shown also that one can read silently much more rapidly if one does not stop to vocalize. The persistence of the older idea of teaching for the purpose of reading aloud thus makes for ineffective habits of silent reading. The recognition of this fact has been important in changing the method of teaching children to read; under modern procedures children are taught to read silently in an effective manner, and less emphasis than formerly is given to oral reading.

Studies have shown that many children fail to acquire good habits of reading, either through some fault in the school system or through some deficiency in the child's experience or physical equipment. Pupils without good reading habits are definitely handicapped in their school work, but many of the brighter ones are able to progress in spite of this deficiency. Thus it is not uncommon to find pupils in high school, or even in college, whose reading techniques are entirely unsatisfactory. Either they read too slowly or they are not able to comprehend effectively what they have read. To overcome these difficulties, programs of remedial reading have been instituted in many school systems, and even in some colleges and universities. Experience with such programs has shown that older pupils whose reading habits are deficient can be taught to overcome their handicaps and to read efficiently, thereby opening up possibilities for further progress in school that were definitely denied them before.

A large number of scientific investigations have been made of the methods of teaching reading. The teacher in a modern school system, particularly in the lower grades of the elementary school, needs to be thoroughly acquainted with the most efficient methods of teaching reading as revealed by these investigations. The question of how to teach reading is one to which a considerable amount of interest always attaches because of the basic nature of the reading process as a tool for further study. As a result of the scientific studies regarding methods of teaching reading, the pupil in a modern school system is taught to read today by methods that are radically different from those of a century ago, and the result is a much more rapid attainment of reading skill and a much greater certainty of the attainment of satisfactory reading techniques by the pupil. Similar scientific studies have been carried on in the teaching of other subjects, such as arithmetic, spelling, and handwriting, with the result that a large amount of information has been accumulated which permits employment of greatly improved teaching procedures in all school subjects.

THE SUPERVISED STUDY MOVEMENT

Even down to recent times it was assumed that a teacher's responsibility was to conduct in the classroom a restudy of the lessons that pupils had previously studied by themselves. That the teacher had any responsibility for the study process itself was not assumed. The teacher's typical admonition to the pupil whose lessons were not well learned was to "study harder," but the pupil was left to his own devices with respect to the method he should employ in order to learn his lessons more effectively.

The supervised study movement, by contrast, assumes that the school must be responsible for teaching pupils how to study and for providing effective conditions under which the pupil may study. One of the first persons to call attention to this necessity was Frank McMurry, who in 1909 published a book entitled *How to Study and Teaching How to Study*. In 1916 Guy M. Whipple published a little book addressed to pupils of the secondary-school level, entitled *How to Study Effectively*. Whipple presents some thirty-eight maxims or rules for effective study, most of which are based on sound psychological observation. These rules are simply stated and can readily be used by a pupil in improving his own study habits.

The introduction of a plan for supervised study in schools called for some rearrangement of the architectural plan of the building. The earlier plan followed in the construction of a building for a secondary school called for a large assembly room or study hall to which all pupils were required to go for study while not in their classrooms. The large room was presided over by a teacher in the rôle of a policeman with no responsibility other than to keep disorder at a minimum. The newer plan calls for the breaking up of the large study hall into numerous study rooms, each in charge of a special teacher who is responsible for seeing that pupils learn to study effectively and that they practice effective study habits.

In secondary schools opportunity for supervised study has sometimes been provided by lengthening the class periods and devoting the last part of each period to the study of the lesson for the next day. Thus instead of the typical forty-five minute period, the class period may be made either sixty or ninety minutes in length. The recitation occupies theoretically the usual forty-five minutes and the remainder of the lengthened period is devoted by the pupils to study under the supervision of a teacher.

One difficulty encountered in this plan is that teachers who are good at lesson-hearing are not always effective in teaching how to study. In practice also, teachers sometimes succumb to the temptation to use the time that should be devoted to study, for the typical routine of class work.

THE UNIT-ASSIGNMENT PLAN

A characteristic common to many of the newer methods of teaching is the development of what are known as unit assignments. The National Survey of Secondary Education reported in 1933 an extensive investigation of several variants of the unit-assignment plan. The investigators were impressed by the fact that, although the schools reported their plans of teaching under many different names, the actual procedures did not differ as much as the names of the plans. The report states:

> Great confusion of terminology exists in the field of plans characterized by the unit assignment. In practice, a number of widely discussed plans, techniques, or procedures characterized by the unit assignment are essentially one and the same thing. These procedures are variously known as the project method, the problem method, differentiated assignments, long-unit assignments, contract plan, laboratory plan, individualized instruction, Winnetka technique, Dalton plan, Morrison plan, or a modification of any one of the last three ... comparative studies amply justify the statement that schools operating under any one of these three last-mentioned terms, or under any modification of them, are doing very much the same type of work done by schools operating under any one of the first seven terms.[1]

The general nature of the unit-assignment plan is illustrated in the method described by Henry C. Morrison in his volume entitled *The Practice of Teaching in the Secondary School.* Morrison first classifies instructional materials into five groups: the science type, the appreciation type, the practical-arts type, the language-arts type, and the pure-practice type. For each of these classifications he suggests that appropriate teaching techniques need to be developed. He then goes on to suggest a method of teaching science-type subjects. The method in this case involves first the organization of the subject into teaching units. In the teaching of any unit five steps are followed:

1. Exploration, or inventory to find out what the pupils already know about the unit;
2. Presentation, or the direct teaching of the unit by the teacher in a single class period;

[1] Leonard V. Koos, *et al., Summary,* pp. 125-27. Monograph no. 1, National Survey of Secondary Education, Bulletin, 1932, no. 17. Washington: Government Printing Office, 1934.

3. Assimilation, or a period during which pupils work independently on the several aspects of the unit;

4. Organization, during which the pupils reformulate the elements of the unit into a logically arranged whole;

5. Recitation, in which the pupils present their organization of the unit to the teacher as evidence of their mastery of it.

An important characteristic of the method is the arrangement of subject matter into units. The teaching unit is defined as "a comprehensive and significant aspect of the environment, of an organized science, of an art, or of conduct, which, being learned, results in an adaptation in personality." It will be observed that the unit may cut across traditional lines of subject-matter organization or may be arranged in any way to meet a given teaching situation.

The expertness of the teacher is revealed in the organization of the units. This task calls both for a comprehensive grasp of the subject-matter field and also a thorough knowledge of the child's nature and of the learning process itself. Textbook makers have been busy in recent years revising their texts to adapt them better to the unit-assignment plan of instruction. The arrangement of subject matter for presentation by the unit-assignment method offers promise of improving considerably the instructional process.

THE SOCIALIZED RECITATION

Another innovation in teaching methods that has been introduced in a number of schools is the socialized recitation. This procedure involves a radical departure from the older type of authoritarian teaching. Under the traditional procedure the teacher dominates the class exercise. The plan for socialized recitation, by contrast, makes the teacher merely one of a group engaged in discussing and informing themselves on the subject matter at hand. The teacher may not even be the presiding officer of the group and is present merely to advise and suggest sources of authority to which reference may be made rather than to settle matters by direct statement.

The successful operation of the socialized recitation demands a special arrangement of furniture in the classroom. The teacher's desk does not occupy a prominent position in the foreground. The children are preferably seated in movable chairs which may be placed in a circle or some other arrangement which seems advisable for effective discussion of the topic under consideration.

A method based on the same principle has been adopted in a number of colleges and universities where it is known as the conference or seminar plan. President Hamilton Holt at Rollins College in Florida has given publicity to such a plan at that institution. He advances the opinion that nobody ever learned anything from a lecture; consequently, Rollins College has abandoned the lecture method of instruction as far as possible and teaching is carried on principally in small conference groups. Class periods are two hours in length, permitting a laboratory type of instruction in all subjects.

The introduction of the socialized recitation seems to be a fundamental step in the direction of democratizing the educational process. If children are to be expected to learn the principles and methods of democratic government, it would seem desirable to expose them to a teaching procedure that is somewhat less dictatorial and autocratic than the traditional methods of instruction. The socialized recitation requires careful preparation on the part of the teacher, however, in order to guide the activities of the pupils so that the expected educational outcomes are achieved without too much or too obvious direction of the instructional process.

VISUAL EDUCATION AND THE RADIO

New educational techniques, depending on the introduction of mechanical devices such as the moving picture and the radio, have opened up vast possibilities for improvement in instructional procedure. The talking picture has proved to be an exceptionally effective adjunct to teaching and many school systems have installed the equipment necessary for the projection of sound films.

The use of sound films has numerous advantages over the ordinary lecture or demonstration method as used by the teacher, particularly in such fields as science. Many phenomena which cannot be reproduced in the lecture room can be filmed and made available for visual presentation. Close-up pictures will reveal details of a demonstration that could not possibly be seen by every student in a classroom no matter how carefully the demonstration is conducted. A perfect demonstration of the process to be shown can be given in the film, whereas in the ordinary classroom demonstration the lecturer is not infrequently embarrassed by a failure of the experiment to go through according to his plan. If it is desired, parts of the film can be run again and again, permitting students to familiarize themselves thoroughly with difficult aspects of the demonstration; in the usual lecture and demonstration process this is impossible except by repetition of the entire experiment. Slow motion or time lapse pictures permit an insight that could never be obtained in an ordinary demonstration. The explanation of the demonstrator as recorded in the talking picture can be made perfect, in contrast to the running account made by a teacher during a demonstration which occupies his whole attention.

Results of careful experimentation lead to the conclusion that the sound film is a useful and effective aid to teaching. All experiments that have been conducted in this area, however, presume that the sound film will not displace the teacher but will serve only as a supplement to other classroom exercises.

Instruction by radio has been experimented with extensively, but little has been done to determine objectively the relative effectiveness of this new device. In certain fields, such as the teaching of music appreciation, the radio seems clearly to be useful. Lectures, drama, and other forms of instruction can apparently also be given effectively by the radio. The possibilities of the use of the radio in the schools are as yet by no means fully explored, and the future will probably see important developments along this line.

LIBRARY METHODS

The source of authoritative materials for use in the instructional process has undergone a considerable change in the course of educational history. As previously pointed out, modern methods of teaching place less reliance than formerly on a single source of information; they suggest consultation of a wide variety of sources. Children are even encouraged to find conflicting points of view in statements of alleged facts, in order that they may be prepared to deal discriminatingly with the types of printed material they will meet in adult life. In order to provide the materials for consultation in the schools, a well-stocked library is necessary today, and the library method of instruction is widely used in well-managed schools. In some schools the library is effectively combined with the study hall.

The introduction of the library method has made new demands on plant space and has necessitated provision of relatively expensive equipment for reading-room facilities in addition to the books and periodicals that are required for effective library service. A new type of staff member, the teacher-librarian, is also needed. The person who occupies this position is not merely a keeper or guardian of books; he or she must also have a good knowledge of sources and be acquainted with the technique for referring pupils to the appropriate materials which they need to consult.

The widespread use of the library method seems to be a real gain in terms of effective preparation for responsible adulthood. Even though the method entails larger costs than the older method of dependence on a single text, the values obtained are well worth the additional expense.

LABORATORY METHODS

In teaching the sciences extensive use is made of the laboratory method. Instead of merely reading about the investigations by which scientific truths have been discovered and verified, pupils are supplied with materials and apparatus and are expected to repeat some of the experiments with their own hands. In many cases laboratory exercises have become altogether formal because the conditions of the experiments have been so fully prearranged that the pupil has nothing to do but follow, without any real initiative on his own part, a series of steps described in a laboratory manual. Careful comparisons of the results of instruction obtained by the laboratory method and by well-conducted demonstrations seem to favor the latter. In any case it can safely be said that a formal laboratory exercise contributes little to a pupil's understanding. A laboratory exercise in which the pupil is required to show imagination and ingenuity is a wholly different matter.

IMPORTANCE OF STUDYING METHODS OF TEACHING

The foregoing review of some of the new methods of teaching is by no means complete. It illustrates, however, what the educational world is doing to devise ways of inducing pupils to think for themselves. It shows also the possibilities of invention on the part of teachers.

Most conscientious beginning teachers try to follow the methods they have seen their own best teachers use. This purely imitative practice has serious limitations because the pupil, lacking training in professional techniques, is likely to overlook some of the elements in a method of teaching which make it effective. Furthermore, it is entirely probable that some teachers are more effective in the use of certain methods than other teachers are, and therefore the development of a good teaching method for any one teacher may be a matter of personal experimentation

to find out the procedure that seems best adaptable to the qualifications of that individual. It is important for the beginning
teacher to study methods of teaching quite as intensively as he
studies the subject matter which he is to teach, in order to gain
as objective a knowledge as possible of the methods that are best
to use under any given condition.

BIBLIOGRAPHY

Bagley, William Chandler, *School Discipline*. New York: The Macmillan
Company, 1926. xiv + 260 pp.
Bossing, N. L., *Progressive Methods of Teaching in Secondary Schools*.
Boston: Houghton Mifflin Company, 1935. xvi + 704 pp.
Breed, Frederick S., *Classroom Organization and Management*. Yonkers-
on-Hudson, New York: World Book Company, 1933. xvi + 472 pp.
Burton, William H., *Introduction to Education*, pp. 533–643.
Butterweck, Joseph S., and J. Conrad Seegers, *An Orientation Course in
Education*, pp. 80–93, 152–63.
Clapp, Frank L., Wayland J. Chase, and Curtis Merriman, *Introduction
to Education*, pp. 469–526.
Douglass, Aubrey A., *The American School System*, pp. 240–70.
Frasier, George Willard, and Winfield D. Armentrout, *An Introduction to
the Literature of Education*, pp. 199–238.
Garrison, N. L., *The Technique and Administration of Teaching*. New
York: American Book Company, 1933. xiv + 594 pp.
Harrison, Margaret, *Radio in the Classroom*.
McMurry, F. M., *How to Study and Teaching How to Study*. Boston:
Houghton Mifflin Company, 1909. viii + 324 pp.
Morrison, Henry C., *The Practice of Teaching in the Secondary School*.
Revised edition. Chicago: University of Chicago Press, 1931. x + 688
pp.
Parker, Samuel Chester, *General Methods of Teaching in Elementary Schools*.
Revised edition. Boston: Ginn and Company, 1922. xx + 336 pp.
Parker, Samuel Chester, *Methods of Teaching in High Schools*. Boston:
Ginn and Company, 1915. xxvi + 530 pp.
Parker, Samuel Chester, *Types of Elementary Teaching and Learning*.
Boston: Ginn and Company, 1923. xvi + 586 pp.
Reeder, Ward, *A First Course in Education*, pp. 229–322.
Simon, H. W., *Preface to Teaching*. New York: Oxford University Press,
1938. 98 pp.

Umstattd, J. G., *Secondary School Teaching*.   Boston: Ginn and Company, 1937.   x + 460 pp.

Whipple, Guy Montrose, *How to Study Effectively*.   Revised edition. Bloomington, Illinois: Public School Publishing Company, 1927.   44 pp.

CHAPTER XVIII

EXAMINATIONS AND TESTS

EXAMINATIONS AND TESTS of various kinds are
familiar means of determining the competency of individuals and
the efficiency of institutions. In the medieval universities the
candidate for a degree was required to appear in public and de-
fend against all comers a statement or thesis which he had proposed. In making his defense the candidate exhibited his ability
or inability to conduct his argument in conformity with the rules
of logic. Often the subject matter of the discussion was purely
hypothetical, but the form of the syllogisms employed and the
internal consistency with which the candidate maintained his
position determined his acceptance or rejection by the guild of
scholars to which he was applying for recognition and admission.
The defense of the thesis against attack degenerated in many
cases because the candidate persuaded his friends to appear and
raise objections which he was prepared readily to answer. In
the course of time the questions raised with the candidate were
left entirely to the professors and became in this way tests of the
candidate's knowledge rather than mere exercises in dialectic.

One of the earliest accounts of the examination of pupils and
teachers in a lower school in England is reported as having occurred in 1562 at the Merchant Tailors' School in London. The
name of this school indicates its origin, for it was founded by the
tailors' guild. The guilds had long required those who were
admitted to membership to prove themselves competent workmen, and naturally, therefore, a school founded by a guild required the pupils and masters to show proficiency. The bishop,
Grindal by name, and other learned men descended on the school

in what was described as a "solemn visitation" and examined the teachers, as to their learning and their manner of teaching, and then the pupils. The headmaster of the school was ill at the time, and when the bishop and his associates made a commendatory report this was "quickly conveyed" to the head of the school and "was received by him with cheerfulness and gratitude."

Written examinations were unknown in universities before 1702 at which date they were introduced at Trinity College, Cambridge. Practical tests in medicine were known long before this date, but examinations in the form familiar to students of today are a product of the eighteenth and subsequent centuries.

The term "test" which is now used to cover certain forms of examinations is a comparatively modern addition to the vocabulary of education. Another term which is also of recent origin and has been extended to include all forms of set examinations is the term "educational measurement." The measurement movement became a recognized phase of educational evolution through the efforts of students of the science of education to make exact and quantitative the evaluation of educational outcomes.

USES OF EXAMINATIONS

Today there are many kinds of tests and examinations, each having a specific purpose and a specific character. Attention will first be devoted to an analysis of the various situations in which examinations are used.

Determination of Pupil's Readiness for Advancement

Among the purposes for which examinations are commonly employed, perhaps the most important is the determination of a pupil's readiness to advance from one stage of learning to the next. Thus a pupil may properly be expected to show ability to read before he is allowed to advance to the study of such a subject as geography, where he will have to secure his knowledge from books. A pupil in secondary school cannot be admitted to second-year Latin until he has shown proficiency in first-year Latin. In an even more comprehensive sense, progress from one stage of the educational system to the next now depends on a pupil's ability to pass examinations, and tests for this purpose are customarily administered at the end of one grade, to determine whether the pupil can be expected to carry successfully the work of the next grade. If the curriculum is well organized and the examinations carefully prepared, progress and ability to pass examinations should correspond.

One of the important points at which examinations are administered for the purpose of determining readiness for advancement is at the time of the pupil's transition from the secondary school to college. Admission to colleges has long been determined by the ability of candidates to pass so-called "entrance examinations." Such examinations were administered in earlier times by each college separately. The conduct of entrance examinations became very burdensome as the number of applicants for admission increased. As was explained in Chapter VIII a group of eastern institutions in 1899 formed a central agency, known as the College Entrance Examination Board, to which was delegated the task of examining all applicants for admission to the member institutions. Each year since 1901 this agency has prepared and administered a series of examinations designed to test the knowledge of applicants for admission to college. The papers of candidates are marked by the central agency and the results for a given examinee are transmitted to the college to which he is requesting admission. Each college then sets its own standard with regard to the particular grade on the examination that is necessary for admission. Most of the eastern institutions now require all their entering freshmen to take the tests given by the College Entrance Examination Board.

In the Middle West, as was also explained in Chapter VIII, an entirely different plan of admission to college arose in the latter part of the nineteenth century. The midwestern states by that time had developed relatively strong state universities which, like the common schools, were under public control. Under such circumstances the plan of admitting students to college on the basis of certificates of competency furnished by the secondary schools seemed feasible because both the college and the schools were in theory at least answerable to the same authorities for the quality of work demanded of pupils. Michigan was the first state to introduce such a plan, and it was later adopted in all the midwestern and western and most southern states.

It will be observed that the certificate plan for college entrance delegates to the secondary school the function of examining applicants for admission to college. The plan adopted by Michigan was based on the example of the French educational system. The plan works well in France because of the highly centralized organization of the educational system.

Some difficulties have arisen with the certificate plan in the United States because the institutions of higher education are not in fact under the control of the same public authorities as the public schools. Local pressures in some cases make local school authorities unable to enforce appropriate standards of attainment, and the higher institutions find that in such cases poorly prepared students are certificated. To guard against this difficulty regional accrediting associations were formed. The nature of these associations and the manner in which they operate were described in Chapter VIII.

There still remains a knotty problem with respect to the agency which should administer the examination for admission to a given unit in the school system. Should the authorities of the unit which the pupil has completed determine his fitness for entrance to the next unit, or should those in the unit to which he expects to go set the examination and grade the answers? This question appears at all levels of education. It becomes prominent at the points of juncture between the units into which the school system is organized, and the issue is especially acute at the point of juncture between the secondary school and college.

As noted above, the thinking on this problem differs sharply in two sections of the country. The East, particularly New England and the middle Atlantic states, holds rather strongly to the view that the college should determine the fitness of its applicants for entrance. The rest of the country typically tends to delegate at least the testing for academic achievement to the secondary schools. Even under the certificating plan some higher institutions impose requirements for admission other than a satisfactory certificate of graduation from secondary school. For example, some colleges accept only the pupils who graduate in the upper half or the upper third of their classes. Some colleges require candidates for admission to pass general intelligence tests.

Stimulation of Learning

A second important purpose of examinations in the schools is to stimulate learning. A knowledge of the fact that an examination or test of some kind is to be given undoubtedly does much to lead pupils to study carefully the materials to be covered on the test. Effective teachers, therefore, employ tests frequently in order to keep pupils constantly stimulated to a high level of achievement.

President A. Lawrence Lowell, in an article some years ago, presented the following well-reasoned argument in favor of examinations as devices for stimulating learners to develop readiness in recalling what they have studied:

Although examinations in single courses, whether in college or in school, have as their primary object to measure the progress of pupils, this is far from being their only object. They can and should be used also as a distinct element in the educational process, and as such can be made highly effective. Even if the sole aim of education at any stage were the knowledge of facts, the formal effort to recall those facts to mind unexpectedly, to exert pressure upon the memory and bring to consciousness things half-hidden there, is of great value by serving to make that faculty readily responsive to a call.

When the writer was a professor teaching a large freshman course he often told the class, before the mid-year or final paper, that the art of passing examinations was one most useful to acquire. This was a surprise, and provoked a laugh; but it was explained that a lawyer trying a case in court was often confronted by an unexpected question of evidence and must at once try to recall any decisions bearing on the point he had ever come across, and that this was passing an examination; that a physician suddenly called to a suffering patient was in a similar position — at the bedside he also passes an examination. Throughout our lives we are constantly forced to muster all we can of our previous knowledge, and the habit of doing so can be cultivated by practice. How often when the occasion has passed do we ask ourselves, as a student does after an examination, why we did not remember some essential fact. The art of recalling quickly, fully, and accurately is certainly a valuable part of mental training. It is a special art, not the same thing as a rich store of knowledge. Some men have all the knowledge they possess ready for use on demand; some require a certain time for reflection before they can produce it; and some can make use of it only in the solitude of their studies. The late Francis A. Walker said that every man had his personal equation, and that his own was two minutes. More than to scholars and writers is the value to men of affairs of recalling rapidly the knowledge that they need.[1]

Comparison of Groups of Pupils

A third purpose of tests is to supply a means of comparing groups of pupils. It is sometimes useful to know whether the pupils in the class this year are doing better than those of past years, or whether the pupils of one school system have learned more than those of another, or whether the pupils taught by one method have attained more than those taught by another method. Tests and examinations are the most effective devices now available for making such comparisons. This use of tests is illustrated by the study reported in 1930 by a member of the administrative staff of the Boston school system. Criticisms of contemporary education as contrasted with education of earlier times led to a comparison, the results of which are described as follows:

1. In 1853 twenty pupils took the examination for entrance to high school. Eighteen were passed as qualified.

[1] A. Lawrence Lowell, "The Art of Examination," *Atlantic Monthly,* CXXXVII:62–63 (January, 1926).

In 1929 two hundred pupils (twenty each from ten different sections of the city) took the same examination under as nearly the same conditions as it was possible to make them. All were passed as qualified by the standards of 1853.

2. The candidates of 1853 had elected to pursue academic or classical courses. That was all the high school had to offer. They had been selected and drilled along such narrow lines as would, if possible, make their admission certain.

The candidate of 1929 had already made a choice of vocational, technical, or college preparatory instruction. The selection was based on scholarship — not on the candidate's decision to attend high school. No special training for the examination was given.

3. In 1853 the examinations were given at the end of nine pre-high-school grades, and in 1929 the same examinations were given to pupils who had not completed eight grades of pre-high-school study.

4. The pupils of 1853 were trained with a concentrated program in only a very limited field of subjects.

The pupils of 1929 were trained in a curriculum far richer than that of 1853.[1]

Evaluation of Instruction

A fourth purpose for which examinations and tests are used is to determine the effectiveness of individual members in the teaching staff or of entire school systems. In the American educational system tests of the achievement of pupils are not often used to evaluate the effectiveness of individual teachers. Indeed, it is sometimes contended that inasmuch as teachers do not determine the curriculum and do not select the pupils whom they instruct, they should not be held altogether responsible for the outcomes of their efforts. The central administrative organization of the school system must carry its share of responsibility. In any case if teachers are to be compared on the basis of the achievement of their pupils, it is certainly necessary to make sure that the groups under their direction are at the beginning of the year equal in ability, promise, and level of advancement. A test given groups

[1] Louis J. Fish, *Examinations Seventy-Five Years Ago and Today: Comparison and Results of Entrance Examinations to High School,* pp. 6–7. Copyright 1930 by World Book Company. Yonkers-on-Hudson, New York.

of pupils at the end of the year may then supply evidence of the relative effectiveness of teachers.

In one state, New York, teachers in the secondary schools may be readily compared on the basis of the success of their pupils on the examination given by the Board of Regents through the State Department of Education. The prospective employer of any teacher who has taught in the secondary schools of New York State can obtain information on the extent to which the applicant has been successful in preparing secondary-school pupils for the Regents' examinations. The feeling generally in the United States, however, is that examinations have not yet reached a degree of reliability sufficient to permit their use for the purpose of judging competence of individual teachers.

The measures of general intelligence and of achievement of learners, as supplied by examinations, have played an important part in the administration of education. Examinations have sometimes been made the basis of the distribution of public funds, but this practice is less common in the United States than in England. The examinations conducted by the New York State Department of Education, known as the Regents' examinations, to which reference has been made in the preceding paragraph, were originally established as a means of determining which school systems in the state had attained a level of excellence sufficient to justify payment of state subsidies.

Determination of the Content of Instruction

Tests and examinations are sometimes used in the schools as a means of determining the content of instruction. In Chapter XI it was pointed out that the arrangement of the curriculum in the schools of the United States involves much overlapping and duplication. In many cases the teacher has little conception of how much the pupils already know about a subject before the study of it is begun. The device known as the "pretest" is useful in determining how much of the content outlined for a given course is new to the pupils and needs to be taught. A similar device is useful in the unit-assignment plan, described in the preceding chapter. A pretest often shows that some of the pupils in the class may properly be excused from the work on a given unit because they are found to have a mastery of the subject matter of the unit before it is actually presented to the class.

When examinations or tests are administered to large groups of students they tend to gain a prestige which often is reflected in the whole teaching program. A single institution does not feel at liberty to depart from the practices that will prepare its students for the generally accepted examinations. Standardized tests thus tend to fix or crystallize the content of the curriculum. Teachers are likely to begin to teach in terms of the learnings that are essential to the passing of the tests rather than in terms of learnings that are valuable for the particular pupil in a given environment. The two types of teaching are in many cases quite different. The danger of overstandardization is by no means imaginary, and great care needs to be taken in the administration of testing programs to make certain that unfortunate outcomes of this kind are not encouraged.

Diagnosis of Pupil Difficulties

Tests may be used in the schools to determine the nature of the difficulties which pupils are encountering, and to prescribe remedial treatment. For example, a pupil who is having difficulty in geography or history is frequently found, through a test of reading ability, to be deficient in the basic techniques of reading. Such a discovery permits the remedial treatment to be applied to his real difficulty in reading rather than to his apparent difficulty in some content subject. Similarly within a given subject such as arithmetic tests have been devised to diagnose the precise nature of difficulties that pupils encounter. A pupil who cannot add correctly a column of three-place numbers may be having difficulty with particular combinations of digits, or he may not have acquired a correct technique for carrying. One who cannot obtain the correct answers to problems in long division may be found,

by means of a diagnostic test, to have a basic difficulty in sub-
traction. Diagnostic testing may thus reveal the precise nature
of the difficulties encountered by a pupil, and indicate where the
learner should concentrate his attention to overcome his difficulties.

Uses of Examinations Outside the Schools

Besides the uses within the schools which have thus far been
described, tests and examinations are used in a wide variety of
situations outside the educational system. Admission to the
practice of many professions is commonly based on examinations
administered to those who have completed their preparation in
professional schools. The selection of persons for many types
of civil-service positions in government is based on examination.
Industrial concerns often employ tests in selecting their employees. Even the issuance of automobile drivers' licenses usually
involves some sort of an examination.

The present treatment is limited chiefly to the ways in which
tests and examinations are used in the educational system, and
little attention is here given to the many uses that are made of
them in situations outside the schools.

CRITICAL EVALUATIONS OF TESTING PROCEDURES

Since the beginning of the twentieth century students of education, recognizing examinations and tests as important elements of
school practice, have subjected them to extended critical investigations. One of the early studies which tended to undermine
confidence in the traditional type of examinations and to question
their reliability for a purpose for which they are often used was
reported by E. L. Thorndike in 1906. The examinations set by
colleges as the tests for admission are assumed to be valuable as
a means of indicating whether or not students will be successful
in their college courses. Two sections from Thorndike's report
may be quoted here:

The facts which I shall present concern the records in entrance examinations and the academic careers of all the students of Columbia College entering in 1901, 1902, and 1903, and especially the relation between their success in the entrance examinations and their success in college. From these facts it will be proved that even so carefully managed examinations as these are an extremely imperfect means of estimating an individual's fitness for college. . . .[1]

The record of eleven or more entrance examinations gives a less accurate prophecy of what a student will do in the latter half of his college course than does the college record of his brother! The correlation between brothers in intellectual ability is approximately .40, but that between standing in entrance examinations and standing in college of the same person is only .47 for junior year and .25 for senior year.

The entrance examinations also bear internal evidence of their inadequacy as measures of fitness for college. If a student who fails in his first trial of an examination gets a vastly different mark a few months or even a year later, it is clear that the examination in so far does not test capacity so much as the carefulness of the coaching or the diligence of the candidate's cram. As a matter of fact, in 150 cases of repeated examinations, the two marks from the same student show a median difference of *over 22* (the scale of marking being the common one of 100 down to 0). The differences between the earlier and later marks of one student are greater than the difference between the marks of different students chosen at random.

Moreover, the marks on which a student is admitted are not so good a test of his fitness to do the work of the college as the marks of his first trials. If the students are ranked by their first trials of the examinations, the order corresponds much more closely to their order of achievement in college than when they are ranked by their official entrance marks.

Where there are several examinations in one general subject, such as Latin, the different marks of the same individual in the one subject vary in such eccentric ways that an individual who is marked the lowest of twenty in one is at times marked the highest of twenty in the other. The average range of difference of an individual's separate marks in Latin in the entering class of 1902 was *over 26*!

The general inadequacy of the entrance examinations from which the colleges suffer is not so important as their enormous individual inaccuracies, from which individual students suffer.

---

[1] Edward L. Thorndike, "The Future of the College Entrance Examination Board," *Educational Review*, XXXI:470 (May, 1906).

The entrance marks often utterly misrepresent the fitness of a student for college work. For instance, there were 10 men out of the 130 who in their junior year got A (the highest mark given) in at least five studies. Their average marks at entrance were in some cases in the lowest tenth of the 130, barely above the passing mark. Had the passing mark been set the least bit higher, one of the very best students of the three college classes would have been debarred from entrance. There is every reason to believe that of those students who did yet worse in the entrance examinations and so were shut out, a fairly large percentage would have done better in college than a third of those who were admitted. Sooner or later there will be some one so barred out who would, if admitted, have been the best man in his class. It is a moral atrocity to decide the fitness of an individual for college by a system which, when required to work to a moderate degree of accuracy, is wrong 47 times out of 50!

From many facts such as these . . . it is certain that the traditional entrance examinations, even when as fully safeguarded as in the case of those given by the College Entrance Examination Board, do not prevent incompetence from getting into college; do not prevent students of excellent promise from being discouraged, improperly conditioned or barred out altogether; do not measure fitness for college well enough to earn the respect of students or teachers, and do intolerable injustice to individuals. There is surely room for improvement.[1]

Another investigation which had much influence in convincing educators of the lack of reliability in the marking of examination papers was reported in 1913 by two investigators then at the University of Wisconsin, Daniel Starch and Edward C. Elliott. The experiment was based on facsimile copies made of a paper written by a secondary-school pupil on an examination in geometry. The investigators sent a copy of the paper to each of the teachers of geometry in the accredited secondary schools in the territory of the North Central Association of Colleges and Secondary Schools, and asked these teachers to mark the paper on the scale used in their schools and also to indicate what the passing mark was on the scale they used. When the copies were collected, the results showed marked disagreement among the

[1] Edward L. Thorndike, "The Future of the College Entrance Examination Board," *Educational Review*, XXXI: 472–74 (May, 1906).

teachers of geometry in their evaluations. Of the 116 teachers who rated the paper, 47 gave it a passing mark and 69 gave it a failing mark; two gave scores above 90 and one gave a score below 30.[1]

Experiments of this type were carried on in several other fields with the uniform outcome that the examination papers were not evaluated in the same way by different teachers. Also it was found that the mark assigned at different times by any one reader often showed wide variations. The explanation of these findings is that some teachers give much attention to the form of answers while others base their judgments entirely on the ability of pupils to show knowledge of the fundamental principles involved. Many teachers are tolerant of minor slips in the answers given while others subtract from the pupil's credit for every point at which error, however trivial, is committed.

The studies described above and others like them were influential in leading school people to give extensive consideration to the purposes and forms of examinations. A voluminous body of literature has developed out of this interest, and many suggestions and inventions have been made for the purpose of improving the techniques of examining. Perfection has by no means been attained as yet, and one of the most recent studies [2] presents a devastatingly critical analysis of many of the newer tests that have enjoyed wide popularity.

CLASSIFICATIONS OF TESTS

For the purposes of analysis, tests may be classified on several different bases. In the literature of education a number of terms are currently used which relate to the various types of tests and examinations, and a knowledge of the meaning of these terms

---

[1] D. Starch, and E. C. Elliott, "Reliability of Grading Work in Mathematics," *School Review*, XXI: 254–59 (April, 1913).

[2] O. K. Buros, *The Nineteen Thirty-Eight Mental Measurements Yearbook of the School of Education, Rutgers University*.

is essential to an understanding of much that is written about the American educational system.

Tests Classified on Basis of What the Examiner is Attempting to Discover

One basis of classification of tests and examinations relates to what the examiner is attempting to discover. On this basis at least three main types of examinations are at present in use.

The oldest type of examination and the one still most frequently used is the achievement test. In this type of test the examiner is trying to discover what the pupil has learned. The test may aim to determine the information that is possessed by the pupil, or the skill that he has acquired, or any other of the outcomes that result from instruction such as the ability to draw inferences from facts.

The second type of test is variously known as a mental test, or an intelligence test, or a psychological examination. The purpose of this type of test is to discover the ability of the pupil to learn. It is often held that tests of this kind measure some innate capacity that is unchangeable during the lifetime of the individual. Recent investigations have thrown some doubt upon this theory of mental tests, and have shown that the results of intelligence tests are affected by the type of environment to which the individual has been exposed.

The third type of test, classified according to what the examiner is trying to discover, is the aptitude test. To a certain extent an intelligence test may be considered a kind of general aptitude test, but the term is ordinarily limited to the tests that attempt to discover aptitudes for certain specific types of learning. For example, it is useful in admitting students to a medical school to know whether they have satisfactory aptitude for the study of medicine. Fairly efficient tests have been devised to show whether individuals are likely to be successful in studying medicine. Aptitude tests have been developed for a number of other lines but thus far the results from their use have been only moderately successful.

Besides these three types of tests classified on the basis of what the examiner is trying to discover, other types are being experimented with and some have come into actual use. Personality rating scales are of this type. Tests have been developed also for the measurement of attitudes. Another type of test attempts to measure character. The number of different objectives for which tests may be developed is limited only by the imagination of experimenters with respect to factors of human personality and development to which measurement may be applied.

Tests Classified According to Method of Administration

A second basis of classifying tests relates to the methods of administering them. Three different types of tests in common use may be distinguished on this basis, the oral examination, the written examination, and the performance test. The oral examination is not often used today in the American school system because it is not well adapted to mass testing. The oral examination must be given individually to each person tested, and to examine any considerable number of persons orally becomes expensive of time and effort. The use of the oral examination is, therefore, limited chiefly to the highest levels of education, particularly to examinations for Doctors' degrees; less frequently examinations for the Master's degree are given orally.

The written examination is the most widely used form of examination because it is readily adapted to mass testing. This type of examination also has the important advantage of preserving the results of the examination in a relatively permanent form so that they may be analyzed at the convenience of the examiner or referred to later, if there is any dispute regarding the evaluation of the examination.

The performance examination is somewhat like the oral examination, except that the response required of the person being examined is an activity other than a spoken statement. Thus the final examination of a candidate for a degree in music may be the presentation of a recital, or the achievements of students in biology classes may be tested in part by observing how well they use the microscope. The performance examination is subject to much the same limitation as the oral test, and hence is not at present widely used in the American educational system.

Tests Classified on the Basis of Administering Agency

Examinations may be classified on the basis of the agency administering them. On this basis there are two distinct types: the instructor-administered examination, and the external examination.

The most commonly used type of examination is that administered by the instructor who has taught the pupil. The teacher sets the goals of learning for the pupil, does the teaching intended to reach those goals, prepares the examination intended to test the achievement of the goals, and evaluates the pupil's performance on the examination. This type of examination, it will readily be observed, is open to several abuses. If the instructor is inclined to be arbitrary in evaluating the results of the examination, the pupil has little or no recourse against injustice, because the instructor is solely responsible for setting the examination and marking the papers. If the instructor is inclined to be unduly lenient, society is not protected against the low standards which he sets and the credits which he gives his students.

To overcome these difficulties of the instructor-administered examination in situations in which the results of the examinations are of some importance socially, a so-called external examination is sometimes administered. It differs from the instructor-administered examination in that some agency other than the teacher who gave the instruction sets the examination and marks the papers. Examinations for admission to the professions, such as law and medicine, commonly are of the external type. The Regents' examinations administered in the secondary schools of New York State, to which reference has been made earlier, are of the external type.

A number of colleges and universities have adopted the external type of examination in determining the fitness of their students for degrees.   Examiners from outside the institution are called in for the testing of candidates who have completed their programs of study.   At the University of Chicago examinations on which certificates and degrees are based are given by a separate agency within the University, known as the Board of Examiners, the members of which have no responsibility for giving the instruction.

Tests Classified on the Basis of Form of Response

The fourth major basis on which examinations may be classified is with respect to the form of the question and of the response required of the person examined.   On this basis two forms of examinations are distinguished: the essay examination and the objective examination.   Sometimes these are referred to as the "old-type" and "new-type" examinations.

In the essay-type test the response is made to a question in the form of a statement written by the examinee.   The required answer may be of any length, from a single phrase or sentence up to a long exposition requiring several hours for writing.   In rating an examination of the essay type the examiner considers such matters as the accuracy of the statements made and the completeness with which the response covers the subject to which the question refers; usually also such factors as the plan of organizing the answer and the evidence of ability to use English effectively are considered; less frequently, factors such as the neatness of the paper and compliance with arbitrary rules of form affect the mark given.

In the objective type of examination, by contrast, the response of the pupil is in the form of a check mark or the writing of a number or word or some other short symbol.   The response is then scored by means of a key so that the rating is the same whoever scores the paper.

There are many different kinds of objective examinations.   A popular form, known as the true-false type, sets up the items of

TRUE–FALSE TYPE. *Instructions:* On the blank in front of each statement that is false write the word "False"; and before each statement that is true write the word "True."

False Test items of the true-false type were widely used in schools in the early nineteenth century.

MULTIPLE–CHOICE TYPE. *Instructions:* Place an X before the statement that correctly completes the sentence.

An objective or new-type test has the advantage of:
_____a. Being easy to construct
_____b. Having high validity
_____c. Covering all educational objectives
__*X*__d. Being reliably scored
_____e. Having a long history of use in the schools

COMPLETION TYPE. *Instructions:* Fill the blank with the word or words that make the sentence true.

A test which seeks to determine the pupil's ability to learn some specific subject, such as algebra or a foreign language, is known as *an aptitude* test.

MATCHING TYPE. *Instructions:* Write the number of the man on the blank in front of the movement for which he is known.

1. Horace Mann
2. William H. McGuffey
3. J. H. Pestalozzi
4. Henry C. Morrison
5. Edward A. Sheldon

__*4*__The unit-assignment plan.
__*3*__Innovations in educational methods in the eighteenth century.
__*5*__Development and expansion of the normal school.
__*1*__Common school revival of the 1840's.
__*2*__Graded materials for school readers.

FIGURE 14. EXAMPLES OF VARIOUS KINDS OF OBJECTIVE OR NEW-TYPE TEST ITEMS

the examination in a series of statements which are to be marked either true or false. Another type is the multiple-choice test, in which the best of a number of suggested statements is to be marked. Still another type is the completion test, in which a statement is presented with some key word or words missing, which can be supplied, it is assumed, only by one who has a knowledge of the subject. Another form requires matching; two series of ideas are presented to the person being examined and he is required to indicate which item in one series corresponds to each of the items in the other series. For example, if it is desired to test the student's knowledge of the persons who made notable inventions, a numbered list of inventors and a list of inventions may be presented with instructions to enter the number of the inventor opposite the invention for which he is responsible.

1 Franklin Roosevelt is: 1 Secretary of State, 2 Governor of this State, 3 President of the United States, 4 A Senator, 5 A member of the House of Representatives............

2 Which of the following is a bird? 1 zebra, 2 mink, 3 ruby, 4 sparrow, 5 beetle........

3 A famous aviator
4 First President of the United States.
5 The President who freed the slaves.

1. George Washington
2. Benjamin Franklin
3. Abraham Lincoln
4. Herbert Hoover
5. Charles Lindbergh

6 Chicago is in the State of Illinois..........

7 All houses are built of brick..............

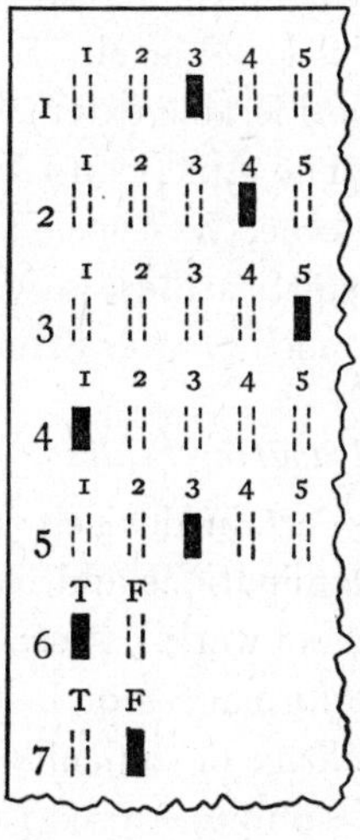

FIGURE 15. METHOD OF RESPONDING TO VARIOUS KINDS OF OBJECTIVE-TYPE QUESTIONS ON THE ANSWER BLANK USED WITH THE TEST-SCORING MACHINE MANUFACTURED BY INTERNATIONAL BUSINESS MACHINES CORPORATION.

Recently a mechanical device has been developed for the scoring of objective-type tests. The machine operates by means of electrical contacts activated by the graphite deposited by pencil marks. The labor of scoring tests of the objective type is by this means greatly reduced when there are large groups of pupils to be tested.

Tests of the objective type may be either standardized or unstandardized. The standardized test is one which has been given to large numbers of pupils so that norms of performance for various age levels and grade levels are available. In order that the test may be standardized, all the circumstances surrounding its administration and scoring, including the directions given to pupils, the time limits, and the credit to be given for various types of replies, must be set forth explicitly and followed absolutely. Standardized tests are now widely available from commercial publishers for all subjects taught at the elementary-school level and for practically all subjects taught at the secondary-school level. Such tests have not yet been developed to any considerable extent for subjects at the college level.

The American educational system is notable for its wide use of objective-type examinations. In the school systems of other countries the essay-type examination is still depended upon to a much greater extent than any form of objective examination.

Measuring Scales

Certain devices, known as scales, differing in character from examinations and tests, are also used in evaluating the results of school work. A scale is a series of illustrative examples of school performances or instructional material arranged in order of excellence or difficulty from a low level to a high level. The series of samples is used for purposes of comparing the achievement of a pupil, his work being matched to that illustrative sample which most nearly resembles the work.

A typical scale is that used in rating handwriting. A collection of specimens of penmanship is made and a series of examples are selected either on the basis of the judgments of experts or by means of measurements of legibility; these specimens are then arranged in order from a low, barely readable example to a high-grade example which shows all the virtues of skillful writing.

Another scale which has played a conspicuous rôle in the determination of general intelligence is that developed by two French psychologists, Alfred Binet and Theophile Simon, commonly known as the Binet scale. Series of questions were presented by these psychologists to children of different ages. When a question was answered correctly by most of the children of a given age it was regarded as a normal test for that age. Questions of gradually increasing difficulty were similarly discovered and arranged in a series. When a child of a given age is tested he is asked the questions appropriate to different ages until his upper limit of ability to answer is found. The highest age, the normal questions for which the child can answer, indicates what is called the child's "mental age." A ratio is then calculated by dividing the child's mental age by his chronological age; to eliminate decimals the calculated ratio is multiplied by one hundred. For example, if a child of ten years of age can answer the questions normal for children of twelve years, the child's ratio is twelve divided by ten or a score of 120. This score is known as the intelligence quotient and is commonly designated as the child's I.Q. If a ten-year-old child cannot answer questions above the level normal for eight-year-old children, his I.Q. is 80.

Comprehensive Examinations

Another important development has been the recent increase in the use of the comprehensive-type examination. The comprehensive examination may be defined as one that covers a relatively large body of subject matter and requires the integration of knowledge obtained from several different courses. This type of examination has long been used in European countries, particularly at the university level. In the United States, after the coming of the elective system in the colleges, the tendency was to require only examinations at the end of each course covering merely the content of that particular course. College degrees were granted on the basis of accumulated course credits without any extensive examination that would test the mastery of a large body of subject matter at any one time or the integration of materials studied in the various courses. In recent years a number of colleges and universities in the United States have introduced comprehensive examinations either as a substitute for or in addition to course examinations. These institutions require the passing of a comprehensive examination, either at the end of the senior year as a requirement for graduation, or at the end of the sophomore year for admission to the upper division, or at both points. The movement for comprehensive examinations seems to be growing rapidly.

Evaluation Instead of Measurement

An idea which has been growing in favor recently suggests the substitution of the concept of evaluation for the older concept of measurement in education. The idea of measurement in education is based on the presumption that the outcomes of instruction can be determined and expressed quantitatively; that is, for example, that a teacher can report that a pupil has progressed in arithmetic during the year from a score of 171 to a score of 193 on a certain standardized test. Because of the limitation to quantitative expression that is involved in the concept of measurement, the experts in the field of tests for a long time restricted their attention to those aspects of the pupil's behavior or characteristics which could readily be measured in quantitative terms. This policy led, for example, to an extreme emphasis on testing for the acquisition of facts, for it was readily possible to invent objective measures which would show how much factual knowledge the pupil had acquired. But other important phases of development that were not easily measured in quantitative terms tended to be ignored or neglected.

More recently the suggestion has been made by Ralph W.

Tyler and others that the concept of measurement is too narrow for an adequate view of all the phases of pupil development that should be considered, and the idea of evaluation has been suggested to replace that of measurement. The process of evaluation permits the taking stock of many important kinds of behavior or characteristics that are not readily reduced to a quantitative expression. For many purposes it is shown that a descriptive account is of great significance, and that the lack of a ready means of quantifying the description should not preclude attention to important characteristics that need to be studied.

Evaluation procedures require first a careful analysis of the objectives of the instruction, and then the devising of appropriate means to determine the accomplishment of these objectives. For example, it might first be determined that the objectives of a course in biology include not only the acquisition of information but the development of the ability to reason by scientific methods, the ability to locate relevant data, and certain characteristic skills. To test the attainment of these objectives various devices are needed in addition to the familiar tests for knowledge of facts; ability to reason scientifically might be tested by presenting the results of an unfamiliar experiment and asking for appropriate conclusions; ability to use a microscope might be evaluated by direct observation.

The development of the idea of evaluation bids fair to reduce somewhat the overemphasis on the testing of factual materials, and to build up a needed emphasis on the recognition of other desired aspects in the development of pupils.

CHARACTERISTICS OF A GOOD TEST OR EXAMINATION

The critical study that has been given during the twentieth century to procedures for testing has led, as was previously noted, to many suggestions for improvement. Certain criteria are now available for judging the quality of a test or examination. Some six characteristics of a good test will be briefly discussed.

Validity

A satisfactory test must have the quality of validity, which means that the test must measure what it purports to measure. The validity of a test is ordinarily determined by checking it against some independent measure. Thus a test purporting to measure intelligence is said to be valid if the results of the test tend to agree with evidences of intelligence secured by other means.

It seems almost self-evident that a test ought to measure what it purports to measure, but tests fail to meet this criterion oftener than might be expected. Not uncommonly, for example, a test labeled as an arithmetic examination is in reality more a test of reading ability, or ability to understand the long and complex sentences in which the problems are phrased, than it is a test of actual ability to perform arithmetical operations.

In order to be valid a test must cover the ground which it purports to cover or it must at least cover an adequate sampling of the area. The test may fail to meet this criterion of validity, for example, if it calls for knowledge of only a few items from the entire list of learnings in the course. In general, the more thoroughly every important item in a course is covered in an examination the better that examination meets the criterion of validity.

A valid test must also measure all the expected outcomes of instruction. If, for example, a course in civics is expected to produce an improved attitude towards the democratic form of government, a test which asks only questions regarding provisions of the United States Constitution is not adequate and therefore lacks validity. To a surprising extent the examinations in use in American schools call only for a knowledge of factual information, and yet almost every statement made about the aims of education stresses the importance of other outcomes of instruction such, for example, as the ability to make valid inferences. To some extent, perhaps, it may be assumed that the learning of factual information is correlated with other types of achievement expected from the instruction, but the degree of correlation between factual information and powers of thinking is probably not high enough to warrant the omission of tests of these higher powers.

Reliability

A second characteristic of a satisfactory test is reliability, which may be defined as the consistency with which a paper written on an examination will be marked with the same score if graded by more than one person or by the same person at different times. Or, an examination is to be considered reliable if a second equivalent form of the examination given to a pupil results in the same score as he received on the first examination.

The reliability of an examination may be affected greatly by the characteristics of the reader who marks the papers, particularly if the examination is not of the objective type. Some readers of examination papers have a permanent bias toward high marks; others fluctuate inconsistently in their evaluation of papers. Even changes in the physical condition of the reader may cause him to vary in the assignment of marks. All variations decrease the reliability of an examination.

In order to obtain a high reliability on an examination it is necessary, therefore, to prepare a type of test which minimizes the opportunities for personal factors to enter into the marking of the papers, or to be careful in selecting readers who have proved to be reliable in evaluating papers of the particular type. The objective test has an important advantage in eliminating personal factors in marking papers and has therefore been widely advocated as more reliable than the essay-type of examination. On the other hand, objective tests have been criticized because they commonly do not reveal a pupil's ability to organize his thinking. The objective tests may have limitations which are not compensated for by their reliability.

Variations in results of tests may be produced by the method of administering them even if they are standardized tests of the objective type. Failure to follow directions precisely in administering tests is one of the most fertile sources of unreliability. Even under the best possible circumstances of administering tests, there are personal factors affecting the pupils tested which make for unreliability of results. The pupil, for example, may be nervous or unwell or may never have taken that particular type of test before.

For all the better standardized tests a coefficient of reliability is available. This coefficient, arrived at by comparing two series of scores obtained by administering two equivalent tests to a given group of pupils, is rarely above .95 for even the best of the standardized tests, and on some tests is as low as .75. The coefficient of reliability of unstandardized tests is usually far below these figures.

Ease of Evaluation

The large numbers of pupils in elementary and secondary schools and the increased enrollment of students in colleges and universities have made the problem of grading examination papers serious because of the time required for careful evaluation. Sometimes this problem is solved in colleges and universities by employing readers to assist the instructor of the course in his task of evaluating papers; ordinarily this procedure is open to serious criticism, for seldom will an assistant, of the type usually chosen for the work, be able to reach as valid and reliable an estimate of the paper as the experienced instructor in charge of the course.

The objective-type examination has a great advantage with respect to ease in scoring, for an intelligent clerk, if provided with the correct key, can mark the papers accurately. As previously pointed out, the invention of a machine for scoring examinations even eliminates most of this clerical labor in extensive testing programs. Except where large numbers are to be given the same examination, however, objective-type tests do not greatly reduce the total burden of setting the examination, for the preparation of the objective-type examination is much more time-consuming than the preparation of the essay-type test. While something can be done in the construction of tests themselves to increase the ease of marking, little hope can be held out that the burden of preparing and evaluating examinations can be completely eliminated as one of the important tasks of the teaching process.

Known Difficulty

In most cases the mark given a pupil's paper is assumed to represent some point on an absolute scale of values. Frequently, for example, the papers are marked on a percentage scale in which 100 represents the best score that can possibly be attained, and 0 represents absolute lack of knowledge. A given mark, such as 80, is regarded as indicating that the paper shows knowledge equal to 80 per cent of the maximum learnings expected. Some point on this scale, such as 75, 70, 65, or 60, is set as the minimum for passing.

Marking on an absolute scale is not fair unless the questions are accurately adjusted to proper expectations with regard to learning by pupils. For example, if only very easy questions are asked, a large percentage of the class may obtain a perfect score; by contrast, if only very difficult questions are asked, perhaps no member of the class will get more than half of the items correct. To give a mark of 100 per cent in one case, and 50 per cent in the other case to the pupil making the highest mark on the examination, is absurd.

The fact is that in most examinations of the unstandardized type the absolute relation of the questions to proper expectations is not known. The teacher who prepares the examination, being thoroughly familiar with the subject matter to be covered, may be able to guess reasonably well what the pupils should know. In most cases, however, it is largely chance that governs the degree of difficulty of an examination prepared by the teacher for a class, and unless some adjustment is made in the marking to account for variations in difficulty, the pupils taking the examination are either favored or penalized according as the examination is relatively easy or relatively difficult.

The difficulty of an examination can be estimated subjectively by having it criticized by other teachers who are familiar with the subject matter, but at best only an approximation to the true difficulty of a test can be reached by this method. An objective method of determining the difficulty is to submit the test to various groups of pupils of different levels of ability.   It is then possible to differentiate the questions that prove easy from those that prove difficult.

Avoidance of " Ceiling Effect "

A good examination must permit all students to register the maximum of their achievement.   Owing to individual differences of children, some will normally achieve more than others in studying the field covered in the examination.   It is usually important, therefore, that those who know the most about the subject matter be given an opportunity to indicate the extent of their knowledge.

A teacher may be gratified to find that a large number of pupils have made a perfect score on an examination, but a result of this kind usually means that the examination was not an adequate test for a large percentage of the class.   If the test had contained some more difficult items, many of those who made perfect scores would have fallen short of perfection, and the pupil or pupils who really knew most about the subject would have had an opportunity to show their superiority.   Any examination designed for testing a comprehensive body of subject matter is therefore open to suspicion if a considerable number of those examined receive perfect scores.   This statement does not apply to an examination covering a relatively small unit of subject matter where complete mastery is expected of practically every pupil.

Differentiated Scores

It is usually, though not always, desirable to be able to classify students who take an examination into a number of different groups.   Sometimes only two categories are essential, passing and failing, but oftener it is important to distinguish at least four or five levels of attainment within the passing group.   For many purposes it is important to make even finer distinctions, and to be able to list each pupil in the appropriate rank order of his performance within the group taking the examination.

If a highly differentiated series of scores is desirable in the case of a particular examination, a relatively large number of items is necessary.   For example, papers written on a test containing only one or two questions of the essay type cannot ordinarily be graded accurately into highly differentiated groups.   If, on the other hand, a test is composed of 200 items of the objective type, it will usually be found that relatively few of those examined have made exactly the same score.   An increase in the number of items on the test is therefore of advantage in securing a differentiated series of scores.

PRESENT INTEREST IN EXAMINATIONS

As has already been indicated, the educational world, particularly during the twentieth century, has manifested a great interest in examinations.   Especially in the United States has this interest been exhibited.   European countries have lately indicated a somewhat similar awakening of interest in improved techniques of examination.   Three international conferences have been held in recent years on the subject of examinations, and some valuable studies of examination procedures have been made in countries such as England, Scotland, and France.   The investigators in European countries, with the exception of those in Scotland, have not been at all enthusiastic with respect to new type or objective examinations.   They have indicated an earnest desire to improve the examinations of the essay type which have long been characteristic of the European schools.

The future will probably see much effort devoted to the improvement of examinations of both the essay type and the objective type.   Undoubtedly there will also be efforts to develop examinations which will have as their purpose the measurement of outcomes of learning and of personality traits that have heretofore not been subjected to measurement.

BIBLIOGRAPHY

Buros, O. K., *The Nineteen Thirty-Eight Mental Measurements Yearbook of the School of Education, Rutgers University.* New Brunswick, New Jersey: Rutgers University, 1938. xv + 416 pp.

Conference on Examinations under the Auspices of the Carnegie Corporation, the Carnegie Foundation, and the International Institute of Teachers College, Columbia University. Conference organized and proceedings edited by Paul Monroe. New York: Teachers College, Columbia University, 1931. 316 pp.

Dearborn, Walter Fenno, *Intelligence Tests: Their Significance for School and Society.* Boston: Houghton Mifflin Company, 1928. xxiv + 336 pp.

Dougherty, James Henry, Frank Hermon Gorman, and Claude Anderson Phillips, *Elementary School Organization and Management*, pp. 132–248.

Douglass, Aubrey A., *The American School System*, pp. 271–302.

Frasier, George Willard, and Winfield D. Armentrout, *An Introduction to the Literature of Education*, pp. 239–66.

Freeman, Frank N., *Mental Tests: Their History, Principles, and Applications.* Boston: Houghton Mifflin Company, 1939. xii + 460 pp.

Greene, H. A., and A. N. Jorgensen, *The Use and Interpretation of Elementary School Tests.* New York: Longmans, Green and Company, 1935. xxviii + 530 pp.

Hawkes, H. E., *et al.*, *The Construction and Use of Achievement Examinations: a Manual for Secondary School Teachers.* Boston: Houghton Mifflin Company, 1936. x + 498 pp.

Judd, Charles H., *Measuring the Work of the Public Schools.* Cleveland Education Survey, X. Cleveland: Survey Committee of the Cleveland Foundation, 1916. 292 pp.

Lang, Albert R., *Modern Methods in Written Examinations.* Boston: Houghton Mifflin Company, 1930. xx + 314 pp.

Monroe, Walter S., James C. De Voss, and Frederick J. Kelly, *Educational Tests and Measurements.* Boston: Houghton Mifflin Company, 1924. xxviii + 522 pp.

Symonds, Percival M., *Measurement in Secondary Education.* New York: The Macmillan Company, 1927. xviii + 588 pp.

Tiegs, Ernest W., *Tests and Measurements in the Improvement of Learning.* Boston: Houghton Mifflin Company, 1939. xxi + 490 pp.

CHAPTER XIX

THE SCIENTIFIC STUDY
OF EDUCATION

In no respect is the relation of education to the general social order more apparent than in the fact that today the solution of educational problems is expected to be sought in scientific studies. There was a time when myths and superstitions dominated the behavior of men, but that time has passed. In every sphere of life, both in the control of physical forces and in the adjustment of human relations, guiding principles are now sought through scientific research. It is no accident that during the past century a science of education has gradually developed. The particular individuals who have contributed to this development are important but they could not have done what they did if there had not been a fundamental background of interest in science based on the accumulated experience of the society to which they belonged.

Step by step the human mind has made progress in comprehending the physical world and controlling many of its forces. During the past century and a half investigations have revealed the laws of human life and have given an increasingly sound basis for the better organization of society. That science should ultimately attack the problems of teaching and learning was inevitable. The trends of intellectual life were the fundamental causes that set individuals at work seeking the scientific solution of educational problems.

The educational system of the United States, as contrasted with the systems of European countries, offers unique possibilities for the development of a science of education. On the other side of the Atlantic, the central governments dictate the policies and the practices of all the educational institutions. Education there is official and, to the degree to which it is conducted under the direct supervision of central authorities, it resists critical examination by disinterested and impartial students of science. In the United States, by contrast, control of schools, as has been pointed out repeatedly, has traditionally been left to the local communities. As a result, widespread variations have appeared in the practices of American schools; experimentation has been uninhibited; and critical study of the results achieved at different centers has been both natural and acceptable.

Local control and freedom to carry on experiments, which have always been characteristics of the schools of the United States, did not result in the early days of American history in scientific studies of teaching and administration because the motives for such studies were not urgent and the techniques were not available. The American common schools of the seventeenth and eighteenth centuries and of the first third of the nineteenth century were primitive institutions determined in their curriculums and methods of instruction by the conditions of a simple agrarian civilization. During the years from 1830 to 1880 the efforts to throw off formalism prepared American educators for favorable reception of certain new ideas concerning methods of attacking scientifically the problems of education. Although the influences that generated these new ideas in American education are traceable directly to European sources, the great development of the science of education has come in the United States rather than in Europe.

THE BEGINNINGS OF THE MOVEMENT FOR THE SCIENTIFIC STUDY OF EDUCATION

A little more than a century ago, in 1831, to be exact, Johann Friedrich Herbart, professor at the University of Koenigsberg, Germany, published a volume the translated title of which is

Letters Dealing with the Application of Psychology to the Art of Teaching. In earlier writings Herbart had laid the foundations for modern empirical, experimental psychology. Through his letters on the applications of psychology and through his other treatises on education, he became the originator of the movement which in modern times has produced a body of scientific materials that are dominant influences in determining the programs of schools in all civilized countries.

Neither empirical psychology nor the science of education gained any great momentum until long after Herbart's day. Furthermore, the two movements which he started, one in empirical psychology and one in the scientific study of education, progressed quite separately in Germany. It was not until the decade 1880–90, when empirical psychology and the study of education had been imported into the United States by American scholars who had attended German universities, that the applications of psychology to the art of teaching and the general scientific study of education developed on a significant scale.

Another German scholar, Wilhelm Wundt, in 1878 established in Leipzig a psychological laboratory where empirical psychology was cultivated along lines stimulated by Herbart and his psychological followers. One of Wundt's American students was G. Stanley Hall, who in 1884 established at Johns Hopkins University a center for applied psychology devoted to the study of children's mental development. Hall, who later became president of Clark University, was the founder of what he called "child study."

At about the same time that Hall was starting the child study movement the McMurry brothers, Frank M. and Charles A., and Charles DeGarmo brought back from their studies at the University of Jena in Germany the Herbartian pedagogy which had been developed by two of Herbart's followers, Tuiskon Ziller and William Rein. The American Herbartians were not psychologists, but practical teachers, and they wrote prolifically about methods of teaching. They did not contribute directly to the scientific movement, as Hall did, but they injected into the schools of this country a new spirit of conscious, critical consideration of the methods and results of classroom procedures.

The child-study movement did not prove to be finally effective in establishing a science of education. The method adopted by Hall and his students in collecting materials was a somewhat loose questionnaire method of inquiry. They asked parents and teachers to make observations on children and to report the results of these observations. Many who made reply to the questionnaires were untrained, and the questionnaires themselves were comparatively unorganized; consequently the materials collected were often lacking in comparability and were unfit for the statistical treatment that was given them. The discussions which were based on the returns from questionnaires were more discursive than scientific. As an example of a typical report on one of the questionnaires sent out by Hall, the following paragraphs from a study of "Children's Lies" may be quoted. The reader will understand that the quotation is here presented not for the sake of its content, but merely to indicate the kind of reporting that characterized the early phases of the child-study movement.

V. Much childish play owes its charm to partial self-deception. Children imagine or make believe they are animals, making their noises and imitating their activities; that they are soldiers, and imagine panoramas of warlike events; that they are hunters in extreme peril from wild beasts; Indians, artisans, and tradesmen of many kinds; doctors, preachers, angels, ogres. They play school, court, meeting, congress. If hit with wooden daggers in the game of war they stand aside and play they are dead. If they step on a crack in walking the floor, curbing, sidewalk, etc., they call it they are poisoned. Protruding spots of earth or land in pools or ponds, or at half-tide in the bay, suggest the geography of a continent, and in one case, for years, Boston, Providence, West Indies, Gibraltar, Brooklyn Bridge were thus designated by all the children of a large school in their plays. In another, a dozen hills and valleys, rills, near by were named from fancied resemblance to the familiar mountains, rivers and valleys of the geography. The play-house sometimes is so real as to have spools for barrels of flour, pounded rotten wood for sugar, pumpkin chairs, cucumber cows, moss carpets, sticks for doors which must be kept shut, sometimes cleaned, twig brooms, pet animals for stock with pastures and yards, all the domestic industries in pantomime, toadstools, lichens and puff-balls for bric-a-brac, while some older boy and girl may play parents with secret pet names, and younger ones as children, often for a whole term and in rare instances for years; all of this of course being almost always in the country. They baptize cats, bury dolls, have puppet shows with so many pins admission, all with elaborate details. They dress up and mimic other often older people, ride on the horse cars and imagine them fine carriages, get up doll hospitals and play surgeon or Florence Nightingale. The more severe the discipline of the play-teacher and the more savage the play-mother the better the fun. . . .

In some games like "crazy mother," younger children are commanded, or older ones stumped or dared, to do dangerous things, like walking a picket fence or a high roof, etc., in which the spirit of play overcomes great natural timidity, and by playing school with other mates, or perhaps parents, they are helped by the play instinct to do hard examples and other hated tasks they had scarcely accomplished in actual schools. The stimulus and charm of the imagination makes them act a part different from their natural selves; some games need darkness to help out the fancy. It seems almost the rule that imaginative children are more likely to be dull in school work, and that those who excel in it are more likely to have fewer or less vivid mental images of their own. Especially with girls, it is chiefly those under ten or twelve who play most actively in our school yards, but those of thirteen or fifteen, who, under the apathy that generally affects girls of that age, walk in pairs, or small groups up and down the yard and talk, are no less imaginative. One early manifestation of the shadowy falsity to fact of the idealizing temperament is often seen in children of three or four, who suddenly assert that they saw a pig with five ears, a dog as big as a horse, or, if older, apples on a cherry tree, and other Munchausen wonders, which really means at first but little more than that they have that thought or have made that mental combination independently of experience. They come to love to tell semi-plausible stories, and perhaps when the astonishment is over to confess. . . . Revery which materializes all wishes, and the mythopoeic faculty which still occasionally creates a genuine myth among children, boys who amuse their mates with long and often clever yarns of their own invention, girls who make up ridiculous things about others — to all these the school has paid little attention, and Mr. Gradgrind would war upon them all as inimical to scientific veracity.[1]

While Hall's writings did not contribute any large body of scientific principles to education, they stimulated enthusiasm for the observation of children and made psychology popular in many quarters where serious study of that subject had never been thought of before. The most pretentious and probably the most lasting of Hall's contributions was his treatise on adolescence. He gathered a great store of anecdotal material and indulged in much speculation about the nature of the physical and mental development which takes place during adolescence. He recorded, however, many significant facts. He may be said to have made the concept of adolescence a permanent factor in educational thought.

A later more scientific system of child study has recently been developed which differs in methods from that which Hall originated. Careful observation of children and measurement of their traits have been undertaken and exact determinations have been made of the stages of physical and mental development. The findings from the researches carried on in these new centers for child study have proved of great value, not only in the development of sound educational programs but also in other areas concerned with childhood and youth.

Another pioneer who has had much to do with the stimulation of modern movements in education is John Dewey, who organized in the 1890's an experimental school in Chicago. In his school and in the books and articles which he wrote Dewey elaborated the theory that the school is a place where activity rather than passive listening to instruction should prevail. He also pointed out and illustrated in his school the view that social adaptation is the purpose of all education and that the school must supply the conditions for such adaptations, especially in

[1] G. Stanley Hall, "Children's Lies," *American Journal of Psychology*, III:64–67 (January, 1890). Also *Pedagogical Seminary*, I:213–15 (1891). Also *Educational Problems*, I:377–80. New York: D. Appleton and Company, 1911.

modern times when the experiences of children are restricted by life in the cramped and limiting environment of urban homes. In the early 1900's Dewey moved to New York, where he proceeded to develop further his educational theories and philosophy. At the time of his retirement from active service a few years ago he was generally recognized as one of the foremost American philosophers. His principal contribution to American education has been in the field of theory rather than in the field of controlled experimentation or scientific analysis of school problems.

It is difficult to give an adequate impression of the enthusiasm which was generated for the study of education during the period when Hall and Dewey were becoming active in the field, the decade from 1890 to 1900. There were others who contributed to this enthusiasm. In institutions of higher education President Charles W. Eliot of Harvard University was developing the elective system, and President William Rainey Harper was introducing the innovations which made the University of Chicago an outstanding center of educational experimentation. Francis W. Parker and William T. Harris were leading the lower schools to undertake novel methods of teaching and administrative organization.

THE TESTING MOVEMENT

Toward the close of the decade of the 1890's — in 1897 — a new note in the study of education was sounded by J. M. Rice, then editor of the magazine, *Forum*, a note which was to be of the first importance in directing the study of education into new channels. Rice had been describing in the *Forum* his impressions of the school systems of various cities. He came to the conclusion that his observations and his personal evaluations could not be relied on as bases for final judgments regarding the merits of the various school systems. He needed objective evidence, so he devised a method of testing to make more reliable his evaluation of the methods and results of teaching.

Rice at the time was interested in comparing the spelling ability of children taught by different methods in various cities. To this end he prepared a list of common words which he asked the children in several cities to spell. The idea of such a test, which now seems so simple, was revolutionary at the time, and the change from mere observation to a definite objective test was a distinct step in the direction of scientific measurement of results. By substituting measured results of tests for personal judgment, Rice introduced into the field of education a concept which can be thought of as basic to all science. When, in addition, he used measurement as the means of comparing the results obtained by various agencies of instruction, he employed a technique which needed only to be refined to make it an instrument of important exact study of educational results.

Rice's measurements were devastating in their revelation regarding the inadequacy of much of the school work in that day. As can readily be imagined, the conclusions to which Rice's inquiries led were not readily accepted by the school administrators of that time. Commenting on the effects of Rice's reports Leonard P. Ayres, himself an important contributor to the science of education, made in 1915 the following statement.

Eighteen years ago the school superintendents of America, assembled in convention in Indianapolis, discussed the problems then foremost in educational thought and action. At that meeting a distinguished educator — the pioneer and pathfinder among the scientific students of education in America — brought up for discussion the results of his investigations of spelling among the children in the school systems of nineteen cities. These results showed that, taken all in all, the children who spent forty minutes a day for eight years in studying spelling did not spell any better than the children in the schools of other cities where they devoted only ten minutes per day to the study.

The presentation of these data threw that assemblage into consternation, dismay, and indignant protest. But the resulting storm of vigorously voiced opposition was directed not against the methods and results of the investigation, but against the investigator who had pretended to measure the results of teaching spelling by testing the ability of children to spell.

In terms of scathing denunciation the educators there present and the pedagogical experts, who reported the deliberations of the meeting in the educational press, characterized as silly, dangerous, and from every viewpoint reprehensible, the attempt to test the efficiency of the teacher by finding out what the pupils could do. With striking unanimity they voiced the conviction that any attempt to evaluate the teaching of spelling in terms of the ability of the pupils to spell was essentially impossible and based on a profound misconception of the function of education.

Last month in the city of Cincinnati that same association of school superintendents again assembled in convention, devoted fifty-seven addresses and discussions to tests and measurements of educational efficiency. The basal proposition underlying this entire mass of discussion was that the effectiveness of the school, the methods, and the teachers must be measured in terms of the results secured.

This change represents no passing fad or temporary whim. It is permanent, significant, and fundamental. It means that a transformation has taken place in what we think as well as in what we do in education. It means that education is emerging from among the vocations and taking its place among the professions.

This profound change in our educational practice has not come thru the slow processes of philosophy, or because we were awakened by the stirring words of voice or pen of any educational prophet. Few school men can claim great credit for having hastened its advent. It was forced upon us, first, by the natural results of compulsory education, and still more definitely and directly by the exactions of the scientific age in which we live.

This new attitude of educators towards education means that we have ceased exalting the machinery and have commenced to examine the product. We have awakened to a startled realization that in education, as in other forms of organized activity, applied science may avail to better even those processes that have rested secure in the sanction of generations of acceptance.

The transformation now taking place in education means that it is our privilege to be part of a movement that is working changes comparable to those that are now remaking almost every form of industrial activity.[1]

[1] Leonard P. Ayres, "Making Education Definite," *Second Annual Conference on Educational Measurements Held under the Auspices of the Extension Division of Indiana University*, pp. 85–86. Indiana University Bulletin, vol. XIII, no. 11. Bloomington, Indiana: Indiana University, 1915.

During the decades which have followed the work of Rice great progress has been made in collecting and interpreting exact objective evidence with regard to the results of teaching and school administration.   Investigators have devised tests in every field of school work.   Tests were developed first where it was easiest to measure definite abilities of pupils, in spelling, arithmetic, and handwriting.   Later, tests were devised for measuring abilities in reading and for measuring mastery of foreign languages and of the sciences.

The popular confidence in tests is today, if anything, too great. As was pointed out in Chapter XVIII, a test which has been extensively employed is sometimes considered by teachers and investigators to be endowed with prestige and authority as an instrument of evaluation far beyond its true desert.   After all, tests are valuable only as means of collecting evidence.   Tests do not automatically interpret their own results.   The science of education has been compelled, therefore, in its use of tests to develop techniques for the critical interpretation of the results of tests.

STATISTICAL METHODS

Studies of education made during the first fifteen years of the present century were devoted largely to the elaboration of instruments and techniques of measurement.   The science of statistics was in an early stage of its development in 1900.   Sir Francis Galton in England had made his epoch-making contributions to this science during the nineteenth century, but mathematical refinements which are now available to students of statistical methodology were lacking.   The field of education has proved to be a fertile area for the employment and refinement of the techniques of statistics.   In 1904 Edward L. Thorndike published a volume entitled *Mental and Social Measurement*. This volume and the numerous later volumes published by the same author and his students have made statistics one of the important special branches of educational science.

The development of statistical methods has given rise to a large number of technical terms with which the student of modern educational problems needs to be familiar. It is quite impossible to read with intelligent understanding current discussions in educational journals without some knowledge of statistical techniques and the terminology associated therewith.

EDUCATIONAL PSYCHOLOGY

Earlier in this chapter reference was made to Herbart's suggestion that psychology supplies many truths which are applicable to education. Herbart's own system of psychology, while it aimed to be empirical, was wholly inadequate as a guide to education. Indeed, even at the present comparatively advanced stage of that science, general psychology throws little light on problems of teaching. For example, the elaborate studies which general psychology has made of the sensory processes, such as color vision and auditory keenness, are undoubtedly of scientific importance, but they give very little guidance to school work. Experimental methods in psychology had to be adapted to the examination of educational processes and had to be elaborated into what is now known as educational psychology before they began to be useful in supplying the facts needed to guide educational practice.

The contrast between general experimental psychology and educational psychology can be illustrated by reference to one of the fields in which educational psychology has been most productive, the scientific study of reading. To the general psychologist, the individual differences exhibited by readers, the stages of development through which individuals pass in cultivating ability to read, and the special nature of silent reading and oral reading are details for which he has scant attention. To the educational psychologist, by contrast, every fact which can be discovered with regard to reading is of cardinal importance. The educational psychologist may be compared to the medical specialist who carries on investigations in such fields as the physiology and chemistry of nutrition, or the diseases of childhood, or the diseases of old age. Educational psychology is more than a mere branch of general psychology. It has taken over and elaborated the techniques of the general science to the point where it has become an independent discipline.

The relation between general psychology and educational psychology can be emphasized by referring to an interesting reflex effect which educational psychology has had on the parent science. A quarter of a century ago no textbook on general psychology had more than a passing reference to the learning process. As educational psychology has investigated many different kinds of learning one after another and has added to the knowledge which adults can gain about their own learning processes, facts that are gathered from experiments with children, general psychology has been compelled to recognize that the genetic method of investigating mental phenomena is far more revealing than the examination of any single stage of mental life. Modern textbooks in general psychology have, therefore, come to devote much space to the learning process. In the meantime, educational psychology extends its inquiries in the field of learning further and further.

The results which have been gathered by the application of scientific methods have produced profound changes in education at every level and in every branch of instruction. This statement does not mean that all educational problems have been solved. Indeed there is one field in which present-day knowledge about the nature of the learning process is lamentably deficient. That is the field of the higher mental processes. It was, of course, only natural that scientific studies should first be undertaken with respect to those phases of education that are fairly simple. Reference has been made to studies in reading. Even earlier than the studies of reading there were studies of handwriting and arithmetic. While much is known with regard to these simpler forms of learning, knowledge about the higher mental processes is still meager.

Some concrete illustration of the truth of the foregoing statement about higher mental processes may be in place. It is usual for teachers of the natural sciences to claim that their instruction cultivates in pupils the power to draw inferences. When one looks at the examinations that are typically set by teachers of the natural sciences, one observes that, in spite of the claim that the study of science develops powers of inference, the real demand imposed on pupils by these examinations is that the statements made by the textbooks or by the instructor be accurately reproduced. Reproduction of items presented, or memory, to use the common term, is recognized by psychology as a form of mental activity lower than inference. The criterion employed by educational psychology to distinguish between lower and higher mental processes is the criterion of participation by the individual in the formation of his own experiences. There is a certain passivity about the receiving of impressions presented to the mind. Impressions are, therefore, low forms of experience; memory as the mere reproduction of experiences is also to some extent passive. Inference, which consists in rearranging ideas and inventing new interpretations of impressions, involves activity and is therefore higher than any mental process which is largely passive.

When it is observed that science teachers demand of their pupils reproduction of impressions rather than active inference, one begins to get a clue to the reasons why modern teaching of science fails to attain the success which is expected of it. One reason for the failure of instruction in science is the eagerness of teachers to acquaint pupils with as many of the results of science as possible, so that class exercises are devoted to recitations on items of information taken up in rapid succession. There is no available time or energy to do more than become superficially acquainted with the methods or even the findings of science. Here and there modern schools are employing methods of teaching which induce pupils to compare and contrast impressions, to discover the points on which authorities agree or disagree, to note the unsolved problems which confront science, and to seek the additional facts that are essential to the solution of scientific problems. If the science of education had never done anything but classify mental processes as higher and lower and direct the efforts of the educational system toward emphasis on the higher processes, it would have effected a change of first importance.

SCIENTIFIC STUDIES OF READING

It was stated in an earlier paragraph that one of the most significant contributions of the science of education is the analysis of the reading process and the light which this analysis has thrown on the different stages in development of the ability to read and on different types of reading. The teachers of a generation ago were misled by superficial indications. Teachers unacquainted with the true nature of the reading process were satisfied if pupils were able to pronounce the words which the printed page presented to their eyes. As was pointed out in Chapter XVII, oral reading was the goal of school instruction in reading. No high degree of penetration, however, is required to discover that oral reading is often quite misleading as an indication of the pupil's true degree of understanding of the words and sentences he is pronouncing. Before the mind can grasp meanings, words must be comprehended and must be combined into phrases and sentences.

A teacher who listens to a pupil pronounce words in reading a paragraph can obtain only a vague notion of the reader's understanding of the content, but science has found a way of determining much more accurately what goes on in a reader's mind and the degree of his understanding of the passage read. Investigators have discovered that the behavior of a person's eyes as he reads is indicative of all that goes on in his central nervous system. Records of eye-movements have made possible studies of the reading process which are revealing in the highest degree.

The eyes of a reader can be photographed as they move along a line of printed matter. The movements of the eyes are not continuous, but the eyes fixate successive points and make rapid movements between the points fixated. Each time the eyes pause the mind grasps more or less fully the meaning of the group of letters fixated. The length of time during which the eyes pause at a given point gives clear indication of the difficulty of the inner process of recognition. Sometimes the eyes, instead of moving forward, move backward. A backward, or regressive, movement indicates that the reader is attempting to get a kind of running start to carry him over the intellectual hurdle he has encountered. The number of pauses which the eyes of an individual make during the reading of a line of printed matter is as significant as the length of the pauses. The greater the number of pauses, the greater the difficulty the reader is experiencing.

Without attempting to describe in further detail the methods by which the reading process has been studied, one can assert with perfect assurance that the work of the schools has been fundamentally changed by the discoveries from scientific studies of eye-movements in reading. A description of a single striking experiment will suffice to indicate the kind of contribution which science has made in this field. A subject is asked to read a simple narrative which he understands readily, and photographs are made of the way in which his eyes move across the page. In the midst of this simple type of reading he is informed that shortly he is to be asked questions about the passage. The injection of the new psychological factor, the expectation of questions, changes completely the mental attitude of the reader and at the same time changes his eye-movements. The pauses become more numerous and are of longer duration. It is evident that concern about the questions which will be asked radically changes the attitude and the mental activity of the reader.

SCIENTIFIC STUDIES IN OTHER FIELDS OF EDUCATION

It would be easily possible to multiply examples of the outcomes of scientific analysis of learning processes. The present effort to give some insight into the character and scope of the science of education will not be complete, however, unless the discussion turns to illustrations of studies which are not primarily psychological.

Measurement of school results and employment of psychological methods of analyzing learning processes are by no means the only lines along which the science of education has developed. Administrative practices have been subjected to investigation by methods quite as objective and detailed as the methods used in examining learning processes.   It is no longer possible for a board of education to conduct its business without being confronted with comparisons of its methods of operation and the results secured with those of other boards of education.   Here the techniques of investigation are adaptations of the methods employed in business, where the study of comparative costs is an approved method of inquiry.

In the fields of both administration and teaching the importance of adequate and comparable records has become apparent. Schools were formerly conducted without much attention to the keeping of records.   The tendency now is to keep every possible kind of record with the hope, sometimes not realized, that the records will some day and in some way be useful in throwing light on school problems.

One of the greatest single financial economies in the conduct of an educational institution results from increase in the size of classes.   The assumption is often made, however, that the effectiveness of teaching is reduced to the degree to which the size of the class is increased, because large classes serve to distribute the teacher's time and influence over many learners.   A kind of dilution is supposed to result, such that each learner receives a smaller share of instruction because of the presence of others in the class.   Personal contact between pupil and teacher is popularly regarded as of great importance.   As against this widely held belief, the evidence accumulated from numerous scientific investigations of the problem in recent years indicates that a teacher's influence does not, like light, diminish in effectiveness the more widely it spreads from its source. A teacher can at one and the same time stimulate hundreds of minds if only his instruction is vital and clear. Indeed, some of the studies have shown that when suitable methods of instruction are adopted, students are aroused to independent effort by large classes more than by small classes in which the teacher is in close contact with each member. Educational organization has been greatly influenced by scientific studies of the problem of class size.

Another type of inquiry which shows the value of objective evidence as distinguished from traditional beliefs is illustrated by the recent efforts of the North Central Association of Colleges and Secondary Schools to improve its methods of making up its list of approved institutions of higher education. The method which this association employed during the period from 1912 until 1934 was that of imposing on institutions certain standards which were supposed to be the proper criteria for judging colleges. One of these standards, for example, prescribed that a college must have a certain minimum amount of endowment corresponding to its student enrollment. It was argued that endowment gives an institution stability. An institution with endowment was not tempted, it was believed, to lower its scholastic requirements in order to secure and retain students.

When the original standards of the North Central Association were adopted, no one thought of asking for definite objective evidence of their validity. There was, it is true, no little friction in applying the standards, but the Association showed the courage of its convictions and insisted on endowments and other requirements. In due course of time, after many surveys of colleges had been made and the characteristics of good colleges came to be fairly well understood, it occurred to the scientifically minded members of the Association that the correlation between endowments and efficiency could be statistically determined. An inquiry was made, and the truth was brought to light that endowments do not correlate highly with efficiency.

The Association saw the necessity of giving a more justifiable basis to its approved list. It set about studying colleges and now has an elaborate system of accrediting procedure arrived at through a scientific study of all the characteristics of the institutions on its approved list. If on the average the colleges of the Association make certain provisions for students and members of the faculty, and an individual institution fails utterly to make such provisions, that institution is regarded as deficient to the extent to which it departs from the ordinary practices. If such an institution cannot show compensating virtues of a high order in other aspects of its organization, the Association refuses it a place on its list of members.

It is unnecessary to add further illustrations of the applications of scientific methods to the treatment of educational problems. This book has in all of its chapters attempted to exemplify the objective attitude which is characteristic of science. It has based its assertions on evidence collected from a great variety of sources. Its discussions have made evident the fact that there are many questions to which present knowledge does not supply the answer. The outcomes of the many experiments now under way in the schools of this country must be awaited before the best methods of teaching and organizing schools can be determined. The educational system is a growing, living organism and as such can never be finally evaluated at any one time in its history, because as progress goes forward, new problems will constantly appear.

Science is more than a method of collecting and interpreting facts; it is an attitude of mind. The purposes of this book and of this chapter will be served if students of education are induced to analyze all the situations which they encounter, to gather the most complete evidence available with regard to methods of dealing with these situations, and to be objective in their criticisms and evaluations of the outcomes of the educational programs which are adopted. The major achievement of the educational system in recent times is that it has substituted scientific study for the blind adoption of programs and procedures, and is able and willing to face the most searching tests of the effectiveness of its efforts.

THE RECENCY OF THE MOVEMENT

It is perhaps not out of place to close this account of the science of education with a quotation from the annual report of the president of Columbia College made in 1882. This quotation will serve to make emphatic the statement that the science of education is a comparatively new addition to the family of the social sciences. Today there is associated with the institution over which President F. A. P. Barnard presided in 1882 one of the largest and most influential centers for the cultivation and dissemination of the science of education. Less than two-thirds of a century ago President Barnard made a plea which is scarcely more than an expression of a then almost hopeless desire for institutional recognition of what in the interval between 1882 and the present has become a reality.

Education as a Science. One defect of our educational system which might have been included in the foregoing enumeration of our wants, has been reserved to be separately considered in this place. It is one which was dwelt upon at some length in the last annual report of the undersigned, and it has lost none of its importance from the fact that its presentation at that time was unattended with the hoped for success from the favorable consideration of the Trustees. It is the want here of a department designed to train young men to education as a profession, by giving instruction in the History, Theory and Practice of Education. The recommendation on this subject contained in the last annual report of the undersigned, just referred to, was not the first presentation of this project to this Board. As early as 1853, when the proposition to remove the college from its original site was first agitated, it was proposed that simultaneously with the removal there should be a change of system, in which, to the course of undergraduate instruction already in operation, a scheme of university education also, either in continuation of the former or otherwise, should be added. This proposition was the subject of much deliberation and of sundry reports; but no definite result was reached until April 5, 1858, when a definite plan was reported and adopted. Immediately after the adoption of this plan, an additional resolution was offered to "add the '*science and art of education*' to the subjects to be taught in the School of Letters." And this, too, was adopted with no apparent opposition. The scheme of university instruction here set on foot was but partially put into execution; and after the experiment of a single year, was abandoned as being premature. Though "the Science and Art of Education" was placed among the subjects to be taught in the School of Letters, no Professor or other Instructor appears to have been appointed for the purpose, and this part of the scheme fell through with the rest. The fact remains, however, that by the adoption of the resolution above cited, this Board distinctly committed itself to the proposition that the Science and Art of Education is a subject worthy to be taught in Columbia College. Had the general scheme proved a success, this part of it would have gone into operation also; and we should now have been able to look back upon a quarter of a century of experience of the inestimably valuable results accruing from the successful attempt, in this city at least, to transform the business of teaching from a trade to a profession. For the influence of the power here put into action would inevitably have reached not merely the educationists of the higher order, but every humblest teacher of the most insignificant primary on the island. Not that every such teacher would have been brought under the direct instruction of this chair. Possibly not one in five might have been so. But through those who were actually subject to this beneficial influence, the substance of the instruction would have filtered through to all the rest. The errors which these had been taught to avoid would have been stamped out, not only in their own schools, but in those of their colleagues, the just notions which they had imbibed would have been imparted casually or designedly to the rest, and the whole system of public education in New York, from the most elementary schools upward, would have been lifted to a higher level and all engaged in its management would now be walking in the light of a sound philosophy instead of groping blindly in the darkness of ignorance or the obscurity of uncertainty and doubt.

Nor is it in Columbia College only that the importance of this subject has been recognized, or that attempts have been made to carry out in practice a system of instruction in Paedagogics. During the past winter an accomplished educationist has been giving a course of lectures at Harvard University upon the Science and Art of Education, and has repeated the same in the city of Boston. Another no less capable has been lecturing with success on the same subject in some of our western cities. But in these cases the object attempted has not been that which is the principal aim we have proposed to ourselves here. Our proposed object has been to reach the teachers of the public schools of the city of New York and its vicinity. By inspiring these with a just appreciation of the nature of their work, and instilling into them a proper knowledge of the principles which should govern it, we should awaken in them an interest in it, and an ambition to do it well, which in the nature of things they cannot under present circumstances feel, and should thus accomplish a public good, the magnitude of which it would be impossible to calculate. For at present they have as a rule no adequate knowledge of the nature of their task, and certainly they have no proper preparation for it.[1]

BIBLIOGRAPHY

Burton, William H., *Introduction to Education*, pp. 117–85.

Clapp, Frank L., Wayland J. Chase, and Curtis Merriman, *Introduction to Education*, pp. 409–68.

Cubberley, Ellwood P., *Public Education in the United States*, pp. 688–704.

Good, Carter V., A. S. Barr, and Douglas E. Scates, *The Methodology of Educational Research*. New York: D. Appleton-Century Company, 1936. xxi + 882 pp.

Judd, Charles H., "The Development of the Science of Education in the United States," *International Education Review* (Koln, Germany), II: 475–96 (1932–33).

Judd, Charles H., *Education and Social Progress*, pp. 229–51.

Judd, Charles H., *Problems of Education in the United States*, pp. 178–86.

Meyer, Adolph E., *The Development of Education in the Twentieth Century*, pp. 125–53.

Monroe, Walter S., and Max D. Engelhart, *The Scientific Study of Educational Problems*. New York: The Macmillan Company, 1936. xvi + 504 pp.

National Society for the Study of Education, *The Scientific Movement in Education*. *Thirty-Seventh Yearbook*, Part II. Bloomington, Illinois: Public School Publishing Company, 1938. xii + 530 pp.

Reeder, Ward, *A First Course in Education*, pp. 96–115.

---

[1] F. A. P. Barnard, *Annual Report of the President of Columbia College, Made to the Board of Trustees, May 1, 1882*, pp. 51–54.

CHAPTER XX

SCHOOL SURVEYS

THE CLOSING YEARS of the nineteenth century and the first decade of the twentieth saw the development of scientific methods of measurement and appraisal not only in education but also in other spheres of social life. Sociological studies were made of the family, of the wages of householders, of the food of the laboring classes, and other like topics. As investigations threw light on single aspects of individual and community life, it became evident that no adequate understanding of social phenomena was possible without an inclusive examination of the relations between these single aspects. If a school system failed in the teaching of arithmetic, the complete explanation of the failure could not be found solely through the study of class exercises in that single subject. If family conditions were unsatisfactory, the causes usually had to be sought in economic conditions outside the family. A realization of the importance of investigating social facts in a broad way led the social sciences, including the science of education, to undertake certain comprehensive investigations which came to be known as surveys.

The first time that the word "survey" was used in connection with a social study seems to have been in 1909 when Paul U. Kellogg and Edward T. Devine, the editor of the magazine now called *The Survey* but then known as *Charities and the Commons*, undertook, under a subvention from the Russell Sage Foundation, a study of Pittsburgh which Kellogg described as:

> ... a rapid close range investigation of the ranks of wage-earners in the American steel district ... a demonstration in social economy made graphic against the background of a single city ... an attempt to throw light on these and kindred economic forces not by theoretical discussion of them, but by spreading forth the objective facts of life and labor which should help in forming judgment as

to their results ... [an attempt] to get at certain underlying factors in this [Pittsburgh's] growth as they affected the wage-earning population ... an inventory of such an American community.[1]

Members of the staff of the Russell Sage Foundation, describing at a later date the Pittsburgh Survey, made the following statement:

Thus, while employing the methods of social research as developed at the time, and also contributing something to their further development, the greatest claim of the Pittsburgh project for distinction lay perhaps in its success in combining the methods and skills of the social investigator with those of specialists in other fields.

The subject matter of the Pittsburgh Survey included the study of wages, hours of work, work accidents, and other questions of industrial relations and conditions for both men and women workers; of family budgets and home conditions among steel workers; typhoid fever and other problems related to health and sanitation; housing of the working population; the local system of taxation; the public schools; city planning and civic improvement possibilities; the hospital and other institutional needs of the city; certain phases of the crime situation and the administration of justice; playgrounds and recreation; dependent children in institutions; and a number of other related questions.

The investigations were made by a special staff who had the co-operation of a large number of leaders and organizations in national social and public health movements, together with organizations and leaders in social and civic work in Pittsburgh, the latter including three outstanding citizens who sponsored the undertaking throughout.

The chief findings were presented graphically in a public exhibition in Pittsburgh, summaries of the various reports were also published as articles in *Charities and the Commons*, and the full reports were issued in six volumes under the titles: *The Pittsburgh District — Civic Frontage; Wage-Earning Pittsburgh; Women and the Trades; Homestead, The Households of a Mill Town; Work-Accidents and the Law;* and *The Steel Workers.* Much of the Survey's data also reached the public through addresses at national conventions, newspaper articles and editorials, discussions at luncheon meetings, and articles in a wide range of magazines.[2]

---

[1] Paul U. Kellogg, *The Pittsburgh District: Civic Frontage*, pp. 493–95. New York: Russell Sage Foundation, 1914.

[2] Allen Eaton and Shelby M. Harrison, *A Bibliography of Social Surveys.* Reports of Fact-Finding Studies Made as a Basis for Social Action: Arranged by Subjects and Localities (Reports to January 1, 1928), pp. xix–xx. New York: Russell Sage Foundation, 1930.

THE DEVELOPMENT OF THE SURVEY MOVEMENT
IN EDUCATION

Although the modern development of educational surveys was undoubtedly stimulated to some extent by the contemporary development of sociological surveys, it must be recognized that certain comprehensive reports of school conditions had been made and published long before the second decade of the twentieth century. These early reports on educational conditions are not usually considered a part of the modern survey movement because, though interesting and informative, they were far less systematic and precise in their evaluation than is now demanded. For example, the reports of Horace Mann on the conditions he observed in the schools of Massachusetts in the late 1830's and in the 1840's might properly be called early surveys, though they were not so called at the time and they lack the scientific techniques of measurement employed by such investigators as J. M. Rice and other research workers of the past forty years.

A similar comment may be made about the reports of several so-called school commissions which were published for several states and cities between 1900 and 1910. The reports of these school commissions, for the most part, were not prepared by experts, but rather by groups of laymen who were interested in the general improvement of school procedures. The survey movement necessarily was dependent upon the development of techniques of objective measurement, and it was only after suitable measuring devices were developed that the modern survey could come into existence.

The first of the modern school surveys in the United States is generally considered to be that conducted in Boise, Idaho, in 1910. The school authorities in Boise were interested in finding out how they might improve their educational services. They hit upon the idea of calling in an outside expert who could appraise their practices and suggest how they might be improved. For this purpose they selected Calvin N. Kendall, who was then

superintendent of schools in Indianapolis, Indiana.   Mr. Kendall
spent a few days in Boise studying the work of the schools, and
at the end of his visit wrote a brief report which was published
in the local newspapers.

The idea of an appraisal of this type proved to be a particularly
happy one.   It was immediately followed by surveys in a number
of other cities.   Among the larger cities in which educational
surveys were conducted in the early years of the movement were
Baltimore and New York with surveys in 1911; Portland, Oregon,
in 1913; Butte, Montana, in 1914; Salt Lake City, in 1915; and
Cleveland, in 1916.   In Boise, Idaho, where the first survey was
made, a second and more extensive one was conducted in 1913.

The interest in school surveys grew at a remarkable rate during
the years following the first survey.   The National Society for the
Study of Education devoted Part II of its *Thirteenth Yearbook*,[1]
published in 1914, to a discussion of surveys, and included a complete outline for the making of a school survey.   In that yearbook
Edward C. Elliott described the purposes of an educational
survey in the following terms:

> To discover the truth about our institutions of education in such form
> and in such manner as will make our profession of citizenship more
> intelligent as to the motive, methods, and machinery of the whole
> school plan and to cause our profession of education to be more
> directly purposeful and more consciously constructive.[2]

The number of surveys made each year since 1910 as listed in
the best available bibliography, that by Henry Lester Smith and
Edgar A. O'Dell, is given in Table 12.   The statistics reported in
Table 12, although probably incomplete, show that each year
large numbers of surveys have been made of school systems and
educational institutions in the United States.   The first World
War brought a temporary reduction in the number of surveys but

---

[1] Henry Lester Smith and Charles H. Judd, *Plans for Organizing School
Surveys, Thirteenth Yearbook* of the National Society for the Study of Education, Part II.

[2] *Ibid.*, p. 25.

the movement became strong again after 1920 and continued until well into the economic depression of the 1930's. The reduction in numbers of surveys since 1933, shown in Table 12, is probably due in part to the fact that some recent surveys have not yet been listed and also to the fact that during the most recent years a number of surveys have been made that have not been published and therefore are not available for listing.

TABLE 12. NUMBER OF SCHOOL SURVEYS PUBLISHED EACH YEAR
FROM 1910 TO 1935 *

Year	Number	Year	Number	Year	Number
1910....	5	1919....	68	1928....	182
1911....	13	1920....	73	1929....	211
1912....	34	1921....	117	1930....	216
1913....	49	1922....	133	1931....	187
1914....	54	1923....	126	1932....	224
1915....	68	1924....	145	1933....	110
1916....	111	1925....	132	1934....	80
1917....	81	1926....	131	1935....	94
1918....	86	1927....	159		

* According to Henry L. Smith and Edgar A. O'Dell, *Bibliography of School Surveys and of References on School Surveys.* Bulletin of the School of Education Indiana University, vol. VIII, nos. 1 and 2 (September and November, 1931), and vol. XIV, no. 3 (June, 1938).

Two forces seem to have been responsible for calling the survey movement into being. The first was the expanding enrollments in the schools and the lengthening period of education, which required increased expenditures for the maintenance of schools. The pressure for funds led both taxpayers and school authorities to become interested in discovering any possible economies that might be introduced. Many surveys even in relatively recent times have been initiated with a view to finding ways to reduce the costs of school systems.

The second source of the survey movement was, as indicated earlier, the desire for a scientific understanding of social phenomena. The survey movement not only originated because of the development of scientific techniques, it supplied opportunities for experimentation with new and promising techniques and for the refinement of these techniques on a scale that was entirely beyond all possibility in the early days of scientific study of school results. Many of the early standardized tests, for example, were developed specifically for use in certain school surveys. Measuring devices, such as score cards for school buildings, grew out of the demands of the surveys. Thus, if the survey movement owes its origin in part to the availability of scientific methods for studying educational problems, the scientific movement in education also owes a real debt to the survey movement because of the opportunities and the stimulation provided in the surveys for the development and improvement of scientific methods.

SCOPE OF THE SURVEY MOVEMENT

The scope of the survey movement is indicated by the fact that the best available bibliography, published in 1931 with a supplement in 1938, lists a total of 3022 different surveys. This list is probably incomplete because many of the survey reports are difficult to locate, having been published in small editions or unpublished. In many cases only an oral report was made of the survey and thus no document is available for listing in a bibliography. In a few cases survey reports have been deliberately suppressed by the agency requesting the survey because of dissatisfaction with the recommendations. Obviously, under such conditions, some surveys are likely to be omitted from the bibliographical list.

Even though probably incomplete, the list of surveys is sufficiently impressive to indicate that the movement has been of great importance to education in the United States. All levels of education have been affected by the survey movement, including kindergartens, elementary schools, high schools, junior colleges, colleges, universities, and professional schools. Both publicly controlled and privately controlled educational institutions have been appraised by the survey method.

The range of topics considered in surveys varies widely. A complete or comprehensive survey includes all phases of a school system or an educational institution; this type of survey is perhaps the most common. Frequently, however, surveys are made that relate to special features of a school system, such as administration and supervision, buildings and equipment, finance and business management, curriculum, instruction and the teaching staff, the achievement of pupils, or special educational programs, such as health, vocational education, library service, physical education, or guidance. Sometimes a survey relates only to special kinds of education, such as rural schools, or the institutions which prepare teachers.

Almost every kind of geographical area imaginable has been covered by educational surveys. Forty-two per cent of the surveys listed by Smith and O'Dell are surveys of city school systems. County school surveys number 641, thus constituting 20 per cent of the total reported. The bibliography lists 655 state surveys, an average of 13 or 14 per state. Some 225 surveys on a national basis have been reported. The Smith and O'Dell compilation lists only 212 surveys of higher institutions; the bibliography is evidently incomplete in this category, for another investigator, Walter C. Eells,[1] found 578 published and unpublished surveys of institutions of higher education.

Certain state surveys have dealt only with institutions of higher education, or with limited phases of the educational system. Most of the national surveys have dealt with limited aspects of the school program, rather than with a complete and comprehensive treatment of the entire program of education. One of the national surveys, for example, was concerned only with secondary education, another with the teaching personnel. The most recent national survey of education, that reported by President Roosevelt's Advisory Committee on Education in 1938, together with its nineteen supplementary staff studies published in 1938 and 1939, is the most comprehensive analysis that has ever been made of educational conditions in the United States as a whole.

[1] Walter C. Eells, *Surveys of American Higher Education*.

SIGNIFICANCE OF THE SURVEY MOVEMENT

The survey movement during the three decades of its progress in the United States has been of great significance to the development of education. A few of the important outcomes may be briefly noted.

Improvement in School Conditions

In the first place, surveys have resulted in much direct improvement in school conditions. The recommendations for changes that have been contained in surveys have generally been sound, and most of these recommendations have been put into practice.

One of the findings that has characterized a great many surveys is that there is need of better support for the educational program. Because surveys have effectively established the fact of this need, constituencies of both publicly and privately controlled school systems and institutions have been stimulated to obtain larger funds for educational purposes. Survey reports of local public-school systems, for example, have frequently stressed the need of new buildings and have suggested the desirability of bond issues for financing the needed construction. The community may have been informed of this need by its own educational leaders, but to have such a recommendation come from a disinterested survey group seems to give it greater weight; and school bond issues are more readily voted, it seems, when recommended in a survey report than when advised only by local school authorities.

In privately controlled institutions, particularly in colleges and universities, the needs for larger endowments and larger supporting contributions have been stressed time and again in the surveys. Fortified by such recommendations, the authorities in these institutions have in many instances been successful in approaching their constituencies and in raising the funds needed for endowments, buildings, or other purposes.

Collection of Valuable Data

In the second place, the survey movement has been significant because of the valuable data that have been collected about the schools of this country. As previously noted, large numbers of surveys have been published, and in these published reports descriptive information concerning the school system is given in some detail. Although the data and information are usually published in a survey report primarily for the purpose of explaining and supporting the recommendations that are made, the publication of these data has served to make available a great deal of factual information concerning the schools of the United States. Laymen have been enlightened about conditions in their own communities, and educators, through compilation of statistics drawn from numerous surveys, have been able to obtain a grasp of the facts relating to the operation of the school systems in the United States that would not have been otherwise possible.

The facts accumulated from hundreds of surveys furnish a basis for comparative studies. Educators have thus been supplied with norms of performance or standards for many aspects of school equipment and activity, such as building accommodations, cost per pupil, teaching loads, and arrangements of teaching schedules. The officer of a school system today does not need to proceed blindly when he proposes some innovation; in most cases he can find an accumulation of information in school surveys that will guide him in making a wise proposal.

Stimulation of Research

An earlier paragraph in this chapter stated that the survey movement was a part of the general development of the scientific study of education, and explained how the two movements operated reciprocally to strengthen each other. Many persons who have distinguished themselves as research workers in education obtained their first experience in the use of scientific methods in survey work. A relatively large staff, including persons with diversified qualifications, is usually needed for the conduct of a survey. The range of talent demanded has made it possible to employ graduate students for many types of staff positions; hundreds of advanced students have thus obtained their first introduction to practical research problems in education by work on surveys.

During the first two decades of the survey movement a survey was considered a satisfactory problem for a Master's, or in some cases, for a Doctor's thesis, and a considerable number of graduate students have in the past undertaken a survey of some local school system or institution as a research project for a dissertation. The making of surveys has become so thoroughly standardized that little or no new contribution to either the methods or general principles of the science of education now seems possible from another survey; at present, therefore, most graduate departments of education do not accept a survey as a topic for a dissertation. Participation in a survey, however, is still considered a valuable experience for graduate students in education.

AGENCIES PARTICIPATING IN THE SURVEY MOVEMENT

A number of different agencies have engaged extensively in the making of school surveys during the past three decades. Perhaps the most important single agency of this type is the United States Office of Education, which has furnished leadership and direction for numerous national, state, and local surveys. The Office of Education has a permanent staff of experts who have been available, when their regular duties permitted, for the direction of or assistance in surveys. Most of the surveys undertaken by the federal Office, however, have relied to a greater or less extent on the services of specialists who have been employed on a temporary basis.

The second type of agency engaging extensively in survey programs has been the endowed foundation. Such organizations as the Russell Sage Foundation, the General Education Board, and the Carnegie Foundation for the Advancement of Teaching, have from time to time engaged in making surveys, and some of these agencies have at times maintained staffs of considerable size for this purpose. The survey facilities of the endowed foundations have often aided state and local systems desiring school surveys when available public funds would not permit a sufficiently extensive program of investigation. The foundations were in many instances willing to finance practically the entire cost of making a survey because of the anticipated benefits that would accrue to the state or local community which was being surveyed. The participation of the endowed foundations in surveys was characteristic of the first two decades of the movement. Endowed foundations do not now engage in the making of surveys as extensively as they formerly did.

Many college and university professors of education have made surveys. In fact, the staffs which have been assembled on a temporary basis for surveys by the United States Office of Education and by the endowed foundations have generally been composed to a large extent of college and university teachers of education who have been given leaves of absence from their regular duties. In a few universities special bureaus have been set up for the purpose of conducting surveys. Examples of this type of organization are the Bureau of Field Studies at Teachers College of Columbia University, the Bureau of Field Studies at George Peabody College for Teachers, and the Bureau of School Service at the University of Kentucky. Large numbers of surveys have been made by college and university faculty members without any formal organization of survey bureaus.

A limited number of organizations for making educational surveys have been established on a private commercial basis. The one organization of this type that is most widely known undertakes to make governmental surveys as well as educational surveys. When this organization undertakes an educational survey of any considerable magnitude it usually employs college and university faculty members for staff positions.

THE SURVEY: A DISTINCT CHARACTERISTIC OF THE
AMERICAN SCHOOL SYSTEM

The educational survey is a distinctly American development. Even though in its early stages it was perhaps stimulated by the work of Sir Michael Sadler in England, the rapid growth of the survey movement into its present accepted place in the American school system has been paralleled in no other country. The widespread use of the survey is therefore an important characteristic of the American educational system.

To a large degree the local control that characterizes the American educational system is responsible for the growth and development of the school survey. In countries where there is centralized governmental control of the educational program, the local schools are inspected rather than surveyed. In fact, there is little or no place for the type of analysis employed in the school survey in a highly centralized school system.

The way in which strong central control over the educational program tends to move in the direction of inspection rather than in the direction of objective, critical surveys is well illustrated in the United States in the case of the federal program of vocational education. The federal and state offices which control the federal grants for vocational education are staffed with a corps of inspectors who visit the local schools benefiting by the appropriations to see that the requirements are being met. Since the passage of the Smith-Hughes Act, which initiated the federal program of vocational education, the procedures of the central agency controlling the program have been those of inspection rather than those of survey.

That school surveys should be fostered by local control is altogether easy to understand. When the local school system is free to set up its program as it sees fit within wide limits, a capable and conscientious management will from time to time wish to have an accounting to assure that affairs are conducted on a sound basis and that proper progress is being made. The survey provides the best possible type of educational audit, for it gives wise guidance and direction to the management of the local school system without diminishing in any way the control of the local community over its own school system. The school survey is thus a procedure that has fitted in remarkably well with both the needs and the spirit of the local control of the school system that is characteristic of the organization of education in the United States.

BIBLIOGRAPHY

Almack, John C., editor, *Modern School Administration*, pp. 217–59.

Caswell, Hollis Leland, *City School Surveys*. Teachers College Contributions to Education, no. 358. New York: Teachers College, Columbia University, 1929. vi + 130 pp.

Eells, Walter Crosby, *Surveys of American Higher Education*. New York: Carnegie Foundation for the Advancement of Teaching, 1937. xii + 538 pp.

Gulick, Luther Halsey, *Education for American Life*. The Regents' Inquiry into the Character and Cost of Public Education in the State of New York. New York: McGraw-Hill Book Company, 1938. xvii + 168 pp.

Judd, Charles H., *Problems of Education in the United States*, pp. 183–85, 201–203.

Klein, Arthur J., *Survey of Land-Grant Colleges and Universities*. Office of Education Bulletin, 1930, no. 9. Two volumes. Washington: Government Printing Office, 1930. xxviii + 998 pp.; iv + 922 pp.

Reeves, Floyd W., *et al.*, *Report of a Survey of the State Institutions of Higher Learning in Indiana*. Indianapolis, Indiana: Survey Commission on State Supported Institutions of Higher Learning, 1926. 206 pp.

Reeves, Floyd W., *et al.*, *The University of Chicago Survey*. Twelve volumes. Chicago: University of Chicago Press, 1933.

Vol. I. *Trends in University Growth*. xxvi + 242 pp.

Vol. II. *The Organization and Administration of the University*. xv + 152 pp.

Vol. III. *The University Faculty*. xxv + 326 pp.

Vol. IV. *Instructional Problems in the University*. xxii + 246 pp.

Vol. V. *Admission and Retention of University Students*. xxxiii + 360 pp.

Vol. VI. *The Alumni of the Colleges*. xix + 126 pp.

Vol.   VII. *The University Libraries.* xv + 250 pp.

Vol. VIII. *University Extension Services.* xv + 174 pp.

Vol.   IX. *University Plant Facilities.* xiii + 154 pp.

Vol.   X. *Some University Student Problems.* xix + 194 pp.

Vol.   XI. *Class Size and University Costs.* xxi + 230 pp.

Vol. XII. *The Oriental Institute.* xxiii + 456 pp.

Russell, John Dale, Floyd W. Reeves, and C. C. Ross, *Report of a Survey of the Public Schools of Shelbyville, Kentucky.* Bulletin of the Bureau of School Service, vol. I, no. 1. Lexington, Kentucky: University of Kentucky, 1928. 192 pp.

Sears, J. B. *The School Survey.* Boston: Houghton Mifflin Company, 1925. xxx + 440 pp.

Smith, Henry Lester, and Charles H. Judd, *Plans for Organizing School Surveys.* *Thirteenth Yearbook* of the National Society for the Study of Education, Part II. Chicago: University of Chicago Press, 1914. 86 pp.

Smith, Henry Lester, and Edgar Alvin O'Dell, *Bibliography of School Surveys and of References on School Surveys.* Bulletin of the School of Education, Indiana University, vol. VIII, nos. 1 and 2 (September and November, 1931), and vol. XIV, no. 3 (June, 1938). 212 pp.; 144 pp.

Strayer, George D., *Report of the Survey of the Schools of Chicago, Illinois.* Vol. V: *Summary of Findings and Recommendations.* New York: Teachers College, Columbia University, 1932. x + 138 pp.

Works, George A., and Dorr E. Crosley, *Philadelphia Public School Survey.* Vol. I. *Summary of Findings and Recommendations.* Philadelphia, 1937. 70 pp.

CHAPTER XXI

Examples of scientific
studies in education

It is the purpose of this chapter to present a number of concrete examples of investigations that have contributed to the science of education. The studies selected for illustrative purposes belong in three fields: administration, curriculum construction, and methods of teaching. The choice of studies to be described is somewhat arbitrary because, from among the thousands of investigations which might have been included, limitations of space permit only the briefest summaries of a few typical examples. The reader who is interested in the full account of these and other like studies should refer to the educational journals, yearbooks, monographs, and other publications in which studies are reported.

ADMINISTRATION

Some five different types of research studies may be distinguished in the field of school organization and administration. Perhaps the commonest type of research in administration may be described as the investigation of present status. A study of this type seeks to answer the question, "What is the present status with respect to certain administrative practices?" An example of this type of study is the investigation made by William C. Reavis and Robert C. Woellner regarding office practices in secondary schools.[1] By collecting and compiling reports from

[1] William C. Reavis and Robert C. Woellner, *Office Practices in Secondary Schools*. Chicago: Laidlaw Brothers, 1930. 240 pp.

high schools of various sizes and types, the investigators were able to present information with respect to the kinds and amounts of office equipment maintained and the practices and procedures followed in the administrative offices of the secondary schools over the country. Another example of this type of study is that by F. H. Bair,[1] which reported extensive data on the personal characteristics of city superintendents of schools in the United States. That, on the average, the superintendents of schools in the United States are very conservative, have a rural background, and have strong church preferences are examples of the types of conclusions reached by Bair.

Another kind of research in the field of administration has to do with trends in administrative practices. This type of investigation is not content to report present status, but inquires, "How did the present situation come to be?" An example of this type of research is Earl J. McGrath's[2] study of the development of administrative offices in American colleges and universities, in which he was able to show how new offices have been added to the administrative organization of higher institutions in the period since the Civil War.

Another study of this type is the one by Thomas M. Gilland on the origin and development of the power and duties of the city school superintendent.[3] In this study Gilland shows how the office of city-school superintendent has achieved its present importance in the organization of the American school system. Still another study which would be classified as an investigation of developing trends is that by James O. Engleman[4] which reports

[1] F. H. Bair, *The Social Understandings of Superintendents of Schools*. Teachers College Contributions to Education, no. 625. New York: Teachers College, Columbia University, 1934. vi + 194 pp.

[2] Earl J. McGrath, *The Evolution of Administrative Offices in Institutions of Higher Education in the United States from 1860–1933*. Unpublished Doctor's dissertation, Department of Education, University of Chicago. 208 pp.

[3] Thomas McDowell Gilland, *The Origin and Development of the Power and Duties of the City-School Superintendent*. Chicago: University of Chicago Press, 1935. xiv + 280 pp.

[4] James Ozro Engleman, *Centralizing Tendencies in Educational Administration in Ohio since 1900*, Kent State College Quarterly, vol. XX, no. 2 (February, 1933). viii + 186 pp.

a study of centralizing tendencies in the educational administration of Ohio since 1900. From this study Engleman concludes that centralization of control over school affairs has increased since 1900 in Ohio, but that local control has not been given up entirely.

Studies of trends are useful for the purpose of predicting the future. A study limited to present status obviously does not give any clue as to the direction in which movement is taking place or should take place. From a study of developing trends, however, it is possible to project past and present tendencies into the future and to suggest what will happen if present tendencies continue. In so far as the purpose of science is to make prophecies of the future on a sound basis, the study of trends seems to be a more valuable scientific procedure than the study of status. As a rule a study of status must first be undertaken, however, before a study of trends becomes possible or meaningful.

A third type of research in the field of administration is the evaluative study, which seeks to compare two or more practices or procedures and to determine which is to be preferred. Thus while a study of status asks, "What is the present condition?" and the study of developing trends asks, "How did the present situation come to be?" the evaluative study asks, "Is the condition good or bad, or better or worse than some other condition?"

An example of the evaluative study in the field of administration is the investigation conducted by John Dale Russell and Floyd W. Reeves for the North Central Association of Colleges and Secondary Schools.[1] As explained in Chapter XIX, the Association was interested in improving its accrediting technique and asked for a study that would indicate what institutional characteristics are significant in determining the worthiness of a college for membership in the accrediting agency. By comparing the characteristics of institutions known by independent

[1] John Dale Russell and Floyd W. Reeves, *Administration.* The Evaluation of Higher Institutions, VI. Chicago: University of Chicago Press, 1936. xx + 286 pp.

criteria to be strong institutions with the characteristics of others known to be weak institutions, it was possible to arrive at certain distinguishing factors that are significant in determining fitness for accreditation.

Another example of a study of the evaluative type is that reported by Nelson B. Henry and Jerome G. Kerwin [1] with respect to the dependent and independent types of school boards, in which it is found that political interference with school operations is equally characteristic of the dependent and independent types of school system.

The evaluative type of study is extremely important, for it alone gives an assured basis for the improvement of procedures. While a knowledge of the present general status with respect to many items of administrative practice is usually interesting, this information may be a false guide regarding the practices that should be followed. To know, for example, that 91.5 per cent of the offices of secondary-school principals have a mimeograph contributes only indirectly to an answer to the question whether a mimeograph should or should not be a part of the office equipment in a well-managed secondary school. The experience of a large number of schools in purchasing equipment may frequently be a safe guide, but it may be on the one hand that purchases are extravagant and unnecessary, or on the other hand that needed equipment has not been supplied. Similarly a knowledge of trends, while possibly useful for the purpose of predicting the future, does not determine whether the trend shown is desirable or undesirable. Evaluative studies are necessary to answer the question of the desirability of practices or trends, and therefore they provide the most important scientific guide that is available for improving the effectiveness of educational procedures.

Unfortunately evaluative research in the field of administration has not as yet been carried on to any great extent. The techniques at present available for conducting evaluative studies

[1] Nelson B. Henry and Jerome G. Kerwin, *Schools and City Government.* Chicago: University of Chicago Press, 1938.　xii + 104 pp.

are usually clumsy and difficult to operate in the field of administration. So many factors are likely to affect the results in a complicated administrative situation that the process of evaluation by scientific methods is frequently difficult or almost impossible. Investigators should not be discouraged by such conditions, however, for the important contributions which can be made to educational procedures by evaluative research warrant great effort to carry on this type of investigation.

Besides the three principal types of research in administration and organization — studies of status, studies of trends, and evaluative studies — two other types may be briefly mentioned. One is research that deals with methods and techniques of investigation. This type of research is, of course, fundamental not only to other researches in the field of administration but to researches in all areas of education. As an example of a study of a research technique widely employed in investigations of administration, the report by Leonard V. Koos [1] on the questionnaire may be cited. Koos presents data showing the frequency with which the questionnaire has been used in research, and he indicates the pitfalls into which the unskilled user of this technique is likely to fall.

The fifth and final type of research in the field of administration is the survey. The origin and development of the school survey have been discussed in the preceding chapter, and the survey needs only to be mentioned here for the sake of completing the list of types of administrative research. The survey is itself a combination of many research techniques; it brings together into a peculiarly effective composite a whole series of research techniques.

INVESTIGATIONS OF CURRICULUM CONSTRUCTION

The plan that has long been used for deciding what shall be taught in the schools contrasts sharply with the scientific method

[1] Leonard Vincent Koos, *The Questionnaire in Education.* New York: The Macmillan Company, 1928. viii + 178 pp.

of curriculum construction.   The earliest plan used in the schools of the United States for determining curriculum content was to leave the matter entirely to local initiative.   The content of the curriculum in a local school was determined largely by the preparation and inclination of the teacher and the opinion of the school trustee and the community.   If, for example, the community employed a teacher who had a knowledge of arithmetic, arithmetic was taught in the school.   If in the following year a new teacher was employed who did not have an adequate comprehension of arithmetic or who did not regard it as important, arithmetic was given little attention or was omitted from the program. The community exercised its influence over the curriculum chiefly in the selection of the teachers.   If the citizens were determined to have a certain subject taught, they took steps to make sure that a teacher who could teach that subject was selected; otherwise the content of the curriculum was left largely to the teacher. When the preparation of the teacher was limited, as was commonly the case, the curriculum was meager.

Realization that the policy of leaving the curriculum entirely to local initiative frequently resulted in a limited program of instruction led to the next stage in curriculum-making, in which some central state supervision was exercised over the selection of subjects to be taught in the schools.   In many cases the legislature of the state undertook to prescribe what subjects should be taught.   As long as the subjects so specified were only those normally to be expected in a program of general education, the process was, perhaps, unobjectionable and even necessary. Legislatures, however, have not been willing to stop with the prescription of obviously desirable subjects but have often gone further, particularly in the last few decades, and have prescribed many special topics and subjects that are of doubtful importance to all public schools.   For the most part legislation of this type has been introduced at the insistence of certain pressure groups representing minority elements in society.   In Chapter VI the objections to this procedure of curriculum-making by state legislatures have been set forth, and it is sufficient at this point to note only that curriculum-making by this procedure is universally considered unwise by those who have made studies in this field.

A later stage in the process of curriculum-making is that in which responsibility is exercised by state departments of education. After being authorized by the state legislature to prescribe subjects, a state department of education or a state board of education sometimes draws up courses of study which schools in local communities are required to follow. State inspectors are charged with the duty of seeing that local schools are using the prescribed courses of study. Local supervision, often exercised through the county superintendent of schools, frequently goes no further than to ascertain whether the teacher is following the prescribed course of study and whether the progress made by pupils during the elapsed period of the school year indicates that the course will be covered completely by the end of the term. In most cases the prescribed courses of study are considered as minimums to which the local community may add anything it desires. As a rule only those communities which maintain school for longer than the minimum required term can do much more than follow the prescribed course of study.

All the plans for curriculum construction thus far described rely to a considerable extent on the judgment of some one person or agency, who has the power to determine or prescribe what shall be taught in the schools. A different plan assigns this function to a committee. The committee plan of curriculum organization has been increasingly adopted in the United States since 1890. One of the earliest instances of committee action on the subjects of instruction was the report prepared by the Committee of Ten, the work of which was described in Chapter XIII. From the time of that Committee to the present there has been a steady succession of committees, national, state, and local, working on problems of the content and arrangement of the curriculum.

The committee plan of curriculum construction has a great

advantage over most of the earlier plans in that it substitutes informed opinion for uninformed.   The members of curriculum committees are generally chosen with care and are usually persons of recognized competence in some scholarly field.   Sometimes committee determination of the curriculum is disadvantageous, particularly when the committees are heavily loaded with subject-matter experts who are narrow specialists.   Persons of this type are likely to have great respect for their own fields of scholarship, and though they may know the subject matter of their fields thoroughly, they frequently do not consider adequately the situations in the public schools, where the program of elementary and secondary instruction is administered.

A recent modification of the committee method has given much more recognition than formerly to the desirability of selecting classroom teachers of broad interests and wide experience to work on the curriculum.   Committees of this type are today working on revisions of the curriculum in large numbers of cities, in several states, and sometimes on a national basis.   The arrangement is made, as a rule, to relieve the teachers chosen for curriculum construction from a part of their classroom responsibilities in order that they may give time to the study of curriculum problems.   Sometimes an expert in curriculum construction is employed to guide and co-ordinate the activities of committees at work on various phases of the curriculum.   This development in the committee method offers much promise of an improved adaptation of the content of the curriculum to the needs and capabilities of the children for whom it is to be administered.

None of the methods that have thus far been described is a scientific method, for obviously in all the cases discussed the selection of materials to be included and their arrangement in the curriculum are determined on a subjective rather than on an objective basis.   While it is a great improvement to substitute informed opinions for uninformed, and to give a prominent part in the work to those who know best the needs and capabilities of the children who are to follow the curriculum, the whole basis of determining the content and arrangement of the curriculum is likely to be personal and subjective opinion. The scientific method, by contrast, seeks an objective basis for the determination of the materials to be taught in the schools. Attention may be given to a few of the scientific studies that have been made to determine the content of the curriculum. One of the procedures that has been widely used will be described in some detail, and others will be discussed more briefly.

Analysis of Frequency of Use

One of the scientific methods that has proved especially valuable in determining the content of the curriculum is the analysis of frequency of use. The principle accepted in employing this method is that the school has as its function the preparation of the child for life; by examining situations in which the pupil needs to use knowledge and skills, it is assumed, the desirable content for the instructional program can be determined. The method is perhaps best illustrated in the field of spelling.

Spelling is a subject that has long been taught with vigor and enthusiasm in the schools. Ability to spell is so obvious a mark of the educated person that instruction in spelling seems clearly desirable and necessary. The teaching of spelling, furthermore, lends itself admirably to the authoritative method of instruction, for the performance of a child can be checked accurately against the established spelling list, and an exact rating of his achievement can be given. Public exhibitions or matches to demonstrate spelling ability came into the school program early, and have continued to the present as a means of demonstrating accomplishments in spelling. Public interest in this phase of school work has been easy to arouse.

The selection of words to be taught in spelling is the central problem of curriculum construction in this field, for when it is granted that spelling needs to be taught, the next problem is what words should be taught. The original plan for the selection of spelling words left the matter to the whims of the individual teacher.   With the publication of Noah Webster's blue-backed speller in the eighteenth century the selection began to be determined by the makers of spelling books.   Those who made these books, however, usually selected words from a dictionary, grouping together those which began or ended with the same syllable. In some cases the author of a speller tried to include in his list words that looked difficult to spell.   It was generally assumed that difficulty of spelling was associated with the length of the word and the spelling book which had the longest and the most unfamiliar words was considered the best.   The makers of spellers vied with one another in trying to find a list of difficult-looking words, and in general the less frequently used words were preferred because they seemed likely to require the most intensive study.

The classic demonstration of the fallacy in the traditional methods of selecting spelling words was made by Leonard P. Ayres during the survey of the public schools of Springfield, Illinois, in 1914.   The following quotation from that survey shows the technique employed by Ayres to demonstrate the unsoundness of the older methods of selecting curriculum content, not only in spelling but in certain other fields as well.

The most serious defect of the present course of study, including some of the suggested revisions now under consideration, is that it makes thousands of children waste tens of thousands of precious hours in the laborious acquisition of facts for which they will never have any practical use.   While the survey was under way the staff attempted to test the practical value of some of the subject matter taught to children in the elementary grades.

For this purpose short examinations were prepared from the material prescribed by the course of study and actually being taught in the upper grades in spelling, arithmetic, history, and geography. Through the co-operation of a woman prominent in social and intellectual circles of the city, 11 of the leading successful citizens were brought together one evening and asked to take these examinations. The object was to find out whether or not the material that the children of the upper grades were being taught was of the sort actually used by able men of affairs in the conduct of their daily business.   For carrying out the test the most prominent and successful citizens were purposely chosen and in making up the examinations the most difficult material was purposely selected. The result of these examinations in spelling, geography, arithmetic, and history of the fifth, sixth, and seventh grades was that no one of the men examined made a passing mark in any subject. The reason is that the material on which they were examined, and which the children in the schools are daily learning, is of a sort that is seldom or never met with in the business of even the most successful men engaged in commercial and professional pursuits. The gentlemen who submitted to the examination were the following:

A state senator	A physician
A former lieutenant-governor	A merchant
The president of a manufacturing concern	A lawyer
	A newspaper editor
The former superintendent of parks	An efficiency engineer
A banker	A clergyman

The test in spelling consisted of ten words taken from the spelling lists of the seventh grade. These words were as follows:

1. abutilon	5. paradigm	8. mnemonics
2. bergamot	6. reconnoissance	9. trichinae
3. deutzia	7. erysipelas	10. weigelia (*sic*)
4. daguerreotype		

Among the 11 men taking the examination, one spelled six of these words correctly. Three succeeded in spelling four words, two got three words right, one got two, three spelled one word correctly, and one failed on every word. It is not surprising that they failed so completely for no citizen in any ordinary walk of life needs to know how to spell these words. When the rare occasion arises that he needs to write one of them, he looks it up in the dictionary. These words and scores of words like them are studied in the classrooms as well as found in the spelling book.

The test described above was suggested by the experience of the director of the survey who went into a sixth-grade room where an examination in spelling was being given. He took the test with the children. It consisted of 20 words and he failed on six of them. These six words are included in the 10 word list used in the examination of the business and professional men. Some of the children in the schools can spell these words correctly but while they are laboriously learning to do it, many of them are still unable to spell short and common words as "which," "separate," and "receive."

The test in geography was taken from the sixth-grade work as pre-scribed by the revised course of study and consisted of five questions which are all included as requisites in the new course.   These questions are the following:

1. What is the distance in degrees from Portugal to the Ural Moun-tains?

2. How many miles long is South America?

3. Name the capital of Montenegro.

4. Locate the desert of Atacama.

5. Where is the Pamir Plateau?

One of the 11 men was able to answer the third question.   All of the rest of them failed on all five questions.

The test in arithmetic was taken from the work of the sixth and seventh grades and consisted of five questions as follows:

1. Italy uses the time of 15 degrees East and Illinois that of 90 degrees West.   When it is noon in Italy what time is it in Illinois?

2. How much pressure will you have to exert on the handles of a pair of shears 3 inches from the fulcrum in order to exert a pressure of 5 lbs. at a point 5 inches from the fulcrum?

3. What is the area of the base of a cylindrical gallon can 10 inches high?

4. Express 150 degrees Centigrade in terms of Fahrenheit.

5. If 2 liters of alcohol weigh 1.58 kilograms, what is the specific gravity of alcohol?

The results in arithmetic were more successful than those in geography.   Three of the 11 men worked the first problem successfully, two got the correct answer to the second and third problems, one solved the fourth, and all failed on the fifth.

The examination in history asked for the identification of 10 dates as follows:

1. 1000	6. 1818
2. 1607	7. 1846
3. 1638	8. April 14, 1861
4. 1763	9. 1873
5. October 17, 1781	10. September, 1901

Among the 11 men, one correctly identified the first date, two the second, none the third, three the fourth, one the fifth, ten the sixth, one the seventh, eight the eighth, one the ninth, and three the tenth. These 10 dates, which meant so little to these men, were selected from the 91 dates which the course lists as necessary to be learned by memory by all pupils with the note that the list may be lengthened to suit the needs of the individual teacher.

Such a series of tests as those described cannot finally and satisfactorily tell us just which portions of our courses of study are out of harmony with the practical requirements of modern life. Undoubtedly it would be possible to pick out details from almost any set of textbooks which could be converted into questions on which many able and successful adults would fail. Nevertheless it is believed that the tests conducted in Springfield do indicate symptoms of the greatest problem that the schools of this and other cities are facing. This problem is the lack of intimate relationship between the work of the schools and the work of the world.[1]

The conclusions reached by Ayres led him to make a scientific study of the content of the curriculum in spelling. Analyses can be made of the words used in life situations, and when these words and their relative frequency of use are known, the spelling list can be readily determined. Somewhat earlier a similar idea had been suggested by English investigators. One of them, Knowles, actually developed a list of words based on the vocabulary used in the Bible and in classical authors. Another English investigator, with perhaps a more realistic view of the actual usage of the language, based his list on the vocabulary found in Sunday newspapers. Both of these techniques, it will be observed, failed to deal with the use made of spelling by the average adult.

Ayres approached the matter in a different way and went to another source for the determination of his list of spelling words. He pointed out that the chief connection in which the adult needs to spell is in the writing of letters. He accordingly collected thousands of letters, both personal and business, and proceeded to tabulate the words used in them. He found that the list of words used with any great degree of frequency was relatively short, and that a surprisingly large percentage of the words in the list of those used frequently consisted of the common prepositions, articles, simple verbs, and a few adjectives and adverbs. Ayres was able by this method of analysis to build the first list of spelling words selected on a truly objective basis, and his procedures changed completely the content of instruction in spelling.

[1] Leonard P. Ayres, *The Public Schools of Springfield, Illinois*, pp. 86–89. New York: Russell Sage Foundation, 1914.

Other investigators followed the same trail, but based their analyses on somewhat different premises. One investigation, for example, assumed that the uses made of words by children, not the usages of adults, should determine the spelling list for use in schools; hence the analysis dealt with school papers, compositions, and other materials written by the children.

On the basis of such investigations it has been possible to determine precisely the words most frequently used in the English language and to arrange the words in accordance with the frequency of their use. E. L. Thorndike has prepared a list of the twenty thousand most common words, rating each word with reference to its relative frequency of use.[1] Every first-class spelling book published since 1920 has been based on a word list of this type.

It will readily be recognized that the method of determining word lists in spelling by analyses of frequency of use has a defect, in that it assumes that the words people use in the specimens of writing on which the count is based are the words that should be used. No one knows the extent to which people in writing personal letters avoid using certain appropriate words because they do not know how to spell them. In general terms this defect can be stated as the difficulty of accepting present practice as the standard or ideal rather than aiming at the discovery of best practices.

The method of studying frequencies of use has been applied to content fields other than spelling. Historical references have been studied to determine what events and persons are referred to with sufficient frequency to warrant teaching them. Geographical references have also been studied. The method in these fields seems less valuable than in spelling, for world interest in historical events or geographical locations shifts considerably from time to time. During one year everybody is reading in the newspapers

[1] Edward Lee Thorndike, *A Teacher's Word Book of the Twenty Thousand Words Found Most Frequently and Widely in General Reading for Children and Young People.* New York: Teachers College, Columbia University, 1931. viii + 182 pp.

about the Italian conquest of Ethiopia, and the papers are full of references to the geography of northeast Africa. At another time the interest may be in Spain, in Czechoslovakia, in China, or in Finland. A thoroughgoing discussion of this method of determining curriculum content in history and geography is given by William C. Bagley in the following extract from a contribution which he made to the *Fourteenth Yearbook* of the National Society for the Study of Education.

At a meeting of the Committee on Economy of Time held in the fall of 1912 it was suggested that current literature could be profitably employed as a standard for determining the kind of geographical information that the school should provide. The proposal was to read current newspapers and magazines, record the geographical references, and determine from the frequency of these references the relative value of the various types of geographical information. . . .

The writer set this problem as one of the topics in his graduate seminary in educational values during the spring of 1913. A large number of newspapers and magazines were read by members of the seminary, the geographical and historical references were recorded and classified, and an attempt was made to evaluate the general procedure as a means of determining minimum essentials in these two subjects. While this preliminary work was not sufficiently extensive to justify anything in the nature of conclusive statements, the writer ventures the following opinions as a result of the trial:

1. A thoroughgoing application of the method might well result in a table showing the relative frequency with which certain geographical and historical references recur in the discussions of current problems, and this table might prove suggestive to teachers and administrators, and especially to textbook-writers, as indicating the relative emphasis to be placed upon different topics.

2. So far as the results of our initial test justify inferences they suggest that the present content of history and geography in the elementary school is not radically inconsistent with the need for geographical and historical information as revealed by a study of current publications; that is, the historical and geographical references that seem to recur most frequently in current literature commonly involve types of information already well represented in the school program.

3. If one were to take the newspapers and magazines of a single month as a basis for applying the method, one would be likely to get

results that would make the materials taught in the school appear to be somewhat ill adapted to real needs; but when "samplings" of these publications are taken representing periods of from seven to ten years the recurring references stand out distinctly. . . .

4. It would be reasonable to infer that, in the material which they furnish to their readers, newspapers are somewhat limited by the basis of interpretive knowledge that they may assume on the part of their readers. This inference is strongly borne out by the results of our initial tests. In certain newspapers we found geographical and historical references very few and far between. In such papers the appeal is largely upon the basis of primitive interests (or instincts) which can be safely assumed to be common to all; hence the so-called "sensational" character of such journals. On the other hand, there are journals that presuppose a large capital of interpretive information among their readers, and which are, for this reason, commonly limited in the number of their readers. This is strikingly illustrated by one periodical which was taken over by a publisher some years ago with the avowed intention of increasing its circulation. He succeeded admirably. We computed the number of historical, geographical, and literary references from an equal number of samplings over a period of five years before and five years after the magazine changed hands. As the circulation increased the number of references decreased, and for some classes of references the decrease was almost precisely in proportion to the increase in circulation.

5. It would appear from these suggestions that any method that attempts to utilize current literature as a criterion for the selection of educational materials should be applied with a distinct understanding that it may simply result in a circular form of reasoning: current literature of a "general" nature is likely to represent pretty accurately the level of "general" education. In some respects, it is just as valid to infer from the content of the school program what the character of current literature *will* be as to infer from the character of current literature what the content of the school program *should* be. Certainly, if there is a causal relationship, it is from the school to current literature, and not vice versa.[1]

---

[1] W. C. Bagley, "The Determination of Minimum Essentials in Elementary Geography and History," *Minimum Essentials in Elementary-School Subjects — Standards and Current Practices*, pp. 131–33. *Fourteenth Yearbook* of the National Society for the Study of Education, Part I. Chicago: University of Chicago Press, 1915. Quoted by permission of the Society.

Attempts have been made to determine the content of arithmetic by studies of frequency of use. One investigator, Guy M. Wilson, obtained records of the use of arithmetic made by the parents of pupils in several public-school systems.[1] The results show a surprisingly small use of arithmetical processes and also show that such arithmetical calculations as are used are of the simplest kind. The difficulty of applying this technique of determining the curriculum content to the study of arithmetic is that arithmetic constitutes a system rather than a series of isolated facts. One cannot learn a few scattered parts of the system but must understand and learn it all if he is to be equipped for the life situations that will likely arise.

The method of determining curriculum content by studies of frequencies of use has been described here in some detail, because it has been widely applied as a scientific method of curriculum construction. The method seems to be more applicable to some subjects than to others. It cannot be safely applied without full regard to the differences between subjects. The investigator must also recognize that the procedure rests fundamentally on a conception of the aims and purposes of education, that the school is effective to the extent that it prepares the child for life. The validity of this conception of the aims of education is not at present determined by scientific methods, but it rests rather on a subjectively determined basis.

The Job Analysis Technique

A method of determining curriculum content that is somewhat similar to studies of frequencies of use is the job analysis technique. This method has been especially fruitful in setting up courses of study to prepare for vocations. As developed by Werrett W. Charters, the method consists, first, in a careful analysis of the operations carried on in a vocation, and second,

[1] Guy Mitchell Wilson, *A Survey of the Social and Business Usage of Arithmetic*. Teachers College Contributions to Education, no. 100. New York: Teachers College, Columbia University, 1919. vi + 62 pp.

in setting up instruction designed to equip the student for carrying on these operations.

A good example of this type of research in the field of the curriculum is the study made by Charters to determine the program for training secretaries.[1]   A considerable number of competent secretaries were asked to keep detailed diaries for a month, reporting exactly what they did in the performance of their work. These diaries were analyzed and a list of the various jobs performed by secretaries was made up.   These different jobs were then rated by employers of secretaries to indicate the relative importance of each type of operation.   The jobs that were shown by this process to be an important part of the equipment of the capable secretary were then analyzed in order to determine their essential elements, and a curriculum was set up to develop the capacity of would-be secretaries along the lines in which proficiency was shown to be needed.

A similar study was made by Charters, Lemon, and Monell in the field of pharmacy.[2]   A single detail of this study may be cited to show how the job analysis technique is carried over into the determination of curriculum content.   In the education of pharmacists it has long been assumed that a thorough knowledge of Latin is necessary.   Doctors' prescriptions, possibly for good reasons, are written in Latin, and superficially it would seem that a thorough knowledge of Latin would therefore be important in order that pharmacists might read prescriptions readily and fill them correctly and intelligently.   For that reason the traditional curriculum in pharmacy had always stressed Latin, and the prospective pharmacist was required to study Caesar, Virgil, Livy, Horace, and other Latin authors in his program of mastering the language.   Charters, however, was interested in finding

[1] Werrett Wallace Charters, *Analysis of Secretarial Duties and Traits.* Baltimore: Williams and Wilkins Company for the National Personnel Service, Inc., 1924.   186 pp.

[2] Werrett Wallace Charters, H. B. Lemon, and Leon M. Monell, *Basic Materials for a Pharmaceutical Curriculum.*   New York: McGraw-Hill Book Company, 1927.   xiv + 306 pp.

out how much Latin a pharmacist really needs to know. Accordingly, he obtained a large number of prescriptions on file in drug stores and analyzed the Latin vocabulary they used. He found that the number of Latin words used in medical prescriptions was surprisingly small, and that the words were mostly nouns, the names of the various drugs and chemicals. Most of the inflected words that appeared were found in only one or two of their forms. The Latin verb *recipio*, for example, appeared only in the imperative mood (*recipe*), meaning "take" — the term that is used to indicate the amount of the dose. Yet generations of pharmacists had been required to master the conjugation of the verb *recipio* in all six numbers, in all the various tenses, in the indicative mood and the subjunctive mood, and in the active voice and the passive voice. None of these complicated forms was ever needed in filling prescriptions. From analyses such as these Charters concluded that, for vocational purposes, the study of Latin might be greatly abbreviated in the pharmacy curriculum so that only the few necessary Latin words would be taught.

The job analysis technique of determining curriculum content has the weakness of accepting conditions as they are, and thus limiting education to present practices. Innovations in the performance of the job are not provided for in the vocational curriculum built by such methods, and improvements must be introduced from some other source if improvements are ever to come at all.

Textbook Analyses

Another method of determining the content of the curriculum on a somewhat objective basis has been through the analyses of textbooks. In its original conception, the textbook was the curriculum in the subject that it covered. As previously explained, however, modern educational practice has tended to discard the plan of depending on a single source of information and to utilize a variety of sources. The curriculum, so far as its subject-matter content is concerned, therefore must be determined independently of any one textbook. The method of textbook analysis determines what materials are common to a considerable number of books and utilizes this information as a guide in outlining the topics to be included in the curriculum.

The textbook has a certain degree of validity as a guide to curriculum content, for it is usually written by an experienced teacher who is well versed in the subject matter to be covered. In the process of teaching the materials time after time, the capable teacher formulates and reformulates them until a pattern of content emerges which seems to be useful in the teaching situation and adequate in covering the field. By comparing the content included in several well-planned textbooks, the investigator can get an accurate and objective determination of the materials that have been considered important in the field by a majority of those who have gone through the experience of constructing a textbook. This information can then be used as a guide in outlining the course of study in the subject.

The analyses that have been made of textbooks have had other uses than that of determining the content of the curriculum. Some of these analyses have been useful in improving the textbooks themselves. For example, a customary technique now employed is to analyze the difficulty of textbooks in terms of the vocabulary used. Some textbooks use a large number of unfamiliar words, while others in the same field are able to convey the same subject matter without excessive use of difficult technical terms. Some science textbooks, on analysis, have been found to consist chiefly of drill on new words; the learning of science from such a source becomes much like learning a foreign language. Analyses of other textbooks in secondary-school science have shown that some of them tend to present merely a series of unrelated facts rather than a systematic view of science as a whole.

Analyses of textbooks have been a popular type of research in the past. It is now generally believed, however, that the research possibilities of this technique are limited. Particularly as the newer concept of the curriculum as something more than mere content, or subject-matter-to-be-covered, comes into prominence, analyses of textbooks seem to be less and less significant.

Analyses of Ideas of Frontier Thinkers

Earlier in this discussion it has been suggested that the studies of frequency of use offer little hope of improving the present situation, and seem not especially well adapted to many fields. Studies of frequency of use are of little value in subjects characterized by rapid change. The social sciences are particularly subject to change; as a consequence serious questions arise with respect to the choice of teaching materials in those fields. If the ideas currently accepted by the majority of adults are taught to children in school, the chances seem large that by the time those children reach adulthood the ideas they were taught will be entirely outmoded. Thus the mere analysis of the present situation, or instruction in terms of only the currently accepted ideas, will fail to prepare the children for the responsibilities they will face in adulthood.

The proposal has been made that curriculum content in a field such as the social sciences be determined by analysis of the writings of frontier thinkers. If the ideas that advanced thinkers are considering are used as a basis for the construction of the curriculum in social sciences, children will become acquainted in the schools with the ideas that are likely to be widely held when they are adults. The plan, it will be observed, is not entirely objective; the analysis of the ideas put forth by the thinkers can be made with reasonable objectivity, but the frontier thinkers themselves are seldom objective in their methods of thinking.

The suggestion has some merit but it entails important difficulty. The determination of who are the frontier thinkers at any given time is not easy, for most generations fail to recognize their true prophets and often give credence to false prophets. Furthermore, the ideas of frontier thinkers are likely to be different from those accepted by the conservative elements in society. Conservatives are altogether likely to object to the teaching of what they deem radical doctrines in the schools. It is a matter of record that large numbers of currently accepted economic and social practices and procedures, when first proposed in a preceding generation, were deemed dangerously radical by most of the substantial citizens of that time. There is real doubt as to whether society would permit the schools to go as far as would be necessary today in teaching the ideas of frontier thinkers.

Studies of Points of Difficulty

The method of assigning pupils their subjects for study frequently seems to proceed on the assumption that every part of a given subject of instruction is of equal difficulty and value. Assignments tend to distribute the time of pupils and of class exercises more or less evenly over the various topics in a subject. Investigations that have been made of the degree of difficulty which pupils encounter at various points in their studies indicate that some parts of a subject are much more difficult to understand than others. An effective adaptation of the curriculum to the needs and capacities of pupils, therefore, demands the distribution of study time and teaching time in such a way as to pass relatively quickly over the phases of the subject that are easy, and to provide much more time for the difficult parts. By means of analyses of points at which difficulties are found, it is possible to eliminate much useless teaching. Adjustments of this type contribute to the interest of pupils in a subject and at the same time open up the way for the cultivation of thorough understanding where such can be secured only by great effort and expenditure of time.

In spelling, for example, certain words are found to be much more difficult for the majority of pupils than other words. On the other hand, some words are so easy that they may be almost completely omitted from the formal teaching of spelling. It has been found, furthermore, that spelling difficulties are different for different learners; one pupil may have trouble in spelling a word that most of the other pupils find relatively easy. In the teaching of spelling, therefore, it seems desirable first to set up a list of spelling words that will include only those that are likely to be difficult for some pupils. The next step consists of an analysis within the required list of words for the purpose of determining for each learner the words that are difficult for him. The pupil then should center his study on the words that give him trouble.

Studies of the incidence of difficulty have been made in the teaching of secondary-school mathematics. Frequently the mere form of presentation rather than any inherent complexity of the learning process required is discovered to be the cause of difficulty.

Investigations of difficulty in reading have been of value both in arranging plans for remedial teaching and in correcting basic difficulties in the preparation and printing of textbooks. Studies have been made of the features of language and expression that make for difficulty in reading a book. Investigations of this kind point the way to vast new possibilities in the preparation of books that will be more easily read and understood, and hence more profitable to the reader.

Grade-Placement of Instructional Materials

One of the important problems on which investigations have been conducted is the problem of grade-placement of the materials of instruction. The level at which a poem, such as Whittier's "Barefoot Boy," should be taught was originally determined wholly by guesswork. Now grade-placement of literary selections has been subjected to scientific analysis and the best location in the school curriculum of any particular item has been determined by a study of the degree to which pupils of different ages are able to master it.

Space is lacking to describe in detail the many scientific studies that have been made in the field of curriculum construction. The reconstruction of the curriculum is at present one of the problems to which the liveliest interest attaches. Fortunately educators are now equipped with scientific techniques so that reorganization may proceed to a considerable extent on the basis of objective investigation, rather than only on the basis of expert opinion or trial and error as was formerly the case.

STUDIES OF METHODS OF TEACHING

Scientific methods have been particularly fruitful when applied to problems of methods of teaching. Large numbers of studies have been carried on to determine which of two or more methods produce the most satisfactory educational results.

Typical procedure in such an investigation consists in grouping pupils into two sections, an experimental class and a control class. The characteristics of the pupils in the two units are carefully measured and equated so that the groups are equal with respect to ability and promise and other factors that might influence the results. All factors, except the one with which the investigation is concerned, are held constant. The control group is then taught by the conventional method, and the experimental group is taught by the method being tested. Standardized tests are administered to the pupils at the end of a period of experimentation to determine whether the experimental method is better or less successful than the conventional method.

As an example, some experimentation has been carried on with the use of talking pictures as an adjunct to instruction. Various types of visual aids to instruction have been compared, such as the silent film with no comments, the silent film with comments by the teacher, the silent film accompanied by a lecture especially prepared for that purpose, and the sound film. From this experimentation has come the conclusion that the sound film is an especially effective device for stimulating learning.

Perhaps more experimentation has been carried on with

methods of teaching reading than in any other field. Such a question, for example, as whether it is of value to teach phonetics, has been investigated; the conclusion has been that the nonphonetic method is in general more effective, but that some value is attached to phonetics and word analysis. Investigations of eye-movements that have been of great importance to methods of teaching reading were described in Chapter XIX.

The subject of handwriting has also been studied scientifically to determine the best method of instruction. The relative merits of manuscript writing as opposed to the cursive style have been investigated with the conclusion that pupils should perhaps be started on manuscript writing in the primary grades, but should be changed to cursive in the latter part of the second grade or at the beginning of the third grade.

The literature of education contains large numbers of reports of experiments which evaluate the various types of teaching procedures in practically every subject. Naturally this experimentation has been most extensive in the common subjects of the elementary school, but much experimentation has also been carried on at the secondary-school level, and some work has been done in the study of methods of teaching at the college level.

THE STATUS OF THE SCIENTIFIC STUDY OF EDUCATION

The scientific method has given educators a most valuable tool for the appraisal of procedures in the school. The techniques of measurement have been reasonably well worked out, so that it is possible to determine the relative effectiveness of various practices and arrangements in the administration of schools, in the construction of the curriculum, in methods of teaching, or in any other phase of educational procedure. Although the techniques of scientific investigation have become widely available, only a beginning has been made in attacking and solving the problems faced by educators. Great improvements may yet be expected from the application of the scientific method. Perhaps the development of new techniques of investigation will be required in order to solve some of the problems of education, and it may confidently be expected that in the future new techniques will be developed as necessary to supplement those that have already been proved valuable in attacking educational problems.

The scientific method is now an accepted and respected feature of the American educational system. When the movement was in its infancy, those who were experimenting with it were looked upon with some suspicion by the practical-minded schoolmen. As the results of scientific study became increasingly significant for the improvement of educational practices, however, this attitude has all but disappeared. A number of capable persons have been equipped by training and experience to carry on the scientific study of educational problems. While the supply of capable research workers has never been adequate to meet the needs, the presence of this new type of person in the educational world has served to stimulate the interest of all educators in the value of research.

Observation indicates that the knowledge of desirable educational practices obtained through scientific investigations has now gone far beyond the actual application of that knowledge to school procedures. In administrative practices, in the development of curriculum, in methods of teaching, and in other aspects of school procedures, the practices at present followed fall considerably short of those that have been shown by scientific experimentation to be most effective. Large numbers of teachers, for example, do not use the methods of teaching that have been shown to be the most desirable in the subjects which they are teaching.

This lag in the application of scientific discovery is a phenomenon common to all fields of modern activity, and is by no means limited to education. The commonness of the lag in other fields, however, is no excuse for condoning it in education. Efforts should be redoubled to apply wherever possible in the schools the findings resulting from scientific investigations. Besides effort to discover new and improved procedures, there is need for continuous effort on the part of teachers and school administrators to inform themselves about what has already been discovered concerning effective educational practice.

The American Educational Research Association, a society composed of persons who have contributed scientific studies of educational procedures, has undertaken an extensive project to inform school people with respect to the findings of research. A bulletin entitled the *Review of Educational Research* is published five times a year, each issue being devoted to a summary of the research in some one aspect of education. The whole field of education is divided into fifteen different sections, so that in a cycle of three years there is reported for each section a summary of the research in that area.

Other means of keeping teachers and school administrators abreast of the latest findings in educational research are the journals published in the various fields, professional books which appear from time to time, summer courses offered in the graduate schools of the country, and the contacts between teachers and well-prepared supervisors in local schools. It seems clear that the scientific movement in education has reached a stage where the practices of the schools will in increasing degree depend on objective studies, thus in greater and greater measure implementing the findings of research.

BIBLIOGRAPHY

Judd, Charles H., *Problems of Education in the United States,* pp. 185–207.
Norton, John K., and Margaret Alltucker Norton, *Foundations of Curriculum Building*, pp. 92–570.
Review of Educational Research. Washington: American Educational Research Association. Five times yearly. Presents in a three-year cycle a comprehensive review covering each of the fifteen major areas of interest in the field of education. The best single source of information regarding research findings from scientific studies in the whole field of education.

CHAPTER XXII

Innovative Ideas
IN MODERN EDUCATION

A REMARKABLE UPHEAVAL has occurred in education in the United States since 1890. The earlier chapters of this volume have traced some of the causes of these changes and have shown how both the scientific study of educational problems and the demands arising from social and economic changes have resulted in marked modifications of the school system.

It must not be thought that the present generation is the first to witness a rapid and significant change in the schools. Demands for changes in education are by no means new and the long history of education shows many periods of reform. Heretofore in educational history, however, the reforms have been chiefly attributable to some one person or at most to a small group of individuals. Points of departure for new educational movements during the past two thousand years have been associated with the names of such men as Quintillian in the first century A.D., Comenius (1592–1670), Rousseau (1712–1778), Pestalozzi (1746–1827), Herbart (1776–1841), and Froebel (1782–1852). The group of men who appeared in the United States in the second quarter of the nineteenth century, including Horace Mann, Henry Barnard, Caleb Mills, Calvin Stowe, and others, was able to effect important reforms in the educational program of the country, but the number included in this group of reformers was relatively small.

By contrast with these earlier movements for reform in education, the present upheaval seems to be not the work of any one man or of any small group of persons, but the result of the efforts of many forces, agencies, and individuals. Some of the persons who have made significant contributions to the modern movements in education have been mentioned in previous chapters. The account of the development of education here presented is necessarily incomplete, for the number of persons who have effectively contributed to the present widespread movement for change in the educational system is far too great to be listed and reviewed in such a small compass.

Perhaps when scholars of a later age write the history of the past fifty years in education in the United States, they will be able to point to a relatively small number of persons whose contributions to the changes in this period have been of outstanding significance. From the present perspective, however, it seems that credit for the changes must be widely distributed among many contributors.

The changes that have come in the schools of the United States during the past half century have not all happened at the same rate. Many, perhaps most, of the changes have come slowly and have seemed to be, when considered singly, only minor modifications of existing practices. A few of the changes, however, have involved marked deviations from the accepted practice. Many innovations of this latter type are now being proposed and experimented with in certain centers. For the purpose of including some of the changes which have not been referred to in earlier chapters, this final chapter is devoted to the review of a number of radical innovations that are being experimented with in modern education.

It is to be hoped that the word "radical" as used in this connection will carry no unfortunate implication to the mind of the reader. In discussing educational innovations under this descriptive term the intention is only to convey the idea that if these procedures were adopted on any extensive scale, extreme modifications in the American educational system would result. A radical innovation is a procedure that differs widely from the accepted practice of the school; it contrasts with change or improvement which affects only minor details or may be expected to alter conditions in the schools only slowly.

The choice of specific innovations to be discussed in this chapter has been arbitrarily made; the attempt is only to list and describe some proposals which have received wide attention in the United States during the past few decades. Some of the innovations have become sufficiently well established so that they perhaps should no longer be classified as radical, but none here described has as yet been introduced into anything like a majority of the public-school systems of the United States.

THE DALTON PLAN

One of the innovations that has had considerable publicity is the so-called "Dalton Plan," originated by Helen Parkhurst and named after the city in Massachusetts in which it was first tried out and developed. The plan is applicable chiefly at the secondary level, including grades seven to twelve.

The inquiry conducted by the National Survey of Secondary Education in 1932 showed that relatively few schools have tried out the Dalton plan, and that most of those which report the use of the plan have modified it considerably in their own practice. In fact, investigators in that survey could find no one school that had adopted the Dalton plan in all its essential aspects, with the exception of Miss Parkhurst's school, the Children's University School in New York.

The Dalton plan seems to have attracted more attention in England than in this country, for a Dalton Association has been formed there and several reports about the plan have been published in Great Britain. Inasmuch as the American schools reporting the use of the Dalton plan for the most part fail to incorporate all the features described by Miss Parkhurst, the description here given will be based on her account, rather than on the plan as it actually operates in most of the schools that have introduced it.

The Dalton plan, according to Miss Parkhurst, is based on three fundamental principles. The first is freedom, which should perhaps be designated as individualized responsibility. The second principle is co-operation, or interaction between members of a group. The third is economy of energy through budgeting the pupil's time. Miss Parkhurst considers the plan as more of a sociological than an academic venture, and the objectives of education under this system emphasize the social aspect of the schools fully as much as the intellectual.

One of the important features of the plan is the organization of the school into "houses," each house consisting of pupils of all grades included in the school. This plan contrasts sharply with the usual practice, by which pupils are grouped homogeneously into classes graded according to the level of their advancement. Miss Parkhurst advocates the house plan of grouping because it is more natural. A school should, in her opinion, be a natural social group, and in a natural grouping such as the family, children of varying ages are found together rather than children of approximately the same age. Consequently, the Dalton school is organized into houses in order to imitate the social situation into which children are normally grouped in the family.

A second salient feature of the Dalton plan is the transformation of the traditional classrooms into subject-matter laboratories. In fact, the plan was originally known as the Dalton Laboratory Plan because of the basic idea that all instruction should be on a laboratory basis. This principle requires appropriate furniture for the classroom, tables and chairs being provided rather than ordered rows of desks.

A third feature of the plan is the abandonment of the daily schedule of classes. Instead of following a fixed routine each pupil budgets his own time and plans his own activities to accomplish the work laid out in the curriculum.

A fourth feature is the manner in which the curriculum is presented to the pupil. Instead of being laid out as a series of courses of study the curriculum is presented in terms of "jobs."

Each job represents one month's work in all subjects. Integration is carefully provided for in the planning of the jobs, and correlated progress is required so that the pupil does not advance more rapidly in some phases of his work than in others. The jobs are broken up into "units," each of which is a day's work in a single subject.

A fifth feature is the bulletin board. In effect the bulletin board takes the place of the daily schedule of classes. The pupil's first task upon reaching school in the morning is to consult the bulletin board and to note the scheduling for that day of group activities in which he will participate. The first fifteen minutes of the day are set aside as a period which the pupil may spend in planning his day's program.

A sixth feature is the independent work by the pupil. Class exercises of the recitation type are not held but instead the pupils work independently on their units and jobs, and consult teachers only for advice and assistance. Some group activities are maintained, for example in music, where the presence of the group is essential, but most of the academic work is carried on individually and independently by the pupils.

A seventh feature of the plan is the careful check that is continually made on the progress of pupils. Tests are given frequently in order to measure pupil achievements. Each pupil keeps a job-book, in which the work he has accomplished is filed, and these job-books are inspected occasionally to see that the pupils are doing the required work. Elaborate graphs are drawn showing the progress being made by each pupil.

INDIVIDUALIZED INSTRUCTION

Another important innovation, involving an arrangement for individualized instruction, goes under many names, but the Winnetka plan has perhaps had the widest publicity and may be considered fairly representative of the modern development in this type of program. The individualized instruction plan was referred to in Chapter XII in the description of methods used to overcome the difficulties of the graded system in the elementary school.   It will be recalled that in this former connection the statement was made that one of the earliest experimenters with the plan was Superintendent P. W. Search of the Pueblo, Colorado, public schools, and that the plan was further developed by Frederick Burk at the State Teachers College at San Francisco. The Winnetka technique was developed by Superintendent Carleton Washburne who was at one time a teacher with Burk in the San Francisco Teachers College.

The Winnetka plan provides group activity for a part of the day's program, but emphasizes individualized instruction in many of the subjects taught.   Some subjects seem to require the presence of a group for effective instruction, and there is also a recognition of the need for group activity for socializing purposes. The drill subjects such as arithmetic, however, seem eminently suitable for individual attack.   Each pupil in the Winnetka schools is allowed to work at his own rate in the drill subjects, and is advanced to the next unit as rapidly as his progress warrants.   The function of the teachers in the individualized progress plan is to give assignments to pupils, to assist them when they find difficulties in their study, and to check on the progress made.

Some have suggested an even more radical departure than the Winnetka plan in the direction of this individualization of the school program.   Professor S. A. Courtis of the University of Michigan, for example, has suggested the need for a radical change in the whole architecture of the school in order that full advantage may be taken of the individualized method of instruction.   Instead of the traditional classrooms he would provide large workrooms in which pupils are grouped in considerable numbers.   He would have the workrooms equipped with all the essential furniture and instructional aids that the pupils would find necessary in their studies.   Conveniently placed around the edges of the room would be a series of cubicles or offices — confessionals, as he calls them — in each of which a teacher would be stationed. The pupils would consult the teachers there as need was found for explanation and advice, and the pupils would hand in to the teachers the evidence of the work they had accomplished during their individualized study.

The idea of individualized study undoubtedly has much merit. Until relatively recently in the history of the schools, practically all education was on the basis of individualized instruction, and in all probability something of value has been lost in the transition to mass instruction by the class method. To recapture the values of individual instruction under conditions which require mass education is a challenging task, and the experiments that look in this direction seem worthy of encouragement, however disturbing they may be to the traditional concept of school organization and procedure. On the other hand, as Search found, it requires great effort on the part of the teacher of a class to keep in mind the particular points which individual pupils have reached in the various subjects they are pursuing. Furthermore, there are in all lines of study certain common difficulties and certain useful suggestions that can be dealt with most economically if the teacher directs the work of a group rather than repeats the same instructions to each pupil.

PROJECT METHOD

The school for many centuries has arranged the content of the curriculum into subjects. Each of these subjects has historical justification. Thus, for example, certain mathematical processes came into the curriculum as algebra and others as geometry, and for a long time these subjects remained separate. Similarly geography was long taught without any reference to the historical facts which show how men have reacted to geographical features of the earth's surface. As knowledge has expanded the relationships between bodies of knowledge have become increasingly evident. The truth of this statement can be illustrated by pointing out that, with the expansion of chemistry and biology, scientists have come to recognize that there is an intermediate subject now known as biochemistry. While the original list of subjects has been greatly increased and the original classification of items has in some measure become inappropriate, the plan of presentation of organized experience to pupils has often continued to follow the old pattern.

Today there is a strong tendency to abandon entirely or in some degree the old classifications of knowledge. General mathematics is advocated in which the fundamentals of algebra and geometry are taught together. Geography and history have been fused in the programs of some schools. This latter combination has been favored by the trend within geography itself to stress the human side of geography rather than the more formal space relations which were formerly prominent.

The examples cited up to this point illustrate trends toward reorganizations which retain the coherence of subject matter in certain compact divisions of subject matter. Radical reformers sometimes advocate the complete abandonment of all subjects, holding that a school subject is artificial and foreign to the experiences of ordinary life. Daily experience, these reformers say, is a mixture of space relations, historical precedents, physical phenomena, mathematical measurements and manipulations, and many other factors. If the schools are to prepare for life, it is argued, the school must offer opportunities to accumulate and apply knowledge in the way in which life presents experiences.

A complete revolt from the subject plan of presenting the material of the curriculum to the pupil is represented by the project method. A number of educators have been responsible for the widespread advocacy of the project method of instruction. Perhaps Professor William H. Kilpatrick of Teachers College, Columbia University, may be regarded as the leader of the movement.

The project method, forsaking subject-matter instruction, arranges for pupils to undertake pieces of work, or projects, in which they are interested. A project may be any purposeful undertaking in which a pupil takes a genuine interest.   For example, the project may be the building of a playhouse.   In the work on this project it will be necessary for the pupils to carry through some operations in arithmetic; they must determine accurately the quantities of materials that will be needed, the cost of materials, and architectural proportions that are to be adopted. Geometry may be needed to cut the pieces so that they fit properly together.   Spelling and English composition may be required in writing letters ordering materials, in describing the project to friends, and in many other situations connected with the project. History may be brought in when a decision is reached regarding the type of architecture.   Civics may be involved in considering the zoning ordinances and the limitations which they impose on the construction in various areas.   In short, almost every subject in the traditional curriculum may be touched upon in the course of an extensive project.   The important requisite in the project method is that the learning shall take place around the project, not in the traditional organization of the logically arranged subjects.

In organizing the curriculum on the project basis it is necessary to take special care to insure that all essential learnings are at some time brought into the experience of the pupils through the projects.   Ultimately these learnings must then be organized into some logical pattern and at this stage the subjects in their traditional organization or in some new organization usually emerge.   The project method sharply distinguishes initial learning from the organizing stage.

The project method is perhaps not as new as it may seem, for in some fields of study teachers have long been accustomed to organize instruction in terms of the accomplishment of certain projects.   In music, for example, an orchestra or a chorus gets ready to present a concert, and the organization of learnings by the pupils group readily around that purpose.   In art, the pupil attempts to paint a picture or to model a piece of sculpture.   In science the laboratory work is clearly arranged on a project basis although the setting of the required experiments in the laboratory probably violates the fundamental principle of the project method which requires that the activity must be one in which the pupil may have a strong personal interest. The project has been widely adopted in the teaching of vocational courses. The regulations governing the program of vocational education sponsored under the federal subsidies provided in the Smith-Hughes Act require each pupil to undertake a project outside of the school, in which he will apply the skills and information he is learning in the instructional program.

Most schools in which the project method has been introduced have not abandoned completely the subjects of instruction. Instead for the most part projects are arranged within the limits of the conventional subjects. The project method, however, lays emphasis on the purely functional organization of subject matter. If this idea were carried to its extreme conclusion, it would result in a complete reorganization of the traditional subjects of the school curriculum.

THE ACTIVITY SCHOOL

Another innovation which has been widely discussed in recent years is the activity school. To some extent the activity school may be thought of as an outgrowth of the project method. The activity school plan is based on the fundamental psychological principle that a pupil learns most readily by doing, and that if learning is to carry over into any practical situation it should preferably be acquired in a similar situation.

Harold Rugg of Teachers College, Columbia University, who has been one of the chief proponents of the activity school, has used the designation, the child-centered school. The adoption of this term is intended to indicate a sharp differentiation of the school advocated from the conventional school, which may be described as the subject-matter-centered school. Here again, as was pointed out in discussing the project method, the departure from long-established methods of teaching is not as radical as it has been described by its advocates to be. Teachers have always sought to induce in their pupils some type of activity even when the chief form of this activity has been verbal. The activity school is new only in its great emphasis on manual activity and other forms of behavior that differ from purely verbal responses to instruction.

Nonverbal forms of activity can be introduced into most of the class exercises where subjects of the familiar type are taught. As a matter of fact the recent emphasis on activity has served to enliven much of the classroom work in even the most strictly traditional schools. The radical character of the proposals of the extreme advocates of the activity program is in the emphasis which is given by these advocates to such subjects as drawing and painting and construction activities of various kinds. The revolt is in reality a revolt against the language arts and such abstract subjects as arithmetic. The activity movement has been objected to because it manifests what its critics call an unfortunate tendency to give up the advantages that come from following the experience of the race in organizing knowledge into well-arranged systematic units of thinking.

The basic idea of the activity school, or the child-centered school, is that the curriculum should not be fixed in advance by some central authority, but that it should grow out of situations as they arise day by day and hour by hour within the class group. The children should choose their own experiences in school in terms of needs as they feel them. Only under such circumstances, the advocates of this plan argue, can real learning take place. All learning under other circumstances is artificial and exercises no important influence over the life and behavior of the child.

The keynote of the activity school is therefore spontaneity. Ideally each child is to be left free to choose for himself the activities in which he will engage. Under practical conditions, however, a considerable amount of planning is done by the teacher, and the successful teacher seems to have a way of suggesting activities that will be enthusiastically adopted by the children and undertaken by them as if they were the originators of the suggestion. The classical remark which illustrates the activity schools in actual practice is supposed to have been addressed to a teacher by a pupil entering the room in the morning who asked, "Well, teacher, what are we going to want to do today?"

At present interest in the activity school is pronounced in several sections of the country. Some prominent institutions engaged in the preparation of teachers have been vigorously disseminating the idea, and the plan has caught the attention of many teachers and school administrators. The plan calls obviously for a new and different attitude toward the curriculum; in some states the courses of study for the schools have been rewritten with distinct leanings toward the activity plan.

The success of most of these newer educational plans seems to depend in large part upon the capability and enthusiasm of the teachers. A competent teacher may make a success of a plan that would be a complete failure in less capable hands. For the most part the schools that have introduced the newer practices are staffed with superior teachers. The success of the plan in such schools may therefore not always be taken as evidence that the plan would be successful under any and all conditions. Especially is it true that competent teachers, having their own knowledge well systematized in the conventional divisions known as "subjects," can guide the thinking and activities of pupils without resorting to the formal instruction against which the project method and the activity school are rebelling.

PROGRESSIVE EDUCATION

A term widely used to describe many modern educational reforms and innovations is "progressive education." The Progressive Education Association has been formed which, by the help of a subsidy from an endowed foundation, has been carrying on a vigorous program for improved practices in the schools. By

pils taught in schools using the traditional methods.   The
aluation procedures are under the direction of Ralph W. Tyler
the University of Chicago.   In order to set up the experiment
was necessary to obtain agreement from colleges and univer-
ies to admit the graduates of these innovating schools without
posing the usual requirements of particular secondary-school
its.   Some thirty schools are included in the experiment and
e results when completed will undoubtedly be of great impor-
ce in determining whether the traditional plan of instruction
he only method that can safely be trusted to produce satis-
tory educational outcomes.

EXPERIMENTATION IN COLLEGES AND UNIVERSITIES

he movement for radical reorganization of the existing edu-
nal practices has also been felt at the college and university
l.   The *Thirty-First Yearbook* of the National Society for the
ly of Education reported in 1932 an extensive investigation
hich 128 outstanding changes and experiments in institutions
gher education were described.   These changes have in many
been designated by the name of the institution in which
were first introduced.   Three of the more important of these
anizations will be briefly described.

Co-operative Plan

e organization known as the co-operative plan has been de-
ed in a number of institutions.   The University of Cincin-
eserves the credit for initiating the idea but it has also been
d out with certain modifications in other colleges and uni-
ies.   The plan involves a combination of an academic
m with practical work experience of a type calculated to
ment the theoretical study.   The students are paired, and
ne member of a pair is studying in the classroom for a given
, usually from five to ten weeks, the other member of the
ters on some practical job in business or industry.   The

means of its publications and its meetings, the Pr
cation Association has brought to the attention
educational world its demands for changes in
and in methods of teaching. Laymen outside t
teachers and administrative officers within th
joined in the movement.

It has been said that the only major characteri
Progressives unite is the negative attitude towar
type of school.   On the positive side the organ
advocates of many diverse and conflicting edu
and practices.   All the movements that have b
this chapter, such as the Dalton plan, the Win
the project method, and the activity school,
within the Progressive Education Association,
ous other reforms that have attracted less atte

The Progressive Education Association is
ganization of reaction against formalism in te
limitations in the curriculum arising from trad
influence has been in stimulating a wide vari
As a result of the vigorous evangelism of this
ulary of new terms and of old words with nev
arising to express certain educational concep
"progressive," which has long been a resp
definite meaning, has been appropriated in s
some educators careful to note whether the
capital letter when applied to any person o

Outside the propagandistic features of t
ment the most significant undertaking ha
experiment in which a group of secondary
the purpose of testing the outcomes of e
under so-called Progressive methods.   T
endowed foundation, funds have been su
program of evaluation to determine whe
under the newer plans advance in their s
and in other desired outcomes of schoo

jobs are arranged for and students are assigned to them by the college. At the end of the period the members of the pair change places, thus carrying on both the job program and the study program without interruptions to the institution and industrial plants concerned. By utilizing the summer months, a student may in this way complete the normal four-year program of study leading to a Bachelor's degree in about five years. During the five years, however, the student has had some extremely valuable experience in holding actual jobs, so that he is much more readily placed than the senior graduating from college without working experience.

Institutions that have used the co-operative plan find that it has certain difficulties. Jobs which are really educative are not easy to find, and there is the temptation to give the student his work experience in whatever type of employment can be found rather than to select rigorously only the employment opportunities that give promise of contributing to the student's educational objectives. The plan tends also to degenerate into an arrangement for assisting needy students to obtain funds to complete their education. Careful supervision is necessary if the work experience is to be fully integrated with the educational program and if the important values that are possible from the work experience are to be assured.

The General College

A second experimental plan at the level of higher education, instituted at the University of Minnesota, is known as the General College. This plan has attracted wide attention and seems to offer great promise as a solution to one of the perplexing problems of modern higher education: the problem of providing suitable educational experiences for young people of college age whose interests and abilities do not lie strictly within the area traditionally laid out in the academic program. The General College has been developed to offer a program differing radically from the customary freshman and sophomore years of the college, for the benefit of secondary-school graduates whose aptitudes and tastes do not conform to the pattern that has long been accepted as necessary for the Bachelor's degree.   Any secondary-school graduate may enter the General College and be assured of a profitable use of his time and talent.   His qualifications may differ from those set up as requirements for admission to any of the other divisions of the University, which are concerned primarily with the education of specialists.   Admission to the General College, however, is not limited to those who cannot qualify for admission to the other colleges of the University; any student who finds the courses profitable may take them.

The General College has a two-year program with courses laid out with a view to giving students very practical general knowledge.   The courses are intended to meet the personal interests of young people and to give them a preparation for the responsibilities they will face as adults.   Instructors under this plan have no necessity for maintaining the standards that have long been customary in subjects that are organized for students who are specializing.   The contents of the courses are selected with reference to students' needs rather than with reference to a rigidly systematic organization of subject matter in the traditional academic classifications.   For example, a course on modern technology is not like a course in engineering but is designed for young people who should know something about the machine age.   The completion of the program leads to a certificate; some of the courses also are accepted by the other colleges and schools of the University toward the requirements for the Bachelor's degree.

The experiment in the General College at the University of Minnesota seems to be the most promising attack yet made on the problem of reorganizing the college program to meet the needs of young people who graduate from the secondary school and are to enter on careers other than those of the professions or technical occupations.   The plan has been adopted in a few other institutions and where tried seems to be proving successful.

The Chicago Plan

The University of Chicago plan has also received wide publicity. This plan is an attempt to bring into the program of every student the opportunity for a reasonable acquaintance with all the broad fields of human knowledge. Under the traditional organization of the college curriculum the whole area of human knowledge has been divided into numerous departments. At the University of Chicago prior to the adoption of the new plan in 1931 there were some forty of these departments, and to obtain even a preliminary acquaintance with all fields of knowledge the student would have needed to take one or more introductory courses in each of these numerous departments. This was manifestly impossible, so the students who graduated under the traditional plan were ignorant of many of the broad phases of human knowledge.

The Chicago plan provides four general survey courses covering the fields of the biological sciences, the physical sciences, the humanities, and the social sciences. Each student is required to be familiar with the materials of these four survey courses, which are taken in the freshman and sophomore years. The remainder of the junior-college period is filled by either second-year survey courses or departmental sequences in one or two of the four fields and by the usual requirements in English composition. Upon the completion of the two-year College, the student enters one of the four Divisions (Biological Sciences, Humanities, Physical Sciences, or Social Sciences) or one of the professional schools. The programs leading to the Bachelor's, Master's and Doctor's degrees are administered by the Divisions and the professional schools.

The University of Chicago plan is further featured by the use of comprehensive examinations as the basis for granting certificates and degrees. Course credits do not have the usual significance in the attainment of certificates and degrees, and the student who can pass the comprehensive examinations as a result of private study without attending courses is permitted and encouraged to do so. This plan has the effect of speeding up the program for brighter students, freeing them from the necessity of class attendance and other routine burdens. It also imposes perhaps a more rigorous test of accomplishment than the ability to pass examinations in particular courses, which is the basis upon which the Bachelor's degree is granted under the elective system of most colleges.

Other Plans

Space is lacking for the description of many other innovations that have been introduced in colleges and universities throughout the country. Institutions in which innovating programs have received wide publicity include the University of Buffalo, Swarthmore College, Reed College, Harvard College, Wabash College, Hendrix College, the University of Florida, Grinnell College, Stanford University, Rollins College, and St. John's College. Each college seems to have a distinctive plan and there has been relatively little copying of complete plans from one institution by another. Many of the new plans that have been announced in various colleges, however, are combinations of some of the standard innovations, such as survey courses, comprehensive examinations, or functional organization of courses.

ATTITUDES TOWARD INNOVATIONS

The question may well be asked, "What should be the attitude of educators toward the multitude of innovations now being proposed for acceptance in the schools?" The large number of proposals that have been made is bewildering and it is obviously not possible for a school system or educational institution to adopt them all. It is difficult for the individual teacher or administrator even to know about more than a limited number of the plans that have been proposed. Among some educators there is evidence of a belief that the old ways are best, and that the possibilities of improving the traditional procedures are small. The great majority of educators, however, do not exhibit this conservative attitude; they show an interest in the newer ideas, although they do manifest at times timidity in accepting and acting on them.

It should be noted that all these newer plans have the common characteristic of tending to break up formalism and routine. This is an objective with which all thinking educators should be heartily in sympathy. The schools, like most other social institutions, have a marked tendency to settle down into fixed ways and to follow traditional practices without attempting to discover whether better ways can be found. Any device that will result in the questioning of accepted practices is useful in overcoming this habit of falling into complacent routine.

Some of the more radical proposals for changed procedures in the schools may be viewed very critically by the practical-minded schoolmen. A critical attitude should not result in complete disdain for the proposals with which one disagrees, though anyone is entitled to suspend judgment until convincing evidence of the effectiveness of a new proposal is forthcoming.

A charitable attitude toward proposals which may seem fantastic to the conservatively minded schoolman seems necessary when it is remembered that most of the features now accepted as fixtures in the schools were radical innovations at the time of their introduction. Such currently accepted practices as the grading of pupils, the teaching of science, the public secondary school, extension teaching by universities, summer sessions in institutions of higher education, and co-education, to name only a few, were perhaps more shocking to the traditionalists at the time they were introduced than any of the new ideas at present widely discussed.

It must not be assumed, however, that every idea is sound merely because it is new. Many innovations that have been proposed and accepted for a time in the past have been ultimately abandoned as useless or harmful. The history of education ordinarily does not give much emphasis to these discarded ideas, but a careful survey of the educational literature of almost any period will reveal numerous proposals that have not proved workable.

The least that can be expected from the advocates of radical reform measures is that they will be willing to have their ideas tested rigorously by scientific methods before expecting their acceptance and adoption by the educational world. It is quite in accordance with the facts to state that many modern reformers are largely propagandists and evangelists, and show little disposition to submit their plans and proposals to careful scientific investigation. Most of the plans are worked out on the basis of theory rather than as a result of empirical demonstration of effectiveness in some practical situation. Sometimes a plan is demonstrated originally in an experimental school where conditions are so highly favorable with respect to the pupil group served, the qualifications of teachers, and the kinds of equipment available, as to supply no legitimate grounds for the conclusion that the plan would be workable if adopted under less favorable conditions.

The suggestion that the advocates of an educational reform should demonstrate clearly the effectiveness of their proposals is reasonable because of two important circumstances in the American educational system today. In the first place, the means for scientific analyses of educational problems are available and can be utilized for objective demonstration of the relative effectiveness of various plans and procedures. In the second place, the American school system, with its tradition of local control, offers almost unlimited possibilities for trying out new educational theories. The happy combination of these two circumstances offers great possibility for the improvement of educational practices and procedures through experimentation with any and all sorts of innovations, be they radical or otherwise.

BIBLIOGRAPHY

Bogoslovsky, B. B., *The Ideal School.* New York: The Macmillan Company, 1936. xii + 526 pp.

Breed, Frederick S., *Education and the New Realism.* New York: The Macmillan Company, 1939. xx + 238 pp.

Butterweck, Joseph S., and J. Conrad Seegers, *An Orientation Course in Education*, pp. 129–51, 203–38.

Cubberley, Ellwood P., *Public Education in the United States*, pp. 513–38.

Dewey, John, *Experience and Education.* New York: The Macmillan Company, 1938. xiii + 116 pp.

Douglass, Aubrey A., *The American School System*, pp. 303–30, 474–81.

Frasier, George Willard, and Winfield D. Armentrout, *An Introduction to the Literature of Education*, pp. 337–73.

Kilpatrick, William H., and others, *The Educational Frontier.* New York: D. Appleton-Century Company, 1933. viii + 326 pp.

Mead, Cyrus D., and Fred W. Orth, *The Transitional Public School.* New York: The Macmillan Company, 1934. xxii + 372 pp.

Meyer, Adolph E., *The Development of Education in the Twentieth Century*, pp. 1–124, 166–91, 214–31.

Mossman, L. C., *The Activity Concept.* New York: The Macmillan Company, 1938. xvii + 198 pp.

Recent Trends in American College Education. Edited by William S. Gray. Proceedings of the Institute for Administrative Officers of Higher Institutions, III. Chicago: University of Chicago Press, 1931. x + 254 pp.

Rugg, Harold, and Ann Shumaker, *The Child Centered School.* Yonkers-on-Hudson, New York: World Book Company, 1928. xiv + 360 pp.

Washburne, Carleton, *Adjusting the School to the Child.* Yonkers-on-Hudson, New York: World Book Company, 1932. xvi + 190 pp.

Wrightstone, J. Wayne, *Appraisal of Newer Elementary School Practices.* New York: Teachers College, Columbia University, 1938. xiii + 222 pp.

Wrightstone, J. Wayne, *Appraisal of Newer Practices in Selected Public Schools.* New York: Bureau of Publications, Teachers College, Columbia University, 1935. viii + 118 pp.

INDEX

INDEX

High school, 39–43, 54, 58, 207, 219, 221, 229, 233, 234, 236–37, 238, 239, 271, 277–78, 279, 285, 286, 291–94, 295, 386, 395, 478. *See also* Secondary school

Higher education, 17–19, 22, 33–34, 43, 60–62, 80–88, 95, 97–98, 113, 118, 148–59, 165–66, 174, 206, 215, 217–19, 221–34, 238, 256, 262, 271, 272, 274, 276, 277, 290–91, 296, 298, 302, 307–46, 347, 356, 360–63, 368, 382, 384–92, 404, 410, 423–25, 430–32, 435–37, 441, 446, 453, 468, 478, 479, 480, 483, 488, 489–90, 511, 526, 528–32, 533

Hill, Frank Ernest, 370

History, as a school subject, 221–22, 239, 261, 263, 267, 274–76, 282, 293, 294, 309, 317, 393, 429, 500–02, 522, 523

Hochschule, 28, 271

Hockett, J. A., 268

Holbeck, Elmer Scott, 168

Hollis, Ernest V., 165, 168

Holt, Hamilton, 415

Home demonstration agents, 362

Home economics, 83, 205, 267, 284, 285, 293

Home membership, education for, 303

Home-and-school relationships, 161–63, 227, 260–61

Home-study courses, 360–61

Homogeneous grouping, 258–59, 518

Hoover, Herbert, 93, 94

Hornbook, 197–98

Houle, C. O., 370

Housing of schools. *See* Buildings, school

Hughes, James M., 304

Humanities, 334, 531

Humphrey, Heman, 372

Hutchins, Robert M., 345

Hutson, Percival, 304

Hygiene, 196–97, 204, 267, 293

Idaho, 182

Illinois, 133, 182

Illinois, University of, 155

Illinois Wesleyan University, 360

Illiteracy, 364

Immigrants on western lands, 45

Implementation of research findings, 512–13

Income, 172, 179, 181–83, 186–87

Independent school systems, 140–44, 490

Indiana, 31, 107–09, 151, 182, 216–17

Indians, education of, 89

Individual differences, 247–48, 250, 255, 289

Individualized instruction, 203, 246, 257, 259, 413, 519–21

Industrial subjects, 63–64, 102, 284–88, 293

Inheritance taxes, 179, 184, 187

Innovations in education, 408, 515–35

In-service preparation of teachers, 299

Inspection of schools, 117, 484, 493

Institutes, technical, 307

Institutionalization of education, 5

Insurance companies, 65

Intelligence tests, 258, 291, 425, 428, 434, 441, 444

Iowa, 182

Iowa State Agricultural College, 61

I.Q., 441

Irving, Washington, 373

Island possessions, 101

Italian, as a school subject, 293

Italy, universities in, 18

Jacksonian Democracy, 77

Jacobson, E. W., 268

Japan, vocational education in, 64

Jefferson, Thomas, 77

Jena, University of, 453

Job analysis, 503–05

Johns Hopkins University, 453

Johnson, Palmer O., 100

Jordan, William H., 61

Jorgensen, A. N., 450

Journalism, 154, 280

Journals, professional, 207, 240, 366, 487, 513

Judd, Charles H., 36, 54, 74, 100, 120, 145, 190, 213, 220, 240, 304, 346, 370, 399, 450, 471, 485, 486, 513

Judicial decisions. *See* Court decisions

Junctures between units in the educational system, 224–25, 232–33, 236–37

Junior college, 54, 87, 207, 236–37, 272, 279, 296–97, 307, 311, 313, 319, 362–63, 386, 478, 531

Junior high school, 54, 207, 233, 234, 236–37, 244, 260, 261, 272, 279, 283

Juvenile delinquency, 354–56, 368

Kalamazoo Decision, 40–41

Kandel, I. L., 36, 74, 120, 145, 190, 240, 269, 304, 305, 346, 370, 399

Kansas, 182

Kansas City schools, 243–44